Engines that bend

Atlantic
PUBLISHERS

Engines that bend

NARROW GAUGE ARTICULATED LOCOMOTIVES

David Joy

FRONT COVER:

MAIN PICTURE: View from the cab of South African 2ft gauge class NGG16 Garratt No 143 on Ixopo to Donnybrook goods, July 1976. (David Rodgers)

TOP INSET: Mallet 99 5901 on the Harz system, February 2005. (David Rodgers)

LOWER INSET: Ffestiniog Railway double Fairlie *David Lloyd George*, October 2005. (James Waite)

TITLE PAGE: Class 20A Garratt No 747 leaving Thomson Junction, Zimbabwe, August 1991. (Keith Chester)

THIS PAGE: An engine that bends – and has gears. Three-truck Shay No 14 rounds a curve on the Georgetown Loop Railroad in Colorado, 2005. (John Clover)

BACK COVER: Garratt No 87 south of Rhyd Ddu station, Welsh Highland Railway, June 2010. (James Waite)

Atlantic Publishers

83 Parkanaur Avenue, Southend-on-Sea, Essex SS1 3JA

ISBN: 978-1-902827-23-0

British Cataloguing in Publication Data
A catalogue for this book is available from the British Library

© David Joy 2012

Designed by Juliet Arthur
Stimula Creative

Printed in China through Printworks International Ltd.

CONTENTS

Introduction

There has been one reason above all for writing this book. When I founded the magazine *Narrow Gauge World* in 1999 and went on to edit it until 2009, by far the greatest number of queries from readers concerned articulated steam locomotives. On relinquishing the editorship I therefore resolved to put together a broad overview of the subject and attempt to answer most of the questions that had arisen. There have been times when I have wished that the top of the queries' list had been almost any other topic, as this has proved to be just about the most difficult of the fifty-plus books I have written! It is a subject compelling in its variety and yet fraught with complexities.

The title *Engines that Bend* trips off the tongue but may strike some readers as too flippant. Yet at the end of the day the prime reason behind articulation was to help locomotives get round sharp curves. Moreover, this book is not a ponderous definitive history but is intended as a readable narrative. Those requiring a more erudite and comprehensive approach need to consult *Articulated Locomotives* by Lionel Wiener. Although published as long ago as 1930, the amount of detail in its 650 pages has never been surpassed and it has been lauded as one of the top four books on motive power. Professor Wiener was a master of classification and managed to cover more than 130 types of articulated locomotive. It was a supreme achievement, even though many had the briefest existence and have long been forgotten. *Engines that Bend* looks at a much smaller number and concentrates on those that either still exist or are especially remembered.

Two definitions need to be clarified. One is 'narrow gauge', which is not straightforward at either end of the scale. In these pages it extends down to fifteen-inch gauge but excludes miniature versions of much larger prototypes. At the upper end, most dictionaries define narrow gauge as a track width of less than the standard 4ft 8½in. This approach tends to be questioned on first sight of the mighty 3ft 6in gauge Garratts of southern Africa, with dimensions and tractive effort way in excess of virtually all UK standard gauge motive power. *Engines that Bend* covers such giants but gives greater emphasis to the more diminutive designs of the narrower gauges.

Questions of gauge immediately raise the thorny matter of metrication, which seems unlikely to achieve worldwide adoption today let alone historically. The approach followed in this book is best summarised as commonsense and uses either imperial or metric dimensions according to the standard in the country concerned. It would be as much a nonsense to convert the three-foot gauge of the USA into 91 centimetres as it would to refer to French metre gauge as 3ft 3in, although equivalents have been included when it comes to distances.

The term 'articulated locomotives' has tricky issues of definition. Wiener was characteristically precise with wording that needs careful thought and may require reading more than once: 'An articulated locomotive is a locomotive in which one or more of the driven axles are able to take up positions where they do not remain parallel to the others and may take angular positions in curves. The axles may be driven by two separate engines or by a single one.'

Others have taken a narrower but more immediately understandable approach in simply stating that the term refers to 'a locomotive carried on two or more bogies'. This does after all cover key evolutionary stages, which on the standard gauge began as early as 1832 with a dubious 2-2-2-2 built in New York. Progress was at first slow and articulated locomotives participating in the famous Semmering trials in Austria in 1851 had the same lack of practical success. They were at least way ahead of anything on the narrow gauge, which then represented little more than horse tramways. It was not until 1869 that a double Fairlie performed sensationally on the Festiniog and led to both articulated locomotives and the narrow gauge rapidly spreading across the world.

An inspirational era ended just forty years later with the advent of the most successful design of them all in the shape of the first Garratt. Between these two landmark events came Meyers of many kinds and a host of other less familiar designs, all using bogies to cope with hauling ever heavier loads round sharp curvature.

Most inventions have initial drawbacks and in this case it was the necessity to use flexible steam pipes with their tendency to develop serious leaks. Engineers soon looked at alternatives and one of the relatively few successful results was the Mallet, which became one of the most enduring of designs with just its front unit swivelling and taking only low-pressure steam. As the rear unit was rigid and fixed to the frame, it clearly did not accord with the simpler 'articulated' definition of a locomotive 'carried on two or more bogies'. It also failed to qualify for inclusion in Wiener's core category of 'articulated locomotives properly so called'. Although the distinction is often overlooked, he pointed out that the Mallet could only be termed a semi-articulated locomotive.

Wiener also took the same approach with several systems that had a single rigid group of driving wheels and achieved articulation through radial axles. They were built in huge numbers but externally often looked little different from conventional locomotives. For this reason, only a relatively few successful types among a host of failures are covered in these pages. They feature with due moderation in a 'Weird and Wonderful' chapter, its title being chosen because their internal mechanisms were often extraordinary.

Included in the same chapter are Shays, Climaxes and Heislers, which became so uniquely associated with the logging industry of the American West. Here too the text is kept in check, even though they are unquestionably proper articulated locomotives. Yet this facet takes second place both in sight and sound to the fascination of their gearing, which

Purists may argue that a Mallet is only a semi-articulated locomotive, but this does little to dent their special appeal. To many they reached perfection on the Vivarais system in France, as instanced by Swiss-built 0-6-6-0T No 404, photographed in July 1991. (James Waite)

has given them lasting cult status and means that a massive amount of material is already in print.

Shays and the like were also highly specialised, whereas most other articulated locomotives had more general application. Primarily manufactured in Germany and Britain, they spread to all corners of the world. These pages look at some of the most fascinating of all narrow gauge locomotives working in conditions ranging from tropical paradise through the battlefields of World War I to high mountains of almost unimaginable severity. Their swansong was in South Africa in the 1950s and it is not surprising that it triggered preservation on a grand scale.

It is a wholly appropriate finale – and a fitting conclusion to this book – that Garratt locomotives built in Britain should return to their homeland. It was a superb moment when they first steamed on the Welsh Highland and thus became destined to operate out of Porthmadog, the birthplace of narrow gauge articulated locomotives.

David Joy

Acknowledgements

An enormous thanks is due to those who have helped with this book in so many different ways.

My quest to see articulated locomotives overseas was made immeasurably easier by tours arranged by David Rodgers, the late David Ibbotson and Travel Bureau Railtours. Accompanying me on virtually all these trips were John Jennings and Mick Johnstone, who were a tower of strength in the wilds of South America and especially in Zimbabwe when I was suspected of being an investigative photojournalist!

Keith Chester, Rob Dickinson and James Waite have read the text and suggested amendments that were always constructive and considered. I am very grateful for the time they have spent on this task. Help with the text has also been given by the late Donald Binns, David Cairns, David Payling and Michael Reilly. Wilfred Mole, the guiding force behind the remarkable Sandstone Steam Railroad in South Africa, has been an enthusiastic supporter at all times.

Many of those named above have contributed wonderful photographs that bring the story of articulated locomotives to life. Others are individually credited in the captions. Several of the images are selected from pictures originally appearing in *Narrow Gauge World*, in some cases so long ago that it has proved impossible to contact the photographers to thank them. In such cases, I shall be pleased if they get in touch with me: dawjoy@aol.com

Finally, I thank Trevor Ridley of Atlantic Publishers for seeing my thoughts through to print. I'm especially grateful to Juliet Arthur, the designer, for applying her vision to *Engines that Bend*.

CHAPTER ONE

The Flawed Genius of Robert Fairlie

FESTINIOG TRIUMPH

The world's first successful narrow gauge articulated locomotive was both a product of genius and an answer to a dire problem on the Festiniog Railway. Charles Easton Spooner, the company's gifted engineer from 1856 until 1872, had already confounded sceptics by introducing pioneer steam locomotives on what was essentially a horse tramway. In a computer age that has scant regard for fractions its gauge is generally rounded up to two feet but in fact was precisely 1ft 11⅝in. The small 0-4-0 tanks, built by George England at Hatcham Iron Works in south-east London in the period 1863-67, proved competent within their limitations but were soon unable to handle rapidly increasing slate traffic already in excess of 100,000 tons per annum.

Eager to find a solution was a Scottish engineer Robert Fairlie, who grandiosely considered that all existing railway locomotives had a common defect. They wasted weight on tenders that were heavy but totally useless except to carry fuel and water. In 1864 he produced a pamphlet arguing a case for superior efficiency by combining two conventional locomotives back-to-back, with the boiler barrels incorporated within an outer casing to form one complete unit. It would rest on four- or six-coupled bogies supplied with steam through flexible pipes, thus creating an articulated locomotive that would use all its wheels for adhesion. It was a concept especially suited to lines like the Festiniog with sharp curves and steep gradients.

Fairlie patented his ideas, which were promptly applied to standard-gauge motive power in 1865 by Cross & Co of St Helens. The following year the same firm built three 0-6 + 6-0Ts for the 3ft 6in gauge Southern & Western Railway of Queensland. Unfortunately, a whole raft of complications outside his immediate control meant that the locomotives proved a failure and severely damaged his reputation. Happily he had an ally in the wings. As summarised in the biographical note, Fairlie and George England had a bruising encounter in court in 1862. Perhaps because this established that they were both of dubious moral character, they patched up their differences and England became a firm supporter of Fairlie's ideas. In September 1868 he wrote to C E Spooner from Hatcham Iron Works:

'We will undertake to make you a Fairlie double-boiler duplex locomotive of the very best material and workmanship, equal in power to any two of the engines you have now working on your line. We have no hesitation in saying that this engine will effect a very great saving over the old type, both in wear and tear of the permanent way, and working expenses, will run round curves down to two chains radius, and at all speeds required with great safety.'

Spooner may have needed little convincing, as he had already received a prophetic letter from his close engineering associate

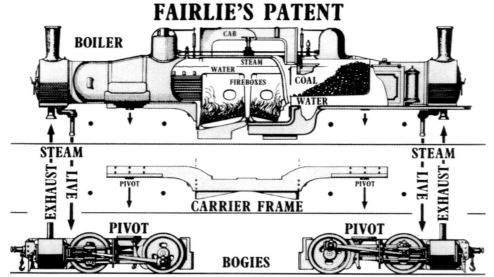

THIS PAGE: Exploded diagram of a 'Fairlie's Patent' locomotive. (Ffestiniog Railway Company)

OPPOSITE: With a chimney emitting smoke at either end and a boiler separating driver and fireman, it is easy to see why a Fairlie 0-4 + 4-0T caused a sensation when it first appeared at Portmadoc. *Merddin Emrys* recaptures the atmosphere in October 2005. (James Waite)

Charles M Holland. Stressing the advantages of flexibility in a locomotive's wheelbase and of having all wheels powered, it also expressed with extraordinary premonition a preference for 'a long centipede style of engine on six or eight wheels to creep steadily and with a great load up your line'.

Nevertheless there must have been some anxiety. The Fairlies so far constructed had been designed for lines with a loading gauge that was far more generous than that of the Festiniog. Its infamous Moelwyn tunnel, constructed with nothing more than horse-haulage in mind, was only 8ft wide by 9ft 6in high. Potentially 730 yards of hell if any locomotive failed inside its stygian depths, it was in contrast with other lines like comparing a mouse-hole with a rabbit burrow.

Any doubts were swiftly cast to one side by the ever-optimistic Robert Fairlie. In July 1869 the Festiniog accordingly took delivery of *Little Wonder*, an extraordinary 0-4 + 4-0T built at a cost of £2,006 (about £140,000 at current-day prices). The name was appropriate, as it was after all a wonder on rails and nothing like it had previously been seen on so narrow a gauge. With a chimney at either end it certainly looked startling, especially when the crew were in place with the driver working at one side of the double boiler and the fireman at the other. The large 'Fairlie's Patent' nameplate left no doubt that this was something distinctly out of the ordinary.

Yet *Little Wonder* was a near-perfect answer to the limitations posed by the Festiniog Railway. It had around twice the power of the earlier England 0-4-0s, but its weight of only 19.25 tons and a light axle loading spared the company's relatively lightly laid track from any grief. It was able to handle both the line's very sharp curves and its restricted clearances – including the notorious Moelwyn tunnel. Any failure at one end was not necessarily terminal, as the two fireboxes generated steam independently and the locomotive could be controlled by one power bogie. Finally, it required no turning and thus there was no necessity for costly turntables.

Little Wonder caused a sensation when it appeared before assembled engineering experts at Portmadoc Harbour station in September 1869 and duly made up a train of 114 tons comprising six loaded carriages, twelve goods wagons and no fewer than 111 empty slate wagons. It stretched into the distance for well over 300 yards. Any doubts were soon dispelled when the climb to Blaenau Festiniog was completed through a storm of wind and rain at an average speed of 23mph. The footplate crew especially appreciated the smooth riding more akin to that of a bogie carriage and very different to the bucking and swaying of an England 0-4-0 tank. As the representative of *The Engineer* commented, they could be prone to break the driver's teeth!

A later issue of the sister magazine *Engineering* evocatively described the view from the footplate in thick mist and driving rain, when it was impossible to see much more than the length of the locomotive. The engine seemed to be flying through the clouds with the long boiler pointing out over the valley – invisible through the mist – at an angle of twenty to thirty degrees to the line ahead. The reporter concluded that, in order to understand the capabilities of the articulated locomotive, 'one wants to travel on the Festiniog Railway in a fog'.

With *Little Wonder* proving much more successful than even George England had anticipated, Robert Fairlie's reputation took a giant step forward. So did the standing of the Festiniog, which overnight found itself the focus of world-wide narrow gauge mania. At the same time its prayers were answered, as among the few alternatives would have been the expensive options of doubling the track or even converting to standard gauge.

The Festiniog lost no time in ordering a second Fairlie with many detailed design improvements. Following the demise of Hatcham Iron Works, the choice of builder fell on the Bristol based Avonside Engine Company. One of the partners was Edward Slaughter – an enthusiastic advocate of articulated locomotives and formerly assistant engineer to Isambard Kingdom Brunel on the Great Western Railway.

Designed by George Percival Spooner and named *James Spooner* after his grandfather and the railway's original engineer, the second Fairlie entered traffic in December 1872. Turned out in full Victorian finery with lined red livery complete with the Prince of Wales' feathers, it must have made a splendid sight. Brass domes, bells mounted on top of the sand pots and disc-pattern wheels were among the other distinguishing features. Typical of the times was a total absence of any comforts for the crew, who were expected to endure the frequently torrential rain of North Wales' weather with only primitive weatherboards and half cab sheets for protection. Like its predecessor, *James Spooner* was worked hard and normally did three round trips a day, notching up over 20,000 miles a year. It was a remarkable performance with average loads of 90 tons on ruling gradients of 1 in 80.

The company's next move took it to new heights. As if to celebrate the tenth anniversary of *Little Wonder* in style, it decided to dispense with a locomotive manufacturer and on 21 July 1879 its works at Boston Lodge turned out a third Fairlie *Merddin Emrys*. The boiler, frame plates and wheel centres were supplied to the works, but it was still an amazing achievement complete with the welcome improvement of an almost fully enclosed cab. Its name was derived from a Head

Bard in the Tales of King Arthur, whom those outside Wales might have insisted was better known as Merlin.

The Festiniog now appeared to be in the happy position of possessing ample motive power, but it was soon to suffer a brief setback. By 1882 *Little Wonder* required a new boiler, the highly acidic local water having taken its toll, and was also suffering from all the disadvantages of being a prototype. In less than fifteen years the sensation of 1869 had become a worn-out anachronism. Rather than spend money on costly repairs, it was decided to build a further locomotive at Boston Lodge. *Livingston Thompson*, named after the company's former chairman and largest shareholder, took out its first train on 29 June 1886 and, along with its sister Fairlies, played a pivotal role in handling over ninety per cent of the Festiniog's train mileage. These were the peak years when the company could scarcely cope with ever-rising demand for Welsh slate created by the building boom of the late Victorian age.

FAME AND FAILURE

The 1880s may have been years of plenty for the Festiniog but its brief glory at the centre stage of world railway development was already over. Immense hopes had been raised and promptly dashed.

The spectacular debut of *Little Wonder* was followed the next month by a series of wildly enthusiastic articles and editorials in *The Times*, which created huge interest overseas. In January 1870 Fairlie was invited to St. Petersburg where he set out his stall to the Ministry of Public Works. He clearly was seductive, for the next month a high-powered delegation visited the Festiniog. The assemblage of the great and the good arrived at Portmadoc in style, their train comprising the London & North Western Railway's royal carriages and the private saloon of the 3rd Duke of Sutherland. One of Britain's richest men, he was also a passionate railway enthusiast and a fortunate choice to head the delegation that comprised numerous representatives of the Imperial Russian Commission as well

Little Wonder poses for the camera with an immensely long train on the Festiniog Railway's Cei Mawr embankment. The photograph dates from 1870, when the locomotive was only a year old.
(Andrew Neale collection)

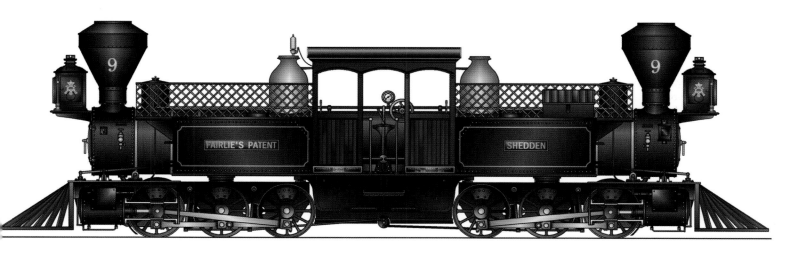

ABOVE: *Shedden*, one of the two pioneer Fairlies produced by Avonside in 1871 for the 3ft 6in gauge lines based on Toronto. Early conversion to standard gauge meant that it lasted little more than a decade. (drawing by Rod Clarke)

RIGHT: *Caledon*, the sister locomotive to *Shedden*. The cages to hold huge amounts of logs were a distinctive feature of a wood-burning engine that had precious little space for fuel.
(Ralph Beaumont collection)

as railways in France, Scandinavia and India. The outcome was the first overseas order for narrow gauge Fairlies in the shape of five wood-burning 0-6 + 6-0Ts supplied by Sharp Stewart of Manchester to the 3ft 6in gauge Imperial Livny Railway. Soon after arrival in early 1871 one of them hauled a 61-wagon train with a gross weight of 400 tons and a commemorative medal was duly struck.

It was a golden opportunity for a natural self-publicist like Fairlie and he seized every minute of it. Untroubled by modesty, he stressed in a paper why the Russian railway had used his locomotives, 'without which the value of the narrow gauge at once sinks into comparative insignificance'. This may have seemed barbed praise, but he went on to write a book that left no doubt on where he stood. Its title was Victorian verbosity at its finest: *Railways or No Railways: Narrow Gauge, Economy with Efficiency v. Broad Gauge, Costliness with Extravagance.*

Fairlie genuinely believed that narrow gauge railways, operated by what he regarded as his proven motive power, would dominate much of the world. It was precisely the time when railways were expanding on all fronts to develop much of the British Empire, and the apparent cost savings represented by constructing to a narrower gauge held great

appeal. By 1871, narrow gauge track had been laid in India, Australia, New Zealand and Canada.

Locomotive manufacturers were primed to build more Fairlies and it was Avonside that rapidly achieved dominance in the export market. Although *James Spooner* proved to be the only locomotive built by the company for a public British narrow gauge line, it was not the firm's first Fairlie. The earliest narrow gauge products in 1871 were destined for Canada and were a pair of 3ft 6in gauge 0-6 + 6-0Ts *Caledon* and *Shedden*, respectively for the Toronto, Grey & Bruce Railway and the neighbouring Toronto & Nipissing line. They were wood-burning and hence their most distinctive features were imposing diamond-stack chimneys and cages astride the boiler to hold copious amounts of logs.

Both systems had the same chief engineer, Edmund Wragge, who in a paper to the Institution of Civil Engineers made some telling comments in comparing the Fairlies with other more conventional locomotives on the two lines: 'The Fairlie engines consume less fuel in hauling the load of 280 tons than the Goods Engines in hauling 250 tons and they are much easier on the Permanent Way. At the same time they require three men to work them instead of two owing to the difficulty in getting the fuel from the crates on the top of the

Boiler; the saving in fuel however is quite equivalent to the wages of an extra hand on the Engine.'

The third man, known as the 'Woodpasser', worked in appalling conditions during the Canadian winters, often having to get logs by crawling along the top of the locomotive in pitch darkness with temperatures of twenty degrees below zero. Wragge seemingly paid little heed to the dangers involved, perhaps taking the view that the riding characteristics of the Fairlies posed few risks: 'The engines pass round our curves admirably, and are very easy on the track; they run so smoothly that our men are apt to run them too fast for economical working.'

In February 1873, Wragge wrote to Fairlie with further favourable comments and also touched on a little-known aspect of their performance: 'Your engines have shown themselves first-rate in snow, running through drifts of four feet or five feet in depth at a speed of twenty miles an hour.'

Avonside continued to expand its export territory, and ultimately supplied Fairlies to such diverse destinations in the far-flung Empire as Nova Scotia, South Africa and Western Australia – where two 3ft 6in gauge locomotives were distin-guished by their unique 2-4 + 4-2T wheel arrangement. Yet the initial dominance achieved by the company could hardly be expected to go unchallenged. Other early suppliers of narrow gauge Fairlies were R & W Hawthorn of Newcastle and the Yorkshire Engine Company of Sheffield, which in the early 1870s built locomotives to stock orders for a selling agency, with the gauge and even wheel arrangements being altered according to demand.

The Vulcan Foundry of Newton-le-Willows built its first Fairlies in 1872 in the shape of a pair of 0-4 + 4-0Ts *Rose* and *Josephine* for the 3ft 6in gauge Dunedin & Port Chalmers Railway in New Zealand. Loaded onto a ship at Bristol in April 1872 and accompanied by Mr Amos, the company engineer, it took them five months to complete what must have been an epic journey to this most distant of destinations.

The next two locomotives to be turned out by the Vulcan Foundry in 1872 were again Fairlies. The pair of 0-4 + 4-0Ts went to Peru for the opening of the 2ft 6in gauge Patillos Railway, built to convey nitrate from the Lagunas area down to the Pacific coast. A further pair followed a year later, all four having a South American style cab with its roof divided

ROBERT FAIRLIE

Robert Fairlie 1831 - 1885.
(Festiniog Railway Company)

Born in Paisley in March 1831, Robert Francis Fairlie received his training at two great locomotive works – Crewe and Swindon. When only twenty-one he was appointed locomotive superintendent of the Londonderry & Coleraine Railway, but was soon made redundant and went to the Bombay Baroda & Central India Railway. Returning to Britain, he set up as a consulting engineer and made the acquaintance of George England, locomotive manufacturer at Hatcham Iron Works.

It proved to be a fateful meeting in more ways than one. Fairlie, then aged thirty, fell in love with England's seventeen-year old daughter Eliza Anne, but her father disapproved of the match owing to the age difference. The couple eloped to Spain and forged a marriage licence, whereupon England had Fairlie arrested and charged with perjury for corruptly making a false statement. If proven it was an offence that carried a prison sentence, but the trial at the Central Criminal Court in April 1862 took a sensational turn when it emerged that England had made Eliza Anne's mother pregnant while he was married to another woman. Under Victorian law he was not therefore her 'legal' father and could not prevent her marrying. The trial thus immediately collapsed in circumstances bordering on farcical.

George England retired through ill health in the summer of 1869 at about the same time as he delivered *Little Wonder* to the Festiniog Railway. Fairlie was one of the parties that then leased Hatcham Iron Works. The partners formed the Fairlie Engine & Steam Carriage Company, but it was plagued by financial problems and ceased locomotive production the following year.

Fairlie had by now become a tireless advocate of the narrow gauge and his own locomotive designs to the point of obsession. His name was rarely out of the columns of *Engineering* and he never hesitated to attack anyone who dared to criticise his forthright views. *Scribner's Monthly* perceptively described him as 'an indefatigable controversialist'. He has also been referred to as complex and full of contradictions – ebullient, flamboyant, extremely prickly and utterly charming.

Fairlie travelled the world in pursuit of his ideals, and it was during a visit to Venezuela in 1873-74 that he contracted tropical fever. It was a misfortune from which he never fully recovered, although he continued as an independent designer of articulated locomotives until 1878 and died seven years later at the age of fifty-four.

ABOVE: *Josephine*, one of the first four Fairlies to be built by the Vulcan Foundry. Loaded onto a ship in Bristol in April 1872, it reached the far-distant destination of Dunedin, New Zealand, five months later! (painting by W.W. Stewart, courtesy of Port Chalmers Museum)

CENTRE: Hope unfulfilled! *Mountaineer*, the Fairlie that failed to find favour in the USA and dashed huge ambitions. This photograph shows it as built by the Vulcan Foundry in 1873. (D. Binns collection)

LOWER: *Mountaineer* proved to be the only Fairlie ever sent from Britain to the USA. Despite the provision of extra fuel space, it clearly received little care and had a short life. (D. Binns collection)

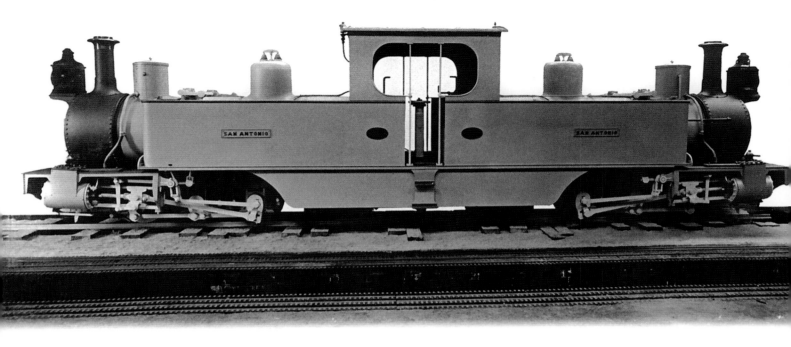

'A very decided improvement' – one of the pair of 0-6 + 6-0Ts supplied by the Yorkshire Engine Company to the Junin Railway in Chile in 1905. It boasted two separate boilers and a walk-through cab. (D. Binns collection)

into two with an air space between. It could not only be hot but also unpleasantly humid on the equatorial plain bordering the coast.

It all seemed very promising but there was one other country that Robert Fairlie knew he had to convert to his cause. The USA, in the grip of narrow gauge fever, was a magnet that seemed to offer so much and yet soon triggered failure. The saga had begun back in November 1870 with a visit to England by General William Jackson Palmer, founder of the most famous US narrow-gauge railroad of them all – the Denver & Rio Grande. He was actually on honeymoon, but this did not prevent him fitting in a visit to the Festiniog and a meeting with Fairlie, who advised him to adopt three-foot gauge.

Anxious that he should personally be linked with this advice, General Palmer's host brazenly referred to the 'three-foot' as the Fairlie gauge and promptly wrote: 'When a Fairlie gauge is worked with Fairlie locomotives and stock, by no other system in existence can such results be obtained.' His persuasive powers must have struck a chord, as it was tracks to this width that were soon conquering the Rockies and taking the quest for gold and silver to new heights. Opening its first line in January 1872, the Rio Grande soon became part of a network that embraced five States and made possible a continuous trip of over 1,200 miles from Denver to Garrison in Montana. Within just thirteen years there were 12,000 miles of narrow-gauge metals in the USA.

Persuading Palmer to adopt the 'Fairlie gauge' may have been one thing but getting him to purchase masses of Fairlie locomotives was another. There was a ray of hope when an order was placed with the Vulcan Foundry for a wood-burning 0-4 + 4-0T *Mountaineer*, which was supplied in 1873. An immediate downside was that it cost £2,900 (about £220,000 at today's prices), which was almost three times as much as a 2-6-0 purchased from the famous Baldwin Locomotive Works in Philadelphia.

On a test run *Mountaineer* hauled a 200-ton load up a 1 in 80 grade and General Palmer insisted he was well pleased with his purchase. Yet those driving the locomotive felt otherwise and in March 1875 Palmer asked his master mechanic to make a detailed evaluation of the Fairlie. On the positive side it found that it was better than a Baldwin in terms of adhesion, haulage capability, smooth riding and tracking curves. Unfortunately, the rest of the findings were devastating. The fuel and water space was too small, the flexible steam pipes could not be kept tight and were always leaking, and the mechanical parts were highly inaccessible for repairs. Moreover, it only ran thirty-nine miles per ton of coal compared with the eighty-one miles of a conventional locomotive.

Such a catalogue of defects could not be countenanced in the context of so expensive a locomotive, especially at a time when there was a rapid movement away from specialised narrow-gauge motive power to scaled-down versions of standard-gauge engines. No other Fairlie was ever sent from Britain to the USA and American enginemen, used to ample cab space, simplicity and ease of maintenance, were no doubt eternally grateful. Nicknamed 'Modoc' after a particularly depressed Indian tribe, *Mountaineer* was demoted to banking duties on the 1 in 25 grades of La Veta Pass and withdrawn in 1883 after a working life of only ten years.

It must have been a disastrous blow to Robert Fairlie but more setbacks were to follow. Despite the promising start, Edmund Wragge ordered no further Fairlies for the two Toronto lines. When additional locomotives were required late in 1873, he opted for conventional products. They were supplied by Baldwin of Philadephia, whose high production

TOP LEFT: Arguably the most extraordinary narrow gauge Fairlie of them all, this was one of three compounds built in Saxony in 1902 and designed for roadside tramway operation between Reichenbach and Oberheinsdorf. Hence the protected wheels and controls at either end. (Uwe Bergmann collection)

TOP RIGHT: All three of the unique compound Fairlies were rebuilt in a slightly more conventional form. The one shown here − 99 162 − remained in service until as late as 1963. (Uwe Bergmann collection)

RIGHT: 99 162 has been restored to its original condition as No 262. It is based in its own museum at Oberheinsdorf, eastern terminus of the line on which it worked. (James Waite)

volumes and low transport costs were by now clearly more than competitive with British manufacturers.

Salt was to be rubbed into the wound, as it soon became apparent that the narrow gauge was a triumph in mountainous areas like the Rockies but offered few advantages in the flat lands of Canada. When both the Toronto lines were converted to standard gauge as soon as the early 1880s there was no case for adapting non-standard locomotives with significant maintenance demands. *Caledon* and *Sheddon* were broken up after a life of little more than a decade.

It was a similar story in many other parts of the world. Of the two pioneer Fairlies sent to New Zealand, *Rose* only lasted until the 1880s. *Josephine* cheated the scrapman when laid aside in 1917 and eight years later was restored for the Dunedin and South Seas Exhibition. She was then placed in a glass cage at the Otago Settlers Museum on the site of the original Dunedin station, finally being removed in late 2010 and taken to a 'secret address' in the city. At the same time

plans were announced to display her in a large new reception building at the museum when its construction was completed in 2012.

Not everyone has enthused over the preservation of *Josephine*, as witness the statement by A N Palmer & W W Stewart in their book *Cavalcade of New Zealand Steam Locomotives:* 'As a revered relic of pioneer days, this flighty old lady has achieved fame to which she is scarcely entitled, for Old Joss as she was known, never was a good locomotive and her contribution to the development of the Dominion was negligible.'

The locomotives that Fairlie's genius had created for the Festiniog were a brilliant solution on a line only thirteen miles long, but the minimal provision for fuel and especially water was simply not going to work in the greater distances of the outside world. As maintenance was difficult, repairs to the double boiler were more than proportionately expensive and fuel-handling difficulties were only solved by conversion

THIS PAGE: Dating back almost 140 years and still steaming, the Michigan-based *Torch Lake* is the only Mason Fairlie in preservation. (Malcolm Peakman)

OPPOSITE: The single Fairlie *Taliesin*, depicted running round at Duffws shortly after it was delivered to the Festiniog Railway. It was built by the Vulcan Foundry in 1876. (painting by David Sutcliffe)

to oil firing. Poor facilities in the more remote parts of the world for servicing non-standard locomotives and patching leaks on their steam pipes meant that much was skimped.

Many Fairlies thus continued to be withdrawn after only a few years, but there were some noted exceptions to this trend. Two 0-4 + 4-0Ts supplied by the Vulcan Foundry in 1875 to the 90cm gauge Porto - Póvoa -Varzim line in northern Portugal survived long enough to be modified when this railway was converted to metre gauge in 1929. No 1 *Rio Douro* was withdrawn in 1938 and No 2 *Rio Ave* lasted until 1945 – a respectable life of seventy years.

It was a similar story when a large order came the way of Avonside in 1879 in the shape of twenty-five 0-4 + 4-0Ts for a proposed metre-gauge line through the Bolan Pass during the Third Afghan War. The military displayed a customary flair for getting things the wrong way round and seventeen locomotives had already been completed by the time it was decided not to proceed with the line. They became part of India Railway stock and, apart from one lost at sea en route, they in most cases managed to have a long and varied career. Four were used in constructing the famous Nilgiri Mountain Railway, where just one of them would today have been a sight to behold on a line that still operates steam-hauled services.

Locomotives continued to be produced in small numbers, but their development was fossilised with no major changes being made to the basic Fairlie concept until 1901. The Vulcan Foundry then adopted a new arrangement with two separate boilers to overcome the problem of variations in water level when standing on steep gradients. This in turn permitted the provision of a roomy walk-through cab, which would have delighted generations of Festiniog enginemen. Five such locomotives were supplied to the metre-gauge Burma Railways, followed by a further two in 1906.

The same modification was made by the Yorkshire Engine Company when it delivered a pair of 0-6 + 6-0Ts to the 2ft 6in

gauge Junin Railway in Chile. Both their length of forty feet and weight of fifty-two tons were exceptional for so narrow a gauge, but they were well received. In its issue of 15 January 1907, *The Locomotive* succinctly commented: 'A very decided improvement is to be noted in connections with the arrangements of the steam pipes. Hitherto the chief weakness of the Fairlie type of engine has been the great number of ball and socket joints, and the difficulty of making them steam-tight.'

Also differing from the basic concept in almost every sense were three metre-gauge 0-4 + 4-0Ts, built outside Britain in 1902 at the Saxon Engine Works in Chemnitz, Germany. At this relatively late date in locomotive evolution, they could benefit from some proven new technology. The only compound Fairlies in the world, all four cylinders were located at the firebox end of the bogie frames. They must have provided more than sufficient motive power for the five kilometres of the Reichenbach - Oberheinsdorf line in the far south-west of Saxony, which in part ran along the public highway. It was thus considered essential for the driver to be at the front and hence there were steam and brake controls at either end. A large canopy with side panels extended the full length of the locomotive and enabled the crew to pass safely from one end to the other. As with many tramway-style engines, the motion was covered by side sheets to protect pedestrians and animals.

Later rebuilt without the extended roof and with driving controls in the centre, they had a longevity that was definitely an exception to the rule. One of the three was reputedly sent to Greece in 1943 and lost at sea en route to the Crimea late that year. The other two of these most unusual of all Fairlies were still working out of Reichenbach until the line closed in 1962. One of them, No 99 162, was saved for preservation and is kept at Oberheinsdorf in a small museum, purpose-built in the style of a Saxon narrow gauge engine shed. An offer by the Harz Railway to restore it to working order was turned down by the museum on the grounds

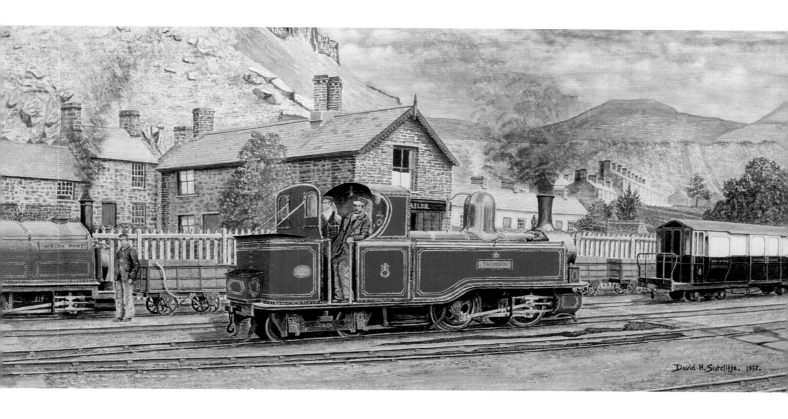

that too much of the original fabric of the locomotive would be destroyed in the process.

A SINGLE SOLUTION

Despite the thumbs down that Fairlies received in the USA, there was one man who did not throw in the towel. William Mason had a machine works in Taunton, Massachusetts, and was a licensee of the Fairlie patent. Only too aware of the American desire for rugged simplicity, he would surely have been impressed by developments at Inchicore Works in Ireland. Here a radical single-boiler Fairlie was completed in 1869 for the Irish 5ft 3in gauge. At first glance it looked like a conventional rather than an articulated locomotive, but closer examination revealed that it did not have a rigid frame and instead comprised a single power bogie and a trailing bogie. A key advantage was that it could negotiate very tight-radius curves without grief. By including a bunker, it also solved the problem of limited fuel space that plagued the double-boiler Fairlies.

Adopting many facets of the Irish approach, Mason came up with a single-boiler locomotive with power and trailing bogies, offering operating convenience, adequate fuel capacity and reduced maintenance liabilities. It generally became known as the Mason Bogie in the USA and the Mason Fairlie elsewhere. The first to be built was *Onward*, completed in 1871 and sold to the three-foot gauge American Fork Railroad in Utah the following year. Subsequent orders were at first slow but rapidly increased once it became clear that double-boiler Fairlies stood no chance of meeting North American needs.

Although a great step forward, the Mason Fairlies were still more complicated and costly than a conventional locomotive.

Problems remained with steam leakage and especially the swivelling bogie, which had a tendency to ride badly and cause derailments by spreading the light narrow-gauge track. Not surprisingly, Mason presented a robust defence in the company's catalogue: 'By means of the flexibility of these bogies the whole working machinery becomes perfectly articulated, which allows the wheels to follow all the undulations of the track. The body of the engine therefore glides along as perfectly and smoothly as a Pullman car.'

Not everyone would have agreed with the comparison with Pullman travel, but the locomotives were far from a failure. Almost a hundred narrow-gauge Mason Fairlies were built by the company in the seventeen years from 1873 until it ceased production in 1890. Often incorporating a tender, they had a bewildering variety of wheel arrangements and sported such colourful names as *Bully Boy*, *Eureka* and *Roaring Fork*. No fewer than twenty-two were supplied to the Denver, South Park & Pacific for use on its lines high in the Rockies, the final development being a 2-8-6 of impressive proportions.

A railroad that refused to be beaten by the closure of Mason Machine Works was the Boston, Revere Beach & Lynn, also in Massachusetts. It purchased the original drawings and patterns and continued to order batches from other manufacturers, the final dozen being built by Alco between 1903 and 1914.

A remarkable survivor is *Torch Lake*, a 0-6-4 nominally dating back to 1873 when it was supplied to the four-foot gauge Hecla & Torch Lake Railroad in the copper-mining region of northern Michigan. Still on the roster in the 1950s, it was donated in 1969 to the Henry Ford museum at Dearborn, Michigan, where it regularly hauls tourist trains.

Although converted to standard gauge, it clearly has narrow gauge antecedents and is both the oldest Fairlie of any kind still in service and the only preserved example of a Mason Fairlie.

The British narrow gauge lagged behind the USA in the introduction of single-boiler Fairlies. The pioneers were two 0-6-4Ts *Snowdon Ranger* and *Moel Tryfan* built in 1875 by the Vulcan Foundry for the embryo North Wales Narrow Gauge Railways. Precursor of the Welsh Highland, this ambitious project was masterminded by the Festiniog and it is therefore not surprising that the original working drawings are signed 'C E Spooner per G Percival Spooner'. The two locomotives were not especially successful and had careers noted for the fact that nothing of any significance happened to them.

A year later in 1876 the Vulcan Foundry delivered the single Fairlie *Taliesin* to the Festiniog. A 0-4-4T taking its name from the Head Bard of Urien Rheged, it featured several design improvements including larger cylinders and driving wheels as well as a bigger boiler. The footplate was spacious and the good-sized bunker had a weatherboard to provide some protection from the Welsh rain. *Taliesin* proved to be fast, free steaming and economical and was held in high regard by footplate crews. More powerful than the old and rough-riding England 0-4-0Ts, it was less demanding than the double Fairlies in that there was only one firebox to fill.

The downside was a reputation as a fire thrower, presumably because the harder the engine was worked the better the boiler steamed. In the end it was the complexities of its design in relation to its power output that told against the Festiniog ordering any more single-boiler Fairlies.

That was not the end of the story. It was apparently on the personal recommendation of Robert Fairlie that Avonside received a contract in 1878 to build fifteen 0-6-4Ts of handsome appearance for the New Zealand Government Railways. Three more single-boiler Fairlies followed a year later and another seven of improved design in 1880/81. Successful locomotives that proved capable of obtaining speeds in excess of 50mph, some examples remained in service until the 1930s. One of them, No R 28, remains on display in Reefton on the west coast of South Island.

WHEN CAPTAIN PÉCHOT MET MONSIEUR BOURDON

Even when taking the single-boiler versions into account, the number of narrow-gauge Fairlies was never vast. It is thus more than a little ironic that they were totally eclipsed in quantity by a locomotive that should arguably have incurred an action for breach of patent. Its origins lay in France with one Captain Prosper Péchot. He was a veteran of the Franco-Prussian War of 1870, which highlighted the need for narrow gauge railways to supply forts and other front-line positions in times of conflict.

In 1880 Péchot teamed up with another French artilleryman, Paul Decauville, who after the war had returned to civilian life and developed the concept of lightweight portable railways using horse haulage. Although intended primarily for agricultural use, they clearly also had great potential on the battlefield. A year earlier Decauville had visited the Festiniog Railway and like so many before him came away hugely impressed. In order to convince the military authorities of the value of narrow gauge lines, Decauville and Péchot

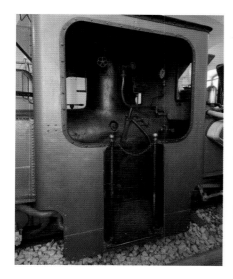

ABOVE: Cab close-up of the Péchot–Bourdon in Dresden railway museum. (James Waite)

RIGHT: The Péchot-Bourdon preserved in the Pozega narrow gauge museum in Serbia. (Alan Heywood)

built a demonstration railway at Fort Vaujours, near Paris. It achieved its object, and in 1882 Péchot was asked to construct a series of 60cm gauge lines to convey supplies from standard-gauge railheads to four massive forts that had been established along the new Franco/German border at Verdun, Toûl, Epinal and Belfort.

It was about this time that Captain Péchot would meet Monsieur Bourdon, a college professor and kindred spirit. The two men addressed the question of suitable motive power for the new lines and were no doubt influenced by Paul Decauville's enthusiasm for the Festiniog and the products of Robert Fairlie.

Adopting an approach that some might unkindly say was typically French, the Captain and the professor decided to pay scant regard to the Fairlie patent and made the most minor of design changes in such areas as position of the steam dome, use of spring compensation between boiler and bogies, and simplification of the steam and exhaust piping. They were then able to obtain a patent in June 1887 – significantly two years after Fairlie's death – for what was clearly a double-boiler Fairlie in all but name. What became popularly known as Péchot-Bourdon 0-4 + 4-0Ts were officially termed 'locomotives articulées Modèle 1888'. Fitted with Walschaert's valve gear and wooden brake blocks, their most distinguishing feature was the pair of huge spark arresters with chimney extensions.

One of the reputed reasons for adopting such an outdated design says much for the military mind. It was a belief that if one half of the locomotive was damaged by enemy fire the other half might still continue to operate!

Paul Decauville was asked to build an initial two locomotives at his works at Evry-sur-Seine, south-west of Paris, but considered the work too complex and sub-contracted the task to the Société Franco-Belge at Raismes. No 1 *France* was delivered in December 1888 to the strategic railways in the Toûl fortified zone, where its duties included hauling heavy cannon mounted on special bogies.

No 2 *Centenaire de 1789* was sent to work on Decauville's 60cm demonstration railway at the Paris Exhibition of 1889, held to celebrate the one-hundredth anniversary of the French Revolution. Unfortunately it failed to distinguish itself on the intensive passenger service and was seldom used. There were also teething troubles with No 1, and in particular with the injectors and safety valves, but Captain Péchot managed to convince the authorities that all would be well and the Péchot-Bourdons were adopted as standard for heavy military use. Production proceeded apace, with Cail building nineteen in 1888 and twelve in 1889/90 with a further twelve coming from Fives Lille in 1892. They all carried plates stating ownership as 'Ministère de la Guerre, ARTILLERIE, Locomotive modèle 1888 brevetée SGDG, no …'.

In 1894 a series of trials at Vaujours involved running no less than 484 trains, but again the Péchot-Bourdons failed to impress and both military and railway observers found them too complex. Drivers and firemen, who had travelled with the locomotives from the various forts, averred that they had not

LEFT: *Merddin Emrys* at the nadir of its fortunes in 1972, just after it had received a longer boiler and looked horribly functional. A benefactor provided funding in 1985 for the locomotive to return to a more traditional Fairlie appearance. (James Waite)

LOWER: The double Fairlie *Taliesin*, originally *Livingston Thompson*, at Blaenau Ffestiniog in the 1930s. The run-down appearance of the locomotive, reflecting the general state of the Festiniog at this time, is all too evident. (Dr I.C. Allen collection)

OPPOSITE PAGE: *David Lloyd George*, the newest double Fairlie on the Ffestiniog, entered traffic in 1992. It is seen crossing the Cob in October 2005. (James Waite)

instead took the form of trench warfare extending all the way from the English Channel to the Alps. It very quickly became clear that a massive expansion of 60cm gauge lines and associated motive power was urgently needed.

The French turned to the only manufacturer in the world considered capable of meeting their needs and in February 1915 asked Baldwin Locomotive Works to supply no less than 280 Péchot-Bourdons. It was one of the largest-ever single orders from Europe for narrow gauge motive power. Construction was undertaken at a pace unhindered by today's layers of self-strangling administration, but nevertheless remains mind-boggling. The first one hundred locomotives were delivered just two months later, with the remainder following by the end of 1916. A further fifteen were supplied by the North British Locomotive Company in 1915.

More conventional motive power also arrived in 1915, but essentially the French went to war with a fleet of oddball locomotives built to a design pirated over twenty years earlier and already considered flawed because of its complexity. If that were not enough, the Péchot-Bourdons could easily trap their crew if derailed and the smoke from two chimneys increased the chance of becoming a target on the front line.

Crews claimed they were always ready to jump, but in fact the locomotives acquitted themselves remarkably well and were retained by the military after the war. They even impressed the Japanese Government, who in 1921 asked Baldwin to build a solitary example so that the design could be copied for use on their military railways. It was duly delivered but nothing further was heard of the proposal.

History repeated itself when construction of vast fortifications on the new border between France and Germany began in 1929. The Péchot-Bourdons remained in use on the fort systems but were regarded as temperamental and did not long survive the German invasion of 1940. Most were broken up for scrap – and especially for their copper fireboxes – and only three are known to have outlasted World War II. Two of these were transferred to the opencast brown coal mine at Kostolac in occupied Yugoslavia, where they worked until the late 1950s. One of them was then sent to the Yugoslavian Railway Museum at Belgrade and later moved to the narrow

performed well because they were unhappy with the accommodation provided for them! Whatever the truth, Captain Péchot stood his ground and fended off any sense of failure by being promoted to commandant.

Cail delivered an additional sixteen locomotives in 1906, some of which were briefly sent to Morocco to work on newly built military lines. They must have been the only locomotives with Fairlie antecedents to be seen in Africa. There was now ample sufficiency for some remarkable military manoeuvres, which saw some forty Péchot-Bourdons being taken on standard gauge wagons to a railhead at Foulain, north of Langres on the Paris to Mulhouse line. From here a steeply graded line was built to a base at Villiers-sur-Suize, high on a plateau above the River Maine, from where feeder tracks were laid to a series of defensive positions. This time all went well and at one stage the locomotives were handling forty-eight trains a day each carrying eighteen tonnes of shells.

It proved to be a spectacular if misplaced curtain raiser to the traumatic events that began only eight years later. On the outbreak of World War I in August 1914 the battle zone was not conveniently located along the line of existing forts but

gauge museum at Pozega, in what is now Serbia, where it remains today.

The third somehow got to Magdeburg, in the Communist controlled German Democratic Republic, where it was used on the Magdeburger Trümmerbahn – one of the 'rubble railways' established in many German cities after the war to clear devastated buildings prior to reconstruction. Out of use by 1950, it was then restored at the locomotive repair shops at Karl Marx Stadt and has been exhibited in Dresden railway museum since 1958.

Thus bizarrely there is no Péchot-Bourdon extant in France. There has been talk of repatriation – and even a return

to steam – on the preserved lines at Froissy or Pithiviers, both of which have working examples of World War I locomotives, but nothing has come of the idea.

BACK TO THE BEGINNING

Soon after the end of World War II it seemed that not just Péchot-Bourdons but also proper narrow-gauge Fairlies had reached the end of the line. There appeared to be no prospect that one would ever steam again in their original heartland in North Wales. Here the peak in terms of numbers had been reached back in the Edwardian age, when the North Wales Narrow Gauge Railways had surprisingly taken delivery of a

third single-boiler Fairlie 0-6-4T *Gowrie* from the Hunslet Engine Company of Leeds as late as 1908. It was thus a sister to *Snowdon Ranger* and *Moel Tryfan*, while on the Festiniog were the similar Taliesin and what were by now popularly known as double Fairlies *James Spooner*, *Merddin Emrys* and *Livingston Thompson*. It was a situation destined to last just seven years.

Gowrie proved to be a poor steamer and was sold in 1915 to the Ministry of Munitions, probably because the railway was short of funds. By this time the two earlier single Fairlies were also struggling, and in 1917 the power bogie of *Snowdon Ranger* was put under its sister engine to make one serviceable locomotive. The hybrid *Moel Tryfan* passed to the Welsh Highland Railway in 1922 and then struggled on for another twelve years until it entered Boston Lodge works for boiler repairs that were never completed. To the consternation of dedicated preservationists ever since, its remains were finally cut up for scrap in 1954.

On the Festiniog, *Taliesin* saw extensive use until 1924 when it was the victim of what is now widely seen as one of the more regrettable decisions in the history of the railway. The management refused to sanction purchase of a new boiler and thus the single Fairlie was placed on stand-by duties until withdrawn in 1932 after fifty-six years' service. It had notched up the impressive total of well over half a million miles.

Livingston Thompson was promptly renamed *Taliesin*. It soon became one of only two surviving double Fairlies, as *James Spooner* was withdrawn in 1933 and then cannibalised

After becoming *Taliesin* and then *Earl of Merioneth*, the double Fairlie *Livingston Thompson* reverted to its original name and its 1910 appearance. It was handed over to the National Railway Museum, but made a return visit to the Ffestiniog in 2005. It is seen standing outside the old engine shed at Boston Lodge. (James Waite)

to keep its younger sisters running. They handled much of the diminishing traffic on an increasingly run-down railway until 1940, when *Taliesin* was partially dismantled for an overhaul that failed to progress.

Merddin Emrys was left to soldier on through the war with minimal maintenance. Sudden closure of the Festiniog in August 1946 led to the locomotive dropping its fire in a cold and decaying Boston Lodge running shed, the lack of hope meaning that it was abandoned with water in the boiler and wet coal in its bunkers. It appeared to be the end of a long era when Fairlies and the Festiniog had been synonymous. The direct descendant of *Little Wonder*, which had so spectacularly blazed a trail in 1869, was surely destined for the scrap merchants, as the chances of the railway ever reopening seemed remote. It appeared to be an ignominious end to a pioneering chapter in the story of articulated locomotives.

Subsequent events that followed the reopening in 1955 are almost tediously familiar. Indeed, the present writer still recalls the time when he was editing *Narrow Gauge World* and received an email from a reader stating in no uncertain terms

ABOVE: The single Fairlie *Taliesin* approaching Pont Croesor with a train from Hafod y Llyn to Porthmadog in January 2011. The works/number plate *(page 24)* must be just about the only part to have survived from the original locomotive. (James Waite)

RIGHT: The *Earl of Merioneth* name was re-used on the locomotive that in 1979 became the first Fairlie to emerge from Boston Lodge Works for 100 years. The slab-sided tanks have never been wholly popular and new tanks are due to be fitted. (James Waite)

that he would cancel his subscription if any further photographs of double Fairlies appeared in its pages! Such threats cannot so easily be made against books and thus it seems safe to summarise the great revival, noting at the same time that a reversion to traditional Welsh spelling has seen 'Portmadoc' become 'Porthmadog' and 'Festiniog' shown as 'Ffestiniog'.

Although it had been out of action the longer of the two surviving double Fairlies, it was *Taliesin* that was the first to return to traffic. The overhaul that began way back in 1940 was finally completed and the locomotive steamed again in September 1956. Five years later it received its third name *Earl of Merioneth*.

By contrast, *Merddin Emrys* had been run into the ground and had suffered from the lack of any attempt at proper storage when traffic ceased in 1946. As a result, it required considerable boiler work as well as new welded tanks, smokeboxes and chimneys. Not until July 1961 was it back in service, bearing more than a passing resemblance to *Little Wonder* as the new tanks would not fit the original design. It therefore had to run without a cab and one cannot help wondering if Robert Fairlie and George Spooner might well have approved.

Equally, they would undoubtedly have been horrified by what happened to the locomotive when it was withdrawn to receive one of two new superheated boilers ordered from Hunslet's in 1968. It returned four years later looking horribly functional, without dome covers and with bigger side tanks failing to balance the longer boiler. Tapered chimneys sat on smokeboxes that looked ludicrously small.

Such was the outcry that plans to use the second of the two boilers on *Earl of Merioneth* were abandoned. In order to preserve the traditional appearance of one double Fairlie, it was decided to keep the locomotive out of service and restore it to its known condition in 1910. Reverting to its original name *Livingston Thompson*, it was eventually handed over to the National Railway Museum at York.

The bold decision was instead made to incorporate the boiler into a completely new locomotive, which reused the name *Earl of Merioneth* but recognised the revival of the Welsh language by also carrying an *Iarll Meirionnydd* nameplate. The Fairlie saga took a dramatic turn when it emerged from

Boston Lodge works in 1979. Exactly one hundred years had elapsed since the last Fairlie was built there, and it was surely an ironic twist that this was the now disfigured *Merddin Emrys*. Even the new locomotive was far removed from traditional Fairlie lines. It had a more spacious cab to provide better working conditions for the crew, as well as distinctive slab-sided tanks with cut-off ends designed to carry enough water to run through from Porthmadog to Blaenau Ffestiniog.

The traditionalists continued to exert pressure and in 1985 a benefactor provided the funding for *Merddin Emrys* to return to a more traditional Fairlie appearance, which included fully-lined maroon livery close to that carried in Victorian times. Two years later the austere outlines of *Earl of Merioneth* were softened by replacement chimneys, smokeboxes, brass dome covers and more elaborate lining.

Lessons were learned and traditional Spooner styling was very much to the fore with *David Lloyd George*, again built at Boston Lodge, which entered traffic in July 1992. Even the brick red livery was similar to that of early days on the Ffestiniog. Yet there was nothing hidebound about its performance, an increased boiler pressure and a larger superheater meaning it could easily out-run any of its sister locomotives. The newcomer quickly became known as the 'super Fairlie'. Its name commemorated the last Liberal Prime Minister, who before entering politics was a solicitor with offices at both Portmadoc and Blaenau and was thus a regular traveller on the line.

By now the construction of replica locomotives was becoming almost commonplace in the preservation movement, and so it was perhaps inevitable that a scheme to build a new single Fairlie should take shape. Emerging from Boston Lodge in 1999, it revived the name *Taliesin*, which had been used not only by the original locomotive but also by the double Fairlie *Livingston Thompson* from 1932 to 1961. Existence of the historic nameplates and sundry bits and pieces from the 1875 engine accounts for the 'Rebuilt 1999' inscription on the smokebox works plates.

Blessed with one single and three double Fairlies, the Ffestiniog now found itself back in the happy position that had prevailed from 1886 to the early 1930s. Moreover, three of the four were relatively new. Doubts were nevertheless expressed as to whether the line really needed another locomotive of relatively modest capabilities, but there could be no question of its key significance. The railway now had examples of each generation of its original motive power in the shape of George England 0-4-0s and Fairlies both double and single.

As the home of four of only eleven Fairlies surviving worldwide, it also now clearly occupied a pre-eminent position for devotees of these remarkable locomotives. The only other working example is the Mason Fairlie *Torch Lake* in the USA, which is not in quite the same league. To see the remaining six static engines would demand a truly heroic journey to take in the National Railway Museum at York, the Péchot-Bourdons in Germany and Serbia, the preserved double Fairlie in Saxony and the two locomotives in New Zealand. Small wonder that Porthmadog is a preferred destination.

CHAPTER TWO
Mallet Dominance

Solutions to problems with articulated locomotives have often been brilliantly and obviously simple. The incessant difficulties with leaks on the flexible steam pipes of Fairlies led to all sorts of experiments, very few of which achieved lasting success. It was left to a Swiss engineer, Anatole Mallet (pronounced 'Malley'), to overcome the problem with a compromise approach to articulation that had one outstanding feature in its favour. It worked well. Bizarrely, he did so as a sideline to his more serious endeavours and yet conceived the most enduring articulated steam locomotive ever created. No other design was built in such quantity over such a long period, with more than five thousand being constructed between 1887 and 1961. Admittedly more than half were giant machines pounding standard gauge tracks in the USA, but this in no way diminishes what he achieved.

Like others in the evolution of articulated locomotives, Mallet was a man of many talents. Born in Geneva in 1837, he worked as an engineer on French railways, the Suez Canal and the dredging of Italian ports. At the age of thirty he began to experiment with compound engines in which efficiency is increased by using steam twice, once at high-pressure and then at a lower pressure.

In 1884 he patented a four-cylinder articulated locomotive, in which steam descending direct from the dome fed high-pressure cylinders at the front of the fixed rear unit. From here it was taken to larger low-pressure cylinders at the forward end of the front swivelling unit. The cylinders were arranged this way round so that the possibility of leaks through articulated pipes was limited to low-pressure steam. As the back unit was rigid and only the front one swivelled, advocates of

Decauville drawing of the pioneer 0-4-4-0Ts built for the 1889 Paris Exhibition. It clearly shows the principles of the Mallet patent articulation with a fixed rear unit and only the front unit swivelling. Also evident are the different dimensions of the cylinders with the larger size at the front for low-pressure steam. (W.J.K. Davies collection)

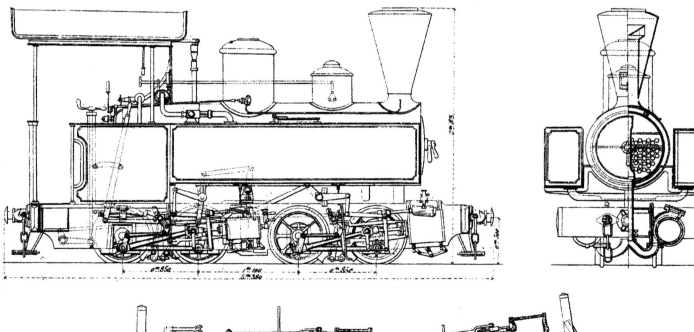

Clearly reflecting the design of Paul Decauville's original Mallets is 22-5, built by Orenstein & Koppel in 1905. Now preserved, it was latterly in service on the Tramway de Pithiviers à Toury and is seen outside its main depot in June 1962. (J.L. Rochaix/BVA)

accuracy have always insisted that Mallet's invention was semi-articulated and not in the ultimate category of a pure articulated locomotive. Visually the difference is not always immediately obvious – and especially so on straight track.

PAUL DECAUVILLE

As with many facets in the evolution of articulated locomotives, the Mallet story has surprising and modest beginnings. It owes much to Paul Decauville, who in the 1860s and '70s had developed his system of 60cm gauge portable railways, initially using horses and then locomotives built at his own engineering works near Paris. In 1885 he visited the Antwerp Exhibition, where Anatole Mallet was displaying a set of drawings for a 0-4-4-0T. Decauville became his first customer, the tiny locomotive weighing only eleven tonnes being built by Ateliers Metallurgique at Tubize, Belgium. Its successful trials prompted him to scale new heights with a demonstration railway at the Paris Exhibition of 1889. Running for three kilometres in the centre of the city from la Gare de la Concorde to a terminus close to the Eiffel Tower, it could hardly fail to be noticed in such an eye-catching location. By this time Decauville had helped in creating the extraordinary Péchot-Bourdon military locomotives, but it is fortunate that he did not choose them as the main motive power on the exhibition line. Well before one of them had proved an

embarrassing failure, he went back to Anatole Mallet with the result that further compounds were duly supplied from Tubize. They played a key role in ensuring that the whole enterprise proved little short of sensational and in its six months of operation it carried more than six million passengers – an amazing average of over 35,000 per day.

The Paris exhibition dramatically changed the fortunes of both Paul Decauville and Anatole Mallet but in very different ways. It convinced many local authorities of the suitability of 60cm gauge for local tramways, with Decauville himself successfully tendering to build three of them. The first, which opened as soon as 1890 and served the seaside resort of Royan on the north side of the Gironde estuary, was initially worked by three Mallets from the exhibition line.

After only a year, they were sent to the second tramway serving coastal resorts in the Normandy region of Calvados. For its opening in 1891 they were joined by two new Mallets built at Tubize and then in 1893 complemented by a further two built by Decauville in his own workshops. Their reign was relatively brief and all of them had been sold by 1908, long before the tramway system suffered the most dramatic of all railway closures when within a few hours it was obliterated by the D-Day landings.

The third of the tramways was a more ambitious affair, extending for 31 km (19 miles) and linking the agricultural centre of Pithiviers in the Département du Loiret with the town of Toury on the mainline from Paris to Orléans. Opened in 1892, its initial motive power was a pair of 0-4-4-0T Mallets, again built in Decauville's workshops. They were eventually numbered 22-3 and 22-4 to harmonise with other locomotives on the line, the first two digits indicating the number of driven axles. None of these pioneer Mallets has been preserved.

Paul Decauville's period of hectic expansion proved to be short-lived, as it was soon evident that he was less skilled at operating railways than building the equipment to run them. In August 1893 his company went into liquidation, although it was reformed as a manufacturing organisation without the original founder at its head. No more Mallets were supplied to the Royan and Calvados tramways but many years later there were further additions on the Pithiviers à Toury line to help it cope with an annual peak during the sugar beet harvesting season.

The most unusual was built at the workshops of the new Decauville company in 1916 as part of a large order for military use in Morocco. This solitary example remained in France and came to Pithiviers in 1923, its number 33-1 indicating that it was a 0-6-6-0. Originally a tender locomotive, it was rather crudely converted to a tank engine with the tender being retained to provide extra water when required.

One of the original Decauville Mallets was transferred from Calvados in 1929 and became 22-2. The numbering sequence was completed by 22-1 and 22-5 to 22-7, four

locomotives built by Orenstein & Koppel in 1905 and acquired from various sources between 1917 and 1930. One of them was destined to have a long history. Closure of the Pithiviers line at the end of 1964 marked a turning point among enthusiasts increasingly concerned about the rapidly diminishing number of 60cm gauge lines throughout France. They acquired 22-5 and went on to save part of the Pithiviers line as the country's first preserved railway. It remains in operation, although the Mallet was later moved to the CF du Haut Rhone at Montalieu, east of Lyon.

THE VIVARAIS SAGA

Anatole Mallet never looked back after the Paris Exhibition and within a matter of months it was clear his primary interest in compounding had led him to an unexpected triumph in inventing what was destined to be the standard form of articulated locomotive for the next three decades. The driving force at the time of the exhibition was the CF Départementaux, formed in 1881 to build and operate railways in areas that were of no interest to the major companies. It ultimately controlled thirteen lines throughout France as well as the system on Corsica, which almost by definition were lightly laid and used featherweight track as they wound over and around natural obstructions. By far the most impressive of the metre-gauge lines was the legendary Réseau du Vivarais, which linked the Rhone and Loire valleys through challenging terrain and ultimately extended to 200 km (125 miles). Construction had already been underway for three years

The unlovely 0-6-6-0T No 33-1, built by the Decauville company in 1916 for military use. It remained in service on the Pithiviers line until 1956.
(W.J.K. Davies collection)

Glory days on the Vivarais line in the 1960s, with Swiss-built 0-6-6-0T No 403 pausing at the now abandoned junction of Le Cheylard. Note the primitive wire-mesh spark arrester on the chimney top. (Colour-Rail)

when the exhibition opened and hence the question of motive power was becoming urgent.

A prototype 0-4-4-0T had already been built in 1888 for the CF Départementaux by the Societé Alsacienne de Constructions Mécaniques (SACM) at Belfort, close to the Swiss border near Basle. Its trials were highly satisfactory and hence the same design and manufacturer was chosen for the first four locomotives on the Vivarais. They were delivered to coincide with opening of the initial 22 km (14 mile) section from La Voûte sur Loire to Yssingeaux in November 1890, with two more joining them the following summer on completion of 32 km (20 miles) at the opposite end of the system between Tournon and Lamastre. They gave excellent service in the early years and one of these historically important pioneers remained in existence until the mid-1960s. Sadly, not a single example has been preserved.

When the Vivarais system was finally completed in 1903, it was noteworthy for long 1 in 30 gradients and many reverse curves. It was clear that more powerful and yet flexible locomotives were required, but it was a boom period and all manufacturers in France were flooded with orders. It was necessary to turn to the Swiss Locomotive Works, which between 1902 and 1905 delivered eight of the world's first 0-6-6-0Ts. Increasingly heavy freight led to two similar loco-motives being ordered in 1927 and then a further four in 1932, both batches being built by SACM.

The Vivarais had become inseparably associated with its Mallets, which were very handsome and unquestionably had great character. A stack of briquettes supplemented by slack coal not only separated the driver and fireman but also produced voluminous quantities of brown smoke that left an acrid aroma hanging over the countryside long after a train had passed. Primitive wire-mesh spark arresters, similar to a domestic chimney cowl, were used in the dry summer months, while a very different addition during the winter was wedge-shaped snow-ploughs to cope with conditions on the 1,060 metre (3,500ft) watershed between the Atlantic and the Mediterranean. A final touch was provided by high-pitched whistles that managed to drown out wheel squealing on the sharper curves.

Diesel railcars took over most passenger workings in the 1930s and the Mallets were relegated to freight traffic. They also hauled wonderful market day specials that were decidedly mixed affairs with cattle and sheep in their own vans and passen-gers piling into coaches with a full complement of chickens and rabbits. It could not last and virtually all the Mallets were out of service by the early 1950s. Two of the Swiss-built locomotives, nos 403 and 404, were retained in working order and became a major focus of attention as closure loomed ever nearer. In the final year in 1968 an unforgettable event on 5 May saw both of them double-heading an enthusiasts' special with every remaining coach pressed into service. It was all over five months later but it was not the end.

Preservation was afoot with the 32 km (20 miles) from Tournon to Lamastre eventually being selected and 403 hauling the first steam-hauled passenger train under the new regime in June 1969. The two Swiss-built locomotives were complemented by the last two Mallets to be supplied to the line in 1932 – Nos 413 and 414 – as well as a smaller 0-4-4-0T with a complex history. No 104 is one of four built in 1906 for the state-owned PO Corrèze line, north of Brive, by Les Ateliers de Construction du Nord de la France at Blanc-Misseron. When this line closed in 1969 it was acquired by a USA museum, which closed before shipment could be arranged. Eventually placed on static display at Lamastre in 1990, it was then decided to embark on restoration to working order. Officially too heavy for the Vivarais track, a customary French approach to regulations found a way round the problem by decreeing that all would be well if speed did not exceed 30kph or 35kph if the tanks were half full! It entered service in 1996, on long-term loan from its American owner.

With such splendid motive power and some outstanding scenery, the Vivarais line soon came to be regarded as one of the leading preserved railways in Europe. A Sunday journey was a very French experience, beginning at Tournon with copious amounts of wine being loaded onto a train of at least twelve coaches. Amid much chatter and excitement, a Mallet coupled up and immediately caused many British visitors to rub their eyes in disbelief. It headed straight onto mixed gauge track under the wires, preserved steam sharing a vital artery of the SNCF electrified at 1,500V dc and much used by freight to the south of France.

After metre and standard gauge had diverged the Mallet began to gain speed as it headed into the Doux gorge, with the sound of traditional French music being clearly audible above the soft exhaust of the locomotive. A pause in the popping of wine corks heralded the approach to a refreshment stop at Boucieu-le-Roi, after which the train headed deeper into the hills to reach the gastronomic centre of Lamastre. There was a mass exodus to restaurant tables, after which the Mallet was left in silence for some three hours. Only after that great French institution of the leisurely Sunday lunch had ended did it commence the return journey.

It all seemed something that would go on forever, but then suddenly and without warning services were suspended at the start of the 2008 season. It was a situation without parallel on a preserved line of such importance, but it gradually became apparent that all had not been well for some time. In particular, the preservation society that had long run the Vivarais was suffering from an acute lack of both funds and volunteers. The line had got through the 2007 season with only one serviceable locomotive – No 414 – which was then withdrawn for a major overhaul. This had taken longer than anticipated and it was clear that services could not be maintained with just a railcar. Moreover, SNCF had given notice to terminate the railway's use of the mixed gauge track forming an essential connection with Tournon where all repair facilities were situated. If that were not enough, the metre-gauge track on to Lamastre was generally in poor condition and the Conseil Général had decided to suspend services on safety grounds.

A warning bell was sounded for other preserved lines of similar stature. There was much apportioning of blame, but any hope of immediate action was delayed by a bankruptcy order served against the previous operators. Only in 2011 did hope emerge with an announcement that the line would be reopened from a new base at the Lamastre end down to St Jean de Muzols, immediately before the former mixed gauge

Essence of the French narrow gauge with Blanc-Misseron 0-4-4-0T No 103 hauling freight on the PO Corrèze in March 1957. Its sister locomotive, 104, entered service on the Vivarais line in 1996. (Neil Sprinks)

section. Services would be provided by a diesel railcar, but steam could return subject to progress by the new operating company in overhauling Mallets 403 and 414. It was at least a move in the right direction for a once great railway that in its early days of preservation had boasted one of the world's finest collections of operable Mallet locomotives.

Ironically, closure of the line caused potential passengers to seek out what had been a struggling enterprise at the opposite end of the Vivarais. The 37 km (23 mile) section between Dunières and St Agrève had been reopened in 1970, forming what was then claimed to be the longest tourist railway in Europe. Initially its sole motive power was 0-4-4-0T Mallet No 101, a sister to 104 on the Tournon - Lamastre section and also coming from the PO Corrèze. When this system closed in 1969, it was the last steam locomotive to operate on a French state-owned narrow gauge line.

Unfortunately, no sooner had 101 arrived than it was clear that it was in dire need of major overhaul. It was withdrawn from service in 1972, and was still in its shed fifteen years later when increasing difficulties stemming from an over-optimistic beginning culminated in the line's closure. A new association, Voies Ferrées du Velay, took over and reopened the railway in 1996. It was still a struggle, as food remains important to French tourists and neither terminus rivalled Lamastre in terms of gastronomy. Nevertheless, the lack of a nearby competing line from 2008 brought much progress in developing operations. In particular, the overhaul of Mallet 101 that had been earmarked to begin almost forty years earlier was finally completed in 2011.

MEDITERRANEAN ISLAND

After the CF Départementaux had chosen Mallets for the Vivarais in 1890, it next turned its attention to the mountainous island of Corsica. A 160 km (98 mile) metre-gauge main line from Bastia, on the north-east coast opposite Italy, to Ajaccio in the centre of the west coast was opened in stages between 1888 and 1894 and complemented by a 74 km (46 mile) branch descending from a junction at Ponte Leccia down to Calvi – the third of the principal towns. Conventional tank locomotives provided the initial motive power, but following their success on the Vivarais it was soon realised that Mallets would be ideal for the Corsican system with its constant 1 in 30 gradients and countless sinuous curves. An initial 0-4-4-0T in 1892 was rigorously tested and then followed by a further three in 1895. As the system and traffic developed, the stud eventually increased to twenty-two near identical locomotives with the last six being delivered as late as 1932. They were all built by SACM at Belfort.

Enginemen on the island took a while to get used to their foibles and especially the tendency of a Mallet compound to slip violently if there was insufficient adhesive weight on the low-pressure front set of driving wheels. There could be even worse problems on the precipitous descents with these wheels sliding just when braking power was most required. Such difficulties were no doubt rarely noticed by passengers, who would be preoccupied with the line's many splendours, ranging from U-shaped bends in

OPPOSITE: No 414 at the Lamastre terminus of the preserved CF du Vivarais in July 2007. It was the last operable locomotive on the line prior to its sudden closure in April 2008. (Colin Boocock)

INSET: The builder's plate of 414, showing its Alsacienne ancestry. (Colin Boocock)

RIGHT: The impressive plates on Vivarais 104. (David Smithies)

precipitous gorges through to the 3.92km (2miles 762yd) long Vizzavona tunnel and the stupendous 80 metre (262ft) high Vecchio viaduct built by the famous Gustave Eiffel.

The Mallets coped well with passenger traffic and especially the prestigious boat train that in terms of comfort was way beyond normal narrow gauge standards. Its bogie composites incorporated a deluxe saloon section, a washroom, one 1st class and two 2nd class compartments opening from a side corridor. It ran from Bastia to Ajaccio one day and then in the opposite direction the next to meet ships from France that used the ports alternately. On one famous occasion the journey was completed in three-and-a-half hours including some stops, which may not sound stupendous but was in fact a remarkable achievement on such a tortuous route.

It must have been a magnificent sight in such a setting and Corsica could today have been an enthusiast's paradise. As it was, railcars came to the island in 1935 and steam traction was abandoned in 1954. Six Mallets were then still serviceable but they had all been scrapped by the early 1960s.

MALLETS IN BRITTANY

The next French system to take Mallets in quantity was a very different affair in a peninsula that came to boast the highest concentration of metre gauge lines in France. The Réseau Breton, comprising five lines radiating from the Brittany town of Carhaix, did not come under the CF Départementaux. It was instead conceived by one of the major main line companies, the CF de l'Ouest, and thus was laid out to metre gauge with a provision for easy conversion to standard gauge should the need arise. Maximum gradients were limited to 1 in 50 and the tight curves so often associated with narrow gauge railways were avoided.

The first part of what ultimately became a 380 km (237 mile) network was opened in 1891 and worked by modest 2-4-0 tanks. Increasing freight traffic quickly meant that something more powerful was required with the result that SACM supplied seven Mallets – Nos E401 to E407 – in 1895/96. They were a larger version of the 0-4-4-0Ts that had earlier been delivered to the Vivarais. During World War I the entire class was

Réseau Breton motive power:

TOP LEFT: SACM 0-4-4-0T No E404, dating from 1894, seen at the main junction at Carhaix in 1957. These locomotives were virtually identical to those supplied to the Corsican system over a lengthy period between 1892 and 1932. (B. Rozé/BVA)

TOP RIGHT: Synonymous with the Réseau Breton were the Piguet 0-6-6-0Ts, which were the most powerful metre gauge locomotives in France. E414 is reposing at Carhaix depot in 1954.
(M. Rifault; J.L. Rochaix collection/BVA)

LOWER: The weighty Corpet-Louvet No 41, which latterly worked freight traffic on the eastern extremity of the Breton system. In November 1958 it paused to take water at St Lubin-Le-Vaublanc. (B. Rozé/BVA)

transferred to Bar-le-Duc on the German border in 1915-16 but returned after the cessation of hostilities and remained in service until the mid-1950s. None has been preserved.

World War I also saw the arrival in Carhaix of the Mallets for which the Réseau Breton is best remembered. There were intended to be nine 0-6-6-0Ts, but these were difficult times and one of them was destroyed by enemy action on the workshops of their builders, Piguet of Lyon-Anzin. On delivery in 1914, two of the remaining eight were immediately requisitioned for military use on the German frontier and were not returned until close to the end of the war. Eventually, Nos E410 to 417 settled down to more than fifty years of service and, as the most powerful metre gauge locomotives in France, they comfortably hauled 350-tonne freight trains.

One other Mallet joined the Réseau Breton fleet in its latter days after a nomadic existence. No 41 was one of five 0-6-6-0Ts supplied by Corpet Louvet to the CF du Centre in Loire in 1913. An impressive and heavy machine weighing 52 tonnes

in working order, it looked far more modern with its high tanks and exposed driving wheels. On closure of the Loire line in 1931, it was transferred first to the Tramway de l'Ain, then the Blanc-Argent and finally the PO Corrèze in 1947. Due to weight restrictions, it saw little service on any of these lines and was moved to Carhaix in 1953. After four years in store, it was finally overhauled and fitted with a larger coal bunker before working freight trains on the eastern extremity of the system between Loudéac and La Brohinière.

By this time the Réseau Breton was a rare survivor and its position close to the English Channel meant it increasingly became a place of pilgrimage for British enthusiasts. Mallets were unknown in their homeland and they were fascinated by what they found, the atmosphere being delightfully captured by Peter Allen and P.B. Whitehouse in their book *Narrow Gauge Railways of Europe:*

'A cloud of dirty brown smoke indicated the presence of steam power, so we made our way across the tracks to find

RIGHT: Europe's only operational narrow gauge Mallet complete with tender is 0-6-6-0 No 12 on Sweden's Jädraas - Tallas Järnväg.
(James Waite)

LOWER: The world's oldest surviving Mallet, No 2 *Lessebo*, built by Munktells in 1891. It is being turned at Laggesta on the preserved Östra Södermanlands Järnväg in Sweden.
(James Waite)

our Compound Mallet No E413 taking water just outside the loco shed. It was a large, imposing, spotlessly clean machine with dark green side tanks sloping down at the front. Close to the shed was the inevitable tiny turntable, for, as on the Irish lines, tank engine or no tank engine, each locomotive is turned at the end of its journey. Just how the Mallets fit on these tables is a mystery, but they do somehow, like an elephant sitting on its upturned tub.'

By the early 1960s it was inevitable that a question mark should hang over the future of one of the largest and most intensively used narrow gauge systems in France. As elsewhere, passenger services had largely been taken over by railcars but both they and the Mallets hauling the freight were now showing their age and transshipment costs were becoming ever greater. Introducing diesel locomotives was not considered to be a viable option and instead complete closure came in 1967, a year before the Vivarais. Two of the lines to the coastal resorts of Camaret and Morlaix could easily have made tourist operations, but railway preservation in France was then in its infancy and such schemes were never even considered. Apart from a short stretch converted to standard gauge the whole system succumbed and left little trace. One of the 1914 Mallets was for a time stored at Racoules-Brossettes on the former Vivarais line before being moved to a private collection in Valence. A more public epitaph is provided by E415, a sister locomotive from the same batch, which was placed on a plinth among flowerbeds close to Carhaix station.

SWEDISH ENTERPRISE

Outside France, the first country to use narrow gauge Mallets was off the European mainstream and somewhat surprising. Sweden took two of Paul Decauville's tiny 0-4-4-0Ts direct from the 1889 Paris Exhibition, which proved to be a major influence on development of its 60cm gauge lines. It then went on to copy the design with several locomotives being

built locally over the next few years. They soon proved too small for their intended use, although amazingly one of them has survived in working order complete with its original boiler!

Lessebo, built by Munktells of Eskilstuna in 1891 as their works number 27, takes its name from its original railway where it remained until closure of the line in 1948. It then moved to the much busier Munkedals Järnväg until this railway was converted to standard gauge in 1954. Acquired by the Swedish National Railway Museum at Gavle, the next development saw *Lessebo* loaned to the Östra Södermanlands Järnväg, a three-kilometre line on the southern shore of Lake Mälaren near Stockholm. First steamed there in 2009, it looks stunning and attracts great interest as the world's oldest surviving Mallet.

Another 0-4-4-0T has been on this line since the 1960s in the shape of No 5 *Hamra*, which came from an industrial line

Pre-electrification days on the Rhaetian Railway with 2-4-4-0T No 26 piloted by 2-6-0T No 7 *Chur*. Built in 1902, the Mallet was made redundant by the new era of overhead wires as early as 1920 and ended its days on the strikingly named Union Espanola de Explosives. It was scrapped in 1954.
(Keith Chester collection)

in the south-east of the country. Once a typical Orenstein & Koppel locomotive, it has subsequently been 'Swedified' and engendered controversy in the process.

In a different league are a magnificent pair of 0-6-6-0s built by Atlas of Stockholm in 1910 for the Dala - Ockelbo - Norrsundet Järnväg, a line of 891mm gauge (three Old Swedish Feet) running eastwards from Linghed to the Baltic coast. They were still there when the railway closed in 1970 and a short six-kilometre (3.75 mile) section running through pine forest was taken over by the Jädraas -Tallas Järnväg. One of the pair has been withdrawn for repairs but the other has been regularly steamed since restoration was completed in 1995. It is unique in Europe as an operational narrow-gauge Mallet complete with tender and together with *Lessebo* gives Sweden a special place in the evolution of articulated locomotives.

BRIEF GLORY IN THE SWISS ALPS

It was entirely appropriate that the next country to opt for the locomotives of Anatole Mallet was Switzerland – the land of his birth. The unsurpassed metre gauge network of the Rhaetian Railway has been electrified for so long that it tends to be forgotten it once had a dozen Mallets operating over such structures as the world-famous Landwasser viaduct and through the bewildering spiral tunnels at Albula. Part of the reason for this lack of appreciation – and the rarity of photographs – is that the Mallet fleet was complete for only eighteen years, six of which coincided with World War I.

The Rhaetian system dates back to 1890 with completion of a 48 km (30 mile) line extending from the standard gauge at Landquart, north of Chur, to the already fashionable resorts of Klosters and Davos. It ran through the narrow Klus gorge and climbed almost six hundred metres (2,000ft) on vicious 1 in 22 gradients that soon proved too much for the initial 2-6-0 tanks supplied by the Swiss Locomotive Works. A year after the opening a much more powerful pair of 0-4-4-0Ts were obtained from Maffei of Munich and overcame operational difficulties by hauling 80 tonne trains up the gradients at an

acceptable 18kph. A downside was that several bridges had to be strengthened to cope with the extra weight.

The next development was the first stage of a line again starting at Landquart but heading towards the golden goal of St Moritz. Following the relatively easy Rhine valley, its opening as far as Thusis in 1896 necessitated the purchase of two additional Mallets, which like all the later engines were not brought in from Germany but instead were built by the Swiss Locomotive Works. Their unusual 0-4-4-2T wheel arrangement, intended to permit greater water capacity in extended frames, did not prove entirely satisfactory. Just one pair of wheels was therefore simply swapped from back to front and the final eight Mallets were all 2-4-4-0Ts.

Their arrival in 1902 was in preparation for completion of the 64km (40 mile) line from Thusis to St Moritz, which in terms of engineering difficulties had few rivals in Europe. It included not just the breathtaking Landwasser viaduct with its southern arch abutting directly into a cliff face but also the highest of the principal Alpine tunnels at Albula – 1,800 metres (6,000ft) above sea level and over six kilometres (almost four miles) in length. Between them the line crossed over itself no less than eight times in sub-surface spirals that come close to defying all sense of direction.

After six years in construction, opening finally took place in 1904. With long stretches of 1 in 28, it is with hindsight amazing that even Mallets managed to cope with such a line – and especially in the winter months. Conditions for their crews must often have been horrendous. It is also entirely understandable why the Swiss, with a potential abundance of hydroelectric power, soon became pioneers of electrification. After an initial decision as early as 1910, several experimental locomotives were in use only two years later. A desperate post-war coal shortage brought a new level of urgency in 1919 and the entire Rhaetian Railway was electrified in just three years.

Funding was helped by the sale of twelve relatively new Mallets, which were promptly dispersed across the world to locations ranging from Brazil to Madagascar. It may have been some consolation that the 1921 demise of the last of

Mallet magnificence during midwinter on Germany's Harz network. Photographed on the Selketalbahn near Drahtzug, 99 5901 is one of the original batch of twelve 0-4-4-0Ts supplied by Arnold Jung between 1897 and 1901. (David Rodgers)

the Mallets coincided with arrival of six C-C articulated electric locomotives of great character that soon gained the nickname of 'Crocodiles'.

GERMAN EXPANSION

When the first two 0-4-4-0Ts for service in Switzerland were purchased from Maffei of Munich in 1891, it was the start of a trend that was soon to see Germany become both the main manufacturer and major user of Mallets in Western Europe. At first they were mainly supplied to standard gauge main lines, but from 1897 numerous German lines of both 75cm and metre gauge took some eighty locomotives from a host of different builders.

Arguably the best known are those surviving on the famous metre gauge Harz network running through an attractive landscape rich in forest. Like so many systems it started with modest tank engines but quickly found that something more powerful was required. Twelve 0-4-4-0T Mallets were ordered from Arnold Jung between 1897 and 1901 and proved to be excellent locomotives. Six of them were requisitioned for use in France during World War I and never returned, but three of the remainder are still in service and are regularly seen hauling vintage trains on what at well over 160 km (100 miles) is now Europe's longest steam railway. Also still in use is an 0-4-4-0T Mallet supplied by the Army and built by Maschinenbau-Gesellschaft of Karlsruhe in 1918 as compensation for one of the engines lost in the war. Known as the 'nimble machine', it achieved fame in the 1990s when it was illegally sold by the state-controlled Deutsche Reichsbahn to a museum line near Bremen. Only after five years of wrangling and a court order was it retained on the Harz system!

Other Mallets came to this network down the years. Two 0-6-6-0Ts supplied by Orenstein & Koppel in 1910 proved too heavy for the track and their bad reputation got worse when one of them left the rails and fell down into a valley, killing the driver and badly injuring the fireman. After only eleven years both locomotives were sold to the obscure destination of a Bolivian tin mine. More successful were two modern-looking locomotives with an unusual 2-4-4-2 wheel arrangement supplied by Borsig of Berlin in 1922/23 principally for use on the line that spiralled its way to the 1,148 metre (3,769ft) summit of the Brocken. They were promptly withdrawn in 1961, when the metaphoric Iron Curtain became an ugly reality and the mountain found itself a Soviet 'listening post' in the heart of a military zone.

The German-built Mallets that survive in operable condition elsewhere often reflect the country's turbulent twentieth-century history. Much of north-eastern France in Alsace and Lorraine was part of Germany between the 1870/71 Franco-Prussian War and the 1918 Armistice. The uncommon gauge of 70cm was favoured by the German military and was adopted for many lines in this area, including one in the vast Forest of Abreschviller straddling the Vosges hills west of Strasbourg.

Now in France, the railway continued to extract timber until closure in 1966, following which a short section was preserved. Its star survivor is a rare 0-4-4-0T, built by Maschienfabrik Heilbronn in 1906, fully restored in 2002 and typical of the German locomotives used on the line in its heyday.

The military connection is also evident at the impressive Blonay - Chamby Museum Railway, north of Montreux in Switzerland, which boasts what is widely regarded as Europe's most impressive collection of metre gauge locomotives and rolling stock. Its 0-4-4-0T *Todtnau* is one of seven Mallets supplied to the German Army by Karlsruhe in 1918. The museum is also home to a handsome 0-6-6-0T *Zell*, built by Hanomag in 1925. Both locomotives saw service on the Mittelbadische Eisenbahn and take their names from its termini.

PORTUGUESE SURVIVORS

After rapidly gaining favour in France, Switzerland and Germany, the invention of Anatole Mallet spread across the world. Ultimately some fifty countries operated Mallets, the sheer quantity meaning that many have been forgotten unless they have in some way been out of the ordinary. It could for example be the remarkably high number of survivors. A prime instance is provided by Portugal, which until the final decade of the twentieth century had one of the most comprehensive narrow gauge systems in Europe and the last to be operated by Mallets. Largely centred on Porto, it was far removed from any image of a bumbling backwater and boasted full signalling

The unusual 2-4-4-2T No 51 – one of a pair supplied by Borsig in 1922/23. They were primarily intended for service on the line climbing for almost twenty kilometres to the 1,148-metre summit of the Brocken mountain on a ruling gradient of 1 in 30. (Terry Martin collection)

Among the most attractive Mallets ever constructed were the metre gauge 0-4-4-0Ts supplied by Henschel in 1905 for use on the Douro Valley lines in Portugal. Indicative of their appeal is the fact that all ten have survived. Of the two shown here at Lousado depot in July 1974, E168 is now in service on the Brohltalbahn in Germany while E163 is in the museum at Estromez, near Lisbon. (Keith Chester)

as well as a busy double- track section through the city. It also ran through highly scenic and hilly countryside demanding powerful locomotives to haul the often heavy trains.

Mallets were seen as the ideal solution and from first to last they were all supplied by Henschel & Sohn of Kassel. The initial two in 1905 were 0-4-4-0Ts for an undertaking rejoicing in the full name of the Companhia Dos Caminhos de Ferro de Porto a Póvoa de Varzim e Famalicão, which for obvious reasons was known simply as the PPF. It was nominally 90cm gauge, although its financial backing from Britain suggests that it may well have been 914mm to equate to the imperial three-foot gauge. They were designed for easy conversion to metre gauge, as adopted on all neighbouring systems, and this duly took place in 1930. Always considered slightly

underpowered for the duties expected of them, one of them had been scrapped by 1987 and the other survived to become one of the many narrow gauge exhibits in the museum at Lousado, north-east of Porto.

In the same year 1905, Henschel also delivered ten larger metre-gauge 0-4-4-0Ts for use on the Douro Valley lines. With their handsome proportions and copper chimney caps, they are widely considered to be among the most attractive Mallets ever constructed. Their enduring appeal accounts for why all ten have survived. Eight remain in Portugal – two of them in museums at Chaves and Estromez; two displayed at stations at Arco de Baúlhe and Vila Real; and four in store. Of the two migrants, one returned to Germany in 2009 to haul tourist trains on the steeply graded Brohltalbahn in the Rhine Valley south of Bonn. The other works on the CF de Jura in Switzerland.

The final Mallet development in Portugal saw eighteen 2-4-6-0Ts being delivered between 1911 and 1923. Their high-pitched boilers and large side tanks robbed them of the charm of their predecessors, while the absence of a leading coupled wheel on the front power bogie was distinctly unusual. They nevertheless proved well able to haul heavy trains up steep gradients, although in places they were too heavy for

ABOVE: The larger 2-4-6-0Ts on the Portuguese metre gauge did not have quite the same appeal as their 1905 predecessors. They nevertheless operated in delightful surroundings, as instanced by E206 approaching Moncorvo with a mixed train from Duas Igrejas Miranda in June 1978. (James Waite)

LEFT: The sheer length of the Portuguese 2-4-6-0Ts is well shown in this broadside view of E211 following its move to the CF de la Provence in France. It is seen at Puget-Théniers in September 1990. (Clifford Schoff)

the lightly laid track. As a result, two of them were for some twenty years converted into tender locomotives by simply removing the side tanks and placing them in an open truck!

A high proportion has again survived, although in this instance the distinction between preservation and rusting relics is all too evident. Four of the fifteen survivors are in working order in four different countries. One is based at Regua in Portugal and used to haul occasional steam specials until closure of the surviving part of the Corgo Valley line, while another is at the Basque Railway Museum at Azpeitia in northern Spain. A third has joined the 0-4-4-0T at the CF de Jura, while the fourth went to the CF de la Provence in the south of France. This remarkable line extending from Nice to Digne has had a chequered history in recent years but steam has survived on the outstandingly attractive section between Puget-Théniers and Annot.

Another of the 2-4-6-0Ts left Portugal for Majorca in 2009, having been acquired by a preservation group dedicated to restoring it to working order. Apart from one locomotive privately preserved in Spain, the remainder are all in Portugal. One is becalmed in the museum at Chaves, now cut off following closure of the upper part of the Corgo Valley line, while two are displayed on plinths at Guifões and Entroncamento, near Lisbon. The others are officially 'in store', which could be equated to 'abandoned to the elements'. Several have been grouped near the turntable at Regua for more than a quarter of a century and have become an increasingly depressing sight.

Nevertheless, it is a remarkable record that twenty-six out of the thirty Mallets delivered to Portugal are still in existence. They have arguably done better than the lines on which they operated, which were gradually cut back until only remnants survived. A E ('Dusty') Durrant, writing his standard work on Mallet locomotives in 1974, looked ahead with some feeling: 'The future of these narrow-gauge branches is "under consideration" and no more capital is being expended upon them. Presumably the outcome is predictable – the clean, quiet Mallets and metre-gauge trackage will be replaced by road-wrecking lorries, spewing noxious diesel fumes into the clean air of wine-growing valleys, costs will escalate, and all will go under the euphemism of "progress".'

EUROPE'S FINEST

At the opposite extreme from Portugal in terms of survivors is Yugoslavia, which once had close on 150 Mallets on Europe's largest and finest narrow gauge network. It says much for this troubled land that only some seven remain – and two of these are in other countries.

The saga begins unexpectedly on a private forestry railway in the middle of nowhere straddling some 100,000 acres of Bosnia-Hercegovina, then part of the vast Austro-Hungarian Empire. Otto Steinbeis adopted the 76cm gauge already being used on the state railways and extracted timber so successfully that he soon had a 400 km (250 mile) network of lines running through mountainous countryside to the north of Split. Beset by steep gradients and sharp curves, they were ideal territory for Mallets and he was not slow to respond to the challenge.

The first 0-4-4-0T arrived from Orenstein & Koppel in 1901 to coincide with completion of the initial part of the system, and just nine years later they and Maffei had supplied fourteen locomotives with three different wheel arrangements (the others were 0-4-4-2T and 0-6-6-0T). For obvious reasons they were wood-fired and specially equipped for forestry work with spark-arresting chimneys. During World War I, harassed enginemen did not help the situation by using freshly cut wet wood and thus playing havoc with the boiler tubes.

The system struggled through this dire period, when shipping in the Adriatic was at a standstill and it found itself the only reliable supply route for the hungry people of Dalmatia. Always known as the Steinbeisbahn, the line later became known far and wide as one of the great railway journeys of Europe. In a region bereft of roads it was also a vital link for local inhabitants, who had few alternatives but to move elsewhere when it closed in 1975. Nothing can be certain in such a remote location, and especially so after the civil war of the 1990s, but at least four of the Mallets have survived. The National Museum at Banja Luka has the pioneer Orenstein & Koppel 0-4-4-0T, while three similar Maffei locomotives of 1903/04 remain at the former stations at Drvar and Oštrelj.

The Steinbeisbahn had one crucial feature in common with the vast and sprawling state network extending through Bosnia-Hercegovina and Serbia for more than 2,400 km (1,500 miles). All narrow gauge railways in what became Yugoslavia were scarcely known or appreciated until after they had gone. Essentially they were forbidden fruit, their locomotives treated as military hardware with dreadful things likely to happen to those caught photographing them.

Little was ever quite as expected. Just as the country's first Mallets were privately owned and in a remote forest, so the first on the state network were totally bizarre. It could perhaps only have been this way in a land that had earlier adopted such weird and wonderful inventions as the Klose articulated locomotives. The first two main-line Mallets were an extraordinary attempt to ease a serious handicap on the 270 km (170 mile) route in Bosnia-Hercegovina linking the capital city of Sarajevo with the Adriatic coast. The ascent to the summit of the 868-metre (2,850ft) Ivan Pass on the closing stage of the journey was so steep that the Abt rack system had to be installed on a crucial section plunging through six tunnels as it climbed over three hundred metres (1,000ft) in thirty-two kilometres (20 miles).

The line was opened in 1891 and all went well with the first relatively conventional rack tank engines, provided by Floridsdorf locomotive works in Vienna which held the sole rights for the Abt system in the then Austro-Hungarian Empire. It was a rather different story in 1906 when Floridsdorf built a pair of more powerful locomotives to take 100-tonne trains over the Ivan Pass but unfortunately overreached itself. Widely considered to be an impressive flop and among some of the most unusual locomotives ever designed, they almost defy classification. A 0-4-6-0 rack and adhesion

One of the pair of extraordinary Mallets built by Floridsdorf in 1906 to take trains over the Ivan Pass on the 76cm gauge line between Sarajevo and the Adriatic coast. The complexities stemming from the Abt rack equipment are self-evident on No 751 and these bizarre locomotives were ultimately considered an impressive flop.
(Josef Pospichal collection)

semi-Mallet with tender more or less covers the situation. The high-pressure cylinders drove the six-coupled rigid rear unit, which was purely adhesion, while the low-pressure cylinders powered the cog-wheels through a series of shafts and rods.

A tender was then an unusual feature of any Mallet, but it did allow supplementary oil firing to be fitted. This was no doubt intended to alleviate a long-standing problem with six tunnels of narrow bore on the rack section, where the poor-quality Bosnian coal could cause engines blasting slowly up the rack to emit thick clouds of smoke containing the horrendous combination of phosphorous, sulphur and arsenic. Men on the footplate reputedly resorted to covering their faces with sponges soaked in vinegar.

The tender had the drawback that it was a deadweight to be dragged upgrade, but a more serious flaw was that the rack mechanism could cause the front unit to oscillate violently on curves, which led to unacceptable vibrations throughout the whole locomotive. This necessitated frequent visits to the repair shops, with the result that these two unique engines had both been withdrawn by the end of the 1930s. They were long outlived by the earlier design of rack tanks, which continued in service until 1966 when this operational nightmare was eliminated by a new standard gauge line.

Nothing as extraordinary as the rack locomotives ever followed, but 1906 also saw Henschel supplying a pair of conventional 0-4-4-0T Mallets for use on the 76cm gauge network that by now extended for some 480 km (300 miles) in the neighbouring independent state of Serbia. A further ten from Hohenzollern of Dusseldorf followed five years later. Steady traffic growth – and especially completion of the steeply graded line between Zaječar and Paraćin – resulted in Borsig supplying five heavy 2-6-6-0Ts in 1913.

The terrible events of 28 June 1914 in Sarajevo ignited a powder keg that had long been simmering and rapidly changed the face of the area's railways. Serbia needed heavier motive power – and needed it quickly. Like France with its Péchot-Bourdons, it turned to the only country in the world that could deliver in the desired time span. What were by far the

largest locomotives ever to grace Serbia's narrow gauge were ordered from Alco of Schenectady, USA, on 9 February 1915. The ten massive 2-6-6-2s of typical American appearance were loaded on a ship just eight weeks later on 9 April! Within six months of their arrival in Serbia, the small independent kingdom was occupied by the combined forces of Austria-Hungary, Bulgaria and Germany.

In the dying months of the war, four of the earlier 0-4-4-0Ts found their way to what was soon to become Czechoslovakia and two of them are now preserved. One of them, U47 002, ended its working life on the children's railway at Prešov in eastern Slovakia and is now preserved on a plinth at the town's main line station. U47 001 has fared even better. Originally earmarked for the Prague Technical Museum, it was restored to working order in 1992 and has become a familiar sight on the preserved lines between Jindřichův Hradec, Obratan and Nova Bystrice in the south of the Czech Republic.

It provides a symbolic link with deeply troubled times, which reached new depths in 1916 with an acute motive power crisis on all fronts. German industry had quickly adapted to wartime conditions and was able to supply new locomotives at short notice, although not as quickly as the USA. The 2-6-6-0Ts built by Borsig in 1913 became the basis for a new design by Henschel with the Austro-Hungarian army placing orders for forty-six in January 1916 and delivery beginning six months later. Shared between Serbia and Bosnia-Hercegovina, they were unpopular from the outset. Austria was then noted for its strong dislike for things German in general and for the Mallet system of articulation in particular, but problems resulting from hasty wartime construction were undoubtedly another factor. A prime difficulty was too rigid a chassis, which gave rise to a tendency to spread the track when running in reverse. Never wholly accepted, they lingered on into the 1950s, while some of the eight locomotives rebuilt to 95cm gauge in 1937 for use in Sardinia lasted until about 1963.

By 1917 the Germans were faced with an acute motive power shortage to work the heavy copper traffic emanating from Bor mine in their zone of Serbia, which had to travel via

ABOVE: A pioneer user of Mallets in Bosnia was the remote Steinbeisbahn, which deservedly gained a reputation for providing one of the great railway experiences of Europe. Its atmosphere is captured in this 1965 view of Sipovo, with 0-4-4-0T No 90.007 waiting in the loop for the passage of the early morning passenger service. (Charlie Lewis)

RIGHT: One of the very few survivors of the vast number of Mallets formerly operating in Bosnia and Serbia is U47 001, an 0-4-4-0T built by Henschel in 1906. It became a familiar sight in all weathers on the preserved lines based on Jindrichuv Hradec in the Czech Republic, although on this occasion in March 2004 it later became stranded in a snowdrift. (Petr Mircev)

TOP LEFT: Largest exhibit at Pozega narrow gauge railway museum is 92.043, one of the massive Henschel 2-6-6-0s supplied to Yugoslavia in 1922 as wartime reparations. (James Waite)

TOP RIGHT: The Steinbeisbahn's pioneer Orenstein & Koppel 0-4-4-0T of 1901 on display outside the National Museum at Banja Luka. (James Waite)

LOWER: One of the more obscure lines in Yugoslavia was the 75cm gauge Antivari - Virpazar railway, which operated from 1909 until 1959. Antivari is now known as Bar − and it is here that Borsig 2-4-4-0T *Sutorman*, built in 1910, is preserved. The locomotives on this line were only known by their names and never carried running numbers. (James Waite)

the fiercely graded Paraćin - Zaječar line. The solution lay in more Henschel Mallets, but this time the Kassel company got it right: the result was a powerful 2-6-6-0 fitted with a large eight-wheel tender to cope with the water shortages in the area. Twenty were supplied in 1917-18 and a further thirty came in the early 1920s as reparations.

The aftermath of war saw enormous changes in the volatile land that had ignited it. Creation of the fledgling Kingdom of Serbs, Croats and Slovenes, known as Yugoslavia from 1927, brought a determination to connect the railways of the former separate states of Serbia and Bosnia-Hercegovina. A prime aim was to link the state capital of Belgrade with Sarajevo and thus form a 670 km (420 mile) main line that would extend all the way to Dubrovnik and have no equals on so narrow a gauge. The missing link was a mere 56km (35 miles) but involved surmounting the Šargan Mountain on the borders of the two states. This time the

lessons of the rack section on the Ivan Pass had been learnt and instead a Swiss-style approach was adopted with a bewildering series of horseshoe loops and spiral tunnels at Mokra Gora on the Serbian side of the border.

On completion in 1924, most trains over Šargan were worked by a 2-6-6-0 but as large numbers of conventional 0-8-2s came on stream as reparations so the Mallets disappeared and many moved to Sarajevo and Mostar sheds where they worked heavy traffic down to the coast. Unlike the Austrians who had determined locomotive policy until 1918, the Yugoslavs had no problems with Mallets and got many years of hard work out of these large locomotives. After World War II survivors were increasingly concentrated on the Paraćin - Zaječar line in Serbia, where the last was withdrawn about 1970.

By this time the clouds of doom were gathering following replacement of much of the narrow gauge beyond Sarajevo by a new standard gauge line in 1966. Virtually all 76cm gauge lines in Yugoslavia were closed by state decree prior to 1980, with the brave new link through the Šargan Mountain succumbing in 1974 after a life of just fifty years.

It was not quite the end. A heroic initiative on the same scale as reconstruction of the Welsh Highland Railway saw local enthusiasts begin reinstatement of the spectacular spirals at Mokra Gora in 1998. The tragic events then tearing apart much of Yugoslavia delayed progress but a short section was reopened and carrying steam specials by 2001. The motive power does not include Mallets, as sadly only one survivor remains of the many that had once briefly pounded on the main line through the mountains. Ironically, it is only forty kilometres (25 miles) away from Mokra Gora at Požega, where the narrow gauge railway museum has a fine collection. Apart from its Péchot-Bourdon locomotive, it also has as its largest exhibit No 92-043 – one of the 2-6-6-0s of 1922. Hopes that it might one day be restored to working order are probably pipe dreams.

MYSTERY MALLETS

Another country that needed additional locomotives with supreme urgency during World War I was Russia, which also turned to the USA. Closure of the Black Sea, its prime outlet to the West for shipping, forced it to look to the frozen north and the 3ft 6in gauge line extending for 633km (400 miles)

from the broad gauge at Vologda to the port of Arkhangel on the White Sea east of Finland. Completed between 1894 and 1897, it had on its opening taken the first Mallets in Russia in the shape of twenty-five massive 0-6-6-0s built by Borsig. In 1914 the Baldwin Locomotive Works supplied thirty similar wood-burning locomotives with the same promptitude as they were to show the following year with the first hundred Péchot-Bourdons for France.

It was a different story in 1917 when a further fifty-three Mallets of 'a strengthened type' were completed for service on the Makinskaya Railway serving the Caucasian front. The first ten had got as far as the dockside when the Russian Revolution halted their export pending payment. It is no surprise that funds were not forthcoming, but the fate of the locomotives is shrouded in mystery. At least one and possibly four went to the Anglo-Chilean Nitrate line at Tocopilla, where a distinguishing feature would be the characteristically Russian handrails along the outside of the running boards. Brian Fawcett, author of the noted book *Railways of the Andes*, referred to a 0-6-6-0 'riding like a wheelbarrow on a cobbled street with a racket that drowned out every other sound'.

Others went to the Philippines and probably to the British War Department for use in Iraq, but the majority disappeared into the realms of doubt. Some were reputedly sold to various

TOP: Closure of the Black Sea at the start of World War I forced Russia to depend increasingly on the White Sea east of Finland, with motive power urgently being needed to cope with Arctic conditions on the feeder line to the port of Arkhangel. In a matter of weeks the massive Baldwin Locomotive Works in the USA promptly supplied thirty of these wood-burning 0-6-6-0s in 1914.
(Keith Chester collection)

LOWER: By 1917 the world had changed and the Russian Revolution meant that a further batch of fifty-three 0-6-6-0s completed by Baldwin were never delivered. The fate of most of them is shrouded in mystery, although one is known to have gone to Pampanga Sugar Mill on the main Philippine island of Luzon in 1924. It was still in use as a stationary boiler in 1980, complete with Russian-style handrails.
(Uwe Bergmann)

customers in Spain and Malaysia, but there are no absolute certainties. The mystery remains.

STEAM AMONG THE CAMELS

Beyond Europe, the African continent was home to well over three hundred Mallets in their heyday. The main user was Tunisia, which by 1920 had 134 metre gauge locomotives from manufacturers in France, Germany and the USA. On the onset of dieselisation in the early 1960s, eleven massive 2-6-6-2Ts

built by SACM in 1922/23 were sold to the Zaragoza - Utrillas coal-carrying line in central Spain where they provided an impressive sight in a country hitherto noted for its relative absence of Mallets.

Another leading user was South Africa, until its 2-6-6-2s and 2-6-6-0s failed to compete with the articulated locomotives featuring in the final chapter of this book. Third in the league was Madagascar with some fifty engines, many of which were unique 0-4-4-0s with both a side tank and a tender. Yet today it

OPPOSITE: Few lines in the world can offer steam-worked journeys to compare with the Eritrean Railway – and especially its upper section between Asmara and Arbaroba. 0-4-4-0T No 442.54 is utterly dwarfed by the mountain scenery at Devil's Gate, way above the Dorfu valley snaking down towards the Red Sea. (James Waite)

THIS PAGE: A pair of Mallets at Asmara engine shed. On the left is 440.02, constructed by Ansaldo in 1914 and working on construction of the Bologna - Florence Direttissima railway before coming to Eritrea in the mid-1930s. On its right is 442.54, one of the line's four surviving 0-4-4-0Ts that were built in 1938. (James Waite)

is a tiny and little known country that is most closely associated with Mallets, simply because some still remain in service in the most improbable circumstances.

Eritrea in the Horn of Africa on the western shores of the Red Sea became an Italian colony in 1890, when a railway to link the main port of Massawa with the capital city of Asmara was already under construction. Although they were only 120 km (75 miles) apart, the capital was over two thousand metres (7,000ft) above the blistering heat at sea level and construction of this spectacular line through wild and danger-ous country was a formidable undertaking. An engineering

masterpiece in the best Italian tradition, its thirty tunnels and hundreds of bridges and viaducts delayed completion until 1911. The Italians termed the line metre gauge by virtue of their traditional method of measuring from the mid points of two rail heads. The approach adopted virtually everywhere else in the world by measuring between the inner edges of the rails meant that in international terms it was 95cm gauge.

Happily this recipe for confusion did not cause any problems with the first three 0-4-4-0Ts, which fitted the rails when delivered in 1907. Built by Maffei, they characterised the then near German monopoly in the supply of narrow gauge Mallets outside France and its colonies. A radical change saw the Italian firm of Ansaldo delivering a further forty-eight locomotives of the same wheel arrangement between 1911 and 1938. The worksplates on the later examples often puzzled visitors, but the Roman numerals on them simply indicated the number of years since Mussolini had become the Italian prime minister! His bid to create a second Roman Empire and the consequent invasion of neighbouring Ethiopia cut short plans to extend the line further inland and connect with the Sudanese railway, although this project was only abandoned after 160 km (100 miles) had been completed through the important town of Karen to reach Bascia.

Eritrea became a British protectorate for twelve years beginning in 1941 and was then federated with Ethiopia. The railway remained busy, its atmosphere in 1959 being well

TOP: Designing a locomotive able to cope with surmounting five-miles of constant 1 in 13 and excruciating curvature would have phased many manufactures but did not appear to trouble the Baldwin Locomotive Works. In 1926 they supplied 2-6-6-2T No 50 to the Uintah Railway on the border of Colorado and Utah. The noted American photographer Otto Perry captured it on the infamous Baxter Pass in 1939 a few weeks before the line's closure. (Denver Library Collection)

LOWER: Sister locomotive No 51, delivered in 1928, had an active life of only eleven years on the Uintah Railway. It then went to the Sumpter Valley Railway in Oregon, where it received a tender before ending its days in Guatemala. (Denver Public Library)

captured by Charles S. Small in his wonderful book *Far Wheels*: 'The Mallet-type tank engine burns soft coal and the passenger cars have wooden seats and are crammed with the locals, who betray little familiarity with soap and water. It is a magnificent trip up the hill complete with smoke, cinders, exhaust beats and the high-pitched squeak of the continental type steam whistle, all in the best tradition.'

Traffic declined in the 1970s and increasing unrest culminated in a war with Ethiopia. It resulted in destruction of not just the railway but also reputedly locomotives with several Mallets being shunted onto viaducts and dynamited. The war ended in 1991 and Eritrea became an independent nation two years later, when its president declared that rebuilding of the line was a priority and would be achieved by the country's own efforts. Foreign loans were refused and railwaymen were brought out of retirement to use salvaged materials that included track from wartime trenches!

Work started from Massawa in 1995 and through remarkable efforts had reached Ghinda by 2002. By the same date the most spectacular section of line working back from Asmara to Arbaroba had also been reconstructed. Four of the 1938 Mallets and an earlier example from 1915 were extant and three of them were quickly brought back into service. By this time there were few lines in the world able to offer steam-worked journeys of this length through such striking surroundings complete with 1 in 30 gradients, precipitous views sandwiched between numerous tunnels, and camels calmly watching smoke rising to the heavens. A worrying snag is that the line has virtually no through traffic apart from just a few charter trains each year, but the enthusiasm of the Eritreans remains undiminished and includes plans for restoration of a further 100 km (65 miles) extending inland from Ghinda.

THE 'SIMPLE' APPROACH

Fifteen of the Eritrean 0-4-4-0Ts supplied by Ansaldo in the mid-1930s differed from all the others in one fundamental respect. They departed from Anatole Mallet's original patent in that they were 'simple' rather than compound locomotives and were distinguished by the cylinders all being of the same size as steam was used just once at a uniform pressure. They were not a total success and the final Eritrean locomotives were again compounds, but this can hardly have been due to experimenting in uncharted territory.

By this date the 'simple' Mallet had been active in the USA on standard gauge railroads for more than twenty years and had conquered all before it. The compound was inherently unsuited to a country where size and simplicity were everything with ever- larger locomotives hauling long freights over big distances. The bigger the locomotive the greater the problem of handling the immense quantities of soggy low-pressure steam exhausted by the high-pressure cylinders. Cold weather did not help and the overall result has evocatively been described as 'constipation at the front end' with sluggish running reaching unacceptable levels. At the same time the American approach of increasing adhesion by simply adding more wheels to a larger rigid frame locomotive had reached its limits.

Although it took a while to happen, the fairly obvious step was to discard the compounding but retain the existing system of articulation. The result was rapid evolution of 'simple' locomotives that became a national standard for heavy haulage at reasonable speed, with increasingly ambitious wheel arrangements culminating in the Union Pacific's famous 4-8-8-4 'Big Boys'. They were still popularly regarded as Mallets, even though purists argued they were a world

RIGHT: At the opposite end of the scale to the Uintah Mallets is the diminutive 0-4-4-0 No 1 on the Cripple Creek & Victor Railroad in Colorado. It was built in 1902 for the Penoles - Avalos mineral railway in Mexico − only nine miles long and in its steam days virtually unknown to the outside world. (Clifford Schoff)

LOWER: The Donna Thereza Christina Railway in Brazil was noted for possessing the last narrow gauge Mallets to be turned out by the Baldwin Locomotive Works. 2-6-6-0 No 203 of 1949 was in store at Turbarao engine shed when photographed in September 1977. (James Waite)

THIS PAGE: Java became famous in the 1970s as the world's last major colony of mainline Mallets. It was also noted for its locomotive depot at Cibatu, thought to be unique in that its entire allocation comprised Mallets. The atmosphere of these years is evocatively captured in this view of CC5012 leaving Cibatu with the morning train for Garut in August 1979. (Stephen Crook)

OPPOSITE : The turntable at Cibatu had an unusually attractive setting, here graced by CC5003 in August 1978. (James Waite)

away from the original concept where the compound element had been so fundamental.

Narrow gauge in the USA was by this time in decline and in any event had always opted for the most basic of locomotives capable of running on the roughest of tracks. Even 'simple' Mallets were conspicuous by their absence, but there was one noted exception so remarkable that it has become legendary. Nothing in the long saga of North American railroads has quite equalled Baxter Pass on the border of Colorado and Utah, which provided a route across the Book Cliff Mountains for the three-foot gauge Uintah Railway. The 62-mile line started out from Mack, an insignificant depot on the standard gauge Denver & Rio Grande Western main line that most passenger trains ran through without acknowledging the Uintah's existence. It terminated in equally desolate surroundings at Watson, virtually the sole reason for the railway's presence being that the Uintah basin had proved to be the source of most of the world's gilsonite. The asphaltene mineral was in great demand for such purposes as the manufacture of paint, printers' inks and insulating compounds.

The Uintah Railway breasted Baxter Pass at a summit level of 8,437ft. This was not unusually high by Colorado standards but it was the way the line was taken over the top that set it apart. The climb heading north – fortunately with empties – involved an incredible five miles of constant 1 in 13, with both the gradient and the curvature being the most severe on any North American common carrier railroad. Even though the Uintah was one of the last US narrow gauge lines to be built in 1904, its engineering standards were more akin to an earlier logging line.

Trains were hauled by conventional engines at either end of the railway but these perforce had to give way to Shay geared locomotives for the assault on Baxter Pass. It was an expensive way of running a railroad. One day the general manager and his master mechanic disappeared into an office and roughed out some ideas for a 'simple' 2-6-6-2T capable of hauling freight over the entire length of the line. Quite what Baldwin Locomotive Works thought when confronted with these sketches from the American outback is not recorded, but they duly took on the detailed design work and in 1926 delivered a magnificent machine.

Weighing in at no less than 118 tons and claimed to be North America's largest narrow gauge locomotive, No 50 was 45ft long and had a tractive effort of 42,000lb. The Mallet was able to handle as much tonnage as two Shays and traverse Baxter Pass in little more than half the time. The only design flaw was that on a grade of 1 in 13 there was a tendency for one end of the crown sheet to be exposed, leading to the risk of a boiler explosion. The story is still told that this problem was due to Baldwin's refusal to believe such a steeply graded railroad could exist, but in any event the flaw was soon corrected. A second Mallet No 51, five tons heavier, was delivered in 1928.

Their heyday was short-lived. The great depression took its toll on gilsonite production and the Uintah ran its last trains in 1939. It had been a brief but glorious era for a unique railroad well summarised by Lucius Beebe and Charles Clegg in their classic book *Narrow Gauge in the Rockies*: 'The grade was achieved over a bewilderment of loops, swirls and hairpin turns, the most abrupt of which was 66 degrees, and crews who had worked head-on or braked on the Uintah smiled tolerantly at mountain railroading elsewhere. They had taken graduate degrees.'

The two Mallets, still in the prime of youth at the time of closure, went to the Sumpter Valley Railway in Oregon and were converted to tender locomotives. They ended their days

at Escuintla in Guatemala, where in 1964 one had been cannibalised and the other was under repair. Asked what he thought of it, an engineer colourfully replied: 'She was the son of a whore, much harder to run than the other locomotives, more places to oil, easy to come off the tracks; things were always coming loose or breaking. But she could sure pull! Once we had sixty cars with her; I think she would have taken more, but they would have torn apart.'

Both locomotives were scrapped shortly afterwards. Had they lasted just a little longer, they might well have become a star attraction on one of the preserved three-foot gauge lines in the Rockies and have formed an amazing contrast with the only narrow gauge Mallet now in the USA. This is the delight-fully diminutive compound 0-4-4-0 No 1 on the two-foot gauge Cripple Creek & Victor Railroad – a preserved line in Colorado running through the remnants of what were once fabulously rich gold mines. The most unusual feature about No 1 is that its existence was unknown until relatively recent times. Yet under the circumstances this is hardly surprising, as along with identical twin No 2 it spent its working life on a

Mexican mining line a mere nine miles long that connected with no other system. Both locomotives were supplied by Orenstein & Koppel in 1902 and both still exist, with No 2 displayed in the town of Saltillo close to the mines.

Two batches of 2-6-6-2s were built by Alco for the Mexican three-foot gauge in 1928 and 1934/36, but the Uintah engines remained the only narrow gauge Mallets in the USA.

As late as 1945, Baldwin delivered three 'simple' 2-6-6-2 tender locomotives to the metre gauge Donna Thereza Christina Railway in Brazil followed by a further two in 1949 and finally in the following year the last two narrow-gauge Mallets to be built by the company. This 267 km (167-mile) line conceived to carry coal to the port of Imbituba was opened in 1884 and took its name from the Italian princess who became the wife of the country's last emperor. It included a branch with considerable twisting curvature from Turbarão to Lauro Müller, closed by flood damage in 1974, on which the Mallets were principally used. Three have been preserved, one of them at the company's headquarters and another at

TOP: Preservation ventures have not surprisingly shown interest in the large number of Mallets in store at Java's sugar mills. The second such locomotive to leave the island was the 60cm gauge 0-4-4-0T built by Orenstein & Koppel in 1909. As seen here, it is now at the Frankfurt Feldbahn Museum. (James Waite)

LOWER: The 75cm gauge 'Pakis Baru No 5' was acquired by the then new Statfold Barn Railway in Staffordshire in 2004. Three years later it had been restored and was standing outside the line's engine shed. (James Waite)

Railway Museum. The next type introduced was a 2-6-6-0T, which became the country's most numerous Mallet with thirty-four being built between 1904 and 1911. Most came from the same German manufacturers as their predecessors, but the final eleven reflected the fact that Indonesia was then the Dutch East Indies. They were the first Mallets to be constructed by Werkspoor of Amsterdam.

Matters assumed a different dimension in 1916 with the arrival of the first of sixty compound locomotives that were to dominate main-line operations until the end of steam. The first twenty were 2-8-8-0s and came in two batches from Alco in 1916 and 1919. Thoroughly American in appearance and especially their vast dimensions, they brought with them the luxury of electric lighting and some were fitted with mechanical stokers. Much of their early career was spent hauling expresses between Purwakarta and Bandung on the tortuous line through the Preanger mountains, winding its way around jumbled ridges and crossing deep ravines by means of awesomely high bridges. The melodious chime whistles echoed among the hills and became a familiar feature of daily life. Not a single example remains, and to see a preserved narrow gauge Mallet built by Alco it is necessary to go to the Glenbrook Vintage Railway in New Zealand. Its flagship locomotive, stored in good condition, is a 2-4-4-2 supplied to a local timber company in 1907 and once described as 'one of the most delightful small Mallets ever built'.

The Alcos proved to be a touch on the slow side for the express services in Java and so a further batch of ten 2-8-8-0s were ordered in 1923. They came from Werkspoor, Hanomag and the Saxon Locomotive Works (formerly Richard Hartmann), but still retained the American looks of their predecessors. One of their main duties was on the more hilly stretches traversed by the Java Express, which ran virtually the full 1,100 km (700 miles) of the country between the administrative capital of Batavia and the commercial capital of Surabaya. Several remained active into the mid-1970s and were then the world's only eight-coupled Mallets still in service.

All the 2-8-8-0s suffered from a tendency for slipping on the rear unit. This raised the cylinder pressure, which in turn caused the front unit to slip and to be followed by another frenzy at the rear. The yo-yo situation could last for some time and create a cacophony that defies description in words. Happily it was recorded in sound by the noted American enthusiast Winston Link, who captured a compound 2-8-8-2

Rio Negrinho, while a third is derelict at Turbarão. They are all far removed from working order.

GRAND FINALE

It is perhaps fitting that the long story of Mallet evolution did not come to a dull ending on a coal-carrying line or even on the desolate heights of Colorado's Baxter Pass. Instead there has been a grand finale – still not quite ended – on an island that can claim to be the most densely populated on earth. Java, the most dominant of the many islands forming Indonesia, has a 3ft 6in gauge state network extending for some 3,000 km (1,900 miles) on which over sixty million journeys are made each year.

As is so often the case, its use of Mallets began modestly with sixteen 0-4-4-2Ts built by both Hartmann and Schwartzkopff between 1899 and 1907. Six of them were still active in the mid-1970s and one of them is preserved among the two-dozen other exhibits at the excellent Ambarawa

ABOVE: Also preserved at Statfold Barn is 'Tjepper No 5', a 75cm gauge Jung locomotive of 1919. It was photographed in working mode in August 1978 at its original home at Tjepper sugar mill (now known as Ceper as a result of place names changing from Dutch forms to more phonetic versions). (James Waite)

RIGHT: Preservation can never recapture such scenes as this one of a heavy train of sugar cane being shunted in August 2000. The location is Pesantren mill in East Java, which at the dawn of the 21st century was home to the world's last concentration of working Mallets. No 217 is one of several locomotives supplied by the Dutch firm of Du Croo & Brauns. (Keith Chester)

A remarkable photograph taken by an international aid worker shortly after the disastrous tsunami of 26 December 2004, which was at its most devastating in Sumatra. The plinth in Banda Aceh supporting BB84 was battered and broken, but the world's last commercially produced Mallet was relatively unscathed. It had been built in Japan in 1961 as delayed wartime reparations. (John Clark)

on the Norfolk & Western Railroad in dire trouble through this problem. It does much to convey why 'simple' Mallets ousted compounds on so many lines as both locomotives and loads became ever larger.

There was some surprise that compounding was still adopted for the thirty 2-6-6-0s ordered in 1927 from Werkspoor and Swiss Locomotive Works, but there was then a chronic fuel shortage and it may have been the thought that using steam twice over was more economical. Thoroughly modern engines designed for hauling fast freight across the Java plains, they lasted into the early 1980s. Many had then joined earlier locomotives at Cibatu, 64 km (40 miles) east of Bandung, which became famous as almost certainly the world's only locomotive depot where the entire allocation comprised Mallets. Three of the 2-6-6-0s have been preserved – one at Ambarawa Railway Museum and another at Jakarta Transportation Museum. A third, built by Werkspoor, has been repatriated to become an impressive exhibit at the Netherlands Railway Museum in Utrecht. Donated by Indonesian State Railways, it carries the nameplate *Sri Gunung* ('Queen of the Mountains').

As if it were not enough, Java came to boast being more than just the last major colony of mainline Mallets. It also had its sugar mills in the central plains and east of the island, where large numbers of Mallets, mainly built by the German manufacturers of Borsig, Jung and Orenstein & Koppel, were delivered between 1903 and 1932 for service on lines of numerous different gauges. Entering the scene a little later

was the Dutch firm of Du Croo & Brauns, which supplied its last Mallet to Java in 1929.

Even more remarkably, over forty 0-4-4-0Ts still survived in 2012. The overwhelming majority were in store, with just a handful belonging to the increasingly select group of locomotives often described as the last gasp of working as opposed to preserved steam. Even some of these were normally just lit up for groups of visiting enthusiasts rather than being steamed on a regular basis, but at least they formed a fascinating contrast with water buffaloes hauling cane wagons out in the fields.

A few Mallets have left the island's sugar mills, beginning in 1987 with 'Krebet 3', a 70cm gauge O&K built in 1909, which went to a private owner in Australia. It was followed in the 1990s by a 60cm gauge O&K from Gending mill, now at the Frankfurt Feldbahn Museum, which reputedly required the involvement of Chancellor Kohl before the Indonesian government would agree to its export. In 2004 the then new Statfold Barn Railway in Staffordshire acquired the pioneer 75cm gauge O&K of 1905 from Pakis Baru mill. It was joined two years later by two Jung engines, one the 75cm gauge 'Tjepper No 5' and the other from the 60cm gauge system at Jatibarang mill. After extensive restoration, it literally had a baptism by fire when it made a first visit to the Welsh Highland in 2011 and extinguishers were required to quell acute hotbox problems!

Java has clearly played a key role in the closing decades of the longest-lived of all types of articulated locomotives. But the neighbouring and larger island of Sumatra was also home until the 1990s to a fleet of Mallets working in its palm oil plantations, with at least twenty still being active in the 1970s.

It is also on Sumatra where the Mallet story really ends. The 75cm gauge Atjeh Tramway running for almost 510 km (320 miles) close to its northern coast took six 0-4-4-0Ts from Esslingen in 1904. Serving what is now known as Aceh Province, the line was left derelict following the Japanese occupation in World War II. It was Japan that in 1961 eventually supplied as reparations the only Mallets to be built in Asia, but the process was so long delayed that the four 0-4-4-2Ts constructed by Nippon Sharyo were all out of service within ten years. BB84, the last of the four, was plinthed in the provincial capital of Banda Aceh and there might have remained relatively undisturbed had it not been for the terrible events of 26 December 2004.

The horrendous tsunami left 170,000 Indonesians dead, primarily in Aceh province. The fate of a preserved locomotive slipped into utter insignificance, but one international aid worker did photograph BB84 still perched on its battered plinth. Fifteen months later it was reported to be in 'a rather poor condition' with its valve gear and piston rods missing. In a land that suffered a major earthquake in October 2010 and has fallen firmly off the tourist map, the subsequent life or death of the world's last commercially produced Mallet remains unclear. All that can be said with certainty is that it formed a metaphorical buffer stop at the end of a long line, starting and finishing with small narrow gauge engines after developing into the largest locomotives the world has ever seen.

CHAPTER THREE

Weird and Wonderful

'BLACKSMITH'S NIGHTMARE'

It is not just in terms of Mallets that the sugar plantations of Java have come to be especially noted. They have been described as having 'a collection of arguably the most weird and wonderful articulated locomotives ever seen anywhere on earth'. Moreover, like the Mallets, this collection has proved long lasting and is still largely extant, although most of the survivors are in store rather than in steam.

There are two reasons why this treasure trove is not as well known as it deserves. Firstly, Java involves many railway enthusiasts in a journey almost half way round the world and so has tended to be off limits to less-hardened travellers. Secondly, most of the locomotives look at first glance to be conventional and it is only on close examination that their special characteristics are evident. Like the Mallets, they represent semi-articulation but using very different principles to the single swivelling bogie. Their intricacies are best understood from the accompanying diagrams.

By far the most numerous are a type of locomotive conceived in Saxony by Ewald Richard Klien and Heinrich Robert Lindner and patented in 1892. Those in Java look from a distance like a normal 0-8-0 and totally disguise the fact that they are very different. Outside frames and the general presence of well tanks prevent any glimpse of the front and back axles, which are in fact considerably thicker than the other two.

Charles S Small explained the reasons why in his classic 1959 book *Far Wheels*: 'For the connoisseur of mechanical devices of the Heath Robinson variety, there is no greater treat than to be confronted with a Klien-Lindner locomotive... The driving axle was inside a subsidiary axle which connected the wheels. The drive was through a ball and socket joint on the inner axle. A pin through the ball drove the outer axle. The internal diameter of the outer axle was sufficiently large to allow radial movement and a subsidiary gadget allowed the axles to slide longitudinally with respect to each other. All of this blacksmith's nightmare was for the purpose of allowing an eight-coupled engine to traverse sharp curves.'

It is a colourful description but the reference to Heath Robinson is perhaps a little unkind. The Klien-Lindner patent created one of the most common if least appreciated forms of articulation, with locomotives incorporating this system still in steam in the twenty-first century. There was at first a tendency for the outer axles to head off in the wrong direction, but this was cured by relatively minor modifications. Orenstein & Koppel, the main suppliers to Java from 1903 onwards, solved the problem by simply adding some springs.

Experimentation in this period never ceased, a prime example being a remarkable Klien-Lindner mutation produced by O&K in 1916 in the shape of a geared 0-8-0. With cylinders mounted extremely high, an internal jack drive and a plethora of flailing rods and whirring wheels at the front end, its noise when underway is out of all proportion to its speed. It is also a touch disconcerting to watch the motion and upper drive shaft rotating in the reverse direction to the coupling rod! No 10 *Salak* has survived against all odds and remains in serviceable condition at the 70cm gauge Rejosari Mill.

Also using gears is a system developed by Gustav Luttermöller, chief engineer at O&K, which like the Klien-

Motive power in Java at its most weird and wonderful. Although totally concealed by the outside frames, the unique 0-8-0T+T No 10 *Salak* has Klien-Linder articulation and an internal jack drive. The motion and upper drive shaft rotate in the opposite direction to the coupling rods – and make a great commotion in so doing. It is stored at Rejosari Mill, where it was photographed in 2000.
(Keith Chester)

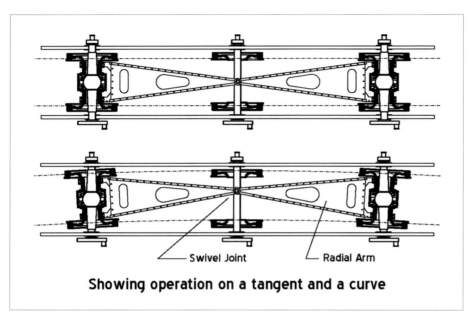

Swivel Joint   Radial Arm

Showing operation on a tangent and a curve

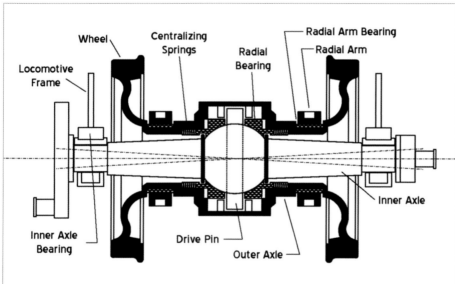

Wheel — Centralizing Springs — Radial Bearing — Radial Arm Bearing — Radial Arm — Locomotive Frame — Inner Axle — Inner Axle Bearing — Drive Pin — Outer Axle

The intricacies of the 'Blacksmith's Nightmare', more politely known as the Klien-Lindner system of articulation.

The upper drawings of the frame detail show how the front and back axles have extra thickness, allowing the driving axle to be inside a subsidiary axle connected to the wheels. There is sufficient play to allow radial movement, as shown in the distinction between operation on a tangent and on a curve. These two drawings illustrate the application of the Klien-Lindner system to a 0-6-0, but the same principles apply with the surviving 0-8-0s in Java. (Jeff Scherb)

The drawing of the axle detail shows in the centre the ball and pin arrangement that drove the outer axle. (Jeff Scherb)

The two drawings are not to scale.

Normally not visible, the ball and pin are clearly shown in this photo of a Klien-Lindner axle sufficiently damaged to expose the contents. (Rob Dickinson)

Lindners is not quite what it might seem at first glance. Outside frames were not essential with this design, but the 0-10-0s could still be mistaken for 2-6-2s were it not for the fact that all the wheels are the same size – and all of them revolve should a slip occur. The outer axles are not connected by rods but instead are coupled internally to the three in the centre by swinging gear-trains so as to permit radial movement. Each set of these gears is totally enclosed in its own oil bath, leading some historians – perhaps with tongue in cheek – to ponder if O.V. Bulleid had heard of this arrangement when it came to designing his infamous 'Merchant Navy' Pacifics!

Proof that development in Java has never quite ended came in 2011 when three Luttermöllers at the 70cm gauge Pagottan Mill took on an even stranger appearance. Built by

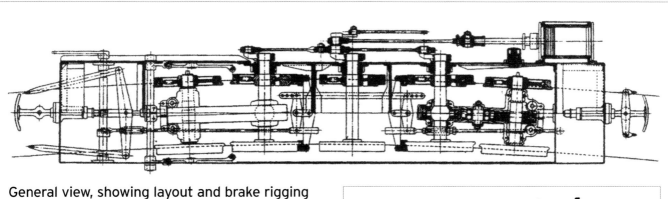

General view, showing layout and brake rigging

TOP: Motive power on the Java sugar lines at its most magnificent. Photographed in 2002 and still working in 2011, Tasik Madu VI is a 75cm gauge Luttermöller 0-10-0 with outside frames. Built by O&K in 1929, it boasts a huge twelve-wheel tender in order to hold ample supplies of bagasse – a fuel that is a byproduct of sugar-making.
(Rob Dickinson)

CENTRE AND LOWER: O&K arrangement for a Luttermöller 0-10-0 with geared drive to the outer axles.
(drawing from W.J.K Davies collection)

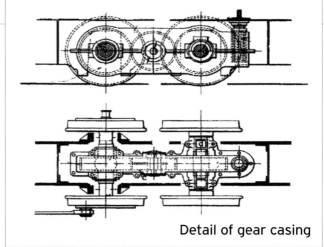

Detail of gear casing

ABOVE: Although it might seem impossible, three Luttermöllers at Pagottan Mill assumed an even stranger appearance in 2011 when they were converted into fireless locomotives. No 7, an O&K product of 1925, is seen taking on supplies of boiling water. (Bernd Seiler)

LEFT: *Bahagia*, one of the Czeczott locomotives on the 3ft 6in gauge Cepu Forest Railway busy at work in August 2002. Logs are being loaded into the cab for burning in the firebox. Visible are the flange-less central drivers and the coupling rods extended to balancing weights under the cab. (Rob Dickinson)

O&K in 1923-25, they have after a life of over three-quarters of a century been converted into fireless locomotives. Abundant supplies of boiling water are a feature of sugar mills and thus future operating costs will be minimal.

Amazing as it might seem with such an unusual wheel arrangement for the narrow gauge, another type of 0-10-0 graces the sugar mills – and again has often been subject to mistaken identity. Although perhaps stretching the definition of articulated locomotives, examples of what look like extraordinary 0-12-0s first appeared in 1926. Unlike the Luttermöllers they have conventional coupling rods, which, apart from their normal function, also restrain axles provided with sideways play. They are extended to what look like rear wheels under the cab, but in reality are just balancing weights and do not touch the track. This simpler and hence cheaper system than its predecessors was developed by Professor Czeczott, a leading Polish engineer, with the locomotives being supplied by Berliner Maschinenbau (BMAG). Apart from those at the sugar mills, there are three that operate erratically on the 3ft 6in gauge Cepu Forest Railway and another is preserved at the Forestry Museum in Jakarta.

On top of these many variants, three totally different articulated locomotives built by Jung in 1924 found favour at the 60cm gauge Soedhono Mill where two still remain. The '+' sign often used in describing their 0-6+4 wheel arrangement immediately suggests that they are out of the ordinary. Instead of being coupled in the conventional way, the tenders are articulated as part of the integral design by means of two arm-like extensions of the frame supported on pivots near the rear driving wheels. This method of increasing adhesive weight was patented as early as 1852 by Wilhelm von Engerth, engineer of the standard gauge Austrian Southern famed as the first railway across the Alps. His system used a geared drive that proved unsuccessful and did not feature on later narrow gauge locomotives, which thus became known as 'Modified Engerths'.

With the sugar lines largely located in central and eastern Java, there can surely be nowhere else in the world that has seen so many different kinds of articulated locomotive in such a relatively small area. Quite how many visiting enthusiasts have appreciated this claim to fame is questionable. With articulation that does not shout to be noticed, it is perhaps understandable that thoughts should first turn to the numerous different gauges, strikingly colourful liveries and the spectacular photographs obtainable at night as a result of locomotives burning bagasse. This by-product of the sugar-making process is prone to send sparks soaring into the tropical skies.

When and if attention is finally paid to the finer points of articulation, enthusiasts may show some interest in radial

axles and focus attention on Klien-Lindner products by virtue of sheer weight of numbers. Even here, they may fail to appreciate that they do not represent the pioneer narrow-gauge use of this ingenious pivotal system with its integral radial axles able to move within a fixed radius. Of all places, this occurred at an English country house.

THE ARISTOCRATIC PIONEER

Arthur Percival Heywood, born on Christmas Day 1849, was an eldest son in a long-established baronetcy. Interested in metalwork from an early age, he had by the time he was eighteen completed a four-inch gauge model railway with a steam locomotive and about a dozen wagons. He was married in 1872 and as a wedding present from his father was given a large house at Duffield Bank, five miles north of Derby.

Heywood was now able to enjoy the life of a country gentleman and at the same time develop his railway passion and bent as a skilled mechanical engineer in some style. Within two years he was building an extensive fifteen-inch gauge line in the grounds of Duffield Bank. This was no toy train but rather a serious intent to develop a railway system for estate, industrial and above all military use. Heywood was influenced by the work on minimum gauge lines already undertaken in France by Paul Decauville. He was also a close contact of Charles Easton Spooner and was thus well aware of the groundbreaking developments on the Festiniog Railway to achieve maximum haulage in the face of steep gradients and sharp curvature.

Duffield Bank was on a steep escarpment and in order to have continuous running the line had of necessity been laid out in what today's modellers call a dog-bone formation. Heywood more picturesquely referred to it as resembling 'a pair of spectacles'. It meant that coping with severe curves was a problem from the outset, but the line's creator did not favour the complicated pipework of the Festiniog double Fairlies that was prone to steam leakage.

Proceeding cautiously, the first locomotive in 1875 was a conventional 0-4-0T. The next was radically different, as

Sir Peter Heywood, great grandson of the narrow gauge pioneer Sir Arthur Heywood, tries his hand at the controls of *Ursula*. This diminutive 0-6-0T is a replica of Sir Arthur's last locomotive, supplied to the Duke of Westminster's Eaton Hall Railway in 1916. It has proved a major attraction at occasional open days on the recreated line at Eaton Hall. (NGW collection)

indicated in a letter that Heywood wrote to *The Engineer* in 1879: 'I myself am now building a six-coupled locomotive, all the axles of which work radially so as to combine the greatest adhesion with the greatest flexibility.' Helped solely by a joiner and a casual worker, it took him a further two years to build the 0-6-0T *Ella*, named after one of his daughters.

Muriel, the last Duffield Bank locomotive completed in 1894, was a 0-8-0T with outer axles that could pivot and inner axles with sliding sleeves. Visitors to a demonstration included the Hon Cecil Parker, agent to the first Duke of Westminster, who wished to connect his vast country seat of Eaton Hall with the Chester to Wrexham main line of the Great Western Railway some three miles distant. A fifteen-inch gauge line was duly constructed and two of its three Heywood locomotives built at the Duffield Bank workshops again had radial axles. They were the 0-6-0Ts *Shelagh* and *Ursula*, respectively delivered in 1904 and 1916.

Arthur Heywood, who succeeded to the baronetcy in 1897, never achieved his major ambition of developing a fifteen-inch gauge system for military use and in estate terms Eaton Hall remained his only major customer. His death in 1916 brought the end of the Duffield Bank line with both *Ella* and *Muriel* being requisitioned by the Ministry of Munitions. The probable intention was to use them in constructing an armaments factory at Gretna. In 1917 they passed to the Ravenglass & Eskdale Railway, then just emerging as a new fifteen-inch gauge line on the original trackbed.

Ella was withdrawn in 1926, although its side mainframes are today preserved as part of the line's Museum Collection and its side tanks are to be found on the ex Dundee Gasworks locomotive *Bonnie Dundee*. The final use of *Muriel* was as a stationary boiler but in 1927 its chassis was incorporated into a new 0-8-2 tender locomotive *River Irt*. This has ever since remained a historic item on the line's motive power roster

and appropriately in 1981-82 it participated in a 'Minimum Gauge Railways' exhibition at the National Railway Museum to celebrate the centenary of *Ella's* completion.

The Eaton Hall Railway survived until 1947 but its steam locomotives were little used after the mid-1920s. *Shelagh* had taken its name from the second Duke of Westminster's wife, but their separation and divorce saw it become *Katie*. Thus, it was *Katie* and *Ursula* that in 1942 succumbed to the wartime scrap drive, which sadly meant that not one of the Heywood locomotives with their innovatory articulation had survived. Yet interest in these pioneers continued to grow and it became inevitable that sooner or later a replica would be constructed.

A Lincolnshire-based enthusiast James Waterfield finally opted for *Ursula*, having rejected *Ella* for aesthetic reasons and the more complex 0-8-0T *Muriel* on cost grounds. The rolling chassis was completed in time for an exhibition held at Chester in 1996 to mark the centenary of the Eaton Hall Railway. The completed replica was first steamed in May 1999 and the following year played a major part in the 125th anniversary celebrations of the Ravenglass & Eskdale Railway. *Ursula* went on to become a star attraction when it visited the recreated Eaton Hall Railway on its rare public open days. Sir Arthur Heywood would no doubt have been delighted.

'A WELL-OILED CLOCK'

Although Heywood was the first to build a narrow gauge locomotive with radial axles, his wider contribution to this form of articulation remains uncertain. Just how many of his ideas were wholly original is difficult to assess. It was an era ripe with railway development when ideas were borrowed, modified and often abandoned only to be revived many years later. The radial axles fitted to *Ella* in 1881 were remarkably similar to a flexible wheelbase system patented in 1877 by James Cleminson for use on carriages and wagons. As a contributor to

One of the most significant narrow gauge designs of all time was the 0-6+2 radial tank developed by Adolph Klose for the 76cm gauge Bosna-Bahn. Thirty-four such locomotives were supplied by Krauss between 1885 and 1896. Spidery and spindly they might have looked, but it wasn't until 1967 that the last was withdrawn. No 189-026, dating from 1893, is reposing at Podlugovi in the 1930s.
(Keith Chester collection)

The Klose 0-6+4 tender locomotives ordered by the Bosna-Bahn in 1900/01 proved as able as the earlier radial tanks. This superb portrait of No 185-003 was taken at Derventa in 1965 just before the photographer was arrested for this then illegal activity. (Charlie Lewis)

The Engineer, Heywood would also probably have been aware of the work of the Swiss engineer Adolph Klose, who in 1880-81 successfully applied radial axles to freight wagons.

Just as developments with rolling stock may well have influenced Heywood, so they also came to the attention of Julius Kraft, chief mechanical engineer of the Bosna-Bahn with its 76cm gauge main line linking Brod with Sarajevo. He was anxious to create a new generation of locomotives to cope with rapidly increasing traffic on this 270km (170-mile)

route with its many sharp curves and steep gradients. Klose was duly asked if he could adapt his ideas for a locomotive with the result that a 0-6+2T was delivered by the Linz factory of Krauss in 1885. It bravely combined two systems of articulation in the shape of radial axles worked by a series of levers and a small articulated tender clearly adapting the principles developed by Wilhelm von Engerth in the 1850s. On the law of averages it could well have been yet one more of the many unsuccessful inventions of the period. Instead it proved to be a masterpiece.

Klose noted with some satisfaction that it 'not only fulfilled all expectations but exceeded them'. By 1896 Krauss had supplied thirty-four such locomotives, which proved ideal in coping with both curves and gradients as well as achieving respectable speeds on the more level sections. Fondly known to generations of Bosnian enginemen as 'radialka', all but one

of the 0-6+2Ts remained in service in 1933 and some endured long enough to challenge railway enthusiasts determined to track them down.

In 1967 the noted author Terry Martin set off across Europe on his motorbike in quest of the last survivor, built by Krauss in 1893. Just days before its withdrawal, he found it on the Steinbeisbahn at Srenetica, one of the loneliest of all junction stations, and later wrote: 'If pressed to offer a description of it working, I would need the assistance of a collapsible clotheshorse to explain the system of double parallelograms. It was certainly an extraordinary spectacle when stationary, but in motion presented the most bizarre sight as it somehow gave the impression of using crutches. But for all its idiosyncrasies it ran with a gentle ease, if somewhat alarmingly as the rear of the cab wriggled about quite independently over the rail joints.'

The outstanding success of the Klose tanks led to sixty compound 0-6+4s being ordered in 1900 and 1901. They were in essence larger tender versions to cope with arid conditions in southern Dalmatia on the newly completed line through to Dubrovnik. If anything they looked even more improbable with both cylinders between the frames and the valves and motion outside. A graphic portrayal was penned by two English travel writers, Jan and Cora Gordon, in the 1920s: 'The engine, a strange-looking construction which had dragged us from Brod, was topped by a fat-bonneted funnel, with tiny axles and an elaboration of complex and ingenious external machinery. It made one think of one of those long-legged beetles of the Congo, for it moved with a ridiculous agitation of mobile members compared with the visible motion achieved.'

Their complexities had by this time led to the 0-6+4s being taken off most main-line activities. This was in part due to the system perfected by the outstanding Austrian engineer Karl Gölsdorf, which, in a way similar to that later developed by Czeczott and still to be seen in Java, gave extra lateral movement to some of the driving wheels on a rigid-framed locomotive. Nevertheless, examples survived into the 1960s and enjoyed a much longer life than the fifty-three supplied to the Württemberg State Railways in southern Germany, which was the only other concern to use Klose locomotives in significant quantity. They had all gone by 1931, perhaps

because there was not the will to cope with maintaining such mechanical intricacies. In Yugoslavia there may well have been no option, and certainly a visitor as late as 1965 was greatly impressed. Seeing a survivor just before he was arrested for photographing it, Charlie Lewis noted: 'The engine seemed to be in excellent good health. When drifting or working lightly no knocks or rattling of the motion could be heard, only a kind of gentle ticking as one would expect from a sewing machine, or a well-oiled clock.'

It is an appropriate metaphor for a system conceived in Switzerland. Yet sadly it is an experience that will never be repeated. Neither in Bosnia nor in Germany has a single example been preserved of one of the most fascinating of all articulated locomotives.

WAR AND ITS AFTERMATH

Heywood must surely have realised that a 76cm gauge main line was worlds away from his work on the fifteen-inch gauge at Duffield Bank. He concentrated his efforts in striving to interest the British military in a minimum-gauge system, which would use locomotives with radial axles suitable for wartime conditions. He must have been disappointed at the lack of any interest and especially so in comparison with what happened in Germany.

A batch of eighteen 0-8-0Ts incorporating Klien-Lindner axles was built by Krauss in 1901-05 for the 60cm gauge State Northern Railway in South-West Africa, where they greatly impressed the German military in charge of operating the line. As the clouds of war started to gather over Europe, it was but a small step to create what became known as 'Brigadeloks' or Feldbahn 0-8-0Ts of the same 60cm gauge. When war finally broke out, the military was thus fully prepared with ideal motive power equipped to negotiate tight curves on temporary tracks. With their relatively modern design, the 0-8-0Ts used on the Western Front could hardly have provided a greater contrast to the bizarre Péchot-Bourdons participating in the French war effort. True German precision records that an amazing total of 2,473 Brigadeloks were built by fourteen different manufacturers.

Although the Western and Eastern Fronts were the main areas of activity, some of the locomotives saw wartime service further afield. A typical example is the plinthed Henschel-

Although built primarily for service in World War I, many 'Brigadelok' 0-8-0Ts had remarkably long lives. Several ended their days on the 168km line in Macedonia linking Gostivar with Ohrid. There was always time to spare, as depicted in this 1964 scene of the crew relaxing at a passing loop near Sbrinovo. Regarded as one of the finest narrow gauge journeys in Europe, the line sadly closed just two years later. (John Phillips)

built 0-8-0T at Sofia station in Bulgaria, which along with many other Brigadeloks operated on an extensive 220km (138-mile) military system through the Rila and Pirin Mountains close to the border with Greece. Both the 60cm gauge railway and many of its 0-8-0Ts survived not just the 1914-19 conflict but also World War II and continued in operation until closure in 1969.

Similar in conception were the field railways laid in Macedonia from 1916 onwards to supply the Central Powers' defensive lines on the Saloniki front, most of which were built by the Bulgarian army using German equipment and bringing in well over two hundred Brigadeloks. Several survived on a line running through dramatic scenery that linked Gostivar with Ohrid, close to the Albanian border. By the 1950s it was recognised as offering one of the finest narrow gauge journeys in Europe, although it certainly needed stamina as the only through train of the day required some fifteen hours for the 168 kilometres (105 miles). Enthusiasts may have revelled in such an experience but the local population increasingly deserted the railway and, with both locomotives and what were seen as coffin-like coaches descending into decrepitude, it was closed in 1966. One of the 0-8-0Ts is preserved outside Kičevo station.

Following the 1919 armistice, large numbers of almost new Klien-Lindner 0-8-0Ts were sold, often to distant purchasers as instanced by the Sena Sugar Estates in Mozambique which took at least thirteen of them. Following the cessation of steam, many of them were again sold in 1998 and ended up at a quarry in Warwickshire, England, from where they were bought for preservation and spread across much of Europe. Even then their journeys were not always over. Sena No 2, built by Henschel in 1915, was purchased by a Swiss enthusiast, who decided to send it to the Sandstone Steam Railroad in South Africa for restoration. It was soon running again, after a life that had seen it exported to Africa twice and to Europe once!

Other locomotives have ended their days much closer to home. Until March 1978 the last Brigadeloks in daily service were to be found on the Waldeisenbahn Bad Muskau in what was then East Germany. Several have been preserved, as has part of the line. Other survivors are at the Feldbahn museums at Frankfurt and at Freiland, south-west of Vienna, as well as on two French lines that have specialised in collections of wartime locomotives by virtue of their locations close to the World War I battlefields. Both the Tramway de Pithiviers à Toury and the Froissy-Cappy-Dompierre (Le p'tit train de la Haute Somme) have become noted for their special events with a wartime theme.

In pre-preservation days the Pithiviers line was the surprising home of three modified Luttermöller 0-10-0s that along with

another two had been ordered by the German army in 1917 on a trial basis. Cessation of hostilities meant the experiment got no further, resulting in a change of circumstances that also applied to Brigadeloks ordered in the closing months of the war. An example completed by Hartmann in 1919 avoided military service and instead went new to a paper factory at Emsfors on the Baltic coast of Sweden, where it remained for the next fifty years. It then went to the Östra Södermanlands Järnväg, where as No 8 it operates alongside the world's oldest Mallet and is named *Emsfors* in recognition of its origins.

FAR AND WIDE
Although the Brigadelok 0-8-0Ts unquestionably reigned supreme in sheer numbers, the full story of Klien-Linder and similar locomotives with radial axles is in more than one sense much wider than the 60cm gauge. In construction terms it began well before the German military placed its first order. Early in the field were nine powerful 0-8-0Ts supplied by O&K between 1901 and 1907 to the Mügeln - Geising line, one of the most difficult to operate on the whole of the 75cm gauge network in Saxony.

A year later in 1902 the 78.5cm gauge Upper Silesian Narrow Gauge Railways in Prussia took their first Klien-Lindner tank engines and by 1912 had twenty-two of them built by

Several Brigadeloks ordered in 1919 never saw wartime service. An example operates on the lakeside Östra Södermanlands Järnväg in Sweden, taking its name *Emsfors* from the paper factory where it went when new and remained for the next fifty years. (James Waite)

RIGHT: One of the 0-10-0s with sleeved axles built by O&K and delivered to the legendary Steinbeisbahn in 1924. Passengers stretch their legs on a sunny day in 1965 as it stops for water and fire cleaning after the long climb out of the Unac valley. These locomotives were greatly favoured by crews as 'they never got stuck in winter service'.
(Charlie Lewis)

LOWER: Equally successful were the Luttermöllers supplied by O&K to Poland in the years between World War I and 1925. This works photograph clearly shows the wheel arrangement and indicates why the 0-10-0Ts could so easily be mistaken for 2-6-2Ts. Four of the locomotives survived into the 1960s.
(Keith Chester collection)

O&K and Hagans. A report in that year commented: 'The 0-8-0T narrow gauge locos have fulfilled all our expectations of them.' The result was a further twenty-six being delivered by O&K between 1915 and 1919, before a quest for yet more power resulted in the same company using Luttermöller axles on thirteen 0-10-0Ts, the last of which were delivered in 1925. Two years earlier, wartime reparations had seen BMAG supply what was now the Polish state railway system with five further locomotives of the same wheel arrangement but using the less complicated Czeczott flexible wheelbase. Java was not the only country far distant from Europe to take Klien-Lindner locomotives from the early 1900s. Another was Argentina, although here the surprise was not so much the location but more the manufacturer. As there were close trading and financial links with the UK, Argentine Estates Ltd turned to a British rather than a German firm and ordered six 0-8-0s for its two-foot gauge lines from John Fowler of Leeds. After minor design adjustments, possibly in order to avoid patent infringement, they were delivered between 1909 and 1920. The same company supplied a single locomotive to the Kalgoorlie & Boulder Firewood Co in Australia in 1916, but no other examples were built in the UK.

Another manufacturer outside Germany was Ansaldo of Genoa, Italy, which in 1922 completed five 0-8-0Ts for the 95cm gauge Eritrea Railway. Here they operated alongside Mallets, many of them from the same builder. Exactly the same situation occurred with the 76cm gauge Steinbeisbahn in Bosnia, when between 1911 and 1915 it took delivery from Maffei of seven superheated Klien-Lindner 0-10-0Ts. The company had already supplied Mallets of many types, as had O&K which went on to deliver three superb 0-10-0 tender

engines with sleeved axles in 1924. For those who ventured there, these remote railways resembled the sugar lines of Java in becoming a showcase of articulation both obvious and hidden.

DOWN IN THE FORESTS

The 76cm gauge was common throughout much of Eastern Europe, including the many Romanian forest railways that have provided a remarkable saga of continuity lasting to the present day. It begins when the country formed part of the vast Austro-Hungarian Empire, and thus the first 0-8-0Ts with Klien-Lindner axles were the celebrated Class 490s produced in Budapest from 1905 onwards. Manufactured in large quantities, examples also went to Yugoslavia, Slovakia and Ukraine as well as Romania and Hungary itself.

Production of the Class 490s continued until 1950, with Reşiţa Works in Romania then adapting the existing design as the basis for powerful locomotives that became synonymous with the country's forestry lines for the next five decades. Major repairs were often undertaken at Reghin Works near Târgu Mures, which entered the record books when it too used the same basic design to produce twelve completely new 0-8-0Ts between 1982 and 1988. Apart from motive power

for tourist lines, they were the only steam locomotives to be built outside China after 1972 and thus were the world's last narrow gauge articulated locomotives to be constructed for commercial use.

Little known until the end of the Communist era in 1989, the remaining forestry railways extending in total to about a thousand kilometres became much-visited survivors. The appeal of being deep in the woods was enhanced by the functional yet attractive locomotives burning the super-abundant supplies of wood and fitted with pumps to draw water from any convenient stream. Most of the lines had closed a decade later, but one survivor – mainly due to the lack of road access – was the Vişeu de Sus system in the Carpathian Mountains with its 44km (28-mile) 'main line' and numerous branches. Following privatisation in 1999, a Swedish company eventually took over the forestry operations and a group of Swiss enthusiasts formed the Wassertalbahn to work tourist services. Locomotives from all three eras are present, ranging from a pioneer Class 490 through various Reşiţas to *Cozia* 1, constructed at Reghin Works in 1986.

Reşiţa locomotives have also found their way to European tourist and preserved railways in Austria, France, Germany, Hungary, the Czech Republic and Slovakia. Not all Reşiţas spent their working lives in the forests. Two built in 1954 went to quarries at Turda and were ultimately destined to

764.408R *Cozia* I is one of a select group of twelve 0-8-0Ts that form the world's last narrow gauge articulated locomotives to be built for commercial use. It was constructed in 1986 at Reghin Works in Romania. Still in service on the delightful Viseu de Sus line, it was captured in July 2003 heading the regular mixed train and pausing at a remote station to pick up an elderly lady and her shopping. (Petr Mircev)

make the long journey to Wales. One was imported by the now defunct Ystwyth Valley Railway near Aberystwyth and then donated to the Welshpool & Llanfair, one of the few lines in Britain that happens to be of the same gauge. The resulting contacts, together with a sudden motive power shortage, led to a visit to Criscior in Romania to inspect its sister locomotive languishing in a field. It was in 'a terrible state' minus many missing parts stolen by gypsies, but was considered a better immediate prospect with the vast Cluj Works offering to do a complete rebuild in six months. This was duly finished on schedule and it left for Wales in time to enter service in July 2007, the earlier arrival henceforth becoming a source of spare parts.

Terry Turner, the Welshpool & Llanfair's general manager, stated his firm belief that the 0-8-0T would be 'ideal for the line, having a total adhesive weight of 24.5 tonnes on four

Klien-Lindner locomotives in the UK.

TOP: 0-8-0T 764.425, built at Resita Works in Romania in 1984, was brought to the Welshpool & Llanfair Railway in June 2007. It is seen being unloaded at Raven Square station. The Klien-Lindner articulation was rightly considered ideal for negotiating the line's sharp curves. (G. Hall)

LOWER: An earlier arrival in the UK was 0-6-0T No 740, built by O&K for the 1907 opening of the Matheran Hill Railway in India. Brought to Britain in 1987, a period of seventeen years elapsed before it was restored and entered regular service on the Leighton Buzzard Railway. This view shows the locomotive, with its striking light blue and white livery, running round at Page's Park station. (Jeff Scherb)

driving axles, the outermost axles being fitted with Klien-Lindner articulation for negotiating sharp curves'. This prediction has proved correct, although frequent breakdowns have not made it popular with crews.

INDIAN CONNECTIONS

The Reşiţa from Romania is not the only locomotive with Klien-Lindner axles to have been brought into the UK. It was preceded by a 0-6-0T that was almost half a century older and had spent its entire working life in India on the two-foot gauge Matheran Hill Railway. Climbing more than 2,300ft in just over twelve miles to serve the hill station above Bombay (now Mumbai), this line has a ruling gradient of 1 in 25 and reputedly boasts 281 curves! It is likely that the railway was well aware of the Klien-Lindner system and without further ado ordered four such locomotives from O&K to coincide with its opening in 1907.

Yet there is a more colourful if perhaps less probable explanation of events. The consulting engineer was Everard Calthrop, who had acted in the same capacity for the Leek &

Manifold Valley Light Railway in the Peak District. It was relatively close to the home of Sir Arthur Heywood, who had been one of its advisors. Both gentlemen were distinguished guests at the grand opening in 1904, when the four-course lunch with champagne and many fine wines no doubt generated a convivial atmosphere and free-flowing conversation. It is tempting to speculate that Heywood had much to say about radial axles and recommended their adoption but the truth remains unknown.

Whatever the case, the four locomotives certainly proved ideal for such a difficult line. Other than an ex Darjeeling class 'A' 0-4-0T and assorted railcars, the quartet worked all services until the advent of diesels in 1956. The striking light blue and white livery undoubtedly contributed to their appeal, with the result that all four remain in existence. Three of them are in India – one restored and remaining serviceable, another preserved at Matheran station, and the third at the National Railway Museum in New Delhi.

It is the fourth – No 740 – that is easily the best known. Brought to the UK in 1987, it initially languished at the

TOP: The 2-6+4s on the metre-gauge Ponferrada to Villablino line in north-west Spain were superbly maintained right up to the end of steam in 1981. PV No 31, waiting to depart from Ponferrada on the midday 'Correo', has been kept in working order to handle occasional tourist trains. (Ron Cox)

LOWER: The paint scheme on this 'Modified Engerth' highlights the system of articulation, with the red applied to the arm-like extension of the tender frame that is supported on a pivot near the driving wheels. 0-8+4 No 399.04 was photographed on Austria's Waldviertelbahn in August 2003. (Tony Nicholson)

OPPOSITE PAGE
LOWER: Definitely in the weird and wonderful category is this 0-6+2T rebuilt in 1920 from a war-surplus Krauss 0-6-0T. In March 1988 it was waiting to leave Mladějov in the Czech Republic with a train for Hřebeč. This line is now part of an industrial railway museum, where the locomotive remains in service. (Keith Chester)

Chalk Pits Museum at Amberley before being moved to Railworld at Peterborough, where it was visible from the East Coast main line. In 2001 it was transferred to the Leighton Buzzard Railway and became a familiar sight on the line prior to moving to the Statfold Barn Railway to await overhaul. It has attracted many admiring glances, but few of these will have centred round its articulation in the same way as happens with the Fairlies on the Ffestiniog. Out of sight is out of mind.

ENGERTH REVIVAL
Even though not spectacularly out of the ordinary, rather more attention is paid to the 'Modified Engerths' as found at Soedhono Mill in Java and more especially associated with two European lines. They continue to represent a prime example of an ancient design that was revived after becoming close to being forgotten.

With their tenders articulated with the locomotive as a whole, a fleet of ten 2-6+4s became a much photographed feature of the 64km (40-mile) metre-gauge Ponferrada to Villablino line in north-west Spain. Primarily built to carry coal, it passed through attractive mountain scenery and remained steam-worked until 1981. The earlier locomotives were constructed by Maffei and Krauss between 1913 and 1920 but these were augmented in the 1950s by a further four built in Spain by Macosa of Valencia. The two dating from 1956 represent the world's last Engerths to be constructed. Two of the 2-6+4s have been restored to working order, while others are at a museum at Ponferrada devoted to the railway and its associated industries.

It is appropriate that the other country where Engerths can still be seen operating is Austria, thus preserving a link with the very first locomotives of this kind dating back to the early 1850s. Six 0-8+4s were built by Krauss in 1906-08 for the 76cm gauge Mariazellerbahn in the Ötscherland mountains west of Vienna. Change came only five years later when this 90km (56-mile) line became the first in Austria to be electrified, following which the Engerths were transferred to other railways. Threats of closure in the 1990s triggered local enterprise to

Sizeable in narrow gauge terms, the 0-8+4s on the Waldviertelbahn were dwarfed by standard gauge wagons on Rollwagen that they handled as part of the regular freight traffic. No 399.01 is steaming away from a few busy moments at Weitra in May 1980. (Keith Chester)

purchase one of the locomotives, restore it to its original condition as No Mh6 and introduce steam services.

Three decades earlier this 0-8+4 and its five sisters became a focus of much attention on one of the last outposts of steam in Western Europe. They had all been allocated to Gmünd motive power depot on the Waldviertelbahn, close to the Czech border in the northern tip of Lower Austria. Here until the mid-1980s they hauled freight on the highly scenic and steeply graded 47km (30 mile) branch to Gross Gerungs, the atmosphere at the time being captured by Keith Chester: 'The freight was not conveyed in narrow gauge wagons, but in standard gauge ones perched seemingly precariously on Rollwagen. Three or four of these represented a full payload for the 0-8-0 at their head and long after its passing the train could be heard thrashing its way through the thick pine forests, with the beat echoing off the steep rock cuttings. All hopelessly uneconomic, but wonderfully romantic.'

All six 0-8+4s have survived, with three of them remaining at Gmünd as part of the ÖBB's heritage fleet. Apart from the Mariazellerbahn and Waldviertelbahn, they also handle steam workings on the Pinzgauerbahn, running through spectacular mountain scenery south-west of Salzburg.

Apart from Spain and Austria, one additional curiosity survives in the shape of what was originally locomotive No 1

on an obscure 60cm gauge line in Moravia, now part of the Czech Republic, which carried clay between Mladějov and Hřebeč. A war-surplus 0-6-0T built by Krauss, it underwent metamorphosis in 1920 with the addition of an extra rear-end and pair of wheels. It thus became a 0-6+2T, using Engerth principles but far more 'Modified' than is normally the case. Amazingly, it survived until closure of the line in 1993 and was restored to handle services at what became an

industrial railway museum. It is in the company of a similar locomotive built new in 1929.

THE AMERICAN WEST

Engerths and the various locomotive types based on radial axles had the common feature of adopting articulation in an unobtrusive way. They may have used gears, as with the Luttermöllers, but they were only semi-articulated. In terms of sheer spectacle they were outclassed by developments centred on the logging industry of the American West, where external gearing was used in such a unique way that it galvanised both the eyes and ears. Moreover, this was on fully articulated locomotives with two or sometimes even three bogies.

The scale of what was then the world's largest coniferous forest was virtually beyond comprehension, but the riches it offered gradually became apparent to the early lumbermen. Horse or oxen were initially used to haul timber on dirt roads and then on primitive wooden tramways, but the required gradients soon became too steep both for animals and conventional steam power.

Ephraim Shay, an experienced Michigan logger with an inventive mind, became convinced of the need for a locomotive like no other. It would have to operate on temporary tracks forcing their way through the trees, cope with rails laid at all angles and surmount climbs of appalling severity. In 1877 he created what in American parlance was a basic flatcar with two trucks (bogies), on which was mounted a vertical boiler and a transverse engine powering the axles via a system of gears.

It was simplicity itself but sufficient to interest Lima Machine Works in nearby Ohio. They had not previously built

An impressive three-truck Shay in the shape of No 14, built in 1916 for the Sierra Nevada Wood & Lumber company, and later one of the fleet of similar locomotives on the long-lived West Side Lumber system in California. Clearly showing the characteristic off-centre boiler and the three vertical cylinders, it was photographed in 1998 on the Georgetown Loop Railroad in Colorado. (Michael Messenger)

a locomotive but only a year later used Ephraim's designs to produce their first Shay. Much change and experiment quickly led to the concept assuming its familiar form as a fully-fledged articulated locomotive with a horizontal boiler. Instead of using pistons, all axles were powered by a lineshaft to achieve maximum tractive effort and at the same time allow the trucks full freedom of movement under the frame. Notable features included three vertical cylinders mounted just ahead of the cab, two of which faced right and one left, thus creating a rapid rhythm and unmistakable sound. In order to compensate for the weight and position of these cylinders the boiler was set left of centre and gave the Shay its uniquely lop-sided appearance.

Like the Klose design conceived for the Bosna-Bahn at about the same time, it seemed such an extraordinary contraption that expectations of swift consignment to the scrapheap must have run high. Instead, it too was a triumph, despite a top speed of little more than 9 mph uphill or downhill. Neither the American logging industry nor Lima Machine Works looked back and the company went on to build 2,661 Shays between 1880 and 1945. Many were

ABOVE: Heislers may not be attractive in appearance but are notable for the 'V'-shaped arrangement of their cylinders canted inwards at a forty-five degree angle. No 2 *Tuolumne* has steam to spare as it pauses alongside the all-American water tank on the Roaring Camp & Big Trees Railroad. Sited among the spectacular Redwoods south of San Francisco, this line is noted for possessing examples of all three of the major types of logging locomotives – Shays and a Climax as well as a Heisler. (John Pitchford)

RIGHT: Close-up of the vertical cylinders that are such a distinctive feature of Shays. Two face right and one left, creating a rapid rhythm and a richly evocative noise. No 12 is another of the former West Side Lumber locomotives. (Clifford Schoff)

standard rather than narrow gauge (generally three-foot), but standardisation was not to the fore and it was said to be difficult to find two exactly alike. As the logging lines expanded, the original two-struck designs were augmented by larger and even more stunning three-truck versions.

It was inevitable that Shays should soon face competition, the first successful challenger being the Climax conceived by another gifted inventor, Charles D. Scott. Looking rather more conventional, it was normally mounted on twin trucks and had inclined cylinders attached to a transmission shaft under the locomotive. There were no side rods on the trucks and all the gears were exposed to the elements. Production by the Climax Manufacturing Company of Corry, Pennsylvania, began in 1888 and many loggers soon considered this design superior to the Shay in haulage capabilities. Yet it had a tendency to develop a sag in the middle and become rough riding. Detractors insisted that 'a Climax would disintegrate itself, a railroad and the engine crews with equal impartiality'.

A further challenge to Shay supremacy came only three years later in 1891 and took its name from the patent obtained by a trained mechanical engineer, Charles L. Heisler. Built initially by the Dunkirk Engineering Company in New York, it was similar to a Climax, except that its two cylinders were canted inwards at a forty-five degree angle to form a 'V' arrangement. A longitudinal drive shaft then drove the outer axles on each powered truck.

Neither the Climax nor the Heisler was ever as popular as the Shay, but between them this great triumvirate of geared steam locomotives took the logging industry to supreme heights. They helped steam to conquer the woods in much of the American West on railroads that crossed ravines on spindly timber trestles and zig-zagged up mountain sides that were almost sheer. It was a glorious but relatively brief era of little more than eighty years. Steam power gave way to diesels and then by the late 1950s most of the traditional logging lines had closed. In many places there was simply no timber left to cut.

A line that gained a special place in the affections of the faithful was the West Side Lumber system in California. The last of the three-foot gauge logging railroads of the American West, it boasted 70 miles of line in the magnificent Sierra Mountains and survived until 1961. There were several attempts at preservation but none succeeded.

It has been a different story with saving geared locomotives for posterity, the opening word of an American website putting the position in perspective: 'Only 116 Shays survive today'. Although this total includes standard gauge locomotives, the implication that there ought to be more does seem to verge on the over-optimistic. It no doubt reflects the continuing appeal of geared locomotives in general and Shays in particular.

Certainly all seven of the three-truck Shays that remained at West Side in its final years found new homes on tourist lines and have been a major attraction ever since. Two went to the relatively nearby Yosemite Mountain Sugar Pine Railroad and three to the Georgetown Loop in Colorado, where they could be viewed clear of trees as they crossed the superb spiral bridge. Perhaps the most visited line has been the Roaring Camp & Big Trees south of San Francisco, not just because it has the earliest of the West Side Shays but also a Heisler and a Climax. Safeguarding all three of the major types of geared locomotives, it claims to have 'the oldest and most authentically preserved narrow gauge engines still providing regular passenger service in the USA'. They operate in a magnificent setting that defies photography, 'Big Trees' referring to the 300ft high Redwoods that dwarf the line at close quarters.

Although geared locomotives are so closely associated with logging in the American West, they have also handled other natural resources. The Uintah Railway in Colorado used Shays to haul its staple gilsonite traffic over the awesome grades of Baxter Pass before they were swiftly displaced in the 1920s by its two Mallets.

Conveying what looked like anthracite coal was hardly glamorous and certainly could not compare with the mineral that was the lifeblood of the Gilpin Tramway. It was the glittering prospect of hauling gold that brought into being this remarkable enterprise centred on Black Hawk over 8,000ft up in the Rocky Mountains to the west of Denver. The first and one of the very few two-foot gauge lines in the West, it was set apart

It was gold high in the Rocky Mountains that created the unique Gilpin Tramway, one of only a handful of two-foot gauge railroads in the American West. Its roster of five Shays included two early examples, No 2 *Russell* built in 1888 and No 3 *Quartz Hill* delivered a year later. In 1896 a pioneer photographer recorded them slogging their way upgrade with a train of coal for the mines.
(Western Collection, Denver Public Library)

ABOVE: Two-truck Shay No 508, built in 1917, spent much of its life in a rarified atmosphere more than 15,000ft above sea level as it worked freight over Cumbre summit in Bolivia. Later it was in more sense than one downgraded to the surprising role of shunting duties at Central station in La Paz, as seen here in 1970. (Roy Christian)

RIGHT: Despite becoming the last place in the world where large numbers of Shays remained in working service, Taiwan and its remarkable railway climbing over 7,500ft from the coast to Ali Shan remained largely unknown. No 31 was shunting passenger stock at the summit station in 1984, the year that finally saw the official end of steam. Most of the Shays remain in existence. (Michael Reilly)

ABOVE: The rare sight of a Climax in steam, as demonstrated on a replica timber line at Shantytown, near Greymouth on New Zealand's South Island. The distinctive inclined cylinders are attached to a transmission shaft under the locomotive. (Brian Webber)

LEFT: New Zealand became noted for its home-built logging 'lokeys'. Few have survived but an exception is the Heisler look-alike constructed by A & G Price in 1943 and thought to be the world's last geared logging locomotive to be built. It is seen in action on the McLeans Island site of the Canterbury Steam Preservation Society in 2002. (Rob Dickinson)

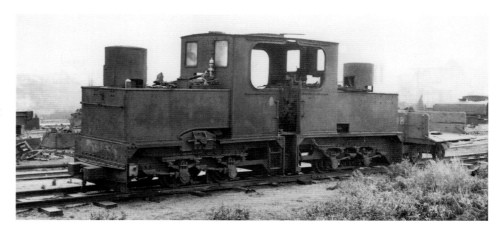

The innovative Sentinel Wagon Works of Shrewsbury dabbled with articulated geared locomotives in the 1920s and '30s, although not with any great success. This 0-4-4-0 was supplied to Kettering Ironworks in 1926 but spent long periods lying idle before finally being withdrawn in 1960. (S.A. Leleux)

by its 1 in 20 gradients, curves reputedly of 50ft radius and more switchbacks than any other American railroad. Built to extend mining beyond what had already achieved fame as 'the richest square mile on earth', its sole purpose was to convey gold-bearing quartz between the immense total of some 280 mines and mills. Opened in 1887, when the first of its five Shays was purchased, it was ultimately some twenty-six miles in length. After only thirty years, the end came suddenly in 1917 due to decline of the mining industry. None of the Shays survived, despite three of them being converted to three-foot gauge and only scrapped after twenty-one years in attempting to find a buyer proved abortive.

FROM THE ANDES TO ALI SHAN

Beyond the American West, the presence of Shays and kindred locomotives has been sporadic. Some went to railways in the Andes where speed was of no consequence, typical of them being a metre-gauge line that never achieved its goal of linking the Bolivian capital of La Paz with the navigable River Beni. Conventional motive power would have been a near impossibility and thus two Shays were obtained in 1917 to coincide with the first phase of construction. They worked freight over the world's second highest railway summit at Cumbre, a dizzying 15,264ft (4,650 metres) above sea level, and then down into the Unduavi Canyon on gradients as steep as 1 in 16. Little more than a tenth of the line was ever completed and by the 1950s the Shays were handling just a twice-weekly service. After being relegated to shunting duties at La Paz, one of them was set aside for eventual display in a Bolivian railway museum but was later reported derelict.

On the other side of the Pacific, few would instantly name the last place in the world where large numbers of Shays remained in working service. It is in fact Taiwan, close to the Tropic of Cancer with mountainous forests soaring to over 13,000ft (4,000 metres) above sea level. Following their occupation of the island in 1895, the Japanese recognised the value of the timber and decided to build a 2ft 6in gauge line climbing from the coastal plain at Chiayi to Ali Shan, which with its altitude of 7,530ft (2,300 metres) claimed to be the

then highest station in Asia. It has been seen as having no equals for awesome engineering other than the legendary Central Railway of Peru, but the Ali Shan line has by comparison remained largely unknown. With the first five miles at a constant 1 in 20 before matters became more serious and steepened to 1 in 16, it was another system where speed took second place and Shays were the obvious choice. Twenty entered service between 1911 and 1917, relying heavily on the faith of a brakesman at the head of the train as they propelled bunker-first uphill. Such a method of working may have helped but conditions in the fifty tunnels must often have been grim. Ali Shan gradually became a tourist resort as well as a logging centre, although the Shays remained in command until road access was provided in the early 1980s. The locomotives had by then become so synonymous with the town that the Forestry Bureau usually arranged for at least one to be in steam to greet visitors, as well as using them occasionally on logging trains.

The formal end of steam in November 1984 saw most of the Shays either plinthed or placed in store rather than scrapped, but there has also been restoration that began in 1999 when one of them was steamed for some special events. Just one locomotive has left the island to find a new home on Australia's Puffing Billy Railway, where it is in the company of the last Climax to be constructed in 1928 and the only one built to 2ft 6in gauge. It was originally supplied to the Tyers Valley Tramway in Victoria, where it replaced a locally built locomotive that proved unequal to the task of extracting timber from the forests on Mount Baw Baw.

It was in New Zealand that the practice of mixing imports from the USA with home production took hold, partly because its forests were on a much smaller scale than those in the American West. They could thus use more modest motive power that was also cheaper. Ultimately there were seven Climaxes and seven Heislers, but in quantity these were dwarfed by almost a hundred home-built 'lokeys' – the name used by Kiwi loggers for engines specifically tailored for forest work. Many were so extraordinary in appearance that they could have been mistaken for a steam appliance rather than a locomotive capable of moving on rails, but others had a long

Twilight of the Shays. Built in 1924, No 10 at Lopez Sugar Central in the Philippines became the world's last active Shay in commercial service. When photographed in April 1983 it was only working nightshifts but looked superbly atmospheric! (Keith Chester)

life and were still at work in the 1960s. Few have survived and even fewer are serviceable, but a notable exception is to be found at the McLeans Island site of the Canterbury Steam Preservation Society. A Heisler copy, it was built by A & G Price as late as 1943 and is thought to be the world's last geared logging locomotive to be constructed.

Despite such brave efforts, the dominance achieved by American manufacturers with their geared and fully articulated products was never seriously dented. One UK firm that might just possibly have succeeded was the Sentinel Wagon Works of Shrewsbury, which by the 1920s was regarded as highly innovative and was enjoying considerable success with its non-articulated geared locomotives. It dabbled with prospects in 1926 by building a three-foot gauge 0-4-4-0 for Kettering Ironworks and later a similar two-foot gauge product for a South African sugar estate. The driving force behind both orders was a need to haul heavier loads over indifferent track, but neither was particularly successful. The builders had to make major modifications to the Kettering locomotive and it spent long periods lying idle before its eventual withdrawal in 1960.

Far more radical were the three metre-gauge 0-6-6-0s of 1934 for the FC del Nordeste in Colombia. Exotic in the extreme, they were evocatively described by the railway author A.E. Durrant as looking 'rather like a pregnant hippopotamus'. Each of the six axles had a compound steam engine supplied by a high-pressure water tube boiler, a complex arrangement that did not augur well for long-term survival on a line climbing from sea level to 10,000ft. Special flaps had to be opened at high altitudes to draw in a greater volume of air and thus obtain the correct amount of oxygen for combustion. It was all just too much in a country that railway-wise became noted for overreaching itself. Reputedly set aside when World War II made it impossible to obtain spare parts, the fate of the three 'hippopotami' became yet another mystery in the annals of South American railways.

Sentinel avoided any more similar indulgences. Although the building of the last Shay was only eleven years away, the Lima factory maintained its supremacy and it became a case of 'first in and last out'. The final Shay to remain in commercial service was supplied to the Insular Lumber Company at Negros in the Philippines in 1924 and later transferred to Lopez Sugar Factory on the same island, where it was still working in 1983.

The aura surrounding Shays remains undiminished. It was well captured by John T. Labbe & Vernon Goe in their book *Railroads in the Woods*, when they summarised the experience of seeing such a locomotive in motion: 'No one who has ever known it could forget it. A Shay thrashing its course up a heavy grade was lost in an aura of sound and smoke and steam. It might strew the right of way with discarded parts, and its gears might be nearly devoid of teeth, but little short of complete derailment could thwart its progress.'

Riding on the footplate could be equally memorable. After a spell in the cab of one of the Shays in Taiwan, Michael Reilly commented: 'The locomotive's angular frame set above the bogies is reminiscent of a Victorian bedstead. In practical terms, it means the centre of gravity is very high and the locomotive sways alarmingly, even at low speeds – perhaps not unlike riding a camel!'

They are apt pen portraits of one of the most weird and wonderful of all articulated locomotives.

CHAPTER FOUR

Meyers of many kinds

SAXON SUCCESS

Shays and kindred locomotives were all very well in coping with exceptional conditions in the North American forests but clearly had limitations in the wider world. Here it might have been thought that the highly successful system of semi-articulation developed by Anatole Mallet spelt the end for fully articulated locomotives with their persistent drawback of leaking steam joints. Yet the fact remained that some lines were too sharply curved for a locomotive with what could impolitely be described as rigid rear end and something more flexible was required.

Way back in 1861, a design pre-dating that of Robert Fairlie had been patented by Jean Jacques Meyer and his son Adolphe. Born in 1804, Jean Jacques was a French mechanical engineer who at the age of only twenty-seven established Mulhouse Works, near Basle, where he built locomotives for German and Austrian railways. His patent 'system of complete articulation for tank engines' involved a single boiler with a rear fuel bunker, cab and side tanks carried on a main frame in a conventional manner. Its distinguishing feature was that this frame was supported by two four-wheel steam bogies coupled by side rods, which were driven from a pair of cylinders mounted at the inner ends of each unit. A special reversing gear meant that one bogie could be in forward motion at the same time as the other was in reverse.

Meyer senior could hardly be accused of false modesty, as he termed his design 'the universal system', but it was not until 1868 that a standard-gauge prototype was completed. Although successful, nothing happened on the narrow gauge

until the Saxon government decreed with classic German thoroughness that every inhabitant had to be within one hour's walk of a railway! The upshot was construction in the 1880s of a network of minor lines, almost entirely of 75cm gauge, serving the more remote parts of the kingdom. Eventually extending to no less than 541km (336 miles), they formed one of the largest narrow-gauge systems in Europe. Many branches were noted for very tight curvature, with radii down to as little as 40 metres, and with rapid traffic growth it soon became clear that some form of fully articulated locomotive was necessary.

A pair of Fairlies supplied in 1885 by R & W Hawthorn did not find long-term favour and experiments four years later with Klose semi-articulated 0-6-2Ts also failed because of their inherent complexity. The situation changed dramatically from 1890 after the Royal Saxon State Railway had introduced Meyer-type locomotives on its standard-gauge lines. Following suit on its narrow gauge network was therefore an obvious step and both varieties were in fact remarkably similar. Their common features included a 0-4 + 4-0T wheel arrangement and four-cylinder compounding using saturated steam. The cylinders were mounted on the inner ends of the steam bogies as per the original Meyer patent and thus were close to each other between the two pairs of driving wheels. In both cases the builder was Richard Hartmann of the Saxon Engine Works at Chemnitz.

A peculiarity was what became known as the 'washing line' running from a reel on top of the cab via wheels and pulleys on the dome and chimney to the front of the loco-

The classic Meyer 0-4 + 4-0T was for generations the perfect motive power solution for the lightly laid 75cm gauge lines of the Saxon State Railways with their many sharp curves and grades. SäStB no 165, built by Hartmann in 1912, duly became DRG No 99 575 in 1925 and was finally withdrawn in 1968.
(Keith Chester collection)

ABOVE : The last line to see IVK's in regular use was the Oschatz – Mügeln – Kemmlitz branch, north-west of Dresden. No 99 713 was heading a train of standard gauge wagons, resting on 'Rollwagen' transporters, in May 1992. (Clifford Schoff)

LEFT: One of several surviving class IVK Saxon Meyers is No 132, photographed in 2002 heading a private charter on the Radebeul to Radeburg line near Dresden. (Keith Barnes)

motive. Its purpose was to operate the bizarre Heberlein rope brake, an archaic system requiring skilful operation to get the correct tension.

Beginning in 1892, no fewer than ninety-six 75cm gauge locomotives were built over the next twenty-five years and Saxony soon had the largest class of Meyers in the world. Known as the IVK, they proved to be extremely efficient and well able to cope with gradients that were commonly 1 in 30

and on one line included a stretch of 1 in 20. Accordingly they had a long supremacy and triumphed over several attempts to introduce successors. Some 0-8-0Ts with Klien-Lindner hollow axles proved to have higher maintenance costs and other designs such as the massive 2-10-2Ts of the late 1920s were simply too heavy for many of the lines.

Some of the IVKs were lost in World War One, but ninety-one members of the class survived to be taken into the stock

Radebeul is now home to 99 1586, which was rebuilt at Gorlitz works in 1965. It was leaving Schmalz for Jöhstadt in wintry conditions in April 1978. (James Waite)

of the newly formed Deutsche Reichsbahn AG in 1924. Sixteen locomotives were withdrawn prior to the outbreak of World War Two, which proved to be much more destructive with many of the class being requisitioned by the German army for work in occupied parts of the USSR. When it was all over, just fifty-seven IVKs survived and most of them were in a sad state of repair.

The post-war turmoil and generally run-down state of railways in what was now East Germany saw nine of them being equipped with air brakes and sent almost literally to sea to save operations on the Rügen Island Light Railways. Part of this remarkable system on the Baltic is still in service. Another three went to the Prignitz Light Railway, north-west of Berlin, but the rest remained in Saxony where they continued

to eek out an existence on a gradually decaying network. Many of the lines closed from the mid-1950s onwards, but the increasingly worn-out IVKs remained the only locomotives light enough to work over several of the surviving branches.

Eventually the moment of truth could be postponed no longer and an extraordinary development saw twenty-two new 0-4 + 4-0Ts being built to a seventy-year-old design between 1962 and 1967. In a bizarre twist they were classed as 'reconstructions' so that they could be erected in the Deutsche Reichsbahn's own repair shops at Görlitz. In the then socialist bureaucracy, time-consuming authorisation would have been required from the Ministry of Industry in order to put the work to an outside builder!

It says much for the success of IVKs both old and new that members of the class continued in service almost to the end of steam. The last passenger-carrying line exclusively operated by them was the scenically splendid Wolkenstein – Jöhstadt, near the Czech border. There was great sadness when it closed in 1986, although it has since largely been

ABOVE: Although over 100 years old, the steam rotary snowplough built in 1910 for the Bernina Railway is still in use today. Enthusiasts pay some £200 to travel in a special train and see the dramatic spectacle of it hurling snow to the side of the line. (Mick Johnstone)

LEFT: The Meyer principle adopted for the 0-6 + 6-0 Bernina snowplough is clearly visible below the rectangular casing that covers most of the unit. (James Waite)

reopened by a preservation group. The last line to see IVKs in regular use was the freight-only Oschatz - Mügeln - Kemmlitz branch, north-west of Dresden, once noted for conveying china clay in standard-gauge wagons resting on 'Rollwagen' piggyback transporters. Following privatisation it was converted to diesel haulage in the mid-1990s.

It is fitting that an impressive number of the Saxon Meyers have survived, including several in working order. Seven came into ownership of the Deutsche Bahn on its formation in 1994 and another fifteen have passed into the hands of private

lines, museums, preservation groups or communities located on former narrow gauge branches in Saxony. There could be no better tribute.

HIGH IN THE SNOWS

Part of the special appeal of Saxon Meyers is that their basic design dates back to the dark ages of articulation. With the Meyer principle already being overtaken by progress when they first appeared, it seemed unlikely that any other design would incorporate the same distinguishing feature of cylinders

The 0-4 + 4-0T Meyers conceived late in the day by W G Bagnall of Stafford were never an unqualified success. All but one of them went to sugar estates in Natal, where *Mbozama* was one of the final pair delivered in 1953. Seen double-heading with a conventional locomotive on the Sezela estate, it was out of use as early as 1975.
(Charlie Lewis, D. Binns collection)

at the inside end of each bogie. The German manufacturer Arnold Jung produced a pair of such locomotives in 1897 for the 60cm gauge Wallücke Light Railway, near Hanover, but they were an isolated example. Few can have anticipated what would appear on the highest adhesion railway in Europe and spectacularly keep it open through the depths of winter.

The metre-gauge Bernina Railway was completed in 1910 to link the famous ski resort of St Moritz with the Italian town of Tirano and at the same time open up the isolated Poschiavo valley. It formed an adjunct of the extensive Rhaetian Railway, which took over the concern in 1943. The original concept of a summit tunnel was abandoned, partly through fears that it would cause a loss of tourist traffic to the Bernina Pass at 2,428 metres (7,403ft) above sea level. From here the line had to descend almost 2,000 metres (6,000ft) to the Italian terminus in a horizontal distance of less than 23km (14 miles). Brilliantly engineered, it spiralled its way down the mountain on a punishing gradient of 1 in 14.

Rack sections were initially considered but abandoned. Steam was never going to cope with such gradients and powerful electric units were introduced from the outset. They performed well in the summer months but the small ploughs fitted to the power cars proved completely inadequate in the winter snows. It was a problem that brought steam to the railway in a totally unexpected way.

Swiss Locomotive Works were asked to provide a rotary snowplough, which in design terms proved challenging. Steam was dictated by the amount of power required for both the rotary plough and its propulsion, which was in excess of what could be obtained from overhead wires that might in any event be damaged by snow. Sharp curves necessitated a single-unit machine and weight restrictions compelled it to be carried on two six-wheel bogies. Hence the adoption of the Meyer principle, with the tell-tale cylinders at the inner ends of the bogies clearly visible below the rectangular casing covering most of the unit.

With the added facility of a device for melting snow by steam, the rotary proved an immediate success following its delivery in 1910. Although requiring a crew of four, it was

joined by a sister plough in 1912 with the pair being respectively housed at Pontresina and Poschiavo on either side of the Bernina Pass. Dramatically hurtling the snow to the side of the line, they coped with falls that in some winters exceeded twenty feet in depth. As the summit stretches were too high for any significant melt, the end result was trains running through a white-walled cutting that often towered above them.

Remarkably the first of the rotary snowploughs is still in use today, as in heavy winters it remains more effective than the pair of electrically powered snow-blowers built in 1967. Inevitably taking place at short notice, the occasions when it is steamed have become a major event for enthusiasts prepared to pay almost £200 to travel in an accompanying special train. Few railway spectacles have quite the same impact, even though the machine is virtually lost behind steam and snow when attacking the drifts under full power.

FAILING FORTUNES

Nothing in subsequent Meyer history was to equal the rotary snowploughs for sheer drama, but the distinctive concept of bogies separated by two pairs of cylinders was not yet dead. It clung to life on a slender thread far from mainland Europe. Taken up in Scotland by the enterprising firm of Andrew Barclay Sons & Co Ltd of Kilmarnock, they completed the 3ft 6in gauge 0-6 + 6-0T *Joan* for a New Zealand timber company in 1913. Little of significance then happened for fifteen years. The end of a long line must surely have seemed imminent in 1928 when *Caledonia*, a functional-looking 0-4 + 4-0 with no side tanks, was supplied to the Straits Settlements.

Yet once again the unexpected happened. It may have been something of an aberration but was certainly not short-lived, with the result that, as in East Germany, locomotives to a design patented in 1861 were still being built around a century later. The throwback to the Meyer design resumed in the 1930s when W G Bagnall Ltd of Stafford were approached by sugar plantations in Natal. They were seeking a locomotive far more powerful than their existing engines for use on two-foot gauge lines that were roughly laid and included both severe gradients and sharp curvature. A Meyer was favoured

ABOVE: *Monarch*, the solitary British-based Meyer, proved to be no more successful than its Natal sisters. Supplied to Bowaters' at Sittingbourne in 1953, persistent steaming problems meant that within ten years it was doing only occasional work. It has now been cosmetically restored and was photographed at Welshpool station in September 2009. (James Waite)

LEFT: One of the two surviving Meyers from the Natal sugar estates is *Nonoti*, which in about 1976 went to the Cripple Creek & Victor Narrow Gauge Railroad in Colorado. (Ian Drummond)

TOP: Baldwin Locomotive Works produced this pioneering standard gauge 0-6 + 6-0T in 1892 to capture sales in the lucrative market of logging railroads. It did much to influence the development of future Meyer locomotives. (D. Binns collection)

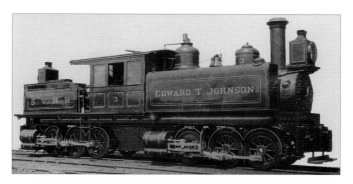

CENTRE: After an awesome sea journey round the perilous Cape Horn, the first three Kitson Meyers were delivered to the Anglo-Chilean Nitrate & Railway Company in 1894. Typical of the Andes, its 3ft 6in gauge line climbed over three thousand feet in its first seventeen miles after leaving the port of Tocopilla. (D. Binns collection)

LOWER: Later and less successful variants of the Kitson Meyer concept included No 139 of the metre gauge Leopoldina Railway in Brazil. It was the second of two 2-6 + 6-4s supplied by Kitson in 1908 to the design of consulting engineers Livesey Son & Henderson. Like its sister on the Antofagasta & Bolivia Railway it was prone to excessive slipping of the rear engine and saw little service; by 1915 it was in store. (Keith Chester collection)

because of its twin power bogies but two problems were never fully overcome.

The first was that the bogies positioned directly under the firebox left no room for an adequate boiler. Instead, Bagnall used a marine-type boiler with a circular firebox, as they had done on various locomotives since the close of the nineteenth century. It was all very well but raising steam could be a protracted process unless a compressed air blower was used.

The second problem was the familiar one of flexible steam joints that were prone to leaking. Bagnall thought they had solved it by incorporating a patent Flextel joint made in Stafford by the then well-known firm of Dorman & Co Ltd. It required proper maintenance and this proved not to be forthcoming.

The first two of seven 0-4 + 4-0Ts were completed in 1936 and respectively delivered to the Illovo and Renishaw sugar estates. Wartime conditions halted further construction until 1946 when two further locomotives, *Tugela* and *Nonoti*, were supplied to the Darnall and Felixton estates. A third pair for the Natal estates were ordered in 1949 but there was then an unexpected delay.

It was probably due to some delicate negotiations centred round Bowaters Lloyd Pulp & Paper Mills Ltd of Sittingbourne, who had become Bagnall's largest UK customer of narrow gauge locomotives. Requiring additional motive power for their 2ft 6in gauge system and knowing of the Meyer tanks, they were apparently at first told they could have two conventional locomotives for the price of a 0-4 + 4-0T. Then the emphasis changed and they were offered an articulated locomotive at a specially reduced price, providing it and the delayed Natal order could go through the works at the same time. In June 1953, four years after they had been ordered, Natal thus finally got the pair that became *Mbozama* and *Umhiatuzi*.

The last day of July saw delivery of what was to be the only British-based Meyer. The lapse between ordering and completion had been reduced to two-and-a-half years, but it was still a disappointing performance made more unfortunate by the name selected for the locomotive. *Monarch* was intended to be in steam to celebrate the Coronation of Queen Elizabeth II but managed to miss the great day by almost two months. Perhaps it was all symbolic of changing times – and certainly it proved to be the last narrow-gauge steam locomotive built for British industry.

These latterday Meyers boasted such refinements as a superheater, seldom seen on such a small gauge, but none of them was particularly successful. In 1954 Bagnall dispatched representatives out to see how the six in Natal were faring under actual operating conditions. The Illovo engine had been abandoned after only twelve years owing to high maintenance costs, proneness to priming, insufficient power and, above all, a worn-out boiler. It was a similar story elsewhere with complaints about the flexible steam joints, over-expanding tubes and boilers taking a horrendous sixteen hours to steam.

A report may well not have pleased the local workforce. It concluded that the articulated design was insufficiently robust to withstand constant abuse in operation and maintenance, and that it was too complicated and delicate for conditions on the plantations. It recommended that the design should

never again be offered in South Africa and that any future manufacture should concentrate on 'rugged simplicity'.

Despite such a damning indictment, there were those on the plantation lines who averred that the Meyers 'performed very well indeed' and loved driving them. Perhaps the truth is that they were just too late in the day and their intricacies proved unacceptable in an age turning against steam.

The last two Meyers delivered to Natal in 1953 were both out of use as early as 1975 and a similar fate befell their sisters. In 1969 the Renishaw locomotive returned to England to be housed in a large private collection, which following a £1.8 million grant from the Welsh Assembly in 2010 was due to be moved to a new restoration workshop at the Vale of Rheidol facilities in Aberystwyth. In about 1976, *Nonoti* went to the Cripple Creek & Victor Narrow Gauge Railroad, where it is in the company of another articulated locomotive in the shape of the ex-Mexican Mallet.

Monarch fared little better and proved very slow in raising steam as well as heavy on maintenance. Within ten years it was doing only occasional work and Bowaters' were soon ready to dispose of it. The final locomotive to be acquired by the company went to the Welshpool & Llanfair Railway in

The world's last working Kitson Meyer copes with arid conditions in the Atacama Desert in 1977. After being abandoned for almost thirty years, it is now preserved in a nitrate railway park at Taltal in northern Chile. (A.E. Durrant, D. Binns collection)

1966. Here too *Monarch* disgraced itself and moved onto the Ffestiniog, where a projected rebuild was abandoned and the final Bagnall-built Meyer returned to Llanfair for cosmetic restoration.

HIGHER AND HARDER

Last of their line, the seven Bagnalls were often termed 'proper' Meyers to distinguish them from a variant that in size and achievement was in a different league. It may have been massive and all-conquering but nevertheless did not have the unique feature of cylinders virtually touching each other.

The evolution of this giant of a locomotive stemmed from an unfortunate trend of the late Victorian era, when many young engineers were dismayed by the rigid hierarchy of UK railway companies. Conservatism and complacency were

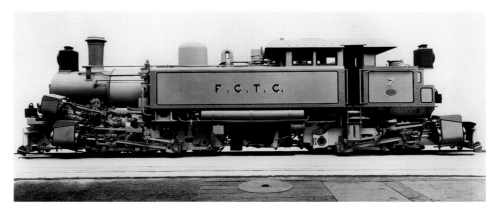

Works photograph of the first 0-8 + 6-0T Kitson Meyer completed in 1907 for the legendary Transandine Railway. The auxiliary cylinders on the front bogie were a design afterthought to power an additional rack pinion. Quickly found to be unnecessary clutter, they were soon removed. (D. Binns collection)

standard practice. The more adventurous turned to the ultimate challenge offered by British-owned railway companies in South America – and especially in the Andes rising abruptly from the Pacific coast for thousands of feet.

Among them was Robert Stirling, son of the Great Northern Railway's locomotive superintendent, Patrick Stirling, who took up the same post on the 3ft 6in gauge Ferrocarril de Tocopilla al Toco (mercifully generally known as the FCTT). Completed in 1890 by the Anglo-Chilean Nitrate & Railway Company, its sole purpose was to open up reserves of nitrate, used both as a fertiliser and in manufacturing explosives, which existed in the barren Atacama desert. Typically in this bleak country, it had no option but to climb over three thousand feet in its first seventeen miles in order to head out of Tocopilla port into slightly easier terrain. It involved zigzags, continuous grade of 1 in 25 and fearsome curves of 180ft radius, and from the outset it was clear that motive power would need to be both powerful and robust.

The 'Nitrate King' in this part of the world was 'Colonel' John Thomas North, son of a coal merchant, who trained in Leeds as a mechanical engineer before making a fortune in his dealings with the riches of the Atacama. It may well have been his connections in Leeds that led the FCTT to obtain its first four locomotives – conventional 4-8-4 tank engines – from Kitson & Co at the city's Airedale Foundry. They quickly proved inadequate as traffic developed, but Robert Stirling was a keen advocate of articulation and it is therefore understandable that in 1891 a pair of Fairlie 0-6 + 6-0Ts was purchased from the Yorkshire Engine Company. The Andes proved too much even for them and it was a matter of coming up with something different.

It proved to be a protracted process. A form of articulation similar to the Meyer principle was used by the mighty Baldwin Locomotive Works in a standard-gauge 0-6 + 6-0T intended to create sales in the lucrative logging railroad market. The prototype appeared in 1892, the same year as the first narrow-gauge Meyers in Saxony. Robert Stirling would be aware of both developments and would realise that taking the best features of both of them could well offer a solution to the problems on the FCTT. He would also know that it would be cheaper to turn to either Baldwin or a manufacturer in Saxony rather

than start the notoriously slow exercise of getting a British builder to develop a new design from scratch.

It seems likely that he was overruled or unduly influenced by John North and it was decided to stay loyal with the existing contacts at Kitson & Co. Fortunately the work was entrusted to a talented designer, Samuel Joseph Lucas, who had been with the company since 1877. One of the unsung heroes of the railway age, his obituary noted: 'When the firm concentrated on their original production of locomotives, Lucas undertook the development in detail of the newer types and in particular the double steam bogie locomotive known as the Kitson Meyer. So well was this carried out, it is said, that the engine went together without a single one of those hitches which so enliven the very human relations between works and drawing office.'

The result was one of the more successful of all articulated designs. When the first Kitson Meyer finally emerged in 1894 it incorporated the most obvious features that distinguished the Baldwin prototype from the Saxon Meyers. The cylinders were repositioned so that they were at the rear rather than the inner ends of each bogie, thus creating greater space for a larger firebox descending between the frames. A compact 0-6 + 6-0T weighing fifty-five tons, it nevertheless had a tractive effort of 27,600lb and immediately transformed operations on the line. Trains of between 115 and 125 tons were hauled up the seventeen-mile climb in some two-and-a-half hours including two water stops. Two more Kitson Meyers were completed in the same year but one was lost at sea and never arrived. It was a disaster taken in its stride, a replacement locomotive duly surviving an almost unimaginable journey of many thousands of miles that involved rounding the perilous Cape Horn.

The two Fairlies soon took second place, but in one respect the Kitson Meyers were reminiscent of them. They had a chimney at both ends, with that at the back being designed to take exhaust from the rear steam bogie. Ultimately the company supplied eleven such locomotives to the line in the years up to 1912, the total including four larger 2-6 + 6-2Ts. The only problem down the years resulted from the side tanks and their considerable overhang, which had a tendency to cause instability on curves. It culminated in a

spectacular accident when one rolled over on the steep seaboard side and plunged down the mountain.

To the south of Tocopilla was a similar nitrate line opened in 1882. The 3ft 6in gauge Taltal Railway extended inland from the coast for ninety-two miles, climbing to a summit of over 9,000 feet. It too acquired a fleet of Kitson Meyers, ten of which were purchased between 1904 and 1907.

When the Tocopilla line dispensed with steam in 1959, the still serviceable Kitson Meyers were sold to the Taltal. It ceased operations in 1977, by which time only one member of the class was still serviceable. Visitors described No 59 as being in 'deplorable condition'. Of uncertain identity owing to this railway's tendency to swap works plates at random, it was nevertheless unquestionably the last of these articulated locomotives to run anywhere in the world. In 1979 President Pinochet signed a decree that deservedly scheduled the locomotive as a national monument,

In Chile scheduling is one thing but devoted care can be another. A protracted dispute over ownership left No 59 abandoned in the yard at Taltal, slowly sinking into the sand and with all the brass and copper parts gradually stolen. Almost thirty years elapsed before the Kitson Meyer took

centre stage in a new nitrate railway park at Taltal, where it has been repainted in a dark green close to its original livery and even sports a copper cap on the forward chimney. Although a decidedly remote location, it is at long last a happier outcome for such a historically important locomotive.

ON THE RACK

Although No 59 is the last of the conventional Kitson Meyers, there are also survivors of a class specially developed to cope with circumstances even more demanding than the nitrate lines. They arose on a mind-boggling railway that in its heyday carried Pullman passenger trains directly across the Andes.

The Transandine was for long the missing piece in a grand scheme to link the great capital cities of Buenos Aires in Argentina and Santiago in Chile. At first it was deceptively easy, the 5ft 6in gauge line heading west from the Argentinean capital for some 175 miles that were dead straight and almost dead level. Mendoza, almost three-quarters of the way to the Chilean capital, was reached with little difficulty, but here the railway builders paused for breath as if aghast at what they saw.

Ahead, and now all too clearly visible, was the backbone of South America seemingly rising sheer out of the plains. A

OPPOSITE: The Chilean side of the Transandine included twenty-six tunnels through which the Kitson Meyers climbed bunker first. Despite special cowls on the chimneys, conditions for enginemen were often horrendous. Depicted emerging from a tunnel on one of the rack sections, No 3349 is now in Santiago's outdoor railway museum. (painting by Lawrence Roy Wilson, GRA)

THIS PAGE: The combined rack and adhesion Kitson Meyers on the Transandine had five different braking systems and forty-nine separate cab fittings. The complexities that had to be mastered by crews are captured in this painting of the cab interior. (Lawrence Roy Wilson, GRA)

rough trail led through rocky gorges and past awesome precipices, running close to the permanently snow-covered 23,380ft peak of Aconcagua. It then breasted the 12,450ft Uspallata Pass to enter Chile before falling eight thousand feet in less than fifty miles to Los Andes, the 5ft 6in railhead for both Santiago and the Pacific port of Valparaiso.

Only 150 miles separated Mendoza from Los Andes but it might as well have been a thousand. The only alternative to the four-day journey, much of it on the bony backs of mules, was to face the notorious sea passage round Cape Horn. Calls to complete the rail link became incessant, but matters were not helped by recurring differences between the two governments. It was the late 1880s before work finally started on the Transandine Railway, conceived as two separate Argentine and Chilean enterprises with construction starting from either end. By now the glory days of steam's conquest of the Andes had already peaked and there was to be no repeat of the heroic endeavour that had taken standard gauge tracks soaring above the 15,000ft contour in Peru.

Instead, the decision was taken to adopt metre gauge for the missing link with the Abt rack system being used for long stretches climbing at 1 in 12. Progress was slow owing to revolutions, bankruptcies and formidable constructional problems, especially with the almost two-mile long Cumbre tunnel through which the line crossed the frontier at a summit of 10,452ft.

As the work finally neared completion, consulting engineers were asked in 1906 to specify the requirements for a type of locomotive that would enable the dream of an international route to retain credibility. They did so with impressive precision, stating that it would need to be capable of hauling 150-ton trains on the rack at 6.2mph uphill and 9.3mph downhill, with adhesion sections scheduled for 18.6mph. Among the many who were sceptical was Dr Roman Abt of Lucerne, creator of the adopted rack system, who averred that the requirements were impossible and 'terrible accidents must be expected if the company tried to haul such loads'.

Waiting in the wings was Kitson & Co, favoured with twelve years' experience of its locomotives at Tocopilla. Keen to develop the Kitson Meyer, the company undertook to meet the consultants' demands and duly supplied a truly impressive 0-8 + 6-0T in 1907. It had few competitors for

complexity, the initial provision of two sets of rack pinions on the rear bogie being raised to still greater heights of intricacy by the Transandine demanding a late alteration to the design. Fearful of wheel slip on the 1 in 12 gradients, it insisted on a third rack pinion being mounted on the leading adhesion bogie. Driven by an extra pair of small cylinders, it merely added unnecessary clutter as the boiler could not cope with the extra demand.

Any reservations were put to one side with eight further Kitson Meyer 0-8 + 6-0T rack locomotives being delivered in quick succession. The local crews must initially have struggled to cope with such complex machines in a situation akin to putting the pilot of a light aircraft in the cockpit of a Boeing. There were forty-nine separate cab fittings and drivers had to master the five different braking systems. The real skills arose in bringing loaded trains downgrade, on and off the rack, and for this reason the descent was always made chimney first, allowing the driver to have a better view of the line with all gauges and brake valves in front of him.

Locomotives were not turned at the summit station of Las Cuevas, the firebox top and water gauges being designed to cope with the steep grades in one direction only. Working upgrade bunker first brought its own set of problems, not least in the twenty-six tunnels on the Chilean section. Backward deflecting cowls helped to disperse smoke, but the poor-quality coal quickly created a poisonous atmosphere.

No 3349, excellently displayed at Quinta Normal in Santiago. This 1993 view shows the changes made to the appearance of the locomotive following removal of the auxiliary rack cylinders.
(David Joy)

Even though oxygen was carried on board, it was by no means uncommon for crews to collapse.

With the summit tunnel finally finished in 1910 and the desired motive power now to hand, the Transandine proudly inaugurated its Pullman International, advertised as 'Latin America's Finest Train with Through Palatial Parlour-Observation Car and Restaurant Service'. With a green-liveried Kitson Meyer at its head, it must indeed have been a wondrous sight to behold, even if the journey required considerable stamina. The 156 narrow gauge miles from Mendoza to Los Andes took a disproportionate twelve hours in the total travel time of two days and one night to get from Buenos Aires to Santiago. At the time there was no alternative.

Against the odds, the Kitson Meyers acquitted themselves well on the international services and proved fully capable of hauling the loads for which they were designed. They proved comfortable with the sharp curvature and had the all-important attributes of being relatively easy to re-rail and competent at snowploughing. Sadly, neither they nor the Transandine were destined to endure. The high cost of importing better-quality Welsh coal led to early electrification of the Chilean side of the line from 1927 onwards. Disaster struck seven years later when sudden collapse of a glacial lake carried away many miles of railway.

It was 1944 before the line reopened, by which time the drawbacks of dual break of gauge and high operational costs were becoming only too apparent. The great South American dream of an international railway linking two of its most stunning capital cities crumbled just as surely as the trackbed, which was repeatedly carried away by avalanches. Paved highways and jet aircraft creamed off the bulk of the traffic and the end came in 1984 when the greater part of the Transandine closed.

Happily, two of the Kitson Meyers that became so symbolic of the railway are still in existence in Chile. No 8 remains at its base at Los Andes, reputedly needing only some boiler tubes and firebox stays to steam again. There have been repeated rumours that it will one day be restored for use on excursion trains along the surviving stub of the line, but the decidedly thin enthusiast market in Chile is bound to raise serious doubts. Looking deservedly resplendent is No 9, which until the 1970s was kept in working order for snow clearance. It is now excellently displayed on a turntable in the impressive outdoor railway museum at Quinta Normal, Santiago.

In a much sorrier condition is No 40, becalmed in a partially roofless shed at Tafí Viejo in the north of Tucuman, Argentina. There was long doubt as to whether it still existed, but today the world holds few secrets. Its continued existence is confirmed on Google Earth!

From a British perspective, it would be wonderful if just one of the survivors could be returned to the land of its birth, but realistically this is as likely to achieve fruition as periodic proposals that the Transandine be rebuilt.

RISE AND FALL

The Transandine rack locomotives may have achieved a complexity and fascination that was never equalled, but development continued of Kitson Meyers both conventional and more than a shade unusual. The latter category owed much to the remarkable 2ft 6in gauge Antofagasta & Bolivia Railway, linking the important port of northern Chile with the world's highest capital city of La Paz. It ran above the 12,000ft contour for an amazing 500 miles but was not noted for its scenic attributes. One traveller commented: 'A more God-forsaken country I never saw. There is not a tree, not a blade of grass, nothing but rock sand and dirty white chunks of nitrate.'

In the early 1900s a nitrate boom led to greatly increased traffic and more substantial motive power was required. With vast distances no doubt suggesting a need for maximum coal and water capacity, the consulting engineers Livesey Son &

Henderson came up with designs for a Kitson Meyer 2-6 + 6-4 complete with tender. The front end was relatively normal but both the back of the cab and the front of the tender rested on the rear steam bogie. Beyond this bogie were the rear cylinders and then the four-wheel trailing truck. Optimistically named *Hercules*, the bizarre contraption entered service in 1908 but proved a failure. It is said to have spent more time off the rails than on them!

Although a conventional Kitson Meyer was supplied in 1911, the lessons that should have been learnt from the earlier contretemps were not entirely heeded. The railway was gradually converted to metre gauge, which was chosen for six locomotives ordered a year later. They were so off-the-wall that Kitson could well have declined to construct them and the order instead went to Beyer Peacock at Manchester. Built to a 0-6-2 + 0-6-2 wheel arrangement, the new arrivals had the cylinders positioned between the driving and bogie wheels. Two chimneys were provided as on early Kitson Meyers, one in the normal position and the other on the bunker. The desire for a tender still lingered, but instead of being placed logically it took the form of a separate eight-wheeled unit coupled to the smokebox end of a locomotive designed to work cab-forward.

The tender carried over five thousand gallons of water and an additional four tons of sacked coal to augment the eight tons in the rear bunker. Yet the only way it could be got to the cab was by two coal carriers, whose job it was to lug sacks across the gap above the couplings and then along the running plate. On a moving train, it was undoubtedly dicing with death and it is hardly surprising that these locomotives were among the first on the railway to be converted to oil burners.

Ironically, they then operated at the Bolivian end of the line with scarcely a hitch. Their travels included a branch to Potosi, which passed through rugged mountain country and was famed for its intermediate station at Condor – the highest in the world at an oxygen-starved 15,814 feet. All six engines were still in service in 1959 but by the mid-1970s had been dumped in the main Bolivian works at Uyuni.

These were not the only locomotives inspired by Kitson Meyers to be built by other manufacturers. A direct copy of

the pioneer sent to Tocopilla was supplied to the same system by Kerr Stuart in 1903, but they lost some £2,000 (over £100,000 in today's money) on the contract and never repeated such an exercise.

In the same year, Andrew Barclay produced what its catalogue described as 'an extremely flexible engine of great hauling power, enabling it to take the sharpest curves with great freedom'. Owing a great deal to the products of Leeds, it was somewhat brazenly described as 'an improved Meyer'. The few examples actually built included *Kakavos*, a 0-4 + 4-0T to the unusual gauge of 2ft 5½in. Delivered to the Anglo-Greek Magnesite Company, it has been described as 'one of the prettiest narrow gauge locomotives ever constructed'.

The company went on to produce a handful of other locomotives with features similar to the Kitson Meyer concept, although they were far from handsome and should not be confused with the 'proper' Meyer of 1913. Other manufacturers did the same, as instanced by the obscure Jensen & Olesen works at Esbjerg in Denmark. So too did the German firms of Orenstein & Koppel and Henschel & Sohn as late as 1939, but they were all spasmodic and in small numbers.

Although not aggressively sold, narrow-gauge Kitson Meyers continued to be in demand in some of the world's most challenging locations. This was not just in other South American countries such as Brazil and Colombia but also in the Philippines and South Africa. In 1928 a pair of 2-6 + 6-2Ts attracted much attention when they were supplied to a line that could scarcely have presented a greater array of difficulties. The 2ft 6in gauge Kalka Simla Railway climbed almost five thousand feet in just sixty miles to serve the famous hill station that formed the summer headquarters of the Indian Government. Opened in 1903, it had long stretches of 1 in 33, curves down to 110ft radius and no less than 103 tunnels. It also had to cope with regular snowstorms in the winter months.

By the mid 1920s road competition had become a serious problem and it was decided that train loads should be doubled to 160 tons. Consulting engineers were commissioned to address the problem of suitable motive power and, after the lengthy deliberation that befits an Indian enterprise, they

Works photograph of the Kitson Meyer 2-6 + 6-2T supplied to Colombia in 1929 as Cundinamarca Railway No 14. A sister locomotive suffered the not uncommon fate of being lost at sea en route to its destination, and thus No 14 was renumbered 12 on arrival. It is virtually identical to the four highly praised locomotives that went to the nearby Girardot line in 1927.
(D. Binns collection)

duly ordered the pair of Kitson Meyers. They had to receive design alterations to cope with the exceptional conditions. One bogie was modified to tilt by over two inches on its east side and the other by the same amount on its west side, thus allowing the locomotive to traverse the many reverse curves without grief. In addition, the single brake blocks fitted on all coupled wheels incorporated an automatic water spray to cool them down after lengthy applications!

A representative of *The Engineer* saw one of the locomotives on a test track before it left the company's Airedale Foundry at Leeds. He was greatly impressed: 'Since the boiler is rigid and the forward end of the bogie projects 12ft or 13ft to the front of its pivot, the bogie twists and inclines by an astonishing amount relatively to the boiler front. We stress this extraordinary flexibility because it is the outstanding characteristic of the Kitson Meyer system.'

Yet no sooner had the locomotives arrived than a decline in traffic led to them being transferred to the less spectacular Kangra Valley Railway in the Punjab where they were used as bankers. Later transferred to Pakistan and converted to metre

ABOVE: The handsome and yet powerful appearance of the four Kitson Meyers supplied to the Girardot line in 1927 was well captured in a limited run of 100 models produced by LGB in 1980. One of the very few to reach the UK is seen on the author's garden railway. (David Joy)

OPPOSITE: The ultimate Kitson Meyer – one of a pair of massive 2-8 + 8-2Ts completed in 1935 for the Girardot line. Although little short of sensational in appearance, their eight-coupled wheelbase was too long to cope with the sharp curves. A similar sized locomotive obtained from Baldwin for comparison purposes came to a spectacular end with a boiler explosion, probably due to its extreme length exposing the crown sheet on the severe gradients. (D. Binns collection)

gauge in about 1951, they were seen dumped near Hyderabad in the 1960s and were subsequently broken up.

Each over fifty feet long and weighing sixty-eight tons, the two Indian locomotives were undoubtedly fine machines

but it is generally considered that they were eclipsed by those delivered a year earlier to the three-foot gauge Girardot line in Colombia. Completed in 1909 and extending for over eighty miles, it provided part of a tortuous link from the coast to Bogota. A climb of 7,500ft took it from Girardot on the navigable Magdalena river to Facatativá, where trans-shipment onto the 3ft 6in gauge Sabana Railway completed a journey to the capital generally taking around twelve hours.

Nineteen Kitson Meyer 0-6 + 6-0Ts had already been supplied to the line by 1924, when the various railways in Colombia were brought under unified government control and P. C. Dewhurst appointed as Chief Mechanical Engineer. Noted for his experience on several lines in the Andes, he made an impassioned and successful plea for larger locomotives to speed up the journey time on the Girardot line. The four 2-6 + 6-2Ts that arrived in 1927 duly sliced an hour off the schedule and also hauled much heavier trains.

Massive machines weighing ninety-four tons with the cab floor towering above the ground at shoulder height, they were at the same time exceptionally graceful and boasted many modern features. These included spring gear and brake apparatus that was easily accessible for servicing, as well as a sizeable generator to power the headlight, further lights in the cab, beneath the water tanks and over the motion, and finally a ten-coach train. Donald Binns, a noted authority on the subject, has unequivocally commented: 'These were the finest Kitson Meyer locomotives ever built, ranking amongst the world's most efficient articulated power.'

Regrettably their appearance deteriorated in the more difficult conditions of the 1930s and derailments became frequent as the track deteriorated. No 31 had already been involved in three accidents when on Good Thursday 1940 a tragic derailment left twenty people dead. It was too much for the superstition of the crews who had the loco-motive renumbered. They attributed the accidents to bad luck brought about by the fact that the number 31 was 13 reversed!

Sadly, no Colombian Kitson Meyer has been preserved and there is little comfort in the fact that this has been attributed to the quality of British workmanship. The argument goes

that the scrap metal was in higher demand than was the case with locomotives built elsewhere.

The 2-6 + 6-2Ts were not in fact the country's ultimate locomotive. Their success encouraged the Girardot line to go what it no doubt thought was one better but proved to be a step too far. The pair of 2-8 + 8-2Ts delivered in 1935 had no equals with their vital statistics of sixty-six feet long, twelve feet wide and nine feet high. The tractive effort of 58,564lb was well in excess of any British standard-gauge locomotive with the sole exception of the solitary LNER Garratt.

Proof of serious intentions was the decision in the same year to order a unique Mallet 2-8-8-2T from Baldwin Locomotive Works in order to compare UK and USA products. The out-come was disastrous, as it ended its life spectacularly with what has been described as 'a boiler explosion due to lack of water'. One cannot help wondering on such a steeply graded line if the near disaster on the Uintah stemming from an exposed crown sheet finally struck home on the Girardot with an even longer locomotive.

The pair of Kitson Meyers ultimately fared little better. Locally described as the most beautiful of all locomotives but operationally a disaster, they had a working life of less than twenty-five years. The eight-coupled wheelbases were too heavy and rigid both horizontally and vertically for a line that, apart from steep grades, was also beset with constant curvature. They were disliked by the crews, who dismissed them as 'the best rail straighteners ever devised'!

This was bad enough, but in 1935 it seemed even more regrettable that Kitson were unable to produce the locomotives. They were instead built at Darlington by Robert Stephenson & Hawthorn, as the Leeds firm failed to survive the slump of the 1930s. It had called in the receivers a year earlier and its heavy cranes had already been dismantled. It was a tragic end to one of the world's great locomotive builders with roots dating back to the 1830s and the dawn of the railway age. Those of more mature years must have pondered how matters might have been very different if the firm had not rebuffed an engineer who contacted them in 1907. He had some highly original designs destined to produce the greatest of all articulated locomotives. His name was Herbert William Garratt.

CHAPTER FIVE

Garratt Supremacy

From First to Last

CHANGING FORTUNES

Herbert W. Garratt must have felt his career had reached rock bottom in 1907 when Kitson failed to show any interest in his radical proposals for an entirely new type of articulated locomotive. He had spent many years in various railway posts in Latin America and was impressed by the success achieved by the company with its Kitson Meyers. They must have seemed the obvious firm to approach when redundancy in Peru forced him to return to Britain.

His spell overseas had made him familiar with railways that had the multiple problems of light track, weak bridges, sharp curves and steep gradients. He was also well aware from personal experience of just how restricted a width were the fireboxes of narrow gauge engines. Having an inventive turn of mind, he was thus well placed to conceive an articulated locomotive that would overcome all these difficulties.

Precisely how Garratt brought his ideas together will never be known, as his unexpectedly early death in 1913 meant that he failed to write anything resembling an auto-biography. The story goes that he once spotted some wagons specifically designed to convey heavy artillery, parts of the equipment resting on bogies at either end with the remainder sitting in a well in the centre. It occurred to him that locomotives could be built in the same way, with the boiler not perched above the wheels but slung between power bogies at either end. As one bogie would carry the main water tank and the other coal plus additional water, the boiler could be wide and short with a deep firebox. It would therefore be cheaper than the double boiler of a Fairlie and more free-steaming than the long narrow boiler of a Mallet.

Garratt's early sketches were far removed from the ultimate outcome, featuring very large driving wheels and a high 'cradle' supporting the boiler, but the fundamental elements were already there. Kitson were not the only firm that rejected his ideas, but he remained undaunted and in July 1907 filed a provisional patent specification. His luck was about to change dramatically.

In August 1907, Garratt was appointed by the New South Wales Government Railways as an inspecting engineer for locomotives built outside Australia. Coincidentally, an order for fifty had just been placed with Beyer Peacock & Co of the Gorton Foundry, Manchester. It was a happy introduction to what was then considered to be the 'Rolls Royce' of British locomotive builders with a world reputation for workmanship

second to none. It was an obvious opportunity to promote his ideas with the management and design staff.

The timing was right. Beyer Peacock was facing severe competition on many fronts, as the age of the electric tram, the motor bus and the private car was dawning. In addition, most of Britain's major railways were now building their own locomotives and this trend was spreading overseas. The company was happy to work with Garratt, whose luck held when his sketches submitted in October 1907 were passed to Samuel Jackson – a brilliant draughtsman destined to become the company's Chief Designer and Works Manager. He was instrumental in the development of a totally new product, with the result that a complete and much improved patent specification was submitted in January 1908 and accepted five months later.

The basis for an articulated locomotive more effective than any other type was now achieved. It easily met the key functions of spreading the weight over numerous axles and providing maximum flexibility on curves. In a locomotive that truly did bend, there were no serious overhang problems. The considerable space between the two sets of axles was destined to be fundamental on lines with weak bridges or light rails. Perhaps more importantly, placing the engine units at either end of the boiler meant the diameter of the wheels could be increased to permit running at much higher speeds than could safely be achieved by a Fairlie or a Mallet. In addition, the size of the boiler could be greatly enlarged, as stated in a letter thought to have come from Beyer Peacock that captures the mood of the moment: 'It is a marvel how Fairlie – and others since who have been engaged in developing the articulated locomotive – could have missed such an obviously simple solution of reconciling a properly designed boiler of large capacity to the limits of the various loading gauges.'

Fired with new enthusiasm and thoughts that he might well have conceived an operating man's dream, Garratt duly terminated his employment with the New South Wales

OPPOSITE, TOP: K1, one of the pair of pioneer Garratts supplied by Beyer Peacock to the Tasmanian Government Railways in 1909. Photographed in 2006 on the Welsh Highland Railway following restoration. (Roger Dimmick)

LOWER: Exploded diagram of K1 showing the then revolutionary concept patented by Herbert W. Garratt in 1908. (Leith Paxton)

GARRATT'S PATENT

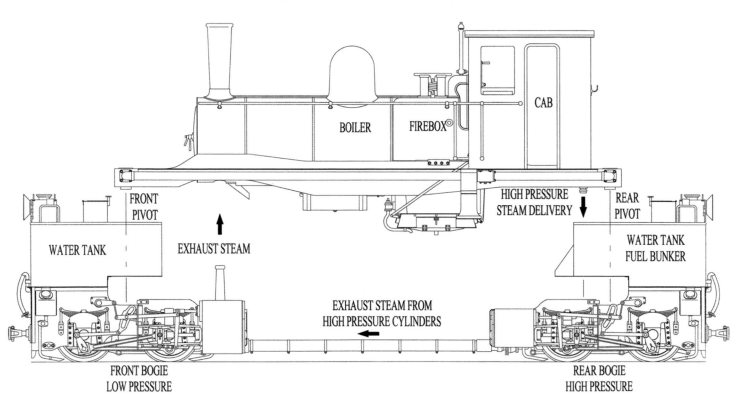

L.PAXTON 2004

The locomotive delivered to the celebrated Darjeeling Himalayan Railway in 1910 is considered the true prototype of all Garratts. The flexibility of the design is shown by the pronounced lean of the front unit on the super-elevated test track at Beyer Peacock's Gorton Foundry. Intended as the equivalent of two conventional engines, this Garratt never quite lived up to expectations owing in large measure to the formidable curvature of the Darjeeling line. (David Joy collection)

Government Railways and in September 1908 entered into a formal manufacturing agreement for Beyer Peacock to build his patent locomotive. The company would have sole manufacturing rights in the UK, in return for which he would receive a royalty of £2 per ton on each completed order. Beyer Peacock was at the time in negotiations to supply a Mallet to the remote North-East Dundas tramway, a two-foot gauge section of the Tasmanian Government Railways carrying lead ore from Hercules Mine to smelters at Zeehan. It seized the opportunity to prove the superiority of Garratt's proposals, with the result that orders for two 0-4-0 + 0-4-0s were received early in 1909. A new age for articulated locomotives was dawning.

THE PIONEERS

The first two Garratts, K1 and K2, were shipped from England to Tasmania on 7 October 1909. The North-East Dundas tramway was only eighteen miles long but had 1 in 25 gradients and 150ft radius curves, on which the locomotives clearly demonstrated their superiority over a Mallet. The firebox, positioned between the two engine units, was broad and deep. Compared with the long and narrow firebox perched over the wheels on a Mallet, it had the ability to burn indifferent fuel and yet still produce plenty of steam. Placing the fuel and water supplies on the engine units enabled ample amounts to be carried without obscuring the driver's view, which in any event had been improved over Garratt's original designs by setting a low-slung boiler on a simple plate frame and providing a tall cab. A feature that was not to be repeated was placing the cylinders in a cramped position on the inside of the bogies.

The 'K' class were compounds with high-pressure cylinders of eleven-inch bore on the front bogie and low-pressure seventeen-inch cylinders on the rear bogie. This helped steady the exhaust blast up the chimney – an unexpectedly important consideration, as they had a tendency to slip when hauling heavy loads. A report sent back from Tasmania foreshadowed a problem that was to persist until the present day: 'The

Garratt slipped very badly with 50 tons. You must bear in mind that Zeehan is one of the wettest and mistiest districts in Tasmania, and the rails are therefore very greasy.'

Apart from this defect, the locomotives were an undoubted success for such a radically innovative product. Beyer Peacock had not previously built any form of articulated locomotive nor – apart from their own works shunters – had they constructed engines to such a narrow gauge. With customary thoroughness they had been determined to achieve steam-tight flexible connections between the boiler and the power units. A description of the spherical joints on a Festiniog Fairlie was carefully studied and a visit made to Portmadoc to observe articulated locomotives of an earlier generation in action.

Both Garratt and the company were understandably keen to build on what they had achieved. They even indulged in what smacks of optimistic modern salesmanship, offering to supply a locomotive on three months' free trial. If successful, its cost would then be paid and two more immediately ordered at the same price! Despite such vigorous tactics and the success of the two Tasmanian locomotives, it was June 1910 before another firm order was received for a Garratt. It came from the celebrated two-foot gauge Darjeeling Himalayan Railway, one of the world's most difficult lines to operate with its 1 in 18 gradients and curves as sharp as 50ft radius on the formidable 7,000ft climb in just forty-seven miles. The cost of the 0-4-0 + 0-4-0 was a pricy £2,625 – over £200,000 in today's money – but the directors anticipated that it would be the equivalent of two of the line's existing 'B' class 0-4-0STs. It was a 'simple' and not a compound engine and in this sense was the true prototype for all future Garratts.

Great disappointment ensued when the assumption that it would haul trains of double the existing length proved to be fatally flawed. With a relatively long locomotive on such gradients it was inevitable that water would first be drawn from the forward tank, which thus became lighter and increased the tendency to slip on curves of such excruciating radius. Longer trains compounded the problem by creating flange friction to the extent that wagons could be pulled off the track rather than obediently going round the curve. If this were not enough, the Garratt was prone to steaming problems and had a voracious appetite for coal, devouring 106lb of coal per mile compared with the mere 40lb of the 'B' class. Used to a very basic locomotive, the crews never took to a more complex machine to cope with the challenges of the hill section and no more were ordered. Yet once confined to the Darjeeling's more normal extension lines away from the mountain, it proved its worth and remained in service until 1954.

All may have been more or less well in the end, but the initial problems were sufficient to cause Beyer Peacock to proceed with caution and hedge its bets. Instead of rushing ahead, it arranged a licensing agreement with the Societé Anonyme de Saint Léonard of Liège in Belgium. It was St Léonard that broke into the ultimate Garratt heartland of Africa in the most modest of ways, supplying four tiny 0-4-0 + 0-4-0s in 1911 to a 60cm gauge line at Mayumbe in the Belgian Congo. Weighing only twenty-three tonnes, they were the smallest Garratts ever built. They certainly had more appeal than the country to which they were sent – the vast labour camp of manacled slaves and mass starvation chillingly portrayed in Joseph Conrad's *Heart of Darkness*.

Later in 1911 a larger 0-6-0 + 0-6-0 built for a 75cm gauge railway on the opposite bank of the Congo river was a prototype for many more that followed over the next fourteen years. St Léonard moved into French territory in 1912 and supplied the Zaccar mines railway in Algeria with a 75cm gauge locomotive that was effectively an enlarged Mayumbe type.

Such expansion could well have prompted Beyer Peacock to build and sell more Garratts itself. The company had an unequalled record of going out around the world to seek work and took the business of selling steam locomotives far more seriously than its competitors. It was skilled at producing first-class sales brochures, although with few examples actually built it had in this instance to use considerable artistic licence for the illustrations!

Despite such enterprise, it was the presence of the two pioneers in Tasmania that led to the first major flush of orders coming from Australia. In 1911 Beyer Peacock had begun production of larger 3ft 6in gauge Garratts with six 2-6-0 + 0-6-2s for the Western Australia Government Railways, which had gradients of 1 in 22 and curves of 328ft radius. Mindful of the steaming problems on the Darjeeling, they were sent out with six different sizes of blast-pipe nozzle, with instructions to report back on which worked best. This customer care proved worthwhile, as in September 1912 an order was placed for a further seven locomotives, specifying precisely the size of nozzle that was required! In turn the Tasmanian authorities decided to try Garratts on its 3ft 6in

HERBERT WILLIAM GARRATT

Born in London on 6 June 1864, Herbert W. Garratt proved to be both inventive and restless from a relatively early age. Between 1879 and 1882 he served an apprenticeship at the Bow Works of the North London Railway, where he showed his ability as both a draughtsman and an artist.

For a time he changed his allegiance to steam ships and became a fitter at William Doxford's Marine Engine Works at Sunderland. In 1883 he went to sea as a ship's engineer and crossed the Atlantic to New York, but his paintings suggest that railways remained his first love. In 1885 he took out a patent for improving steam engine valve gear and also became an inspecting engineer for Sir Douglas Fox, ironically the man blamed for the failure of the notorious Fairlies supplied to Queensland eighteen years earlier. Some goods locomotives were being built at his Glasgow works for the Central Argentine Railway, a company that soon tempted Herbert

Garratt overseas and provided what appear to have been the happiest years of his life. His various posts ranged from a head draughtsman to a locomotive superintendent.

Returning to England in 1899, he continued to be industrious on many fronts with inventions ranging from a spark extinguisher to a patent improved boiled-egg opener! Further long-term employment eluded him, but in 1900 he was appointed locomotive superintendent on the Cuban Central Railways and two years later took a similar post on the Lagos Government Railway. He found a chaotic state of affairs with only three engines capable of moving but turned matters round within seven weeks. His reputation was greatly enhanced when he supervised the assembly of a new locomotive in the record time of thirty-two hours from taking the parts out of a crate to raising steam.

A return to London was short-lived and in 1904 he was abroad again to become resident engineer and locomotive superintendent of the Lima Railway in Peru. Unfortunately, a take-over and electrification plans meant he was made redundant after only a year but was given a first-class passage home in 1905. This gave him the opportunity to develop his ideas for the locomotive that became indelibly associated with his name. It also led to him moving to Levenshulme, near Manchester, where he set up his own office in his new home. Here he dealt with publicising Garratt locomotives, seeking fresh outlets and producing new ideas.

In 1911 he moved to Richmond, Surrey, where he was in a better position to expand his interests by visiting offices of the many British-owned overseas railways. He may have sensed that troubled times lay ahead, as he was also busy taking out a patent for mounting guns on locomotives. His plans were cut short by his untimely death on 25 September 1913, aged only forty-nine.

gauge main line and in 1912 ordered two 'L' class 2-6-0 + 0-6-2s for freight work and two 'M' class 4-4-2 + 2-4-4s for passenger duties. Initial problems with the exhaust nozzle were soon overcome and the 'M' class proved capable of hauling heavy corridor trains at 55mph. When one of the locomotives derailed on a curve, it was claimed that the driver was unaware of his excessive speed because the Garratts travelled so smoothly! Their excellent riding qualities quickly helped to persuade other railways that they were suitable for main-line passenger use as well as heavy freights.

With these orders the Garratt had finally made the grade and was destined to go ever upwards for the next half century. Sir Vincent Caillard, chairman of Beyer Peacock, had no hesitation in stating: 'Our experience in the trade leads us to believe with great confidence that the Garratt has come to stay, and that it is destined to supersede most existing types of articulated engines, and, indeed, to extend the use of that particular type of locomotive altogether.'

CONQUERING THE WORLD

Herbert Garratt must also have been optimistic that great days lay ahead. Another significant order in 1912 was the building of two locomotives with a unique 4-6-0 + 0-6-4

ABOVE: The Class NGG11 2-6-0 + 0-6-2s were the first two-foot gauge Garratts in South Africa. No 54 looks superb in its natural homeland as it leaves Hankey on the Avontuur line's Patensie branch at first light. (David Rodgers)

OPPOSITE: Beyer Peacock drawing for the first batch of three NGG11s supplied to South Africa in 1919. (David Joy collection)

wheel arrangement for the Mogyana Railway in Brazil. They were the first metre-gauge Garratts and the first of many for Latin America.

Now based in Richmond, Surrey, he personally secured an order in 1913 for a pair of 0-6-0 + 0-6-0s for the Arakan Flotilla Company's 2ft 6in gauge Buthidaung-Maungdaw Tramway in Burma. Only half a ton heavier than the Mayumbe locomotives built by St Léonard, they were unique in having skirts fitted around the wheels and motion in recognition of the tramway status of the line. Sadly, it closed as early as 1926 and there was no further use for these two very attractive locomotives.

In 1913 Herbert Garratt was discussing future orders with South Africa, South America and India and all looked promising. Then came his untimely death closely followed by the outbreak of World War I. Contrary to what might have been expected, these two drastic developments did not diminish Beyer Peacock's interest in the locomotive he had patented. The company continued to promote the concept in every way possible until it eventually became the mainstay of production at Gorton.

Once the war was over, it quickly picked up the threads and soon realised that Africa was a land waiting for Garratts to happen. The noted American writer David P. Morgan summed up the opportunities: 'Africa required the impossible. Africa needed a steam locomotive that could climb any grade, negotiate any curve, burn indifferent fuels, be built in gauges from two-feet to standard, be overhauled by unskilled labour, work passenger and freight trains indiscriminately, possess axle loadings of less than four tons upon occasion, and be unaffected by climate… The Garratt was and is such a machine.'

Priority was given to South African Railways, which had intended in 1914 to place orders on an experimental basis for two 3ft 6in gauge Garratts for main-line use and three much smaller locomotives for its 600 miles of two-foot gauge lines in Cape Province and Natal. The smaller locomotives came first with three 2-6-0 + 0-6-2s being built in 1919 and designated Class NGG11. These muscular machines were way beyond the size and specification of anything that was being used elsewhere on so narrow a gauge. They began work in Natal on the Umzinto to Donnybrook line, abounding in curves down to 150ft radius and gradients of 1 in 33, and yet carrying a heavy traffic of timber and sugar cane. In performing the work of two conventional locomotives they halved the required number of man-hours. Their success was such that two more NGG11s followed in 1925, this time with the benefits of superheating and piston valves.

Dramatic as were the developments on this gauge, they were quickly eclipsed by what happened on the South African main lines. The first 3ft 6in Garratt delivered by Beyer Peacock in 1920 was by far the largest ever built at the time. As had been the case with both Meyers and Mallets, the 2-6-0 + 0-6-2 was subject to comparative trials from which it emerged triumphant. Further orders soon assumed massive proportions and culminated in some 400 Garratts being hard

at work in a country that was ideal for them. The striking haulage capabilities markedly increased line capacity in a country with long stretches of single track abounding in curves and gradients.

South Africa may have erred in adopting the 3ft 6in or 'Cape' gauge as it was also known, rather than the standard 4ft 8½in, but at least it avoided Britain's severely restricted loading gauge. This in turn led to the evolution of Garratts that ran on tracks a shade over fourteen inches narrower than those in much of the world, but otherwise were of such enormity that they had nothing in common with the cuddly conception of tiny narrow gauge locomotives. When Beyer Peacock delivered the eight GL class 4-8-2 + 2-8-4s in 1929/30 they were both the largest locomotives in the whole of Africa and the largest narrow-gauge locomotives in the world. Equipped with mechanical stokers and over 210 tons in weight, they had a mind-boggling tractive effort of 89,130lb that was never remotely equalled on the British standard gauge.

Africa became and remained the Garratt heartland and was eventually home to more such locomotives than all the rest of the world put together. Their affinity with the continent was not matched elsewhere and the number running on standard-gauge metals was always relatively small. They quickly spread from South Africa to neighbouring 3ft 6in gauge systems, Rhodesia Railways gaining a head start in 1926 with the largest single Garratt order then placed for twelve 2-6-2 + 2-6-2s. It was the beginning of an allegiance that was to last for almost thirty years, with Beyer Peacock supplying some 250 locomotives to handle not just heavy freight but also main-line expresses to such evocative destinations as Victoria Falls.

In the following year the Portuguese colony of Angola took delivery of six large 4-8-2 + 2-8-4s for the remarkable 3ft 6in gauge Benguela Railway. Fifteen more followed in 1929. Stretching for over 800 miles from the Belgian Congo border, the prime purpose of the line was to convey Katanga copper down to Lobito Bay. The 1 in 40 gradients meant that most trains required two locomotives, the second being cut into the middle in a mode of working known locally as 'dupla'. The Garratts were specially designed with a fifty

Elevation of left-hand (Fireman's) side

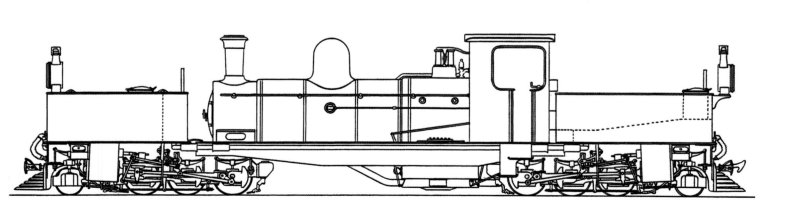

OPPOSITE: Garratts on the South African 3ft 6in gauge had nothing in common with the cuddly conception of tiny narrow gauge locomotives. Epitomising their enormous size and power is this 1990 view of a 4-8-2 + 2-8-4 climbing the last few yards of 1 in 40 to the summit of Lootsberg Pass. (David Rodgers)

THIS PAGE: Even more so than in South Africa, Garratts quickly became the dominant motive power on Rhodesia Railways. Typical of them is Class 16 2-8-2 + 2-8-2 No 601, which was rebuilt in 1979 during the political turmoil that brought increased dependence on steam power. (David Joy)

square-foot grate to burn eucalyptus logs, which were piled high on the bunker and consumed at such a prodigious rate that the railway company employed three thousand men in its own forests to fell some 16 million trees a year. The locomotives were likened to flame-throwing dragons when they emitted voluminous amounts of glowing orange-red char into the dark African night.

A slightly narrower gauge proved no barrier. Quick to join the Garratt empire was the metre-gauge Kenya & Uganda Railway, which placed its initial order for four similarly massive 4-8-2 + 2-8-4s in the same year as Rhodesia Railways. Here again, the trickle soon turned into a flood with another twenty being delivered two years later in 1928 and many more following. Later examples were designed for easy conversion to 3ft 6in gauge should the system be connected to its neighbours to the south but this proved to be a laudable goal that was never achieved.

The dominance of Garratts in Africa was due in no small measure to W. Cyril Williams, who was on the staff of the Assistant General Manager in Durban and carried out the first acceptance trials in 1920. He was highly impressed with what he saw and three years later became the London representative of Beyer Peacock. It was soon clear that the company had one of the greatest locomotive salesmen in the world, able to sell a relatively expensive product against all competitors. This was not just in Africa but in many other far-flung places. He visited every continent looking for new customers, checking how existing Garratts were performing and making them one of the most successful steam locomotives ever exported from Britain. In 1926 alone he travelled 45,000 miles in one tour – and this long before the days of Boeing 747s!

Yet Cyril Williams must more than once have reflected on the uneven geographical spread of Garratts. Starting at home,

the LMS had its standard-gauge examples and a solitary locomotive was produced for the LNER, yet not a single Garratt was ever built for the British narrow gauge. The only railway for which they might have been suitable – the Welsh Highland – was too impoverished in the 1920s and '30s to afford one!

Working round the world from east to west, the position was even more extreme in the USA. Herbert Garratt had entered into a licensing arrangement with Baldwin Locomotive Works but it was never exercised. The country that rejected Fairlies after a brief trial was even less captivated with Garratts, with not one solitary locomotive of any gauge appearing there until preservation days. Big as they were, they did not have the coal and water capacity that most American railroad companies favoured.

South America was a different story. The hesitant beginning in 1912 with the supply of just two locomotives was followed in the late 1920s with further orders from Brazil as well as Argentina, Bolivia, Chile and Ecuador. Garratts proved ideal for notoriously difficult lines on the flanks of the Andes and thus two of these orders were of special fascination. One comprised four 2-6-2 + 2-6-2s delivered to the famed Transandine Railway in 1929. They were for use on the Argentine stretch of line, which was primarily adhesion worked but included a seven-mile rack section where the Garratts were sometimes banked by a Kitson Meyer. It must have been a stupendous spectacle.

The other railway where the use of Garratts must have set the pulses racing is the 3ft 6in Guayaquil & Quito in Ecuador. Supremely challenging even by Andean standards, it rises almost 10,000 feet in fifty miles on a ruling grade of 1 in 18. Not for the faint hearted or sufferers of vertigo is the ascent of the Devil's Nose by means of a Z reverse carved

THIS PAGE: G42, one of a pair of 2-6-0 + 0-6-2s purchased by Australia's Victoria Government in 1926. They transformed operations on the 2ft 6in gauge lines from Colac to Crowes and Moe to Walhalla. (Colin MacKay)

OPPOSITE: Expiry of the Garratt patent in 1927 coincided with a period when Beyer Peacock was working to capacity. As a result, German manufacturers supplied numerous Garratts to South Africa including all twelve two-foot gauge NGG13s. No 59, delivered by Hanomag in 1927, was heading the daily mixed from Weenen to Estcourt in August 1976. The 'Liliputian' headboard was a regular feature. (David Rodgers)

into the near vertical mountain side. The line was built by American enterprise, which accounts for the initial articulated motive power in the shape of a pair of Shays in 1901, followed four years later by two Baldwin 0-6-6-0 Mallets. Against the odds, the owners were finally persuaded by Beyer Peacock in 1929 to try three 2-6-2 + 2-6-2s. Unfortunately they only just beat the depression with the railway's tonnage falling from 164,000 in 1928 to 116,000 just four years later. No further examples were ordered.

Across the Pacific, Garratts could sometimes overreach themselves, as was decisively the case in New Zealand. Three handsome-looking 4-6-2 + 2-6-4s were supplied to the 3ft 6in gauge system in 1928 but they proved a total embarrassment. They were far too powerful for the couplers then in use and were also prone to slipping. The use of unfamiliar Gresley valve gear exacerbated the problems and after only eight years they suffered an ignominious fate. All three were dismantled and the parts used to build six Pacifics!

It was a different story in Australia where most of the main lines operated either 3ft 6in or standard-gauge Garratts, although smaller-scale versions were also to be found. The two pioneers in Tasmania were complemented when the Victoria Government decided to boost the existing 2-6-2Ts employed on its 2ft 6in gauge branches from Colac to Crowes and Moe to Walhalla. In 1926 it purchased two 2-6-0 + 0-6-2 Garratts, G41 and G42, that could handle trains of double the length without the need to improve the existing light trackwork.

In Asia, a system with a long history of articulated locomotives was the metre-gauge Burma Railways with its Lashio branch. Despite a Z reversing section between Mandalay and Maymyo, there was still a ruling gradient of 1 in 25 for eleven miles as it climbed away from the Irrawaddy plain. After using

Fairlies from 1901 and then North British 0-6-6-0 Mallets, it purchased an experimental 2-8-0 + 0-8-2 that was the first eight-coupled Garratt to be constructed. In terms of both haulage capacity and coal consumption, it was greatly superior to the Mallets and a further four followed in 1927. One of them proved to be the only compound Garratt ever built apart from the Tasmanian K1 and K2.

In the same year, five 2-6-2 + 2-6-2 Garratts went to the metre-gauge Assam Bengal Railway, noted for its thirty-seven tunnels and difficult terrain, and in 1929 a one-off locomotive with a unique 2-4-0 + 0-4-2 wheel arrangement was ordered for a 2ft 6in gauge line running through tea-growing country in Ceylon. In 1932, a 2-6-0 + 0-6-2 of the same gauge was supplied to the Nepal Government Railway. Its main function was hauling a daily freight from Birgunj to Amlekhganj, from where a track and ropeway took goods onto the fabled destination of Katmandu. Greater glory came on the occasion of the monthly fair at Amlekhganj, when the special passenger train was so long and overloaded that a tank engine piloted the Garratt.

After India, a Beyer Peacock representative such as Cyril Williams would no doubt spend considerable time in Africa as there would be little to detain him in Europe. Here the one country that boasted a few narrow-gauge Garratts was Spain – and the company had only built two of them. These were a pair of 2-6-2 + 2-6-2s purchased by the 3ft 6in gauge Rio Tinto Railway in 1930.

LICENSED TO BUILD

By virtue of its existing licence, St Léonard of Liège continued to be a significant builder of Garratts through the 1920s, supplying previous customers in the Belgian Congo as well as metre gauge lines in Madagascar and Spain. Otherwise, Beyer

Peacock preserved its monopoly but no doubt was only too aware of what was likely to happen when the basic patent expired at the end of 1927. So too were other companies – and some could not wait.

One of them was the Newcastle firm of Armstrong Whitworth, which in 1924 built a pair of 4-6-0 + 0-6-4s for the three-foot gauge Colombian Pacific Railway in South America. It was a surprising move by a company that had only just entered the locomotive building market and had never previously constructed an articulated machine. Beyer Peacock became aware of their existence and apparently managed to inspect them at Liverpool docks just prior to shipment. Armstrong Whitworth had to admit patent infringement and agree not to build any more Garratts in the immediate future. It was nevertheless quick off the mark on expiry of the patent and soon delivered a pair of 2-6-2 + 2-6-2s to the metre-gauge Great Western of Brazil Railway.

Beyer Peacock's great rivals – the North British Locomotive Company – also created problems. Once suppliers of numerous Mallets to South Africa, the Garratt supremacy caused orders to dwindle away. In 1925 the company attempted an outflanking move by designing what it termed a 'Modified Fairlie' but looked very much like a Garratt. Although it was not received with favour, the company

refused to be defeated. When it later won an order to build ten 4-8-2 + 2-8-4s for the Kenya & Uganda Railway, these too were unquestionably Garratts but were described as 'North British Articulated Locomotives'!

Expiry of the patent coincided with a period when Beyer Peacock was working to capacity and yet failing to cater for the needs of existing customers. The result was that the company left itself open to being undercut in terms of both price and delivery dates. In just two years four German manufacturers delivered well over a hundred Garratts to South Africa. The largest supplier was the armaments firm of Krupp of Essen, which also won an order from Burma Railways for eight 2-8-0 + 0-8-2s.

This proved to be the last straw for Beyer Peacock's chairman, Sir Sam Fay, who had played a key role in guiding the Great Central Railway through World War I. A major row erupted at the company's annual general meeting in 1931 and it was a very long time before German builders again supplied Garratts to a British possession. The company resolved to take decisive steps with new patents and a new name, which meant that officially all future locomotives were termed 'Beyer-Garratts' to distinguish them from those of unlicensed competitors. It was now able to protect its position and at the same time could either grant licences or simply

No 109 at Kenterton on the Umzinto to Donnybrook branch in September 1980. The first NGG16 to be built by Beyer Peacock, it was purchased by Pete Waterman in July 2009 for restoration prior to service on the Welsh Highland Railway. (Neville Fields)

ABOVE: Cab details in an NGG16. A single regulator handle admits steam to both engines. It is often possible to see how the pressure rises more quickly in the front bogie (gauge second from right) than in the back bogie (right hand gauge). After a few moments the pressures equalise and the needles settle at the same readings. (Cliff Thomas)

LEFT: The restricted view from the cab of an NGG16. These Garratts were originally fitted with a seat that could be swung outside the cab, thus providing both cool air and a better vista along straight stretches of track. It can be seen in use in the photographs on pages 99 and 107. (Cliff Thomas)

subcontract should its order books be brimming with work. Unhappily, it was to be many years before such a state of affairs again arose. The consequences of world depression were no doubt behind much of the trauma at the 1931 annual meeting and in the coming five years the company was destined to build just eleven Garratts. Only in the late 1930s were there signs of improvement.

The changes in this era were clearly reflected on the South African two-foot gauge. Following the initial NGG11 2-6-0 + 0-6-2s, all subsequent locomotives had an extra pair of bogies and were 2-6-2 + 2-6-2s. In 1927 Beyer Peacock allocated works numbers for two NGG12s, designed for use on especially light track, but then subcontracted the work to Franco-Belge of La Croyère, Belgium. One of the two principal classes, the NGG13s, then evolved with South Africa able to place orders for all twelve locomotives with Hanomag of Hanover. Two of them initially went to the Otavi Railway in South West Africa (now Namibia) before joining the others in Natal and Cape Province.

The interlude created by the depression was followed in 1937 by orders for the virtually identical NGG16 class. German manufacturers were by now definitely off the agenda, the first four thus proving to be the only Garratts ever built by John Cockerill of Seraing, Belgium. Beyer Peacock itself constructed a further eight, thus making a grand total of thirty-two such locomotives on the South African two-foot gauge.

By this time the clouds of war were again gathering over the horizon, an early consequence being the only Garratts ever built in Italy. After the Italian conquest of Ethiopia, the firm of Ansaldo was commissioned in 1939 to supply six 2-8-2 + 2-8-2s for the metre-gauge line climbing almost 8,000 feet from Djibouti in French Somaliland to the capital of Addis Ababa. Three finally arrived in 1943-4, but the other three

were instead sent to Tripoli. One was in a ship that was torpedoed and its remains must lie at the bottom of the Mediterranean. The other two were so badly damaged by bombing that they were scrapped in 1945.

GARRATTS GO TO WAR

It says much for the basic simplicity of Garratts that they were considered suitable for wartime conditions, beginning in March 1943 when the British War Department received an urgent demand from the Far East war zone for additional locomotives. There was no time for Beyer Peacock to prepare a new specification, so existing designs were used and the first ten 2-8-0 + 0-8-2s were steamed just seventeen weeks after receipt of the order. Unfortunately they proved insufficient for haulage requirements, so this time fresh drawings were prepared for another fourteen larger 2-8-2 + 2-8-2s. All other work was relegated to second place and the design, procuring of materials and complete manufacturing took just 118 days. Two of the Garratts were lost at sea, but all the remainder initially went to the metre-gauge railway in the hills of Assam where the front line with the Japanese army lay after they had invaded Burma and were threatening to advance into India. They did spectacular work and played a vital role in the 14th Army's re-conquest of Burma, where they continued to be active following the Japanese retreat.

Further wartime locomotives bore codenames. Twenty-five 4-8-2 + 2-8-4 SHEGs (Standard Heavy Garratts) were delivered in 1943-44, six of which were allocated by the Ministry of Supply to the 3ft 6in Gold Coast system that had not hitherto used such locomotives. Here they hauled heavy manganese traffic needed as war material. Others went to Rhodesia Railways to assist with increased demand for coal traffic and to the Kenya & Uganda Railway, which was carrying

The basic simplicity of Garratts is such that they were considered suitable for wartime conditions. No 837 was part of an order in 1943 for fourteen 2-8-2 + 2-8-2s that remarkably were designed and built in just 118 days. After spectacular wartime service in Assam and then Burma, it looked decidedly neglected when photographed in long grass at the back of Insein Works, Yangon (formerly Rangoon), in February 2006. (James Waite)

No 32086, one of the wartime 4-8-2 + 2-8-4 'Standard Light Garratts' sent to Assam in 1945. It was still there in March 2004, when photographed in store at Guwahati depot, but was later moved to Tinsukia Junction and repainted in a lurid lime green. (James Waite)

men and supplies to the battles in North Africa. Existing designs were modified as little as possible in order to speed production, although there had to be some economies. Heavy steel slab was needed for battleship armour and thus resort had to be made to plate frames.

The ASG (Australian Standard Garratt) applied to locomotives primarily required in Queensland, which had the misfortune to be closest to the Far East fighting and was in crisis following the bombing of Darwin in 1942. Hitherto not a Garratt customer, its 6,500 miles of line ranked second only to South Africa as the largest 3ft 6in gauge system in the world. As Beyer Peacock was under intense pressure, it was decided in 1943 to build sixty-five 4-8-2 + 2-8-4s in Australia. After just three months spent on design, the construction work was entrusted to over a hundred scattered firms. Not surprisingly, the locomotives were a disaster and proved to be so rough riding and prone to derailment that drivers often refused to handle them. Some were never fully assembled and most were withdrawn immediately after the war.

Although evolved in the war, the major role of the 4-8-2 + 2-8-4 STALIGs (Standard Light Garratts) proved to be post-war recovery. It was a chaotic time owing to rapidly changing requirements, as instanced by eighteen locomotives sent to Assam in 1945. Nine of them stayed there, but the remainder quickly moved to Burma the following year. In 1948 four of them were sent to Tanganyika just before it became part of East African Railways, where the other five joined them in 1952.

As the war ended, it was South Africa that was considered to have the greatest need. Closure of the Mediterranean to shipping meant all convoys to the Far East were having to go round via Capetown, where re-fuelling created massively increased coal traffic on the railway and hence an urgent requirement for more motive power. The result was the

largest single order ever placed for one type of Garratt with fifty 4-8-2 + 2-8-4s being built in 1945/46. By the time they were delivered the war was effectively over and Beyer Peacock must have wondered what lay round the corner.

BOOM TO BUST

Fears of a dearth of work after the war and into the 1950s could not have been more misplaced. The problem was the other way round, with orders growing so rapidly that the company struggled to cope. Part of the reason was the appointment in 1945 of the now legendary Cyril Williams as sales director, four years before he became President of the Institution of Locomotive Engineers. By now popularly known as 'Garratt Williams', he was soon off on another world tour and returned with bulging order books. Not only were new locomotives needed but traffic requirements meant they had to be ever more powerful and larger. As might be expected, the African railway systems were at the heart of it all.

Beyer Peacock was able to meet orders in the late 1940s for 3ft 6in gauge Garratts, including forty-five of various classes for Rhodesia and six for the Luanda Railway in Angola. On the metre gauge the newly formed East African Railways similarly experienced no major problems with its first two orders in 1949 for twenty-four Garratts. Like virtually all the post-war locomotives, they were 4-8-2 + 2-8-4s.

It was in the 1950s that the company became overwhelmed, despite introducing a day and night shift seven days a week. The sheer volume of work – coupled with shortage of materials and skilled labour – meant that many orders were either subcontracted or licensed. Twenty out of thirty locomotives ordered by Queensland Government railways in 1951 were constructed by Henschel, the German firm that in the post-war years was second only to Beyer Peacock in the number of Garratts built. In turn it was the Société Franco-

ABOVE: The Garratt output from Beyer Peacock in the early and mid-1950s was astounding, although it received remarkably little attention in Britain. The zenith of orders from Rhodesia Railways was represented by the sixty-one members of Classes 20 and 20A – almost 100 feet long and boasting mechanical stoking. No 730, built in 1954, is leaving Thomson Junction with a lengthy mixed train for Lukosi. (David Rodgers)

RIGHT: Bulawayo shed, Rhodesia, in February 1978 when it was still a Garratt heaven. Class 15 No 372 was built by Beyer Peacock in 1948. (James Waite)

TOP: The East African Railways' Class 59s were the largest and most powerful locomotives ever built for the metre gauge. Looking superb in its crimson livery when seen outside Nairobi shed in February 1978, No 5904 *Mount Elgon* was one of the large batch of 4-8-2 + 2-8-4s delivered in 1954 and 1955. (James Waite)

LOWER: The Class 59s were one of the very few Garratts to boast names – all of them deriving from the numerous local mountains. A welcome touch was to include the peak's height. Pride of the pack was No 5928 *Mount Kilimanjaro*, its 19,340ft representing Africa's highest mountain. (James Waite)

Belge that supplied ten to the neighbouring South Australian system the following year, when it also delivered six to the Great Western of Brazil.

Beyer Peacock managed to cope in 1951/52 with orders from the Benguela Railway in Angola for a further eighteen Garratts, but one from Rhodesia Railways for ten locomotives was passed to Franco-Belge. Twelve locomotives ordered by Mozambique Railways in 1952 were supplied by Haine St Pierre in Belgium and four years later another five came from Henschel. Breaking the scales in more senses than one were the 120 massive GMA/Ms, which went to South Africa over the six years from 1952 and ensured that the country was the world's largest user of Garratts. Henschel built almost half of them and it was symbolic of changing times that a further thirty-two were subcontracted to a once great rival in the shape of the North British Locomotive Company.

It was on the East African system that difficulties were really highlighted. The first nine of a new Class 59 were ordered in 1950, but five years elapsed before Beyer Peacock delivered a single one. Nevertheless, East African Railways

were both patient and sufficiently confident to have meanwhile increased the number required to thirty-four. It was worth waiting. These phenomenal locomotives were both the biggest in Africa and the largest and most powerful ever built for the metre gauge. In the 1970s, following the demise of the American steam giants, the Class 59s were also the world's largest steam locomotives in regular service. Their vital statistics included a length of 104 feet, a weight of 251 tons, a tractive effort of 73,500lb and a boiler of 7ft 6in diameter – more than twice the rail gauge! They comfortably hauled 1,200-ton freights over the section of line that climbed from sea level at Mombasa to more than 5,000ft at Nairobi in little more than 300 miles. Named after local mountains – complete with the peak's altitude on the nameplate – they looked superb in their crimson livery as they pounded up the long climb with trains of maroon and cream carriages.

The Class 59s did so well that they stopped development work on an even larger Garratt that would have had no equals. The Class 61s would have been 4-8-4 + 4-8-4s with an 8ft 3in diameter boiler and a phenomenal tractive effort of 110,000lb. Sadly the dream was never realised and the next locomotives ordered by East African Railways were diesels.

Nevertheless, motive power performance on the system moved up a notch in 1957 when the work of Dr Giesl-Gieslingen of Vienna led to a Garratt being fitted with a trial Giesl ejector to improve its front-end efficiency. A full-scale 'Gieslisation' programme was implemented in 1961 with impressive results not just in terms of fuel economies but also available power. Working timetables gave separate schedules for 'goods' and 'Giesl goods', with the better uphill performance reducing the overall journey from nineteen to sixteen hours.

The Class 59s were part of the glorious final flourish on East African Railways and were on a par with the GMA/Ms

The wonderful atmosphere of Nairobi shed at night in February 1978. The Class 59 prominent on the left is No 5927 *Mount Tinderet*. (James Waite)

of South Africa. They in turn were complemented on Rhodesia Railways by the equally impressive Classes 20 and 20A, almost 100 feet long and boasting the luxury of mechanical stoking. Sixty-one of these most modern of steam locomotives, supplied by Beyer Peacock between 1954 and 1958, had no difficulty in taking 1,400 ton trains over such noted climbs as the 1 in 64 between Kafue and Broken Hill. The later examples each cost £76,010 (over £1,200,000 in today's money).

Even allowing for orders fulfilled in Europe, the Garratt output from Beyer Peacock in the early and mid-1950s was astounding with locomotives of daunting proportions constantly leaving the Gorton works. Yet such was the parochialism in those days that scarcely a mention of them appeared in the British railway press. Instead, it got excited about Standard class 'Clans' of dubious worth.

It was a wonderful era, but rarely can events have moved downhill with such awesome rapidity in a way that had not been anticipated. When British Railways decided in 1955 to abolish steam locomotives, it created a chain reaction that spread across the former Empire. It was still a colonial age and many countries were determined to follow suit rather than be left behind in any modernisation programme. Diesel

power swept the globe, as succinctly described by David P. Morgan: 'English Electric and GE salesmen are doing to the Garratts of Africa what the ivory hunters did to the elephants of the same continent.'

The downturn was exacerbated by a world recession with devastating results. Beyer Peacock, a company that four years earlier had been struggling to cope with orders, found itself facing disaster. The final sad end centred on the South African two-foot gauge, which had been supplied with a further seven NGG16s in 1951. Capable of hauling loads of 180 tons up a 1 in 33 gradient and as much as 600 tons on easier sections, they were also far from slow and could happily bowl along at some 40mph. The success of the world's most powerful two-foot gauge locomotives avoided the expense of converting lines to 3ft 6in gauge and instead an order for a further seven was placed in 1958. Beyer Peacock was now belatedly attempting to switch to diesel production and the last of the seven proved to be the final steam locomotive built at Gorton. It was fitting it should go to South Africa – a country that had ordered more Garratts than any other.

Matters now went from bad to worse. When South Africa sought a further eight NGG16s in 1965, Beyer Peacock was in the throes of total closure. The order was passed to the Hunslet Engine Company, which entrusted assembly to its South African associate, Hunslet Taylor & Co (Pty) Ltd. Two were delivered in 1967 and the remaining six the following year. It was truly the end of an era that had begun in 1919 with the three locomotives supplied to the Umzinto to

ABOVE: The swift downturn at Beyer Peacock in the late 1950s meant that No 143 became the final steam locomotive to be built at Gorton Foundry in 1958. Now preserved on the Welsh Highland Railway, it is seen in July 1976 hauling the morning goods from Ixopo over dual gauge track into Donnybrook. (David Rodgers)

LEFT: Ixopo shed in July 1976. On the left is No 151, one of the last Garratts that was constructed in South Africa only eight years earlier by Hunslet Taylor & Co. No 87 on the right is one of the four NGG16s built in Belgium by Cockerill and is now on the Welsh Highland Railway. (David Rodgers)

Garratts handling limestone traffic on the Avontuur line were a stirring spectacle prior to dieselisation in 1973. No 81 was photographed near Thornhill in March 1970. (C.J. Gammell)

Donnybrook line in Natal. Over a period of almost fifty years, a total of sixty-four two-foot gauge Garratts had been delivered to South Africa.

In a broader context, the wheel had come full circle in just the same way as with Mallets. The first and last were relatively small compared with the majority of intervening locomotives that almost defy superlatives. Statisticians looking beyond the narrow gauge noted that an amazing tally of 1,651 Garratts had run on eighty-six railways in forty-six countries! A total of 1,023 had been built by Beyer Peacock and the remaining 628 by other manufacturers, but now there would be no more of the greatest of all articulated locomotives.

'REAL' STEAM

It may have been symbolic that the last Garratt was built in the same year as the end of steam on British Railways. Certainly it did not take British enthusiasts long to make the most of photographic expeditions for recording 'real' steam in South Africa, although few of them got to see a spectacular operation on the two-foot gauge that had only a few years to run. The Donnybrook line was still active, as were three other branches in Natal, but it was 'the premier narrow gauge railway

of South Africa' that provided the finest action. Hardly a mere branch, it started from Port Elizabeth and ran close to the Indian Ocean all the way to Avontuur for a total distance of 177 miles – the same as a journey from Euston to Stockport.

It was a quarrying operation at Loerie, forty-four miles out of Port Elizabeth, which created the major operating challenge. Both places were effectively at sea level but between them were rolling hills that had to be surmounted. Loaded limestone trains had immediately to face eight miles of twisting and tortuous 1 in 40 to reach the top of the bank at Summit, some 650ft above Loerie.

Double-heading by a pair of Garratts was not favoured for fear of stressing their articulation pivots, so instead a second locomotive was cut in some eight or ten wagons behind the leading engine. It was what the Beguela Railway would have termed 'dupla' working. The consist then set off up the bank on a schedule that generally allowed fifty-five minutes for the eight miles, the sound and volcanic efforts being phenomenal and the pace such that some of the footplate crews used to prove their prowess by running alongside the locomotive.

The train paused at Summit loop so that the rear portion could be detached and the second locomotive released to return down the bank and assist the next train. The Garratt at the front then coupled to the remaining wagons and the complete train headed across the world's highest two-foot gauge bridge, towering 254ft above the Van Stadens river gorge. Soon afterwards it was the start of a gentle fall to

Photographers flocked to the Cape Town to Port Elizabeth 'Garden Route' in the 1970s to see steam power battling up the Montagu Pass. They were able to record such majestic sights as this GMA/M attacking the start of the climb near Oudtshoorn in July 1976. (David Rodgers)

Chelsea, where the working was handed over to a private line leading down to a cement works near Port Elizabeth.

It was wonderful while it lasted but there was a growing problem that was rare on the two-foot gauge. Limestone traffic had increased from under 150,000 tons per annum in 1945 to some 400,000 tons in 1969 and the tortuous ascent of the bank meant there were insufficient paths for train movements. The problem was compounded by the ever-increasing quantities of apples and pears brought down from the famous Langkloof orchards around Avontuur and also seasonal citrus fruit traffic carried on a short seventeen-mile branch from Patensie to Gamoos Junction. Loads on the limestone trains were reduced in an effort to solve matters, but this was of little avail and 1973 saw the introduction of a fleet of twenty new diesels. Most of the Garratts were transferred to Natal and another 'big show' of the steam age was over.

Relatively few went to see it because of the even bigger show on South Africa's 3ft 6in gauge. Lines such as the noted 'Garden Route' from Cape Town through Oudtshoorn to Port Elizabeth became a centre of worldwide pilgrimage to see Garratts battling up the Montagu Pass. Change when it finally came was sudden with a purge of relatively new locomotives in the late 1970s culminating in withdrawal of the last of the once numerous GMA/Ms in 1984 owing to high maintenance costs. The spectacle that was lost was memorably captured in words and pictures in an evocative Australian book *Famous Last Lines*.

'The Garratts on Oudtshoorn bound trains made a rapid departure in anticipation of the climb ahead. Eventually the characteristic stammer of the two engine units faded into the darkness, only to return the best part of an hour later, slower and quieter this time, as the train neared Power, halfway up the mountain. A ride over the pass was always exciting. The line twists its way around the barren mountainsides, clinging to tiny ledges with drops of up to a thousand feet immediately below. The train wound its way upwards, seemingly forever, the wheel flanges screaming their protest at every curve and the mighty Garratt roaring away up front.'

It was the potent combination of outstanding scenery, perpetual sunshine and a great variety of locomotives that brought photographers and devotees of 'real' steam to South Africa. Other systems such as East African Railways, which had a far higher concentration of Garratts, did not receive quite the same attention. Here steam finished in mid-1980 but it was a very different story in Rhodesia where the same year had been fixed as the target for total dieselisation. Then came UDI and sanctions, and what were now the National Railways of Zimbabwe (NRZ) became the only system in the world with a policy geared to the non-availability of oil supplies. A complete rebuild of eighty-seven Garratts was put in hand to take them

into the 1990s and at the same time surplus GMA/Ms were hired from South Africa. Existing smaller locomotives were withdrawn and NRZ set another record by becoming the first and only railway in the world where every operable steam locomotive – passenger, goods or shunting – was a Garratt.

In the country's growing political turmoil the brave hopes were destined to perish through new diesels and lack of traffic, but rail enthusiasts enjoyed an extra decade of glorious opportunities found nowhere else. Those of a certain age look back to the early 1990s when one Garratt-hauled train after another pounded out of the vast Wankie Colliery. They raised the echoes to such an extent that on a calm day they could be heard coming from miles away. Delight had few equals to relaxing on the terrace at the Baobab Hotel, high above the line a few miles from Thomson Junction shed. Serious beer consumption was essential in such a climate, but it was still possible on hearing the first sound to get down to the lineside and go through film as if there was no tomorrow.

Footplating was also easy to arrange, although on a line running on the edge of the great Hwange Game Reserve it was wise at water stops not to go too far from the locomotive to take photographs. The crew would reinforce the point by relating the tale of the driver who only escaped the jaws of a lion by scrambling up a signal post! It was also at first disconcerting on sharp curves to experience the coal bunker and the centre part of the Garratt moving in different directions. Nevertheless, there can be no question that this was among the most glorious of railway experiences, only surpassed a little further north.

The sight of a majestic locomotive on the bridge over Victoria Falls, vast and yet utterly dwarfed against the backdrop of the greatest wonder of all Africa, never lost its appeal.

The thrills of a mass of 'real' steam in a land of Garratts did not have a celebratory end but simply faded away to leave just memories and a time for tributes. Many bewailed the loss of regularly seeing the fascinating rhythm of the fore and aft units wandering in and out of synchronisation during hard work upgrade. Those with Freudian inclinations dwelt on the 'wiggle' factor and alluded to a locomotive moving in all sorts of directions as it snaked along curvaceous tracks. Perhaps the finest description of a Garratt came from Brian Fawcett, best known for his groundbreaking book *Railways of the Andes*. Writing in the US magazine *Trains*, he perceptively commented: 'The bucking engines beneath the tanks heel and sway in opposite directions but the fat boiler slung between them – like a comatose Roman patrician in his litter – scarcely cants.'

Although it would still be possible to see Garratts in several other continents, nothing would henceforth equal the excitement of hunting them down as they stormed through the wilds of Africa to no known timetable. A.E. ('Dusty') Durrant said it all in a South African context in his classic book *Garratt Locomotives of the World:* 'The sight and sound of two GMA/Ms battling up the 1 in 30 to Claridge summit, with full load, perhaps slipping in the frost of a winter dawn, will never be forgotten by those who have experienced it. No tame preservation railway, however polished their locomotives, can ever provide such an orgasmic thrill to the beholder!'

Garratts Today

It was estimated in 2011 that some 250 Garratts remained in existence, some of standard or broader gauges but mainly of 3ft 6in or less. The overwhelming majority are to be found in southern Africa in conditions ranging from museum standard down to utter dereliction. The lack of precision is due to surprisingly difficult and almost philosophical questions such as when does a locomotive cease to exist. It is especially pertinent with Garratts, comprising three separate units and taken in considerable numbers by countries that have descended into devastating civil war. Making an exact count of locomotives that have been split asunder by explosives, with say one third in the shape of the coal bunker totally destroyed, can never be an exact science.

A prime example is provided by Angola, which for three decades following its independence in 1975 was locked in a bitter civil war. The once splendidly maintained Garratt fleet was soon nothing more than a series of rusting hulks, most of them displaying signs of damage that was sometimes extreme and suggested rocket attack. Even when the position became less volatile, it was hardly to be expected that a Marxist government would allow visits by railway enthusiasts. The number of Garratts that might be defined as surviving, rather than just a heap of shattered pieces, was mere guesswork. As with the

hitherto doubtful existence of a Kitson-Meyer in Argentina, the miracle of Google Earth finally removed much doubt and by late 2008 there came the surprising claim that Angola contained the largest number of Garratts in the world. It is now unlikely to be true, as greater stability saw cutting up for scrap proceeding apace in 2010.

The end of a steam locomotive is a depressing subject, but there is a much happier picture elsewhere. It inevitably continues to change, although Garratts remain of such perennial interest that comprehensive listings of all surviving locomotives can be found on the Internet. A useful site is 'http://users.powernet.co.uk/hamilton'.

'SHEER GRAFT' IN SIERRA LEONE

War has not always been totally disastrous. There has been an unexpected twist in Sierra Leone, a West African country tiny in extent but nevertheless once boasting a 2ft 6in gauge system with a route length of over three hundred miles. Always slightly outside mainstream Garratt developments in Africa, it took its first 2-6-2 + 2-6-2 in 1926. It proved so popular that a further twelve were ordered over the next seventeen years, five of them later being rebuilt as 2-8-0 + 0-8-2s and thus forming the smallest eight-coupled Garratts ever built.

In the absence of any local coal, all locomotives had to burn expensive briquettes imported from Wales. There was talk of early dieselisation, but instead a big surprise came as late as 1955 when Beyer Peacock supplied fourteen 4-8-2 + 2-8-4s that were unquestionably the largest and most powerful locomotives ever built for so narrow a gauge and for such light rails weighing only thirty pounds per yard. Sadly their heyday was brief as the entire system had closed by 1974. A Hunslet 2-6-2T and three coaches were repatriated to the UK for service on the Welshpool & Llanfair Railway, but

The largest and most powerful locomotives ever built for the 2ft 6in gauge were the fourteen 4-8-2 + 2-8-4s supplied by Beyer Peacock to Sierra Leone as late as 1955. Withdrawn in less than twenty years, it was assumed they had all been scrapped when the country was plunged into protracted civil war. It came as a major surprise in 2004 when one of them was found to be still intact in an abandoned shed. These two contrasting views show No 73 before and after the subsequent restoration. (Steve Davies)

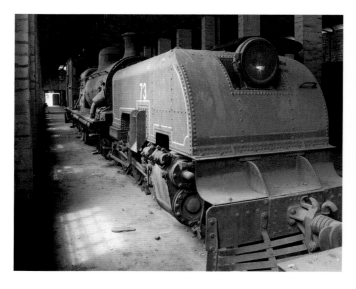

This unusual wood-burning 2-8-2 + 2-8-2 constructed by Henschel in 1936 was attractively displayed when photographed at Kanchanaburi station, Thailand, in December 2007. (James Waite)

soon afterwards the country lapsed into its lengthy civil war and it was assumed that everything had been scrapped. A major study of the world's Garratt locomotives published in 1981 specifically stated that none remained in Sierra Leone.

There matters rested for some thirty years until September 2004 when Colonel Steve Davies was posted to Sierra Leone's armed forces as an advisor to the Ministry of Defence. Apart from being a serving Army officer, he was also a lifelong railway enthusiast. Understandably, one of his first tasks was to search for remnants of the railway system and he soon came across a former carpentry and carriage shed within the one-time workshops on the eastern edge of Freetown. Rather than a mass culling, there had clearly been an attempt to safeguard key items of rolling stock by placing them under cover. The most amazing survivor was Garratt No 73, one of the massive 4-8-2 + 2-8-4s built in 1955.

Everything was in a depressing state. An estimated ten thousand refugees had lived in the workshops at the height of the conflict and any items not firmly bolted down had been taken by people striving to exist below the poverty line. It was also clear that scrapping of the remaining contents was imminent. Colonel Davies took a firm military line and made immediate contact with President Kabbah to stop such a tragedy. He then volunteered to devote his spare time to overseeing a project that would prevent any further deterioration and prepare the contents of the shed for display.

Having only been used for twenty years and then under cover for the next thirty, the Garratt was in fact in far better condition than its accumulated dirt and grime suggested. Although stripped of most of its non-ferrous fittings, all was clearly well with the boiler, platework and the motion. Remarkably, both of the Beyer Peacock worksplates had survived, no doubt because they were so caked in layers of paint that no-one had realised they were brass. Also still in place were the words 'Queen of Tonga', painted onto the headlamp when No 73 hauled the royal train during a state visit in 1964.

Through 'sheer graft', a team of the young unemployed did much of the hard work required to create a national railway collection. In just six months it was ready for opening, with the Garratt now restored to its lined-out green livery and undoubtedly the jewel in the crown. Six thousand visitors came to see the display in the first five weeks following the formal opening by

ABOVE: The only surviving narrow-gauge Garratts in Europe that have run in 'real' service – as opposed to preservation – are to be found in Spain. No 146, built by Beyer Peacock in 1929 for the 3ft 6in gauge Rio Tinto Railway, survives at the company's Nerva depot. Unfortunately its leading pony truck is missing. (James Waite)

LEFT: Restoration can often be an expensive and agonisingly slow process. G42 was acquired by the Puffing Billy Preservation Society in Victoria, Australia, in 1964 but there was still much to be done when it was photographed in 1979. A further quarter of a century elapsed before the work was complete and it hauled its first passenger train on the line in April 2004. (Colin MacKay)

Andrew Scott, the then Head of the National Railway Museum in York. Looking down the grapevine, it was appropriate that his successor in this post was to be Colonel Steve Davies.

ON DISPLAY

The Sierra Leone Garratt is one of many displayed in non-operating condition in all corners of the world, thus reflecting the numerous countries to which they were supplied.

Some survivors are in locations firmly on the tourist map such as Australia with its Franco-Belge 4-8-2 + 2-8-4 in the National Railway Museum at Port Adelaide. A locomotive from the same batch, built in 1953 and last steamed on Boxing Day in 1969, is at the Zig-Zag Railway eighty miles west of Sydney. In the same league is Thailand, where an unusual wood-burning 2-8-2 + 2-8-2 constructed by Henschel in 1936 for what was then Siam is preserved in an attractive setting at Kanchanaburi. Arguably at the other extreme is seldom-visited Myanmar (Burma), where one of the wartime 2-8-2 + 2-8-2s moved from Assam in 1946 is at Insein Works and another is at Thazi on the main line between Rangoon (now Yangon) and Mandalay.

The successor wartime class of 4-8-2 + 2-8-4s is represented in Assam by 32086, which was once preserved in poor condition in Guwahati shed before being moved to Tinsukia Junction and repainted in a lurid and wholly non-prototypical lime green. One of the locomotives from the same class that was transferred to East Africa is preserved in Nairobi Railway Museum along with other Garratts.

As might be expected, southern Africa has much to offer. There are five 3ft 6in gauge Garratts at Outeniqua Railway Museum, George, including the second to be delivered to South Africa in 1921. There are another seven at the NRZ Museum in Bulawayo and a further three well displayed outdoors at Livingstone Railway Museum in Zambia.

The only surviving Garratts that ran for real in Europe are to be found in Spain. They include one of the two supplied to the Rio Tinto Railway by Beyer Peacock, as well as a metre gauge 2-6-2 + 2-6-2 built by St Léonard for the Catalan Railways in 1925 and now housed at Manresa in a purpose-built store for heritage stock.

Most 3ft 6in gauge Garratts are so vast that few have moved from the land where they last worked, but there are some notable exceptions. In the UK it is clearly appropriate that one should be in the Beyer Peacock home city of Manchester. No 2352, a 4-8-2 + 2-8-4 of Class GL and thus the most powerful of all Garratts when built in 1930, was repatriated in 1983 after being out of use for twelve years. It has since been at the city's Museum of Science & Industry, where it has been restored to lined grey livery and mounted on a curved track to show the articulation.

Beyer Peacock's main competitor in the UK, the North British Locomotive Company, is similarly represented by one of the later GMA/Ms dating from 1957. In service until shortly before being brought back to Britain by a preservation group in 1982, it is now displayed at Summerlee Heritage Park in Coatbridge, Scotland, just a few miles from where it was

built. It was donated by South African Railways, although dock fees and road transport reputedly cost almost £20,000.

A more recent development has occurred in New Zealand with its railway system the same 3ft 6in gauge as southern Africa. This compatibility has encouraged the Mainline Steam Trust to import two Garratts, with ex Rhodesia Railways 2-6-2 + 2-6-2 No 509 arriving early in 2008 after overhaul in Bulawayo. It was joined by GMA/M No 4083 from South Africa, and then Steam Incorporated brought over Class 15A No 398 from Zimbabwe.

Bringing such massive locomotives back to operating condition is a major undertaking requiring substantial resources. It has been achieved in Kenya, where 5918 *Mount Gelai* was taken out of Nairobi Railway Museum in August 2001. Restored to its magnificent crimson livery, it made its first test run less than three months later. A similar happening in Australia has seen 4-8-2 + 2-8-4 No 1009, the sole remaining Garratt in Queensland, removed from an open-air museum and brought back to working order. It looks equally splendid in the same striking crimson livery.

PUFFING BILLY

The difficulties facing preservation societies opting for restoration have been demonstrated elsewhere in Australia. Even on the smaller gauges it can be an agonisingly slow process. Just how long may not have been by appreciated by those who started the restoration of G42, one of the pair of 2-6-0 + 0-6-2s dispatched to Australia in 1926 for use on 2ft 6in gauge branches in Victoria. It spent its last days hauling heavy trains of pulpwood and local produce between Colac and Crowes, but in June 1962 the line closed and the locomotive faced an uncertain future.

It so happened that just one month later the Puffing Billy Preservation Society reopened part of another 2ft 6in gauge line in the Dandenong Ranges outside Melbourne. It initially extended from Belgrave to Menzies Creek and is famous for its Monbulk timber trestle. The Society was collecting as much rolling stock as possible from all narrow gauge lines in Victoria and in 1964 acquired G42. It was placed on static display and in the mid 1970s plans were initiated to restore it to working order.

The task was daunting, as the locomotive had been worked hard and had received little maintenance. Over twenty years elapsed before a Commonwealth Employment Project Grant funded the labour that enabled serious restoration to begin in 1986. The main frames were cracked and in a poor state, but with support from Australian shipbuilder Transfield Amecon some new frames were cut to shape. The Society then started the long and arduous task of machining them. Similarly, the boiler had been stripped and all brass tubes as well as the copper firebox had been removed. This time the plight came to the attention of the Australian Portland Cement Company, whose railway at Fyansford had recently closed. They were able to donate a spare Garratt boiler and a new steel firebox. Finally, a Society member funded the provision of steel so that new tanks and a coal bunker could be constructed.

G42 hauled its first passenger train on the Puffing Billy line in April 2004. It had been silent and lifeless for almost

TOP: The remote El Tren del Fin del Mundo on Tierra del Fuego was claimed in 2012 to be one of only two places in the world where a Garratt was likely to be seen in daily service (the other was Bulawayo). The 0-4-0 + 0-4-0 *Nora* was built in 1994 for the opening of the 50cm gauge line that holds the title of 'The Southernmost Railway in the World'. (David Joy)

LOWER: In 2001 *Nora* was renamed *Ing L D Porta* after the famous Argentinean engineer who visited the line and advised on improvements to the locomotive. The subsequent rebuild may not have improved its appearance but certainly revolutionised performance. It was now capable of hauling sixteen coaches up a 1 in 23 gradient. (Chris Parrott)

forty-two years – a period six years longer than the time it had spent in service! It then became a familiar sight and impressed passengers, who found the Garratt 'amazingly quiet like a whispering giant'.

FURTHEST SOUTH

Other working locomotives are to be found in distant and sometimes surprising places.

Wikipedia has become an invaluable resource, but many of those consulting it in 2012 for a broad overview of Garratts might have well have scratched their heads on reading the concluding paragraph: 'There are only two places in the world where one can with reasonable confidence view a Beyer-Garratt in daily operating service – Bulawayo and Ushuaia.'

The key word is 'daily', as there are other more familiar locations where Garratts can be seen on a seasonal basis. That said, it is the last word that might cause doubt, as even the existence of a railway in one of the most remote places on earth is not widely known. The Southern Fuegian Railway – or El Tren del Fin del Mundo as it is more evocatively named in Spanish – is an unlikely feature of the Tierra del Fuego archipelago at the very tip of South America. Its prime purpose is to take passengers arriving on cruise ships from the capital of Ushuaia into the magnificent mountain surroundings of the National Park bordering Chile.

The 0-4-0 + 0-4-0 built for the opening of the line in 1994 is in many respects a hybrid. It was clearly inspired by

the pioneer K1, but has numerous differences and is not a replica. Nor could it seriously challenge the 1968 claim that a South African NGG16 was the last Garratt to be built. It is a scaled-down locomotive that would normally be treated as intended for a miniature railway, where the gauge is usually no more than fifteen inches. In this case it is a significantly wider 50cm – almost 1ft 8in.

Although arguably not quite the real thing, this tiny Garratt undoubtedly has many features of special interest. One of the very few locomotives to be built – as opposed to erected – in Argentina, it has close connections with the work of one of the greatest of latterday railway engineers. Above all it operates on a line that holds the title of 'The Southernmost Railway in the World'. When it was first steamed at Ushuaia, no other articulated locomotive had ever worked so close to the Antarctic Circle.

The Garratt was initially named *Nora*, which seems more akin to northern England but was so called after the wife of the line's creator Quique Diaz. Its performance was initially erratic but fundamental improvements were gradually made. Among those closely involved was Chris Parrott, who had the enviable lifestyle of a Talyllyn volunteer during the British summer before travelling across the world for a second summer acting as technical assistant and seasonal driver at Ushuaia. Extra water tanks were initially fitted, although this still left problems with unlagged steampipes that failed to deliver adequate steam to the cylinders in the frequent sub-zero temperatures at 55 degrees South.

Advising on the various problems was Livio Dante Porta, the legendary Argentinean engineer credited with having made the most significant contribution to the development of ultra-efficient steam locomotives in the latter half of the twentieth century. He visited the line to inspect progress prior to the Garratt receiving a major rebuild, its boiler now mounted higher on the cradle with sweeping pipes carrying steam to the power bogies. In honour of his involvement, *Nora* was renamed *Ing. L D Porta* in December 2001. It was now a totally different machine, able to haul sixteen coaches up the maximum 1 in 23 gradient with only slightly increased consumption of fuel oil. Like many Garratts it was still prone to slipping, but this tendency has been greatly

The mainstay of the Alfred County Railway when reopened in 1988 was timber traffic. Displaying the attractive red livery is No 140, hauling a block train of pulpwood and passing Aloe Ferox in bloom near Bongwana. (Allen Jorgensen)

reduced by adding sanders and even steam jets to clear ice from the rails.

All these improvements cleared the way to order a second Garratt, which was built in 2006 by Girdlestone Rail at Port Shepstone, South Africa. It is named *Ing. H.R. Zubieta* after the Argentinean naval engineer who played a leading role in the development of the line. With the one other steam locomotive – a conventional 2-6-2T – under major repair in Buenos Aires, the line claimed in 2011 to be the only railway in the world worked entirely by Garratts.

AFRICAN HEARTLAND

The Wikipedia reference to Bulawayo would come as less of a surprise to most users. Although 'real' steam on the main lines of Zimbabwe has gone, the politically induced time-warp is such that a remnant of a former age still survived in 2012. Amazingly, an average of four Garratts – based at the last still-functioning steam shed in the world – continued to handle shunting duties around Bulawayo on a daily basis.

Restored locomotives still work steam specials, as is also the case in South Africa. Here, with the many relatively new Garratts, it might have been expected that the world's largest

With the Indian Ocean providing a perfect background, a freight charter crosses the Mbango river outside Port Shepstone in May 2005. Sadly, the Alfred County Railway suffered from intense competition by road hauliers and all services were withdrawn less than a year later. (Dick Manton)

two-foot gauge network would long endure as an enclave of working steam. Yet all but one of the five remaining lines had closed only eighteen years after the last Garratt had been delivered. Two of them in Natal were by South African standards short branches under thirty miles in length, operating on a 'mixed train daily' basis to serve the agricultural centres of Weenen and Mid Illovo. There was little surprise when they respectively became casualties in 1983 and 1985, but the demise a year later of the spectacular line climbing 4,500ft in its 97-mile journey from sea level at Umzinto to a junction with the Cape - Natal railway at Donnybrook caused great dismay.

A second closure in 1986 was the 76-mile line extending from Port Shepstone to Harding and twisting a switchback course through Alfred County, so named after the younger son of Queen Victoria. It sparked a development hitherto unknown in South Africa in the shape of a private railway company formed by two well-known enthusiasts, Charlie Lewis and Allen Jorgensen. After agreement had been reached to lease the line from South African Transport, it re-opened as the steam-worked Alfred County Railway in July 1988. Phil Girdlestone, a mechanical engineer from the Ffestiniog, joined the railway to introduce some of the principles developed by L D Porta to improve locomotive efficiency. These included

a Lempor exhaust and a gas producer exhaust system designed to reduce coal consumption. Garratts provided the sole motive power, eight of them having been restored to operating condition by the end of the first year.

The mainstay was carrying timber traffic, but advantage was taken of the fact that the line ran through banana plantations alongside the Indian Ocean before climbing into the hills. Hence the introduction of the Banana Express running the twenty-four miles between Port Shepstone and Paddock. Both the ocean views and the Garratts proved popular with passengers, but sadly the line suffered from increasing competition by road hauliers receiving high subsidies. All services were withdrawn in April 2006, leaving four NGG16s in a shed gradually falling to pieces.

It has been a similar sad story on the 'premier narrow gauge railway' from Port Elizabeth to Avontuur. First the

Paton's Country Railway, with its main base at Ixopo, takes its name from the now classic book *Cry, the Beloved Country* by Alan Paton. Its motive power includes one of the pioneering Class NGG11 Garratts, No 55, here photographed in May 2005. (David Joy)

farming cooperatives switched to road haulage and then the cement company went the same way in May 2000, leaving little traffic other than the Apple Express. A few Garratts had been retained to help in working this tourist passenger service, which dated back to 1965 and initially ran up the line as far as Loerie. It became increasingly sporadic and in December 2010 was suspended owing to the loss of its government funding.

'THE BELOVED COUNTRY'

The demise of steam on South Africa's two-foot gauge had three very different consequences. The first was a desire to turn part of one of the closed lines into a full preservation operation, as opposed to the leasing arrangement on the Alfred County Railway. Providing a perfect opportunity was the one-time seventeen-mile branch off the Umzinto - Donnybrook line, extending from Ixopo through woodland and pastures to the agricultural centre of Madonela.

The prime mover behind the project was a local farmer, Julian Pereira, who saw the railway's restoration as a means of kick-starting small scale economic development through tourism. Ironically enough, the Welsh Highland Railway had acquired much of the track, but rebuilding started in 2000 and three years later it was possible to operate over the first nine miles of the branch from a rebuilt station at Ixopo through Carisbrooke to Ncalu.

The importance of Garratts in encouraging visitors was recognised from the outset.

One of the two owned by the line, NGG16 No 116, is waiting overhaul and return to service. The other has attracted great interest, as it is one of the pioneering NGG11s built in 1925. No 55 was sold to Rustenburg Platinum Mines, where it was still in steam in 1967. It was later preserved in what was described as 'doubtful fashion' at Weenen, terminus of the first of Natal's two-foot gauge lines to be closed in 1983. Twenty years later it was removed for restoration.

The line has one other feature of inestimable worth in its favour. Just as no one can calculate exactly how much the Brontës and the literary shrine of Haworth contribute to pas-

senger numbers on the Worth Valley Railway, so the same applies with what has been called Paton's Country Railway. The name derives from Alan Paton and his now classic book *Cry, the Beloved Country*, which in 1948 awoke the world to conditions for non-whites in South Africa. The opening pages were set on the line and give a wonderful flavour of both the countryside and narrow gauge railways:

'The small toy train climbs up on its narrow gauge from the Umzimkulu valley into the hills. It climbs up to Carisbrooke and when it stops there, you may get out for a moment and look down the great valley from which you have come. It is not likely the train will leave you, for there are few people here, and everyone will know who you are. And even if it did leave you, it would not much matter; for unless you are a cripple, or very old, you could run after it and catch it yourself... The train passes through a world of fancy, and you can look through the misty panes at green shadowy banks of grass and bracken... It is interesting to wait for the train at Carisbrooke, while it climbs up out of the great valley. Those who know can tell you with each whistle where it is, at what road, what farm, what river.'

Technical details are understandably lacking, but the locomotive would very probably be a Garratt!

WORLD CLASS

A second consequence of the two-foot gauge collapse was a determination by a group of individuals to acquire, restore and operate within South Africa as much as possible of what remained. Formed in 1997, the Sandstone Heritage Trust was soon claiming to possess the world's largest collection of narrow gauge locomotives. It also established superb workshops at Hoekfontein in the Eastern Free State, close to the Lesotho border some nine miles from Ficksburg. This became the operating centre of the privately-owned and purpose-built Sandstone Steam Railroad, sixteen miles long and with gradients as steep as 1 in 22, running through a vast agricultural estate embracing both arable land and striking hill scenery.

Spearheading these achievements has been Wilfred Mole, who has never been in any doubt about his objectives: 'The

ABOVE: The privately owned Sandstone Steam Railroad in the Eastern Free State quickly became immensely popular with visiting photographers. Soon claiming to possess the world's largest collection of narrow gauge locomotives, it was also blessed with a magnificent landscape and the exceptional quality of South African light. The spirit of the line, with its locomotives that are attractively restored without being over pristine, is captured in his view of Nos 49 and 113 at Mooihoek siding in May 2005. (David Joy)

LEFT: The Sandstone Steam Railroad established a record in April 2011 when it operated a train quadruple-headed by four Garratts, each constructed by a different manufacturer. They were NGG13 No 49 (Hanomag) and NGG16s Nos 88 (Cockerill of Belgium), 113 (Beyer Peacock) and 153 (Hunslet Taylor). (Aidan McCarthy)

A garden centre near Brugg in Switzerland is one of the more surprising destinations for a preserved NGG13. This LGB model faithfully captures the red livery of No 60, now named *Drakensberg*. Not everyone loves the colour, with many traditionalists claiming that black is an unbeatable Garratt livery.

(David Joy)

Sandstone Steam Railroad has simply pursued a policy of trying to accommodate on one site as diverse a cross-section as possible of two-foot gauge items. There appeared to be no single preservation centre that was focused on this activity and as a result it seemed appropriate that Sandstone should take up the mantle and assume full responsibility for flying the flag for South Africa. We hope that men of goodwill from around the world will work with us to complete a project that has true global merit.'

It is certainly a strategy that has impressed visitors, one of who commented: 'Very clearly Sandstone is one of the world's premier locations for photographing the two-foot gauge. It has the beguiling combination of a demanding railway, locomotives that are attractively restored without being over pristine, a magnificent landscape and the exceptional quality of South African light.'

The impressive total of ten two-foot gauge Garratts has no equal elsewhere and includes four that have been fully restored. They are all subtly different. The only NGG13, No 49 built by Hanomag in 1928, had been out of service for around thirty years, lost in scrub and overgrown by a large tree, when it was rescued in May 2002. Bringing it back to life had to wait the priority restoration of the NGG11 for the Paton's Country Railway, but it was still rebuilt virtually to the last nut and bolt in less than two years before being steamed again in November 2004.

Of the three operational NGG16s, No 113 was built by Beyer Peacock in 1939 and ended its days at Donnybrook. It worked the last train in 1986, after which the fire was dropped and it was left exposed to the elements. The same happened to No 153, which comes from the world's last batch of Garratts built by Hunslet Taylor in 1968 and had been in service for a mere eighteen years. A recent addition to the active fleet is No 88, one of the four NGG16s built by Cockerill of Belgium. Its restoration enabled the Sandstone Steam Railroad to claim a record in April 2011 when it operated a train quadruple-headed by four Garratts each constructed by a different manufacturer – Beyer Peacock, Cockerill, Hanomag and Hunslet Taylor.

Sandstone's many other acquisitions include three 3ft 6in gauge GMA/Ms, one of which is in full working order and

has been named *Lyndie Lou* after the wife of Wilfred Mole. It is on loan to Reefsteamers at Germiston and remains in full operable condition.

OUT OF AFRICA

It was the presence of redundant but relatively new locomotives that provided the third and final development stemming from closure of the two-foot gauge lines. From the mid-1980s numerous Garratts were potentially available for preservation projects overseas. It was not long before they started to leave South Africa in such numbers that Wilfred Mole and colleagues at the Sandstone Steam Railroad became concerned about loss of the country's heritage.

Locomotives spread far and wide and for the first time ever a Garratt could be seen in the USA when NGG13 No 50, built by Hanomag in 1928, went complete with a train of South African passenger carriages to the Hempstead and Northern Railroad in Texas. Two more NGG13s delivered by Hanomag in the same year have returned to their home country of Germany and one of them is on display in Berlin Technical Museum. Despite the gauge difference, two later NGG16s built by Beyer Peacock in 1951 have gone to the Puffing Billy Railway after attracting the fastest fund-raising operation in the line's history.

One of the most surprising destinations has to be an obscure garden centre near Brugg in Switzerland with a two-mile line in its grounds. The Schinznacher Baumschulbahn is not well known further afield, but apart from the challenges of correct pronunciation has two claims to fame. First it is Switzerland's only 60cm gauge steam railway and second its operational motive power includes what in this confined setting is a decidedly large NGG13 Garratt. To say that it looks out of the ordinary among potted plants is an understatement. No 60, now named *Drakensberg*, was obtained in 1985 and restored to working order thirteen years later, but was then seldom steamed as sharp curvature prevented it traversing the complete circuit.

It was perhaps only to be expected that the greatest number of two-foot gauge Garratts should go the UK, where many were returning to the land of their birth. The main driving force initially came from an ambitious but sadly abortive

ABOVE: The landmark reopening of the complete Welsh Highland Railway in 2010 provided a superb setting for the NGG16 locomotives obtained from South Africa. No 138, one of the last batch built by Beyer Peacock in 1958, is making its way through Aberglaslyn Pass in June 2010. (James Waite)

LEFT: Restoration of Cockerill-built No 87 was greatly helped by photographs of it virtually upside down following a spectacular runaway on the Ixopo branch in September 1972. They gave a unique overview of the underside of a Garratt! (Terry Hutson, SA Rail collection)

TOP: The shade of green originally applied to No 138 was not to the taste of all enthusiasts. There was greater praise for the striking deep blue carried by No 87 in April 2010, six months before it participated in the official opening of the Welsh Highland. (James Waite)

LOWER: This low-level shot of No 138 on the Welsh Highland captures the awesome sense of power created by an NGG16 Garratt. It was taken at Pas-y-Nant in August 2003. (Douglas Robinson)

scheme to build a new two-foot gauge railway at Robin Hood's Bay in Yorkshire. Five Garratts were acquired, three of them originally built by Beyer Peacock, one by Hanomag and one by Cockerill. When the scheme collapsed they went to the Exmoor Steam Railway, where three still remained in 2012.

The next development came in 1989 with the controversial decision by the Ffestiniog to restore the complete Welsh Highland Railway from Porthmadog to Dinas, over fifty years after its closure, and then extend it onto Caernarfon, thus completing twenty-five miles of new line. It was soon decided that Garratts from South Africa would be ideal motive power, as they had after all coped well with steep grades and ferocious curves that would be so prevalent on the re-born railway. They would also meet the requirements demanded by sophisticated travellers in the 21st century, who would not tolerate the interminable journeys behind inadequate locomotives that were a crucial factor behind the line closing in 1937. There was every confidence that Garratts would meet the perceived need to haul trains of ten or twelve carriages at speeds up to 25mph.

Two NGG16s, Nos 138 and 143, were therefore purchased in late 1996 from the Alfred County Railway at a cost of £90,000 each. They had both been built as recently as 1958, with No 143 being the historic last steam locomotive to be constructed by Beyer Peacock. It was No 138 that hauled the inaugural train between Caernarfon and Dinas on 13 October 1997, whereas the first working onto the Welsh Highland proper reached Waunfawr on 5 August 2000 behind No 143.

Removed from the locomotives on arrival in North Wales were the seats that adventurously swung outside the cab, reputedly to get adequate doses of fresh air in the summer heat. However, such is the length of a Garratt that they probably had as much to do with the problem of being able to see what was in front when running on long straight stretches of track.

It was already clear that additional Garratts would be required once the line was completed. A third locomotive,

the red-liveried No 140, had been acquired in 1997 for a nominal £100 from a group of German enthusiasts and was under long-term restoration as a volunteer project. The timescale was uncertain and attention therefore turned to No 87, the Cockerill-built Garratt dating from 1937 and still at the Exmoor Steam Railway. In 2005 a budget of some £250,000 was agreed with an anonymous donor for purchase and restoration, and the following year the locomotive was moved to Porthmadog for what many regarded as the largest engineering project undertaken at Boston Lodge works for more than a century. The enormous task included replacement of many fittings that had been stolen when it was abandoned following closure of the Umzinto to Donnybrook line.

On the plus side, the fact that No 87 had suffered a spectacular runaway and derailment in 1972 proved a great help. Photographs of it virtually upside down gave a broad overview of the underside of a Garratt and its complicated pipe runs that is normally impossible to obtain. The massive project made good progress and No 87, still in workshop

grey livery, made history on 23 March 2009 when it became the first steam locomotive to travel from Porthmadog to Dinas since closure of the Welsh Highland seventy-two years earlier. It was in a striking deep blue when it took part in the long-anticipated official opening of the line on 30 October 2010.

A second Garratt at the Exmoor Steam Railway was by now also earmarked for the Welsh Highland, funding of its purchase and restoration having been undertaken by Pete Waterman in July 2009. No 109 was the first NGG16 to be completed by Beyer Peacock in 1939, although a remarkable chain of events that began in Australia has undoubtedly overtaken its historical significance.

BACK TO THE BEGINNING

The working life of K1, the pioneer Garratt delivered to the North-East Dundas tramway in Tasmania back in 1909, ended when the 1930s' depression brought closure of the line in 1932/33. Remarkably, the locomotive was not cut up and lay in the deserted engine shed at Zeehan until 1947. It was then re-purchased by Beyer Peacock and brought back to England to become a historic exhibit at the company's Gorton Foundry, where apprentices gave it a mechanical overhaul. To celebrate its years in service, it came complete with a plaque of Tasmanian Blackwood, carved in the shape of the island and sporting a likeness of K1 in relief.

When the works closed in 1966 this now unique survivor escaped extinction for the second time and was acquired by the Ffestiniog Railway for £1,000 plus £400 transport costs. There were plans to place it in operation, although severe trimming would have been required to fit the cramped loading gauge and happily second thoughts prevailed. Perhaps the mutilation inflicted on *Russell* in the 1930s in an unsuccessful attempt to bring it down to size had not been entirely forgotten.

K1 was displayed in the open at Porthmadog station before being placed on loan to the National Railway Museum for a twenty-year period beginning in 1975. By the mid-1990s re-birth of the Welsh Highland made the world's first Garratt a clear contender to join its younger brethren on a line with a much more generous loading gauge than the Ffestiniog. Restoration – complete with a new boiler and firebox – was begun at Birmingham Railway Museum at Tyseley and then continued at Boston Lodge. K1 made its first test run on the Welsh Highland in February 2005, subsequent modifications including the fitting of steam sanding equipment recovered from scrapped ex-BR Class 08 shunters. It reduced the tendency to slip first noted in 1909 – and it was soon decided to extend this provision to the line's NGG16s.

K1 celebrated its centenary in style at Manchester's Museum of Science & Industry in August 2009. The event attracted 136 other Garratts ranging from models in many scales up to 7¼in miniatures and size-wise culminating in the resident 3ft 6in gauge South African Class GL. It was a poignant moment when K1 was then taken to Gorton and placed in steam only a few feet from where it was built. Former Beyer Peacock employees watching the ceremony were visibly touched.

Restoration of K1 and completion of the Welsh Highland has placed Porthmadog in a unique position. From 2011 it has been possible to see here double Fairlies built more than a century apart, a single Fairlie, the very first Garratt, and the last steam locomotive to be built by Beyer Peacock. The tally was briefly augmented in 2011 by a Mallet from Java, which was visiting the Welsh Highland following its restoration at the Statfold Barn Railway in Staffordshire. Nowhere else in the world can offer so much to those captivated by articulated locomotives.

Bibliography

(Magazines: Btk = Backtrack; FRM = Ffestiniog Railway Magazine; IRR = Industrial Railway Record; LGB = LGB Telegram; NGW = Narrow Gauge World; NIRM = Narrow Gauge & Industrial Railway Modelling Review)

GENERAL

Allen, Peter & Whitehouse, P.B.: *Narrow Gauge Railways of Europe* (Ian Allan, 1959).

Chester, Keith (ed): *Narrow Gauge Steam Locomotives of Russia and the Soviet Union* (Trackside Publications, 2003).

Hilton, George W.: *American Narrow Gauge Railroads* (Stanford University Press, California,1990).

Johnson, Peter: *An Illustrated History of the Welsh Highland Railway* (Oxford Publishing Co, 2002).

Ransom, P.J.G.: *Narrow Gauge Steam: Its origins and world-wide development* (Oxford Publishing Co, 1996).

Rutherford, Michael: 'Bogie Steam Locomotives', in *Btk*, Vol 12, Nos 6 and 7, Jun and Jul 1998, pp 333 - 340, 387 - 393.

Rutherford, Michael: 'Some Reflections on the Narrow Gauge', in *Btk* Vol 21, Nos 4, 5, 6 and 7, Apr to Jul 2007, pp 242 - 249, 311 - 318, 358 - 366, 437 - 445.

Whitehouse, P.B. & Allen, Peter: *Round the World on the Narrow Gauge* (Ian Allan, 1966).

Wiener, Lionel: *Articulated Locomotives* (Richard R Smith, New York, 1930).

Wolf, Adolph Hungry: *Narrow Gauge Railway Scenes* (Canadian Caboose Press, Skookumchuck, B.C., 1992).

Website:
Dickinson, Rob: *Articulated Steam Locomotives of the World* (www.internationalsteam.co.uk/articulateds)

1. THE GENIUS OF ROBERT FAIRLIE

Abbott, Rowland A.S.: *The Fairlie Locomotive*, David & Charles, 1970.

Binns, Donald: *Fairlie Articulated Locomotives on the American Continent*, Trackside Publications, 2001.
Binns, Donald; *The Nitrate Railways Company Ltd,* Trackside Publications, 2007.

Boyd, James I.C.: *The Festiniog Railway*, 2 vols, Oakwood Press, 1975.

Clarke, Rod: *Narrow Gauge through the Bush: Ontario's Toronto Grey & Bruce and Toronto & Nipissing Railways*, Rod Clarke and Ralph Beaumont, Ontario, 2007.

Clover, John: 'Josephine of Dunedin', in *NGW* No 27, Jul 2003, pp 45 - 47.

Davies, W.J.K.: *Narrow Gauge Railways of Portugal* (Plateway Press, 1998).

Dobson, John: 'Fairlie Rare', in *FRM* No 210, Autumn 2010, pp 425 - 429.

Graham, Adrian: 'Steam, Bogies and Passion', in *Btk* Vol 24, No 9, Sep 2010, pp 541 - 543.

Gwyn, Dafydd: '*The Little Wonder Trials Revisited*', in FRM No 212, Spring 2011, pp 559 - 565.

Holmes, Paul: 'It's Little Wonder', in *NIRM*, No 84, Oct 2010, pp 160 - 167.

Horton, Philip: 'A Very Peculiar Locomotive' [Péchot-Bourdon], in *NGW* No 38, Mar/Apr 1905, pp 20 - 25.

Johnson, Peter: *An Illustrated History of the Festiniog Railway 1832 - 1954* (Oxford Publishing Co, 2007).

Neale, Andrew: 'The Locomotive Builders: Avonside Engine Company', in *NGW* No 52, Jul/Aug 2007, pp 18 - 21.

Neale, Andrew: 'The Locomotive Builders: George England & Co', in *NGW* No 57, May/Jun 2008, pp 18 - 19.

Wilson, Andrew: 'Taliesin – A Singular Fairlie', in *NGW* No 17, Feb/Mar 2002, pp 26 - 29.

Wilson, Andrew: 'The Fairlie Locomotives of the Festiniog Railway', in *Btk*, Vol 13, No 2, Feb 1999, pp 62 - 70.

Wilson, Andrew: 'Fairlie Spectacular', in *NGW* No 2, June 1999, pp 21 - 24.

2. MALLET DOMINANCE

Badcock, Peter: 'Steam among the Camels' (Eritrea), in *NGW* No 13, Jun/Jul 2001, pp 7 - 13.

Beebe, Lucius & Clegg, Charles, *Narrow Gauge in the Rockies* [pp 176 - 189: Uintah] (Howell-North, California, 1958).

Bender, Henry E.: *Uintah Railway: The Gilsonite Route* (Heimburger House, Illinois, 1970).

Best, Gerald M.: *Mexican Narrow Gauge* (Howell-North, California, 1968).

Chester, Keith: *The Narrow Gauge Railways of Bosnia-Hercegovina* (Frank Stenvalls Förlag, Malmö, 2006).

Chester, Keith: *Bosnia-Hercegovina: Narrow Gauge Album* (Frank Stenvalls, 2010).

Davies, W.J.K.: *Minor Railways of France* (Plateway Press, 2000).

Davies, W.J.K.: 'The Decauville Railways', in *NGW* No 9, Oct/Nov 2000, pp 37 - 42; No 10, Dec 2000/Jan 2001, pp 36 - 40.

Davies, W.J.K.: *A Contrast in Islands: The Narrow Gauge Railways of Corsica and Sardinia* (Plateway Press, 2002).

Durrant, A.E.: *The Mallet Locomotive* (David & Charles, 1974).

Gravett, Gordon: *Réseau Bretton: A Rail Network in Brittany* (Oakwood Press, 1999).

Horton, Philip J & Bell, Leslie M.: 'Belgrade to Dubrovnik', in *NGW* No 24, Feb/Mar 2003, pp 7 - 14; No 25, Apr/May 2003, pp 32 - 35.

Kalla-Bishop, P.M.: *Mediterranean Island Railways* (David & Charles, 1970).

Martin, Terry: 'The Ace of Harz', in *NGW* No 30, Nov/Dec 2003, pp 30 - 35; No 31, Jan/Feb 2004, pp 26 - 31.

Organ, John: *Vivarais Narrow Gauge* (Middleton Press, 1999).

Organ, John: *Northern France Narrow Gauge* (Middleton Press, 2002).

Organ, John: *North East German Narrow Gauge* (Middleton Press, 2004).

Organ, John: *Portugal Narrow Gauge* (Middleton Press, 2010).

Rozendaal, Jack: *Steam and Rail in Indonesia* (Locomotives International, 2000).

Small, Charles S.: *Far Wheels: A Railroad Safari* [pp 14 - 27: Eritrea] (Cleaver-Hume Press, 1959).

Waite, James: 'Swedish Splendour' [Jädraas-Tallas Järnvag], in *NGW* No 52, Jul/Aug 2007, pp 26 - 28.

Waite, James: 'Last Train on the Vivarais?', in *NGW* No 57, Jul/Aug 2008, pp 26 - 28.

Waters, Paul E.: *The Donna Thereza Christina Railway* (P.E. Waters & Associates, 1985).

3. WEIRD AND WONDERFUL

Chester, Keith: *East European Narrow Gauge* (Channel View Publications, 1995).

Chester, Keith: 'Steam in the Waldviertel', in *NGW* No 13, June/July 2001, pp 26 - 29.

Drummond, Ian: 'Getting the Gold from Gilpin', in *NGW* No 44, Mar/Apr 2006, pp 13 - 15.

Eatwell, David: 'The Sweetest Steam' [Java], in *NGW* No 11, Feb/Mar 2011, pp 29 - 35.

Koch, Michael: '*Steam and Thunder in the Timber: Saga of the Forest Railroads*' (World Press, Denver, 1979).

Labbe, John T. & Goe, Vernon: *Railroads in the Woods* (Oso Publishing, Arlington, Washington, 1995).

Mahoney, Paul: *The Era of the Bush Tram in New Zealand* (IPL Books, New Zealand, 1998).

Martin, Terry: 'Klose Encounters in Yugoslavia', in *NGW* No 18, Apr/May 2002, pp 11 - 16.

Organ, John: *Northern Spain Narrow Gauge* (Middleton Press, 2010).

Organ, John: *Romania and Bulgaria Narrow Gauge* (Middleton Press, 2008).

Reilly, Michael and Edmonds, Tim: 'In Search of Shays', in *NGW* No 35, Sep/Oct 2004, pp 26 - 30.

Scherb, Jeff: 'Motive Power from Matheran', in *NGW* No 59, Sep/Oct 2008, pp 22 - 26.

Smithers, Mark: *Sir Arthur Heywood and the Fifteen Inch Gauge Railway* (Plateway Press, 1995).

Turner, Terry: 'The Resita from Romania', in *NGW* No 55, Jan/Feb 2008, pp 6 - 9.

4. MEYERS OF MANY KINDS

Baker, Allan C.: 'Bagnall Articulated Locomotives', in *IRR* No 16, Dec 1967, pp 121 - 131.

Binns, Donald: *Kitson Meyer Articulated Locomotives* (Locomotives International, 1993).

Binns, Donald: *The Anglo-Chilean Nitrate & Railway Company* (Trackside Publications, 1995).

Binns, Donald & Koch, Günter: *Meyer Articulated Locomotives* (Trackside Publications, 1997).

Binns, Donald & Middleton, Harold A.: *The Taltal Railway* (Trackside Publications, 2010).

Davies, W.J.K.: 'Narrow Gauge in Saxony', in *NGW* Nos 66 and 68, Nov/Dec 2009 and Mar/Apr 2010, pp 18 - 22 and 31 -36.

Fawcett, Brian: *Railways of the Andes* (Plateway Press, 1997).

Joy, David: 'Rack and Ruin' [the Transandine], in *NGW* No 17, Feb/Mar 2002, pp 7 - 12.

Marshall, John: *Metre Gauge Railways in South and East Switzerland* (David & Charles, 1974).

Neale, Andrew: 'Paper, Pulp and Diamond Stacks' [Bowaters', Sittingbourne], in *NGW* No 19, Jun/Jul 2002, pp 34 - 39.

Rutherford, Michael: 'What's in a name? – Kitson's of Leeds', in *Btk* Vol 12, No 2, Feb 1998, pp 97 - 103.

Turner, J.M. & Ellis, R.F.: *The Antofagasta (Chili) & Bolivia Railway* (Locomotives International, 1992).

Waite, James: 'Out with the Snowblower', in *NGW* No 63, May/Jun 2009, pp 12 - 13.

Wyss, Mark: 'Switzerland's Spectacular Berninabahn', in *LGB*, Summer 1994, pp 19 - 25.

5. GARRATT SUPREMACY

Ballantyne, Hugh: *South African Two-Foot Gauge* (Middleton Press, 2009).

Brinkman, Bryan & Payling, David: 'South Africa's premier line', in *NGW* No 36 (Nov/Dec 2004, pp 10 - 15.

Davies, Steve: 'Sheer Graft in Sierra Leone', in *NGW* No 41, Sep/Oct 2005, pp 30 - 31.

Durrant, A.E.: *Garratt Locomotives of the World* (David & Charles, 1981).

Durrant, A.E.: *The Smoke that Thunders* [Rhodesia Railways locomotives] (African Publishing Group, Zimbabwe, 1997).

Durrant, A.E.; Jorgensen, A.A.; & Lewis, C.P.: *Steam in Africa* (Hamlyn, 1981).

Hills, Richard L. & Patrick, D.: *Beyer, Peacock – locomotive builders to the world* (Venture publications, 1998).

Hills, Richard L.: *The Origins of the Garratt Locomotive* (Plateway Press, 2000).

McAllum, Steve; Payling, David; & Whalley, John: 'Restoring NG87', in *NGW* No 62, Mar/Apr 2009. pp 6 - 10.

MacKay, Colin: 'Puffing Billy's G42', in *NGW* No 52, Jul/Aug 2007, pp 8 - 10.

Martin, Terry: *Halfway to Heaven – Darjeeling and its remarkable railway* (Rail Romances, 2000).

Moir, Sydney: *Twenty-Four Inches Apart: The two-foot gauge railways of the Cape of Good Hope* (Janus Publishing, Benoryn, South Africa, 1981).

Mole, Wilfred: 'Sandstone: A World-Class Experience', in *NGW* No 42, Nov/Dec 2005, pp 6 - 10.

Neale, Andrew: 'The Locomotive Builders: Beyer, Peacock & Co Ltd', in *NGW* No 54, Nov/Dec 2007, pp 16 - 22.

Parrott, Chris: 'Deepest South' [Tierra del Fuego], in *NGW* No 25, Apr 2003, pp 20 - 23.

Paxton, Leith & Payling, David: *Narrow Gauge Super Power: Limestone to Port Elizabeth* (Narrow Gauge Railway Society, 2006).

Richardson, Dave & Molyneux-Killik, Joanna: *The Sandstone Steam Railroad* (Sandstone Heritage Trust, Bryanston, South Africa, 2006).

Index

Garratts at rest in Bulawayo shed, Rhodesia, February 1978. (James Waite)

PEOPLE

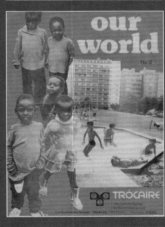

BRAND NEW RETRO

Brian McMahon

First published in 2015 by Liberties Press
140 Terenure Road North | Terenure | Dublin 6W
T: +353 (1) 905-6072 | W: libertiespress.com | E: info@libertiespress.com

Trade enquiries to Gill & Macmillan Distribution
Hume Avenue | Park West | Dublin 12
T: +353 (1) 500 9534 | F: +353 (1) 500 9595 | E: sales@gillmacmillan.ie

Distributed in the United Kingdom by Turnaround Publisher Services
Unit 3 | Olympia Trading Estate | Coburg Road | London N22 6TZ
T: +44 (0) 20 8829 3000 | E: orders@turnaround-uk.com

Distributed in the United States by
Casemate-IPM | 22841 Quicksilver Dr | Dulles, VA 20166
T: +1 (703) 661-1586 | F: +1 (703) 661-1547 | E: ipmmail@presswarehouse. com

ISBN: 978-1-910742-17-4
2 4 6 8 10 9 7 5 3 1

A CIP record for this title is available from the British Library.

Designed by Joe Collins.

Cover photography Micky Kelleher & Johanne Betty Conlon from pixelated.ie

Introduction

The roots of Brand New Retro go back to 1978. Inspired by the DIY ethos of punk, my brother Eamonn and I produced a fanzine called 'Too Late', which offered a humorous and irreverent look at life in Dundalk for the young and single.

Punk also made me realise that you didn't have to be a great musician to make great music. So in 1977 I took up bass guitar. One of the groups I played with appeared on the same bill as U2 at the Dandelion Market whilst another won RTE TV's Youngline Group of The Year.

When my father died suddenly in March 2011, I went into the attic of our family home to retrieve old photographs. While there, I discovered lots of my own bits and pieces, like magazines and photos, from 30 years earlier. With these, I could create a permanent digital record of our early foray into publishing and my musical adventures. As I scanned my own personal stuff, I realised that loads of other interesting Irish content from my collection had no online presence. And so began my blog, Brandnewretro.ie, which in turn led to a continuing personal mission to hunt down more and more material.

I had unearthed a vast collection of photos, adverts and articles with some stunning content from the 1960s. These were my childhood years, a time of sustained economic expansion in Ireland when ordinary people like my parents, now with disposable income, could afford exciting consumer goods such as televisions, records, motor bikes, fashions and more. The magazines, and the ads in them, captured the new spirit of consumerism.

The articles and adverts from this era that I posted on Brandnewretro.ie seemed to amuse younger followers and resonate with older ones. Visitors enjoyed the fact that we only included Irish content previously unavailable online. And in true Irish fashion, people began talking. Brandnewretro.ie flourished and we won multiple web and blog awards.

I've now teamed up with my designer pal, Joe Collins, to bring you a selection of these scans in the format in which they first appeared, and the format in which they are best appreciated. Print.

We hope you enjoy the memories.

Brian McMahon

For my wonderful wife Sinead

Acknowledgments

Words cannot express my gratitude to the hard working, dynamic and very creative Joe Collins for collaborating with me on this book.

Thank you to everyone who kindly provided permission to allow their content to be reproduced. I'd like to specifically thank the Coughlan family for use of New Spotlight content and to its contributors Pat Egan, Roy Esmonde, Kevin O'Brien and Mark Nolan.

To those magazines, still going strong after all these years, I'd like to thank the editorial teams at Woman's Way, the RTE Guide, Hot Press and Mojo.

To Sinead Kenny, for her inspiring support and help with curating and digitising content.

To my children Oisin, Maisie and Isabella for travelling with me to every market and secondhand shop in Ireland on my search to find old Irish magazines. You are tremendous!

To my brother Eamonn for donating his collection of magazines to the Brand New Retro vault and for his editorial input to the book.

To my other siblings Sinead, Orla, Conor and Niamh for donating content and allowing me first dibs on our parents collection of magazines and print ephemera.

To Audrey Farrelly for her never-ending support and Louis for his sublime footballing skills.

To Micky Kelleher and Betty Joanne Conlon of pixelated.ie for the cover photography.

To Chris Smith and Fran Fox for use of their newspaper stand on O'Connell Street, Dublin.

Thanks to the Cawley Nea\TBWA crew, particularly Natacha, Marty, Adam, David, Dylan and Corina. To Kevin Murray, Chris Williamson, Brendan Delany, Gerry Hampson, Gerard Crowley, Maria Dickenson, Gemma Barry, Jim Fitzpatrick, Tony Clayton-Lea, Eoin McHugh, Arthur Mathews, Jude Carr, Pete Price, Louise Coughlan, Catherine Lee, Eimer Murphy, Jake Walsh, Enda Murray, John King, Áine Toner, Garry O'Neill, Simon O'Connor, Conor McMahon and the Outlaw and Crackmice crews for all their help.

And to Sean O'Keeffe at Liberties Press.

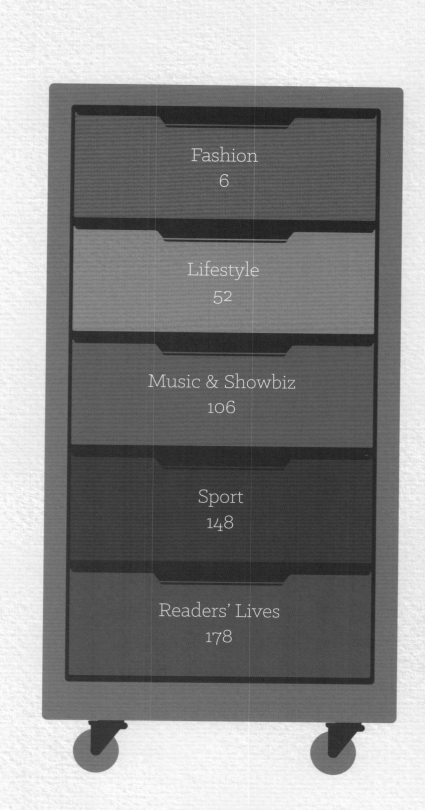

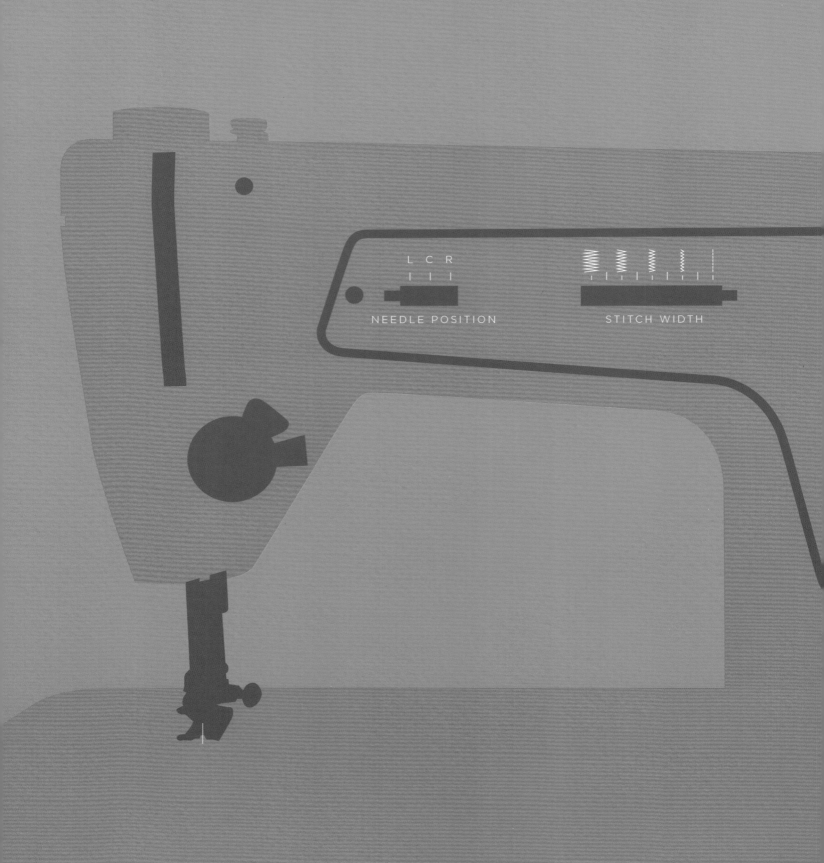

Fashion

'Now, isn't it just as well I kept all of these', said my mother glancing over at my laptop at a set of photos that I had scanned from her collection of old fashion magazines.

How right she was!

I still stop and marvel at how fresh and beautiful these 1960s Irish fashion photos look today and how, over time, they have acquired an almost surreal quality.

The attraction of a still photo is that it allows your imagination to conjure up all kinds of scenarios. I can't but wonder what the people involved are up to now. I recently said to my wife, 'You know that woman we see at the bus stop going to the post office, well she was young in the 1960s and she could be one of the Irish models in those shoots'. 'No. I don't think so', she replied. 'All those 1960s models married Aer Lingus pilots and are living comfortably today on Dublin's Southside'.

Wool is Wild
Promotional Brochure 1969
This Page: Dress by Glen Abbey, carpet by Youghal, sofa by Jersey.

'In a tame world, wool is wild.' So said the blurb of this 8 page fashion brochure
shot in the Wicklow mountains promoting Pure New Wool and Irish designs.

Left: Suit by ROK Styles, carpet by Navan,
suite by O'Dea
Below: Dress by Emor
Middle right: Coat by Barry McDonald
Bottom right: Bedspread by Robert Eadie
Bottom left: Dress by Donald Davis, rug by
Crock Of Gold

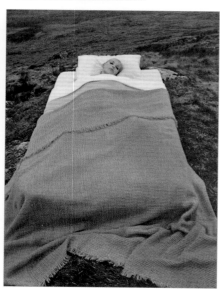

FASHION FREAK OUT

PHILIP LYNOTT, leader of Thin Lizzy joined dancer and model, Niki Adrian, for this week's fashion session in Dublin's Drury Street.

Smock dress in beige khaki is button through with large collar. The bodice and pockets are smocked with coloured thread. Also available with matching hot pants.

Here Niki's in a green white jersey cotton maxi dress with short sleeves and high neck-line buttoned at the front.

Phil Lynott

New Spotlight 1971

Phil Lynott with Niki Adrian modelling clothes from Dublin's Drury Lane Boutique. Photos by Roy Esmonde.

Phil Lynott

New Spotlight 1972

Phil is with Pat Harrison who is modelling mini dresses
from Cinderella Boutique, Mary Street, Dublin 1
Photos by Roy Esmonde

Alias Tom Promotion with Johnny Logan
Success 1984

Shot on location at 'a house in Killiney'
to promote the launch of the new look
Alias Tom Menswear in Duke Lane,
Dublin 2.
Editor in chief of Success magazine was
Noelle Campbell Sharp, Neil Campbell
Sharp responsible for photography.

Plane girls' guide to fancy flying

New Look for Aer Lingus Girls
Woman's Way 1970

Aer Lingus introduce new uniform by Irish fashion designer Henry Digby Morton.

AN air hostess hands out little Cellophane lunches, pours tea and calls you "Madam"; she soothes babies, braves thunderstorms and deals with airsick passengers who need not only little paper bags, but also assurance that they will set foot on solid ground again. She must smile too and considering all this it might seem incredible that an aura of glamour has attached itself to her demanding career.

Consider the other side of the picture, however. An air hostess represents her country. She serves out first impressions of Ireland along with the boiled sweets and during a 3-hour flight there is nothing much to think about except whether or not the Irish crew measures up to the brochures' promises of friendly people and beautiful girls.

When viewed in this light, the designing of a new Aer Lingus uniform takes on a kind of breathless significance.

Top couturier Digby Morton has handled this tricky diplomatic mission with a great deal of flair and expertise. Shunning the old military look which has haunted post-war airline wardrobes like a Vera Lynn song, he has planned for an elegant outline combining flattery with commonsense. A design competition held in the Aer Lingus corps yielded a number of clever, usable ideas which have been incorporated into the finished outfit.

"Please," the girls asked, "forget the old skirt and blouse routine." This twosome was becoming tedious and tended to part company when the wearer was bending or stretching. The answer is a slim, clean-cut pinafore in washable, crease-resistant Courtelle twill worn over a short-sleeved drip-dry Terylene lawn blouse with neat turtle neck. This basic combination plus a well cut jacket and warm topcoat will be happy anywhere from Yokohama to the Yukon.

THE colour scheme is cool and exciting, featuring a true emerald green contrasted with St. Patrick's blue — a fresh pale blue which shows off the green to perfection. Blue is used for the blouse and also for the tabard, a sensible steal from "Richard II" fashioned in non-crease, liquid-repellant cotton twill for protection while serving food.

Lighter green saddle-stitching outlines the seaming on coat, jacket and pinafore, emphasising the smooth trim line which gets a top-to-toe look with sheer dark green tights and emerald casual shoes with medium heels. The handbag is green leather and the overnight holdall is designed in green canvas and PVC while gloves are in a neutral sand colour.

The new Aer Lingus hat is inspired. Morton's colleague Frank Saunders dreamed up a jaunty, feminine style with a squared-off front peak and flat rainproof PVC top in St. Patrick's blue and two neat bands which come down to fasten beneath the chin in windy weather.

The hemline stops well above the knee, but there's a 2¼" turn-up. That should suffice unless the maxi engulfs us completely within the next four years, which is the time-lapse reckoned to be the average life of any uniform design.

New look for Aer Lingus girls

ONE MOD DAY

It started so casually. Hi, he said.

Why not, said my bird - brained buddy. She a l w a y s gets involved.

So we had a drink while we planned our grand strategy. Not too g r a n d, they warned us sadly. For these latterday cinderellas had but fleeting hours to spend . . .

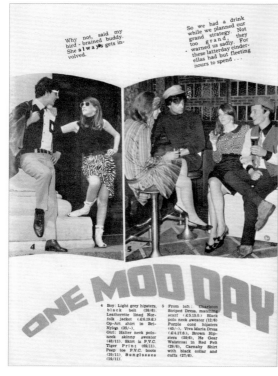

ONE MOD DAY

4 Boy: Light grey hipsters, black belt (59/6). Leatherette lined Norfolk jacket (£6.19.6.) Op-Art shirt in Bri-Nylon (35/-).
Girl: Halter neck polo-neck skinny sweater (45/11). Skirt is P.V.C. Tiger Print (69/11). Peep toe P.V.C. boots (39/11). Sunglasses (19/11).

5 From left: Charlston Striped Dress, matching scarf (£5.15.0.) Black polo neck sweater (12/6) Purple cord hipsters (45/-), Viva Maria Dress (£4.17.6.), Brown Hipsters (59/6). He Gear Waistcoat in Red Felt (29/6), Carnaby Shirt with black collar and cuffs (27/6).

I was all for giving him the deep cool, but next thing I knew his friend was showing mine the sights . . .

How about kicking this town around some, his friend asked me.

1 She's wearing a lovely brown check worsted trouser suit (£11.4.0). The boy has purple cord hipsters with white belt (45/-) He Gear waistcoat in red (29/6) and black polo neck sweater (12/6). His Donovan hat costs 7/6.

2 The lad in the left is wearing a Carnaby Shirt with black collar (27/6), Op-Art Tie (8/6), Camel Jacket with patch pockets and brass buttons (£7.19.6) and brown hipsters (59/6). The girl on the left is flaunting a skinny sweater (48/11) and white She Gear trousers (49/11). Sunglasses (19/11).

3 He's wearing bell bottom Hipsters with matching belt (79/6), and pink casual shirt (39/6). She has a lovely linen play suit (£4.4.0) French sunglasses (7/11) and crochet wool beret (8/11).

MORE OVERLEAF

As for Liz . . . she was falling too.

I'll be back again next week, he said. Will you meet me? Yes, I said.

And then, before we knew it, it was all over, our wonderful Mod mad day in Dublin . . .

6 The girl is wearing a beige skinny sweater with a Cord quilted skirt (49/11 and 59/11).

7 She is wearing a lovely Harlequin two piece crepe suit (£5.17.6.)

IN DUBLIN

One Mod Day in Dublin
Miss 1966

Fashion shoot story set in Dublin city centre with all the clothes from the newly opened She Gear and He Gear boutiques in Roches Stores, Henry Street, Dublin 1.

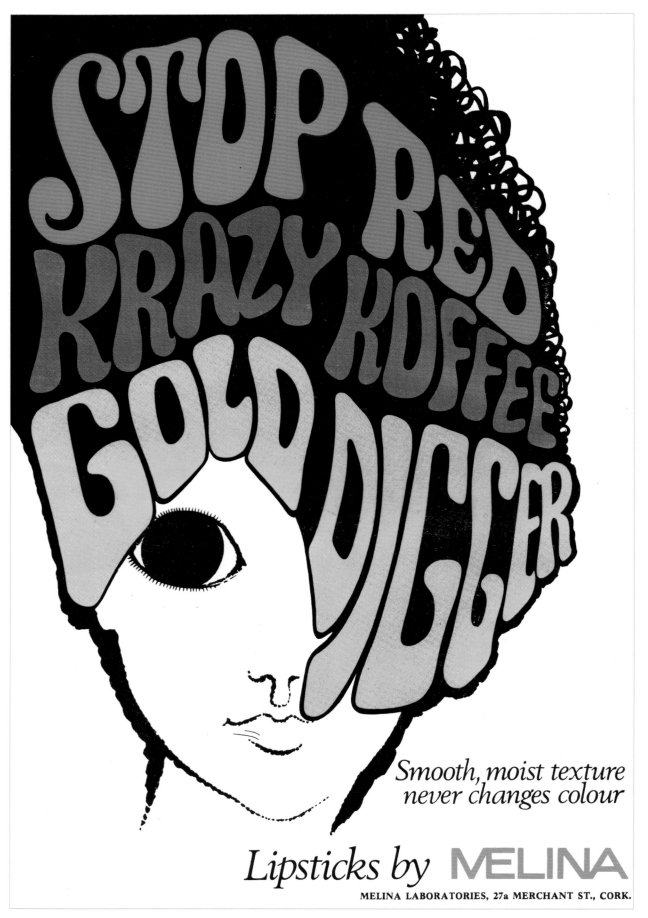

STOP RED
KRAZY RED
KOFFEE
GOLD DIGGER

Smooth, moist texture
never changes colour

Lipsticks by **MELINA**

MELINA LABORATORIES, 27a MERCHANT ST., CORK.

Advert for Melina Lipstick

Woman's Way 1969

Made at Melina Laboratories, Merchant Street, Cork.

Living In Depth:
The profile is Pure New Wool.

Soft-surface Sunbeam sweaters for men. With the deep, living, breathing texture of pure new wool. Style T778: Shetland Jumper, two-colour jacquard front in many colourful combinations. Approx. £3.30. Style T729: Shetland Cardigan in a shoal of natural colours. Approx. £3.75. Style K352: Lambswool polo sweater, long sleeves, in white, thistle, redwood and other versatile shades. Approx. £3.35. All in sizes 38-44.

And for skimming over land, the wild, streamlined beauty of an Opel Manta. A fast-back for five, with a "take everything" boot. Power brakes, four headlights, flow-through ventilation, fully reclining seats. And up to 30 mpg. £1,465. De-Luxe £1,527. Rallye £1,720, (1600 cc. 'S' engine £43 extra). 1900 cc. 'S' engine £81 extra).

Photographed at Bulloch Harbour.

Outlook Luxurious:
With the rich potential of living wool.

From the wealth of qualities which live in pure new wool, Brian Tucker evokes sculptured elegance in worsted wool double jersey, crisp style in wool gaberdine. Style 190: Wedgewood blue jersey coat and pants. Also in brown, pink, navy, aubergine. £24.00. Style 257: Gaberdine Battle Jacket and skirt, with pleat back and front, contrasting stitching. In navy blue, beige, black, brown. £25.25.

Photographed at Cloghran Stud.

Brian Tucker
Dublin

Match Play:
The winners are always Pure New Wool.

Pure new wool swings in colour, matched with the easy styling of these Danus Casual outfits. Jackets: top-scoring Glencheck plaid designs, in red and blue basic shades. Approx. £15.75. Partnered by smooth fitting, slightly flared trousers; with dark blue herringbone stripe, and yellow checked patterns. Approx. £5.75.

Superb executive motoring—the impressive Opel Commodore. 4-door, 2.5 litre, 6 cylinders. Safety and luxury features include radial tyres, power steering and brakes, vinyl roof, fully reclining seats, electrically heated rear window and sliding sun roof. £2,159. (automatic trans. £194 extra).

Photographed at Delgany Golf Club.

Báid agus Báinín:
That's living in any language.

"Gaeltarra" branch Aran's traditional, unswerving bainin is new, high-fashion styles — Safari Jackets", but anti fort, machine knit or custom handknit in pure new wool. Live our rough weather and love it in these new classics. Prices ranging from £7.50 to £15.00.

*Safari Jackets take like ducks to water—they're washable, shrink resistant, pure new wool.

Up on shore, take the wheel of an Opel Commodore Coupé and rule the high road—with 2,500 cc. engine, 6 cylinders, power steering and brakes, radial tyres. Electrically heated rear window, vinyl roof with sliding panel for sun. Fully reclining seats. Price: £2,197 (automatic trans. £194 extra).

Photographed at Howth Pier.

GAELTARRA

Tomorrow's Scene Stealer:
Just Pure New Wool and an Opel.

Wherever the action is, classic Tailteann sweaters in pure new wool are always in focus. For people on the move or relaxing : Style NL35: Casual lambswool shirt in sniperic blue. Sizes 38-44. Approx. £4.20. Style TL3: Ladies turtle neck in super soft Geelong lambswool. Sizes 36-42. Approx. £3.15. Both in a wide range of vibrate shades. Like all Tailteann sweaters in pure new wool, they're washable and shrink-resistant.

Look out for the Opel Ascona 16—another attention-grabber. Way ahead in design with roomy interior. 10.8 cu. ft. boot, fully reclining seats, flow-through ventilation. Power and safety with 1600 cc. engine, front wheel discs, emergency flasher system. £1,547. De-Luxe £1,629 (1600 cc 'S' engine £43 extra).

Photographed at the Delgany Inn.

Tailteann

Pure New Wool and Opel Cars
Promotional Brochure 1971

A mini 8 page brochure promoting Pure New Wool and Opel Cars shot at various locations close to Dublin.

Top left: Sunbeam tops and the Manta at Bulloch Harbour, Dalkey.
Left: Brian Tucker coats and the GT at Cloghran Stud.
Middle right: Gaeltarra Aran and the Commodore Coupé at Howth.
Bottom right: Tailtean knitwear and the Ascona 16 at Delgany Inn, Wicklow.
Bottom left: Danus jackets and trousers and the Commodore 4 door at Delgany Golf Club.

Top men want
leisure shirts for
modern living
with real easy-care
comfort and style..
THEY ARE RIGHT
TO INSIST ON
BRI-NYLON

BUY IRISH

BRi NYLON

SMYCO LEISURE SHIRT IN BRI-NYLON
Available in a variety of shades at all leading stores.
Approx. Retail Price 29/11 — 31/11 (according to size).

BRI-NYLON means nylon yarn or fibre which has been produced by ICI Fibres Limited and has been used to their satisfaction
for approved merchandise. *Bri is a registered trade mark and is not authorised for use except in this manner.

Top men want
leisure shirts for
modern living
with real easy-care
comfort and style..
THEY ARE RIGHT
TO INSIST ON
BRI-NYLON

BUY IRISH

BRi NYLON

VEDONEIRE LEISURE SHIRT IN BRI-NYLON
Available in Coke, Burgundy, Gun Metal, Moss Green, Bronze, Rust, White, Stone and
County Green at all leading stores. Retail price approx: 39/11.

BRI-NYLON means nylon yarn or fibre which has been produced by ICI Fibres Limited and has been used to their satisfaction
for approved merchandise. *Bri is a registered trade mark and is not authorised for use except in this manner.

Various Adverts for Men's Shirts
Woman's Way 1966
Top left and right: BriNylon
Bottom left: Sunbeam
Bottom right: National by McCarter
& Co, Buncrana, Co. Donegal

KNITWEAR OR JERSEYWEAR?

Smooth, sophisticated sweater
shirt in Botany wool. Black,
or a choice of 5 up-to-the-
minute shades. About 49/11.

Handsome smoking jacket in
wool jersey. Diagonal brick
design or in crisp checks. 5 smart
colour combinations. About 72/6.

sunbeam brings colour to life

Choose from the full range of Sunbeam Knitwear and Jerseywear now in the shops.

30

FOLLOW THE SUN

DEANTA IN EIRINN

Cool, crisp cotton is the perfect
foil for warm days and rigorous
exercise. Launders perfectly, keeps
its shape and colours, and lasts and
lasts and lasts. National, long famous for
fine knitwear, this season offers a variety
of shades, patterns and sizes in cotton
sports shirts both for men and boys.
They're at all leading stores.

national

W. P. McCarter & Co. Ltd., Buncrana, Co. Donegal.

WILSON HARTNELL

in Fashion

Fashion, like food, sex or drink comes down to whatever turns you on. And it was with this in mind that we decided to ignore the staged fashion pictures in the studio and sent photographer Tom Collins into the streets to see what the man in the street was wearing. Tom made fashionable Grafton Street his headquarters and snapped the strutting sartorial gents as they passed. And what he came up with is a lot more down to earth than the space age moon suits normally featured in the glossy magazine fashion pages.

'Barney didn't give either his age or his surname. But he did tell us that he was a stripper. A pine-stripper. And that means he can take the paints and varnish off old dressers and antique furniture and restore them to their original and natural wood finishes.

Barney buys all his clothes in Ireland and has about 10 suits and 40 shirts. He has casual clothes for what he considers suitable occasions but he prefers what he calls dressing up. And that means suits and those are tailored for him by Dublin tailor Paddy Sweeney.

In our photo Barney is wearing a check lounge suit, with a button down oxford shirt set off by a bright pink tie.'

'23 year old Ephrem Santiago adds a dash of cosmopolitan colour to our capital city. He was born in Nairobi and came to Ireland to study at Rockwell and Trinity College. Ephrem likes to dress flamboyantly and hates the dull greys and navy blues that still dominate Irish Male Fashion. He lives up to his ideas and owns — he reckons — 60 shirts, 14 pairs of shoes and boots and about 18 different outfits.

Ephrem is pictured wearing a lightweight linen jacket that costs £15.00 from Jeffsons Boutique in Duke Lane. The shoes would set you back £7.95 at Couples and the white satin shirt with the Fred Astaire print is a snip at £10.95.'

'Michael Reilly is a hairdresser who learned his art at the famous Vidal Sasoon saloon in London. He works at the Witches Hut Salon in Dublin now and seems to be 'making out'. His fashionable frame can be seen zooming around Grafton Street in his M.G.B.

But being 'artistic director' with the Witches Hut means he can keep in touch with international trends when he visits shows in London, Paris and Rome.

His dressing habits are casual. And he buys most of his clothes in London. In our picture he is wearing a leather jerkin bought in London for £35.00 and a blue and white print cheese cloth shirt from Couples, Duke Lane that set him back £4.95.'

Dublin Street Fashion
Man Alive 1974

Page one of a two page feature from Man Alive. Keep an eye out for hairdresser Michael Reilly, above right with Trinity College in background, later in this chapter.
Photos by Tom Collins.

Adverts for Dingos Jeans
New Spotlight 1970

Dingos Jeans were made in Co. Louth and competed with the likes of Wrangler, Lee and Levi's in the burgeoning Irish jeans market in the early 1970s.

Dicke Rock

New Spotlight 1969

Dickie is dressed by Louis Copeland while Pam Conway models outfits from both the Topaz and Drury Lane boutiques. The Jaguar E-type, Honda, Rover and BMW cars were supplied by Murphy & Gunn.

Men's Fashion in Dublin

Executive 1979

This session shot in and around Grafton Street 'shows what the well-heeled man about town will be wearing this Autumn… with emphasis on a casual, unstructured look, with muted colours dominating'. Clothes from FX Kelly, Brown Thomas & Switzers. Pints from Davy Byrne's pub.

Men's Fashion in Dublin
Executive 1979

Shot at The Hole in the Wall, Dublin 7 with clothes from the shops of Michael Barrie, 'Frends' and John Taylor. Shoes from Da Vinci. White socks models' own. Photos by Paul Harvey.

Adverts for Stockings and Tights

Right: Ballito at Arnotts, Woman's
Choice 1969
Below: Tendrelle, Woman's Way 1967
Bottom left: Bear Brand, Miss 1966

'Tendrelle' stockings are here!

WONDER NYLON BRINGS NEW GLAMOUR TO LEGS
Every woman knows that it is only when stockings
really fit that legs look really attractive.
Only Tendrelle gives you glamour fit and value
because ICI invented Tendrelle—the new 'Wonder Nylon
to make stockings that tenderly fit you.
Tendrelle are sheer, soft super nylons that won't wrinkle,
crease or sag—so step out in style in Tendrelle BRI-NYLON.
Price about 4/11 per pair—Such Good Value !

ICI 'Tendrelle' — A NEW BRI NYLON YARN

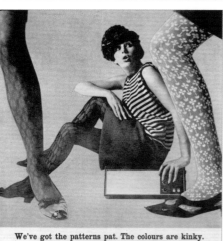

**We've got the patterns pat. The colours are kinky.
Who isn't wearing them? Grandma.**

She seems to be the only one. Everybody else goes for them in
a big way. Bear Brand Pot-o'-Plant, Daisy-Chain and Conifer
patterns, in champagne, brown velvet, tree green, navy,
black, white, in sizes to fit everyone: 8/11. Buy a pair for yourself, a pair for Grandma. Time she followed the trend, too.

BEAR BRAND

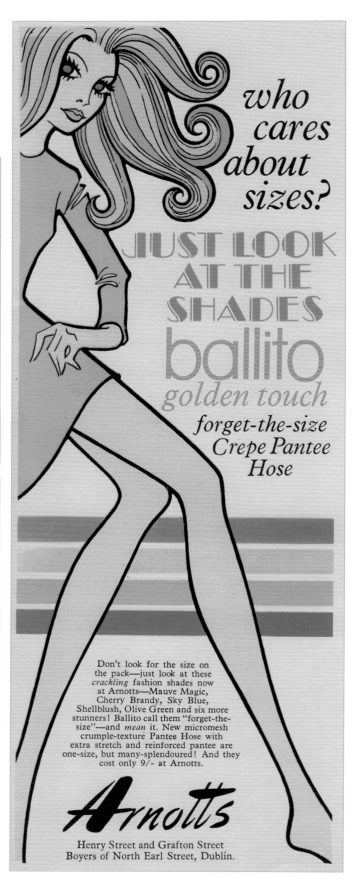

who cares about sizes?

JUST LOOK AT THE SHADES

ballito

golden touch

*forget-the-size
Crepe Pantee
Hose*

Don't look for the size on
the pack—just look at these
crackling fashion shades now
at Arnotts—Mauve Magic,
Cherry Brandy, Sky Blue,
Shellblush, Olive Green and six more
stunners! Ballito call them "forget-the-
size"—and *mean* it. New micromesh
crumple-texture Pantee Hose with
extra stretch and reinforced pantee are
one-size, but many-splendoured! And they
cost only 9/- at Arnotts.

Arnotts

Henry Street and Grafton Street
Boyers of North Earl Street, Dublin.

Keep it dark.

She's wearing the sensational new shade: 'Tambourine'

Legs look so wickedly wonderful in Tambourine — Glen Abbey's great new dark-and-devastating shade for being sensational in!

Tambourine — deeper than brown in the pack — turns to a sultry shadow on the leg. It's a shade that moves with the midi-times. Planned to team with the longer skirt look. It shapes, tapers, lengthens your legs. It's dark and exciting. Dark and enticing. A new kind of dark that makes you feel different. Daring. Fatally feminine.

Don't delay — wear Tambourine — rightaway. The never-till-now new colour. And (keep it dark!) sheerly scandalous the way it gets those second glances.

'Tambourine' in Skintights by *Glen Abbey*

ARK5

Skintights
cling a little closer...

IN SHEERS-STANDARDS-RUN-RESISTS-SERVICEWEIGHTS BY
Glen Abbey filion YARN

TOP DRAWER
TIGHTS FOR GREAT OCCASIONS BY *Glen Abbey*

New from Glen Abbey — Top Drawer — the party touch in luxury tights for great occasions! Top Drawer are planned for wearing when you want to look specially wonderful. Plain knit with the briefest cut away bikini top, sandal heel, Top Drawer give your legs a million dollar look. In five fashion-fresh shades, Top Drawer tights are sheer spoil-yourself luxury. Go buy a pair today. It's always a great occasion when you wear Top Drawer tights by Glen Abbey.

AT ALL HIGH FASHION STORES 45p.

Adverts for Glen Abbey Tights
Above: New Spotlight 1970
Bottom right: New Spotlight 1972
Bottom left: Woman's Way 1971

WEEK ENDING FRIDAY, SEPTEMBER 4th, 1970

woman's way weekly

1s. 2d.
plus 2d. tax

IRELAND'S LEADING WOMAN'S MAGAZINE

The other women

Housewife-of-the-year 1970

The search starts this week!
See inside for competition details

Woman's Way

Above: 1970
Top right: 1969
Middle right: 1982
Bottom right: 1971
Bottom left: 1971

Woman's Way began in 1963 and is one of Ireland's longest running magazines. Initially a monthly it moved to weekly in 1967. With its practical advice, hints and tips on fashion, beauty, health, travel, recipes, parenting and more it remains very popular today. Brand New Retro would be a lot less enjoyable without it.

Top left: 1970
Top right: 1966
Bottom right: 1970
Bottom left: 1971
Middle left: 1969

★ See also Clerys selection of smaller furs including Jackets, Stoles, Mink Scarves, Boleros and the new Fun Furs.

CANADIAN SQUIRREL JACKET 95 GNS.

CANADIAN SQUIRREL 115 GNS.

SOUTHERN MUSQUASH 69 GNS.

CANADIAN SQUIRREL ¾ length 105 GNS.

NATURAL BLACK MUSQUASH 99 GNS.

MINK COAT 699 GNS.

McEvoys

Some of the superlative Fur Fashions at Ireland's greatest fur buying opportunity. Unbelievable savings!

Clerys
OF DUBLIN

Autumn Hat Trick!

All one price . . . 59/11 . . . all in fabulous Peach Bloom Velour—with a super variety of the very newest of new season colours. See the three now at Clerys Millinery Salon where the Small Profits policy means the best of value always.

An eye-catching Robin Hood style with long quill in a colour to tone. A good choice of colours. Price 59/11

A dramatic hat in Bowler style with pheasant feather trimming. Peach Bloom Velour in a selection of good colours. 59/11.

Fashionable Trilby style trimmed with Petersham colours. Clerys price 59/11

Clerys

Adverts for Clerys of Dublin
Woman's Way 1967

Bedtime Beauties
in easy brushed nylon!

Clerys

Three cheers for Spring
from the vast fashion collection at Clerys!

Clerys
OF DUBLIN

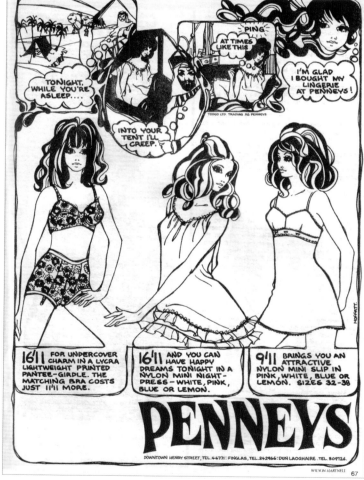

Adverts for Penneys & Dunnes Stores

Above and right: Penneys, Womans Way 1969
Illustrations by Moffatt.
Top right: Dunnes Stores, Miss 1966

MOOD MAKER!

IN **Levi's** CORDS
the cord garments with the style
for the young set Cut slim, cut cunning—
styled so cool you can't
keep the men—or the girls—away from them. Only
LEVI'S could produce that kind of cords.

FROM

"O'CONNORS"

UPPER ABBEY STREET,

THE LARGEST STOCKISTS OF "LEVI
CORDS" IN IRELAND.

PROMPT ATTENTION TO POSTAL ORDERS

EVEN is STEVEN now OPTICALOOVEY

So why not take in a psychedelic pupil-full of our store.... INSIDE AND OUT...

for gear that is Transcendental and Meditative.

Optic us all the way from O'Connell Street at **150 CAPEL ST**

Magee
-masters
of masculine
colour - *and cut!*

You will be delighted you brought
him to Cannock's men's department. You will love the true
Masculine Colour of Magee, subtle
and sophisticated for business and
formal suits — gayer and bolder
for leisure suits, jackets and
matching trousers. Ask to see the
new season's range of Magee twist-
worsteds, thornproofs and Donegal
tweeds and see what the work of
international stylists can do for him.

Magee

at **CANNOCK'S** you get
THE REAL **MAGEE**

Best **49**
FORTY NINER

Internationally designed.
Comes in luxurious Pantawool.
Classically informal. Available in
a variety of today's shades.
Outstanding value at
£49.50. Only at Best
shops for men.

'Chargecard'
Account
Interested in joining
an exclusive club?
Open a Best
'Chargecard'
Account. Pick up a
brochure today.

Best
Shops for Men

THE YEAR : '68
THE CLOTH : MOHAIR
THE SUIT : SUPERB
THE MAN : MAGNIFICENT
THE SHOPS : BEST'S

We at BEST'S are pleased to tell you the news that we
have a magnificent selection of ready-to-wear mohair
suits in bronze, blues, greys and greens
at the interesting price of £21.
Or if you prefer, have your
suit personally — and
expertly tailored for £24.

BEST LIMITED

"The camera doesn't lie — that's why I rely on Vitapointe"

says top Telefis Eireann announcer, Nuala Donnelly.

"Spending a lot of time under hot arc lights in front of the cameras makes it difficult to appear always well-groomed. And no amount of studio make-up can take the place of basic good grooming, for you just can't fool the television camera. A woman's hair, especially, can easily look dull and lifeless on the screen. So that's why I always use Vitapointe before appearing in front of the cameras. It's really remarkable how just one minute with Vitapointe brings out all the natural highlights and leaves hair shining and full of life. Now I use Vitapointe regularly and find that my hair stays neat, shining and manageable all day long."

Well, there's an 'inside' fashion hint for you, then, from a top Telefis Eireann announcer. Discover new life and hidden radiance in *your* hair by using Vitapointe from now on. It's so easy to use, takes only a minute, and is very economical—a small tube costs only 3/6 and lasts a month. Double size for 4/9. Buy Vitapointe today.

Vitapointe of Paris.   Cream beautifier and conditioner for the hair.

"Beauty starts with beautiful hair, that's why I use Vitapointe"

says fashion model Helen Kelly

"One of the first things people notice about a woman is her hair. That's why I was so glad to discover Vitapointe. When I use Vitapointe, my hair is manageable, full of life and shining with natural beauty. Now I make Vitapointe a regular part of my make-up."

Give *yourself* a head start on good looks to-day by using Vitapointe. Vitapointe dressing and conditioning cream keeps your hair beautiful and manageable all day long. It takes only a minute to apply and costs so little – just 3/6 for a supply that lasts a month. Or 4/9 for the double size.

START USING VITAPOINTE TO-DAY.

VITAPOINTE OF PARIS. CREAM BEAUTIFIER AND CONDITIONER FOR THE HAIR

"Flattery goes to a girl's head"

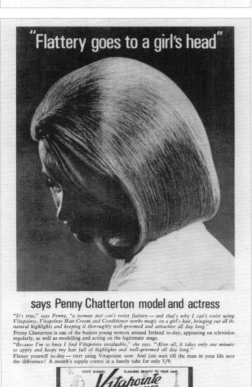

says Penny Chatterton model and actress

"It's true," says Penny, *"a woman just can't resist flattery — and that's why I can't resist using Vitapointe. Vitapointe Hair Cream and Conditioner works magic on a girl's hair, bringing out all its natural highlights and keeping it thoroughly well-groomed and attractive all day long."*

Penny Chatterton is one of the busiest young women around Ireland to-day, appearing on television regularly, as well as modelling and acting on the legitimate stage.

"Because I'm so busy I find Vitapointe invaluable," she says. *"After all, it takes only one minute to apply and keeps my hair full of highlights and well-groomed all day long."*

Flatter yourself to-day — start using Vitapointe now. And just wait till the man in your life sees the difference! A month's supply comes in a handy tube for only 3/9.

VITAPOINTE OF PARIS. CREAM BEAUTIFIER AND CONDITIONER FOR THE HAIR

Adverts for Vitapointe

Miss

Above: Nualla Donnelly, RTE announcer 1966

Top left: Helen Kelly, fashion model 1967

Left: Penny Chatterton, Abbey actress 1967

TONY RODGERS
THE WITCHES HUT
CUTTING AND STYLING
FOR MEN·AND WOMEN

30 STH. FREDERICK ST.
Phone 64260

20 NASSAU ST.
Phone 771252

Advert for The Witches Hut

Woman's Way 1971

Robert Chambers was one of the original staff and posted this comment on the blog: 'I was in the Witches Hut from 1965 to 1973. It was terrific – such an exciting time there and to be in hairdressing. We were the superstars, we were passionate about cutting hair (I still am). Tony and Vidal Sassoon were our inspiration'.

McGONIGAL — GRANT HOGAN — ZORRO — MICHAEL REILLY — DARCY

MARIAN DOYLE — PHILIP YOURELL — ROBERT CHAMBERS — PAUL CUMMINS — VINCE CORRIGAN — TROY

Peter Mark knows a great wig when he sees it.

He looks for the subtle Ginchywig crown—set so that a stylist can pour his craftsmanship into innumerable natural-looking styles.

He looks for the Ginchywig stretch base—for the supreme comfort it brings.

He looks for the Ginchywig fullness—so easy and quick to shape.

He looks for the perfect Ginchywig fit—deep into the nape of the neck, firm round the ears.

He looks for this name—Ginchywig. He knows it's his guarantee of a happier you!

He looks for the Ginchywig colours—a whole wonderful wide range to suit every woman's dream.

Ginchy Wig
The wig your hairdresser knows is best

Ann Davis wearing a Peter Mark Ginchywig.

A Peter Mark Ginchywig with hairpiece added for evening wear.

HAIRPIECES

The Ginchy Magic Box
Makes you bewitchingly different... in seconds

Nowadays, wearing a wig is as natural as powdering your nose. And natural's the word for a Ginchywig (Ask Peter Mark). So natural, you'll hardly believe it's not your own hair. So incredibly soft, light and secure you forget you're wearing a wig. So perfectly cut and styled before you ever buy it that you can brush, comb or flick it into any shape that takes your fancy.

There are over 200 styles to choose from—in a wide range of colours—at prices from five to fifteen guineas. All modacrylic Ginchywigs have a new stretch base that covers any shape or size of head, fit deep into the nape of the neck, snugly around the ears. You can shampoo your Ginchywig in cold water. It drips dry. And keeps on looking marvellous.

But be wise as well as beautiful. Not every wig is a Ginchy. So do be sure you get a genuine Ginchywig. Available from Peter Mark. Or the leading hairdresser in your area.

Ginchy Wig
by Peter Mark

Grafton St., O'Connell St., Stillorgan, Terenure, Dun Laoghaire.

instant hair styles

before

A Maison Prost wig like this (hand-made, from colour-matched European hair, from 36 guineas) means that you can be ready for an important date in a matter of seconds.

after

TOP-TO-TOE BEAUTY is the motto at Maison Prost, 25 St. Stephen's Green, Dublin with three floors devoted to chiropody, electrolysis, sauna baths, manicures, facials, massage and hairstyling, plus a well-stocked perfume, cosmetics and jewellery shop.

Wigs and hairpieces are made on the premises. Current fashion trends have kept this department very busy lately and Maison Prost wigs are now being worn as far afield as New York.

Prices for a full wig of hand-made, colour-matched European hair start at 36 guineas. Hairpieces cost as little as £4. 10s.

A sauna bath, which includes body massage after your session in the "sweat box" and cold shower, costs £1. 5s. Electrolysis costs 10s. a session of 15 minutes and chiropody (by Miss Bernadette Muldowney, M.C.S.Ch.I., resident chiropodist) 12s. 6d. (both feet). Facials, which include cleanse, massage and make-up cost £1. 1s. and £1. 5s.

Wig Adverts from Peter Mark and Maison Prost
Top left: Peter Mark Ginchy Wig, Woman's Way 1969
Top right: Peter Mark Hairpieces, Woman's Way 1967
Above: Maison Prost, Stephen's Green, Dublin, Woman's Way 1967
Bottom left: Peter Mark Ginchy Wig, Woman's Way 1970

GIRL OF THE YEAR
GLADYS WALLER
(SEE INSIDE)

JANUARY 1966 ONE SHILLING

miss

Miss 1966

Published through Creation Ltd, Miss was an alternative to Woman's Way and ran from the mid to late sixties. This front cover features Miss Ireland and Miss World runner up Gladys Waller, sitting on an Austin Seven at Bull Island Bridge, Dublin. Gladys is dressed in a red Emcar suit, white patent leather boots and a Pompadour handbag all from Brown Thomas.

WOMAN'S VIEW and
Vol. xxxix, No. 1.   NOVEMBER, 1965

Model Housekeeping

Ireland's Leading Woman's Magazine

9ᴰ

woman's choice weekly

1/2

EDNA O'BRIEN'S
new novel
A Pagan Place
STARTS INSIDE
free competition
What breaks up
Irish marriages?

June 1982
70p Incl. Tax

U
YOU MAGAZINE

IRELAND'S REVIEW
FOR WOMEN TODAY

'IN' WEDDINGS
PILL WARNINGS
TOO PERFECT PEOPLE!
BLACK FASHION MAGIC
TENNIS COURT TOFFS
ELTON JOHN'S HANG-UPS
PLUS:
The Bride's story, food from China, Greek Islands,
Pat Kenny's albums, Lynn Geldof's travels, Tony
Gregory's whirl and how to react in a crisis.

YOUNG WOMAN

THE TRUTH ABOUT FALLING IN LOVE   •   EXCITING WAYS WITH CHICKEN
HIPPYISM A LOST CAUSE   •   DIARY OF A PREGNANCY   •   AT HOME WITH
MRS. DICKIE ROCK   •   BORN UNDER ARIES-1st OF A SERIES   •   MISS IRELAND

The
Eight
Women in
Mountjoy
— Exclusive
Report and
Pictures

Fashion in
Knitwear
by Dralon

Various Women's Magazines
Top left: Model Housekeeping 1965
Top right: Image 1982
Middle right: Woman's Choice 1970
Bottom right: Young Woman 1967
Above: U 1982

SUMMERTIME AT **GAYWEAR**

Gaywear and Libra Designs have combined to bring to you a range of beautiful designed casual summer lightweight suits available in Jade, Navy, Red, Turquoise and Royal Blue and Cerise.

Style No. 6330 (photographed here)

£32.25 (retail price)

Libra Designs are available in Gaywear branches throughout the country.

6-7 Castle Market, Dublin 2.
Telephone: 775831.

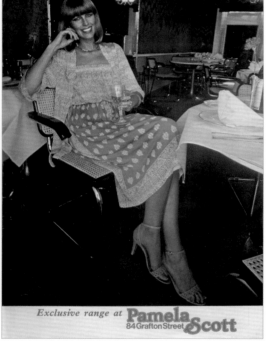

Exclusive range at **Pamela Scott**
84 Grafton Street

The best dressed lady in town

William Elliott
wicklow street,
Queens old castle
Cork,
High street
Bantry.

MONICA JOHN

Fashion Store Adverts
Above: Pamela Scott, Magill 1980
Top Left: Gaywear, U 1982
Bottom Left: Monica John, U 1982

GO KOOKY
in new op fabrics!

Arnotts are out to dazzle this Spring with the greatest splash of Op fabrics—printed Tricels that are really on the scene. Hop into Op you've made yourself—Arnotts have the fabrics, the newest patterns and everything else you need. And Arnotts Tricel prices are really keen: **9/11, 10/11** and **12/11** a yard. Drop into Arnotts for your big with-it opportunity.

Arnotts

Hello there!
This is Kathleen Watkins

inviting you to join me on R.T.E. each Monday on the House of Cassidy International Fashion Programme at our new time of 2.15 p.m.
You'll hear the very latest news on International Fashion and Comment.
We feature the top International Stars on the *Current* European Charts—and you'll be bound to enjoy something that's quite new, topical and different.
Meet Mirrielle Mathieu, Vicky, Adamo, Hildergarde Knef, Victor Torrianni, Georges Moustaki—and a host of others too—

including Gitte, Katja Epstein and Karel Gott—all big names on today's European Scene.
Hope to meet you on Monday next—so until then I'll say Farewell and Slán and leave you with "Music to Watch Girls by".

the house of cassidy
GEORGES STREET, HENRY STREET, DUBLIN DUN LAOGHAIRE, STILLORGAN, 89 PATRICK STREET, CORK.

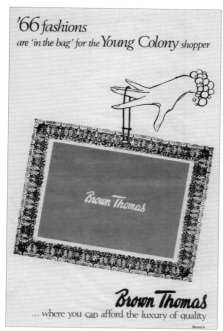

'66 *fashions*
are 'in the bag' for the Young Colony *shopper*

Brown Thomas

Brown Thomas
... *where you can afford the luxury of quality*

Kenny's

Make the scene - and make it move!

Linen shifts into top gear at Bolger's

Hi hi hi and hello squad, glad you could make the scene. Because the big hitsville happening right now is the lithe, lissom linen kick like they're swinging it at Bolger's. Cool for chicks and hot for cats, all that zowie red, zooming blue, and white like night was never invented.
Panels? You got 'em. Portholes? Take a peek. So? So don't just stand there. Plug in. Switch on. And start moving. This way.

CHICK ONE: *straight down linen weave style in scarlet—diamond patterned in navy and white, with central flower motif. In 3 other colour combinations also. A Bolger exclusive.* 49/11
CHICK TWO: *shifty sheath with a nautical air in navy linen weave. White inset outlined in red. Available in 3 other colour combinations. A Bolger exclusive.* 49/11.
COOL FRED: *Don't tell him it's a guitar. He thinks he's bought an egg-slicer.*

Bolger's
WHERE FASHION IS FUN AND THE PRICE IS RIGHT - NORTH EARL ST., DUBLIN. ALSO, CORK, LIMERICK, WATERFORD.

ARKS

Fashion Store Adverts
Above: Brown Thomas, Miss 1966
Bottom: Bolgers, Miss 1966
Top left: Arnotts, Woman's Way 1966
Top centre: House of Cassidy, Woman's Way 1971

Have you heard the latest? Clarks new group:

THE REVOLUTION

The Revolution is four great shoes for trendy guys. Go-anywhere shoes to team up with today's exciting clothes.

Andy, Matt, Buddy and Deano are the wildest foursome on the shoe scene. Moulded soles and heels. Smooth and grained leather. Square toes. And the craziest punch-out patterns. Brown or Black.

Better come in and take a look at the Revolution. The big noise in young men's shoes. Tie-up, buckle-down or slip-on. It's all happening in our shop.

Clarks

DEANO in Black and Oak Leather.
2 – 5½ —**55/11d.**
6 – 8 —**59/11d.**

BUDDY in Black and Oak Leather and Brown Suede.
2 – 5½ —**55/11d.**
6 – 8 —**59/11d.**

MATT in Black and Oak Grain Leather.
2 – 5½ —**55/11d.**
6 – 8 —**59/11d.**

ANDY in Black and Oak Leather.
2 – 5½ —**55/11d.**
6 – 8 —**59/11d.**

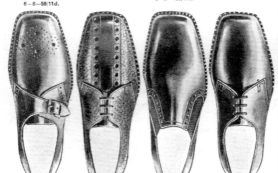

DEANO   MATT   BUDDY   ANDY

Made in the Republic of Ireland by Clarks of Dundalk.

Various Clarks Adverts

New Spotlight

Above: 1968

Top and bottom right: 1969

Opposite: Woman's Way 1967

Note the 'made in Dundalk' tag on these Clarks adverts. In the early 1970s over 1200 people were employed in shoe manufacturing in my home town of Dundalk.

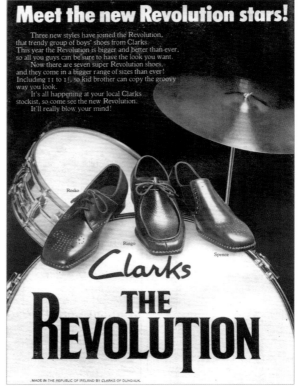

Meet the new Revolution stars!

Three new styles have joined the Revolution, that trendy group of boys' shoes from Clarks. This year the Revolution is bigger and better than ever, so all you guys can be sure to have the look you want.

Now there are seven super Revolution shoes, and they come in a bigger range of sizes than ever! Including 11 to 1½, so kid brother can copy the groovy way you look.

It's all happening at your local Clarks stockist, so come see the new Revolution. It'll really blow your mind!

Rosko   Ringo   Spence

Clarks

THE REVOLUTION

MADE IN THE REPUBLIC OF IRELAND BY CLARKS OF DUNDALK.

Six great numbers.

This year the Revolution is bigger and better than ever, so all you guys can be sure to have the look you want.

Now there are six super Revolution shoes and they come in a bigger range of sizes than ever! Including 11 to 1½, so kid brother can copy the groovy way you look.

It's all happening at your local Clarks stockist, so come see the new Revolution. It'll really blow your mind!

THE REVOLUTION

Clarks

SOS... Taking off on Roman Holiday. Need perfect shoes. What to do?

Clarks to the rescue with a shoe called JEANNIE·
Easy elegant. Casual enough to see all the sights in.
Formal enough to do the bright lights in.
I wouldn't call it Jeannie, though. I'd call it Versatility.

Clarks

Jeannie. In Black, Navy, String and Tan Buffalo Calf. 79/11d.
Made in the Republic of Ireland by Clarks of Dundalk. Wool dress with cowl-hood by Donald Davies.

Maxi, Dick and Twink
New Spotlight 1970

Maxi *(bottom left)*, Dick *(top left)* & Twink *(bottom right)* modelling outfits from Richard Lewis Boutique, Lower Baggot Street, Dublin 2

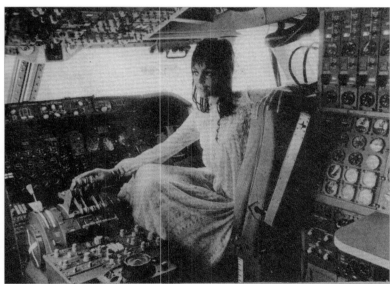

Maxi and Dick
New Spotlight 1969

Maxi and Dick at Dublin Airport modelling clothes
from Simon Richard and Cassidys of Dublin.
Photos by Mark Nolan.

Luke and Ronnie

New Spotlight 1967

Dubliners Ronnie Drew and Luke Kelly with model Vera Hempenstall in
Dublin's dockland modelling clothes from Even Steven, Capel Street, Dublin 1.

Fashion Session with Joe Mac

New Spotlight 1966

Joe Mac of Cork band The Dixies 'dolls up for
laughs' for this Trixie Smith fashion feature with
model Breda. All clothes from Cork stores.

...and just wait until you get to the top!

The top-note this season is obviously Bear Brand knitwear.
In smooth clinging Courtelle, Bear Brand knitwear brings you
new flying-high styles and colours. Look out for humming bird blue,
fuchsia, tan, beech green, orange and many more.
High living this, in easy-care Courtelle.

BEAR BRAND
fully fashioned knitwear in Courtelle

Adverts for Wool Sweaters

Above: Bear Brand, Miss 1967
Right: Tailtean, Woman's Choice 1970
Top right: Round Tower, Woman's Own 1968

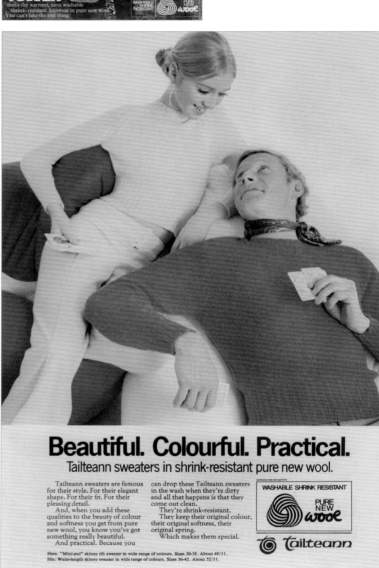

No swimming to-day.

Too cold.
Tough. But everybody's
as warm as toast in chunky
Round Tower knitwear.
Who's worried
about swimming
anyway?

ROUND TOWER
make the warmest, most washable
shrink-resistant knitwear in pure new wool.
You can't fake the real thing.

WASHABLE SHRINK RESISTANT   PURE NEW wool

Beautiful. Colourful. Practical.
Tailteann sweaters in shrink-resistant pure new wool.

Tailteann sweaters are famous
for their style. For their elegant
shape. For their fit. For their
pleasing detail.
And, when you add these
qualities to the beauty of colour
and softness you get from pure
new wool, you know you've got
something really beautiful.
And practical. Because you

can drop these Tailteann sweaters
in the wash when they're dirty
and all that happens is that they
come out clean.
They're shrink-resistant.
They keep their original colour,
their original softness, their
original spring.
Which makes them special.

WASHABLE SHRINK RESISTANT

PURE
NEW
wool

Tailteann

Hers: "Mini-pul" skinny rib sweater in wide range of colours. Sizes 30-38. About 49/11.
His: Waist-length skinny sweater in wide range of colours. Sizes 36-42. About 52/11.

Slender button-
through dress in
raised design on
white background.

Carina
by
Woolcraft
in
Orlon

DUPONT
Representatives: E. K. O'Brien Ltd.
39 Fitzwilliam Place, Dublin 2.

What's New for Autumn
Promotional Brochure 1969

The photos from this 8 page brochure for Carina by Woolcraft in Orlon fashions
were taken in and around Lansdowne Road stadium, Dublin 4.

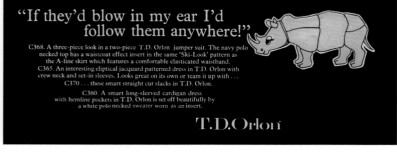

Wild Autumn Fashion by Sunbeam
Promotional Brochure 1970

This 8 page brochure for the Sunbeam 1970 autumn collection featured these photos taken at Dublin Zoo.

"That lean lithe look makes me so envious I could scream!"

C356. A long line Pure New Shetland cardigan in Moonbeam Yellow, long sleeves, cable stitched down the front and trimmed with gold buttons. For cool weather comfort team up with . . .
C355 . . . Matching Pure New Shetland slacks with elasticated waistband and gentle flare at ankles.

C354. Take a long slinky sleeveless Pure New Shetland cardigan, V-necked and double cabled and strike a match with . . .
C355 . . . Pure New Shetland slacks with elasticated waistband and flare at the ankles.

Various Footwear Adverts

All Woman's Way, all 1970

Top right: Brevitt Boots. Advert shot at Howth Castle featuring model Inga Lil in the foreground.

Above: Dunlop. Made in Cork

Right: Q Shoes. Made in Edenderry.

A 180

C 381

Sunbeam Beachwear 1971

Helanca®

A 178

A 182

sunbeam

A 171

A 177

A 181

C 393

C 398   C 379   C 397

designed to make you look
stunning when summing

Helanca®

A 173

Sunbeam Beachwear

Promotional Brochure 1971

Photography taken on location in and around Derrynane Hotel,
Caherdaniel, Co. Kerry.

Lifestyle

'How about... A Bubbling Cocktail of Trash and Style?'
It was 1981 and we were searching for a tag line for issue
5 of our fanzine 'Too Late' and this suggestion, from my
brother and editor Eamonn, was the one we went with.
Too Late #1 hit the streets in 1978 and was our home-
produced fanzine offering a humorous and irreverent
look at life in Dundalk in the late 1970s and 80s.

Each of the 5 issues sold just under 1,000 copies and it
was our little foray into publishing and producing what
was essentially a lifestyle fanzine.

All magazines are lifestyle. Even if the content does not
seem to reflect this, the adverts will.

House of the Year Cabinteely

Woman's Way 1966

High on a hill with a view of the mountains, this 4 bedroom home at Auburn Rd, Kilbogget Estate, Cabinteely, Co Dublin was chosen by Woman's Own as House of the Year 1966. Builders CA Jenkins, Sandycove, Dublin.

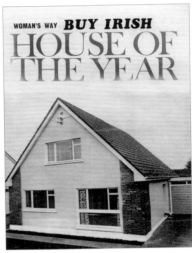

House of the Year Willow Park, Ballymun
Woman's Way 1967

Willow Park Grove in Dublin 11 is often addressed as
Glasnevin, Finglas or, as in this case, Ballymun. It is
nestled alongside the childhood homes of Gavin Friday
and Bono in Cedarwood Road.

House of the Year - Pinebrook

Promotional Brochure 1974

Pinebrook, located off the Malahide Road, Dublin 5, was chosen by Woman's Way for the annual House of the Year award 1974. The brochure 'gives you just an impression in words and pictures of a house that an all-Irish enterprise has created to give superlative value for money'.

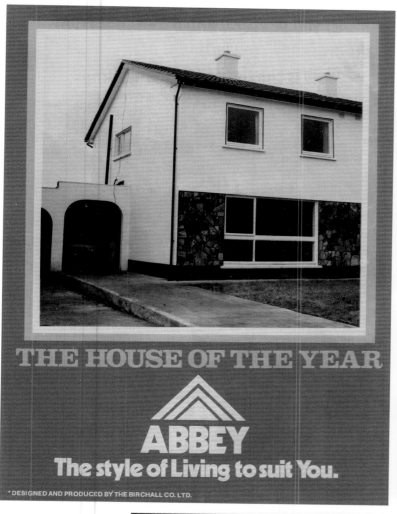

THE HOUSE OF THE YEAR

ABBEY
The style of Living to suit You.

* DESIGNED AND PRODUCED BY THE BIRCHALL CO. LTD.

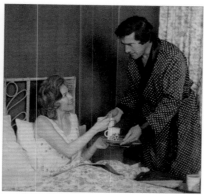

Advert For Valspar Paint
Woman's Choice 1970

Dulux is the colour of pleasure

Pleasure is laughter shared, comfort enjoyed, a colourful modern home. Pleasure is Dulux Emulsion Paint gliding on to walls as smooth as silk. Pleasure is a clear pure Dulux Colour which always looks the way you like it. Home is a pleasure you'll enjoy even more when Dulux adds colour.

DULUX

EMULSION PAINTS in 24 shades of pleasure

■ GLOSS   ■ EMULSION   ■ EGGSHELL FINISH

Arrow   Made in Ireland by HARRINGTONS & GOODLASS WALL LTD. CORK & DUBLIN

Adverts for Dulux Paint
Womans Way 1969

Dulux is the colour of harmony

Harmony is a home where shades and shapes blend beautifully against a background of pure, clear Dulux Colour. Harmony is Dulux Emulsion Paint, flowing as smooth as silk from brush to wall. Harmony makes a modern home attractive; Dulux Emulsion provides the background for attractive modern homes.

DULUX

EMULSION PAINTS in 24 harmonious shades

■ GLOSS   ■ EMULSION   ■ EGGSHELL FINISH

Arrow   Made in Ireland by HARRINGTONS & GOODLASS WALL LTD. CORK & DUBLIN

When white is right Dulux is brilliant

Dulux Brilliant White Gloss is perfect for doors and windows and skirtings. It glides from brush to surface smooth as silk, and dries to a dazzling gloss finish that shrugs off the years brilliantly. Cleans with a wipe too. White doors, windows and skirtings make all the other colours in your home look purer, brighter, clearer. And remember, when white is right, Dulux is brilliant.

DULUX

BRILLIANT WHITE GLOSS & EMULSION

Arrow   Made in Ireland by HARRINGTONS & GOODLASS WALL LTD. CORK & DUBLIN

the good life begins with Navan

navan

Navan's Kazak design reflects the rich tradition of the province of Kazak in the Caucasus, incorporating stylised variations of a Greek Cross and the Imperial Russian coat of arms. Kazak comes in Diadem Axminster quality and is woven from a hard wearing blend of 80% pure new wool and 20% Bri-Nylon. It is available from any good furnishing store in 27" and 12' widths.

A presentation pack of Navan's "Scene setting" leaflets is available free from Navan Carpets Ltd., Navan, Co. Meath.

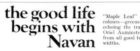

the good life begins with Navan

navan

"Maple Leaf" (Design 3/2716). All the richness of warm Autumnal colours—greens turning to gold and deep rust. A skilful pattern of foliage echoing the traditional shape of the maple leaf appears in this lovely Oriel Axminster carpet by Navan. Available from all good furnishing stores in 27" and 12' widths.

"House of the month" carpets by Navan. Showrooms:—Navan, Dublin, Cork, Limerick, Belfast.

Build your home around
KINCORA CARPETS
Ireland's finest Axminsters & Wiltons

Youghal know why the longest-wearing carpets wear the Woolmark:

You can't fake the real thing.

Various Carpet Adverts
Woman's Way
Top left & above: Navan Carpet 1970
Top right: Kinvara 1969
Bottom right: Youghal 1968
Opposite: Youghal 1967

When you buy a carpet insist on seeing the BRI-NYLON label. This is your assurance of a quality carpet. Tested all the way from the fibre to the carpet you buy That's why carpets in BRI-NYLON blends wear so well; keep their colours; keep their spring; and look good always.
BRI-NYLON + wool gives you luxurious carpets that stay luxurious throughout their long long life.

Youghal

GOLD/quality carpets in BRI-NYLON-80% pure wool 20% BRI-NYLON. Illustrated above is Pattern No. 263/407 available in 27", 36", 9' and 12' widths.

Also available in the following colour combinations: Yellow, Red, Blue Pattern No. 720/407, Greens, Orange Pattern No. 905/407

for carpet luxury that lasts and lasts, choose

QUALITY TESTED

BRI*
NYLON

winter warmth with kosangas

the stylish
Super-Ser room-heater

Enjoy glowing warmth instantly with this modern 3-heat unit. Built-in safety valve, completely mobile on four ball-set rubber wheels. Attractively designed for stylish comfort. See the Super Ser at your Kosangas Dealer's. Cash Price £32.1.8. complete with 1 cylinder of Kosangas. Attractive easy terms available.

Kosangas

Kosangas Ltd., Kosangas Corner.
O'Connell Bridge House, Dublin 2. Tel. 774774

Who says electric firelight isn't romantic?

Take a second look at the blazing beauty in the photograph. It's one of the new Sunhouse heaters — giving firelight to dream by . . . to see visions in . . . to toast your toes at. Sunhouse have put paid to those obsolete fuel effects which were used to imitate coal — and fooled nobody! These new Sunhouse heaters have large, leaping flames which weave upward in a dance of delight—more welcoming and convincing than ever you coaxed from many a 'good old-fashioned' coal fire. So cosy and realistic that all the hearth and fireback are alive with the winking warming welcome of romantic firelight. Nothing like this has ever been seen before

Illustration is of the 3 kw 'Royal' (at £32 15s.), hardly distinguishable from the smaller 2 kw 'Regent' (£22).

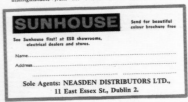

SUNHOUSE

Send for beautiful colour brochure free

See Sunhouse first! at ESB showrooms, electrical dealers and stores.

Name...

Address..

....

**Sole Agents: NEASDEN DISTRIBUTORS LTD.,
11 East Essex St., Dublin 2.**

Which Fuel ?

PEAT BRIQUETTES, of course

Quickly changing temperatures, sharp breezes, showery—in fact the weather we usually experience at this time of the year. Chilly evenings when a bright glowing fire, for a few hours before bedtime, is most welcome. Peat briquettes because they light quickly are the ideal fuel for this purpose.

Obtainable from fuel merchants and grocery stores.
In case of difficulty contact:—
Bord na Mona, 26/22 Upr. Pembroke St.
Dublin 2.

PEAT BRIQUETTES

HOT • BRIGHT • CLEAN • LONGBURNING

no sticks, no paper, no mess, no fuss . . .

ZIP the sure firelighter

For a quick, sure fire, add fuel to a Zip, light it and leave it. Forget about splintery sticks, messy paper; you'll get a cheerful cosy fire in no time with Zip. No mess. No fuss. You get 12 Zip firelighters in every pack; 12 quick-off-the-match fires. Wonderful value for a busy housewife. That's Zip for you.

The most convenient way to light your fire

ZIP firelighters

the sure firelighter

Made by Kay Brothers (Ireland) Limited, Castlebellingham, Co. Louth

Adverts for Home Heating
Woman's Way

Top left: Kosangas 1970
Top right: Sunhouse 1966
Above: Sunhouse 1967
Left: Zip Firelighters 1969
Bottom left: Peat Briquettes 1966

We have
revolutionary connections

The new 4" collar boss

For those who want an advanced plumbing system, connecting all appliances above floor level. Approved for Local Government Grants.

lower internal socket

MARLEY PLUMBING

Manufactured and marketed by Concrete Products of Ireland Ltd., Lucan. Telephone 280691.

INTO THE 80's with the STARS

- See Gay Byrne's Livingroom, Valerie McGovern's Kitchen, Geraldine Branagan's Bedroom and Larry Gogan's Leisure Room.
- Free Competitions
- DIY Demonstrations
- New Concepts in Kitchens
- The latest in decor, furnishings, carpets, audio–visual equipment . . . and that's just a sample of all you'll find at

RDS Ballsbridge Dublin 11th–17th March 1980
Tuesday 11th to Friday 14th: 2–10 p.m.
Saturday 15th to Monday 17th: 12 noon–7 p.m.
incl. St. Patrick's Day

BRIGHTER HOMES & DIY EXHIBITION

Admission £1.00 Children 50p

From 5th to 13th March the Irish furniture and furnishings industries combine in the biggest and most interesting fair ever seen in this country. At ENVIRO 70, the best in modern design and styling blend with traditional craftsmanship to give an exciting indication of the future. From quality Irish furniture to floor coverings, from kitchen fittings to soft furnishings, this unique fair will give a fascinating glimpse into the homes of tomorrow.

Opening Times
6 pm – 10 pm   Thursday 5th March
1 pm – 40 pm   Other Weekdays
11 am – 10 pm Saturday 7th March
2 pm – 7 pm   Sunday 8th March

ENVIRO 70
Irish Furniture and Furnishings Fair

R.D.S. Ballsbridge Dublin 4 5th–13th March

Adverts for Homes and DIY

Above: Enviro, Woman's Way, 1970
Top right: Brighter Homes & DIY, In Dublin 1980
Top left: Marley Plumbing, Architectural Survey, 1971

How Naas and Carlow proved that Electricity is the cheapest way to cook

Everybody knows that electricity is the cleanest way to cook. But is it the cheapest? There was only one way to find out. In the towns of Naas and Carlow, the E.S.B. carried out a special test.

Special recording meters were fixed to cookers in 110 homes. All sorts of homes, all sorts of families—384 people altogether. Many of the people taking part in the test were using electricity for the first time—this showed that skill was not necessary to get good results. The test was carried out over a six week period. When the results of the test were added up, it was found that the average cost of electric cooking was 1.2d. per person, per day. Or less than 5/- for 6 people for 7 days.

Electric cooking costs 5/- for 6 people for 7 days

 the cleanest cooking at lowest cost

GALA make everything to make the housewife happy —except a husband!

Washing machines, refrigerators, fires, cookers, spin dryers, table ironers, heaters, kettles. You name it—Gala make it. And what's more, they guarantee it for a full year. And it's a proper guarantee, mind you—covering parts *and* labour.

GALA
have the biggest range of quality domestic appliances in Ireland.

Some people take a lot of trouble to take home a Maid

Maid is a sink. Shiny, smart, modern and easy to clean. Maid is the only stainless steel domestic sink made right here in Ireland. So when you go looking for a new house make sure it's got a Maid . . . And if you're building or converting your own house put in a Maid . . . and start with the best!

FOGARTY

h HAMMOND LANE GROUP
PO BOX 156 111 PEARSE STREET DUBLIN 2 TEL 775861

Happy Birthday Husband!

Talk him into buying his own birthday present — a Maid stainless steel sink! He'll appreciate helping you with the washing-up — it's not a chore — it's a pleasure when you've got a Maid. Every sink and drainer is guaranteed to keep it's lasting sparkle. Even when you reach your 90th birthday it will have kept it's spotless elegance. Maid to fit the house of the future in all popular sizes with single or double drainer.
Maid the only domestic stainless steel sinks manufactured in Ireland, give life a lasting sparkle!
Manufactured in Ireland by Irish Containers Ltd., Marketed by *GROUP MARKETING DIVISION*

HLG HAMMOND LANE INDUSTRIES LTD.
HAMMOND LANE IRONFOUNDERS LTD.
IRISH CONTAINERS LTD.

P.O. BOX 186,
111 PEARSE ST.
DUBLIN, 2.
TEL: 775861.

fogarty

Various Home Appliance Adverts

Top right: Gala, Irish Housewife 1965
Top left: ESB, Irish Housewife 1965
Bottom right: Maid, Woman's Way 1969
Bottom left: Maid, Woman's Way 1972

Joe Collins, the designer of this book, got his first job in advertising with Fogarty, who created the Maid adverts.

When you buy a washing machine—look inside a Servis

(You'll find 'Hi-zone'—the world's finest wash action)

When you're choosing your new washing machine, make sure you see the Servis Supertwin and Servis Compact. They're the machines with the best wash action in the world—Servis 'Hi-zone'. Built tall and wide to make all the water work, Servis 'Hi-zone' works more efficiently than any other agitator, to get your wash perfectly clean, yet it treats delicate fabrics really *gently*.

The Servis Supertwin is the twin tub with all the important features. It boils. It has spray and soak rinsing for perfect cleanliness. And it will spin dry one load of clothes really *fast*, while it washes another load.

The Servis Compact is Ireland's top selling washing machine—and no wonder! Designed to take a full 6 lb. washload, it fits neatly into any small space after use. And the power wringer can be stowed away inside the Compact—another space-saving Servis idea.

Servis make the Supertwin and Compact in Ireland, and their Servicing Organisation covers the whole country. Wherever you live, you need never miss a washday if you own a Servis.

Whichever Servis you choose, you'll be getting a washing machine of world-renowned quality, plus the finest wash action ever designed—Servis 'Hi-zone'.

SERVIS

SUPERTWIN 78 GNS.
COMPACT 57 GNS.

Made in Ireland with the world's finest wash action—Servis 'Hi-zone'

Servis Washing Machine

Woman's Way 1967

Manufactured in Artane, Dublin 5

Set 6 adds a little colour to everyday life

It's the best idea we've had in years. A completely new way to buy tableware. Part by Part. From six different designs. When you want it. The way you want it. Bright and beautiful. And you can build up a collection to your own special liking.

Set 6 is made from Erin Stone — durable Irish stoneware with a unique "speckled" look.

You can easily get replacements. And you will never have to worry about the availability or continuity of any Part.

It's all set up for you !

Add a little Arklow to your shopping list

Arklow set 6

Parts :—
(1) Three cups & saucers. (2) Six tea plates. (3) Three breakfast plates. (4) Three dinner plates. (5) Three soup/dessert bowls. (6) Milk jug & sugar bowl.

Kennys

Adverts for Arklow Pottery

Womans Way

Above left and right: Double page spread 1972
Right: 1970

Made in Arklow, these sets were ubiquitous in the 1970s.
We still use ours.

Green Shield Stamps

Top: Stamp book and stamps 1974

Middle left: Dundrum store, catalogue 1974

Bottom right: Audio gifts from catalogue 1974

Bottom left: H. Williams, Woman's Way 1969

Green Shield Stamps originated in the UK but had an Irish operation with its own catalogue and a handful of stores in Dublin (Mary Street and Dundrum), Cork, Limerick and Waterford. You would get 2 stamps for every shilling (5p) spent in selected stores and petrol stations. As a book contained 1,280 stamps you had to spend an awful lot in order to redeem a gift. That record player above, for example, required 60 books. In the UK, Green Shield Gift Houses became Argos Stores.

All that's best in home entertainment

PHILIPS FOR 'SOUND' VALUE

PHILIPS ELECTRICAL (IRELAND) LIMITED, NEWSTEAD, CLONSKEAGH, DUBLIN 14

HENNESSY'S GO PORTABLE

the only snag about PHILIPS portables is knowing which one to choose

Conquest

Concord

Popular

Popmaster

Popmajor

HENNESSY'S
Record, Radio, T.V.
47 Oliver Plunket Street,
Cork. Phone 21430.

It has arrived!
...at Tony Wall Hi-Fi

THE NEW SONY ZR 220

£475 cash, or £4.60 per week

TONY WALL HI·FI
4 Grafton Street, Dublin 2
Tel. 779719

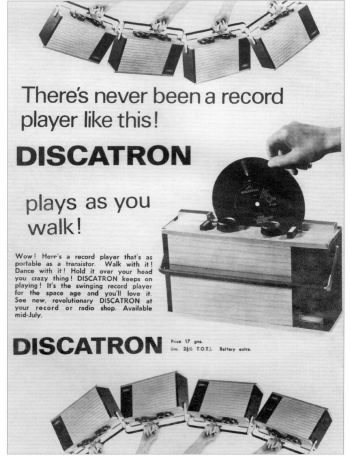

There's never been a record player like this!

DISCATRON

plays as you walk!

Wow! Here's a record player that's as portable as a transistor. Walk with it! Dance with it! Hold it over your head you crazy thing! DISCATRON keeps on playing! It's the swinging record player for the space age and you'll love it. See new, revolutionary DISCATRON at your record or radio shop. Available mid-July.

DISCATRON Price 17 gns.
(inc. 2½% T.O.T.). Battery extra.

Adverts for Audio Entertainment
Above: Discatron, New Spotlight 1966
Bottom left: Tony Wall, Magill 1980
Top right: Philips portables from Hennessy's Cork,
New Spotlight 1967
Top left: Philips home entertainment, RTE Guide 1962

TV Times Four

The Normende Spectra SK2 DeLuxe is an ideal present for those who cannot abide the *RTE Guide*. The 27" colour screen can carry your favourite programme while the three black and white screens ranged beneath let you know what's happening on the other channels. None of this boring flicking through a news-paper or magazine to arrange an evening's viewing. All four screens accept video games, recorders or remote cameras. Headphones are provided to carry the sound from the three small screens. A must for families who can't agree on whether to watch Gaybo or *Match of the Day*. A mere £1895 at Switzers.

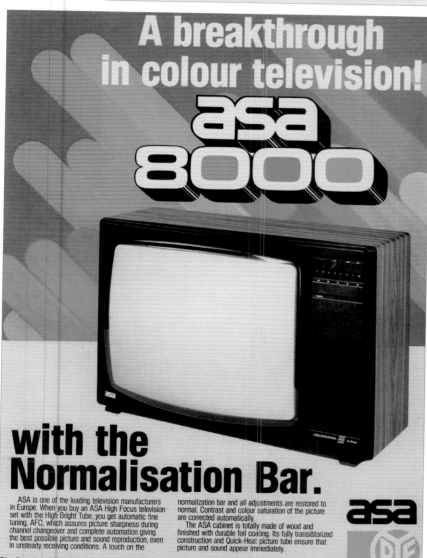

A breakthrough in colour television!

asa 8000

with the Normalisation Bar.

ASA is one of the leading television manufacturers in Europe. When you buy an ASA High Focus television set with the High Bright Tube, you get automatic fine tuning, AFC, which assures picture sharpness during channel changeover and complete automation giving the best possible picture and sound reproduction, even in unsteady receiving conditions. A touch on the normalization bar and all adjustments are restored to normal. Contrast and colour saturation of the picture are corrected automatically.

The ASA cabinet is totally made of wood and finished with durable foil coating. Its fully transistorized construction and Quick-Heat picture tube ensure that picture and sound appear immediately.

Distributed and Guaranteed by **PYE (IRELAND) LIMITED, DUNDRUM, DUBLIN 14, IRELAND.**

"Why choose a Sony Betamax Home Video, Siobhán?"

"Because you can't beat the system, dear."

SONY

Special Christmas Bonanza

VHS E180 Tapes only £8.95
3 for £23.85

Visit our showrooms now while stocks last and see the latest in video equipment and pre-recorded tape libraries.

Irish TV Rentals

Doesn't it make more sense to rent from the experts?

Adverts for TV and Video Players

Above: Pye TV, Executive 1979

Top: Normende Spectra SK2, Magill 1979

Middle right: Sony Betamax video, Hi-Fi Video Review 1982

Bottom right: Blank video tapes at Irish TV Rentals, RTE Guide 1983

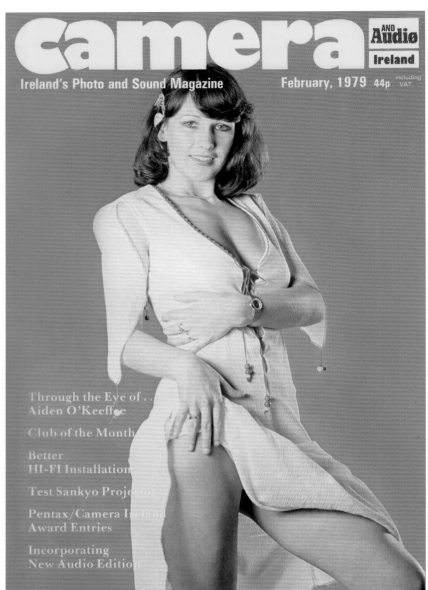

Camera and Audio Magazine
All from 1979

The first issue of Camera, Ireland's only photographic magazine, was published in April 1978. By February 1979 it had become Camera & Audio, Ireland's Photo and Sound Magazine, extending content to include reviews of audio systems and new album releases. The content was quite technical, containing tutorials, folios, interviews and details of photo exhibitions.

200

Reasons To Stay In Dublin

AS TOLD TO CHARLES HUNTER

1. If you are buried here, like Jonathan Swift (to the right of the entrance porch, St Patrick's Cathedral) or Paddy Dignam (Glasnevin Cemetery). Check with the Dublin Cemeteries Committee, telephone 301133.

2. A seat on the Bray train (now the DART) at the moment it leaves Dalkey Tunnel and the darkness becomes Killiney Bay.

3. It is one of the safest cities in the world for jaywalking.

4. So, you're feeling less than human. Go to the Dublin Bird Centre, Market Arcade, off South Great George's Street. Contemplate the axolotls, newtlike amphibians of Mexican origin, one of evolution's more unsettling passages. Be grateful.

5. The first Gaelic typewriter, Dev's penknife, the Countess Markievicz's automatic Mauser and other national treasures in the National Museum, Kildare Street. Tues-Sat, 10am-5pm; Sun, 1-5pm.

6. Every Sunday, in Peter Street (by the Adelaide Hospital), from 10.30am to midday, the Dublin Bird Market is in action; linnets, finches, canaries and other aviary-bred birds.

7. Kavanagh's sweetshop on Aungier Street, featuring liquorice torpedoes, mint humbugs, dimple fruits, and cinder toffee, in big jars or long trays. Mon-Sat, 10.30am-7.30pm.

8. On 16 July 1876 the temperature in Dublin reached 33.4°C (92.1°F); it could happen again. Even if it doesn't, a lot of Dubliners like weather.

9. O'Connell Bridge is as wide as it is long, or almost: 155 feet long by 151 feet wide.

10. Setting your back firmly to the Loopline Bridge to view James Gandon's Custom House, completed in 1791. When it was begun, the city merchants, who didn't want to move their business downstream, hired a mob 'for the purpose of filling up the foundation-trenches, but as it was a warm summer's day they amused themselves by swimming in them instead. (Maurice Craig)

11. Maurice Craig's 'Dublin 1660-1860', tracing and enjoying the two most spectacular centuries of the city's history, and revealing more than any guide-book. Published by Allen Figgis. Adrian MacLoughlin's 'Guide to Historic Dublin' (Gill & Macmillan) is the best formal guide.

12. Playing hoopla (rubber rings on to nail-hooks) in Kavanagh's pub in Prospect Square, Glasnevin.

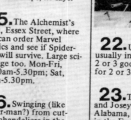

13. Bull Island. Created by the silting caused by the Bull Wall, which was built in 1820. The Brent Geese are only the most famous of the various birds finding sanctuary there; they arrive November/December, depart (for Iceland) February. The hares stay all year. Bus 30.

14. Louis Stewart. Jazz guitar you won't hear anywhere else. Why does he stay? Dublin humour and friendships, he says.

15. The Alchemist's Head, Essex Street, where you can order Marvel Comics and see if Spider-man will survive. Large sci-fi range too. Mon-Fri, 10.30am-5.30pm; Sat, 11am-5.30pm.

16. Swinging (like Spider-man?) from cut-glass chandeliers in the Abbey Mooney after rugby internationals. Alternatively, observe the garish plaster fruit around the ceiling.

17. The bench-eating elm in the King's Inns Park, Constitution Hill.

18. The black marble tops on the radiator blocks in the first room of the Hugh Lane Municipal Gallery, Parnell Square. The warmest seat in town. Tues-Sat, 9.30am-6pm; Sun, 11am-5pm.

19. The Radio 2 Dublin City Marathon. Take a B&B room on the South Circular and watch the masochists from your own bed. Or start training today for 29 October.

20. Limerick.

21. Kabanossi (fresh or dried), Krainer, Cervelat, Setchi, Bratwurst and the other sausages in Magill's, Clarendon Street. Worth visiting just for the aroma. Mon-Sat, 9.30am-6pm.

22. Underground gigs, usually in the Ivy Rooms. 2 or 3 good young bands for 2 or 3 £s.

23. Telling Dwight and Josey from Centerville, Alabama, who are standing in the Front Square of Trinity, that you've never heard of a 'Book of Kells'. But if you have, stay for a year and see sixty-three page turnings.

200 Reasons to stay in Dublin

In Dublin 1984

To celebrate its 200th issue, In Dublin magazine ran a 7 page listing of 200 reasons to stay in Dublin, as told to Charles Hunter. We've included the first page, listing reasons 1 to 23.

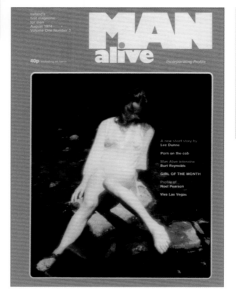

Man Alive

Above and below: 1974

Left: 1975

Launched in April 1974, Man Alive described itself as 'the first general interest man's magazine in the modern international mould. Our package is aimed at today's increasingly sophisticated Irishman in his 20's and 30's'.

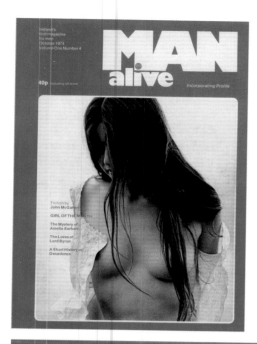

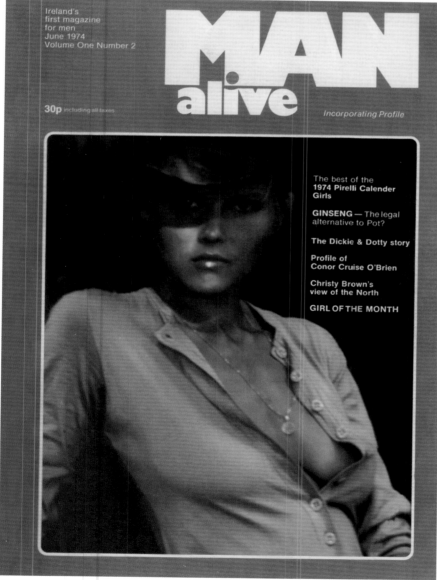

Man Alive
Above: 1975
Left and top left: 1974

Streaking in Ballsbridge, Dublin 4
Man Alive 1974

Pictured in the Wellington Road area of
Dublin 4 on a spring day in 1974, these
photos appeared as part of a feature on
streaking in Man Alive issue 1.
The '■' is part of the original article.
Photos by Tom Collins.

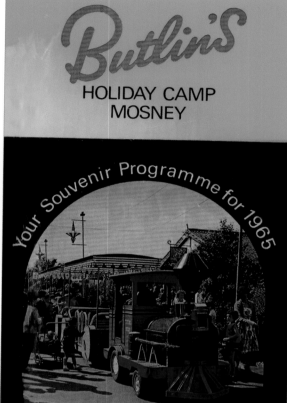

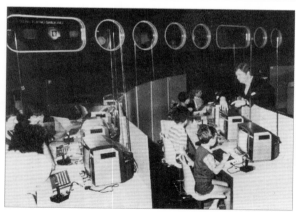

Butlins Mosney

Top left: Souvenir programme 1962

Top right: Souvenir programme 1965

Bottom left: Advert, RTE Guide 1963

Bottom middle: Advert for Computer Centre, Drogheda Independent 1984

Bottom right: Photo of Computer Centre, Success magazine 1984

The souvenir programmes were kept by my mother from our many memorable family holidays at Mosney in the 1960s and early 70s. Butlin's left a run-down Mosney in 1982 and it was taken over by Drogheda businessman Phelim McCluskey, who introduced the Atari Computer Base pictured above.

Travel and Holidays in Ireland
Above: Westport House, Magill 1978
Left: CIE Bus Timetable 1983
Middle left: CIE Go Places, RTE Guide 1962
Top left: Air-Camping, RTE Guide 1965

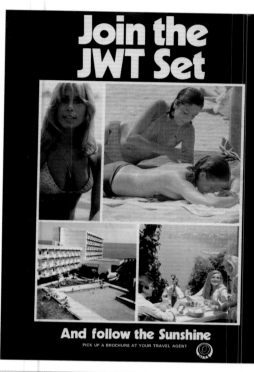

This is Ethna Murphy from Tulla, Co. Carlow. She has nothing to do with music, films or books. Although a life long member of Fianna Fail, she is disappointed with the Green Paper, especially because of the over precipitious drop in the borrowing rate as a percentage of GNP.

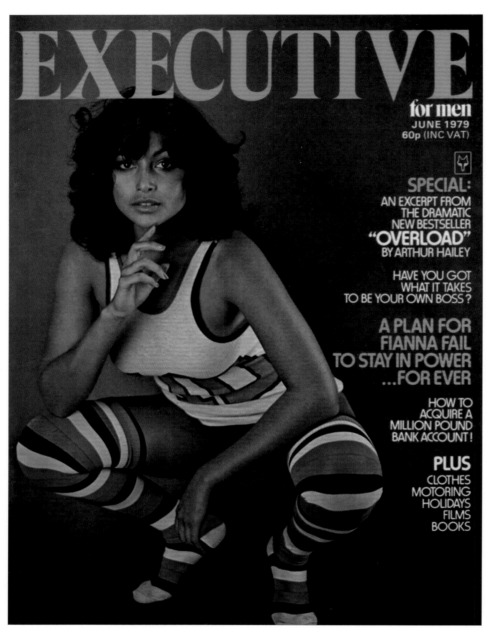

EXECUTIVE

for men

JUNE 1979
60p (INC VAT)

SPECIAL:
AN EXCERPT FROM
THE DRAMATIC
NEW BESTSELLER
"OVERLOAD"
BY ARTHUR HAILEY

HAVE YOU GOT
WHAT IT TAKES
TO BE YOUR OWN BOSS?

A PLAN FOR
FIANNA FAIL
TO STAY IN POWER
...FOR EVER

HOW TO
ACQUIRE A
MILLION POUND
BANK ACCOUNT!

PLUS
CLOTHES
MOTORING
HOLIDAYS
FILMS
BOOKS

Executive

Issue 2, June 1979

Executive Magazine came out in 1979, adopting a similar format to Man Alive (1974),
covering men's fashion, cars, photographic essays (semi-nude women), lifestyle, eating
out, short stories and some politics. It later became 'New Executive', ditching what little Irish
content it had and replacing it with generic international reviews and photographic essays.

Executive
Below: 1979
All others: Circa early 1980s

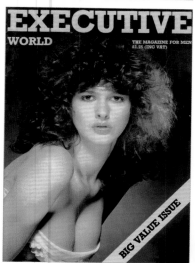

Come alive with Manta the one to be seen with

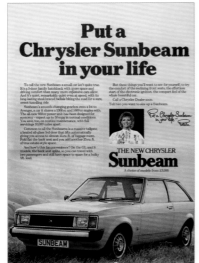

Put a Chrysler Sunbeam in your life

THE NEW CHRYSLER
Sunbeam

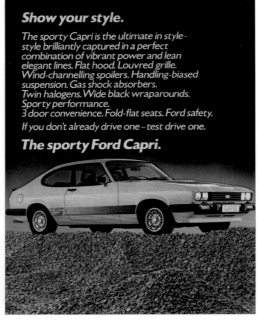

Show your style.

The sporty Capri is the ultimate in style -
style brilliantly captured in a perfect
combination of vibrant power and lean
elegant lines. Flat hood. Louvred grille.
Wind-channelling spoilers. Handling-biased
suspension. Gas shock absorbers.
Twin halogens. Wide black wraparounds.
Sporty performance.
3 door convenience. Fold-flat seats. Ford safety.

If you don't already drive one – test drive one.

The sporty Ford Capri.

Step out of the crowd. Step into Citroën.

Fashioned to your demands

The new Datsun Cherry is equipped to handle any
demands made on it by a modern, busy, motorist.
Reliable and economic in the true Datsun tradition, extra-
smooth styling, front-wheel drive for easier handling,
and roomy interior ensures it is every inch a winner.

The four-door Saloon looks so compact from the outside
that the roominess of its interior, with more leg and head
space, is a constant surprise.

The Cherry hatchback, simple to park, ultra-sleek lines
and the ease of loading and unloading luggage of a
much larger car.

Like all models in the Cherry range, the two-door Saloon
comes with a choice of fifteen colours, luxury cloth
upholstery, radio, cigarette lighter, hazard warning lights
and heated rear screen.

DATSUN

Datsun Limited, Datsun House,
Naas Road, Dublin 12. Telephone 504877.

Motor Car Adverts

Top right: Ford Capri, Magill 1979

Bottom right: Datsun Cherry, Magill 1980

Bottom left: Citroen, pictured outside Shelbourne Hotel, Dublin, Executive 1979

Middle left: Chrysler Sunbeam with Petula Clark, Magill 1978

Top left: Opel Manta, pictured outside Killiney Castle, Man Alive 1974

Motor Cars

Left: Motoring Review, Irish Business and Finance 1978
Below: Irish Motorist, front cover picture at Dollymount Strand with Jim O'Neill 1983
Bottom right: Spitfire Triumph, Magill 1980
Bottom middle: BE Princess, Executive 1979
Bottom left: Opel Manta Hatchback, Executive 1979

Adverts for Honda Motor Bike

New Spotlight

All from 1970 except Powerscourt 1973
and Grand Canal 1971

MAIN YAMAHA
DEALERS

HANOVER
CYCLE
CO.

43 OLIVER
PLUNKETT
STREET,
CORK

introducing the
new 50cc bike
that anyone
can afford

the Yamaha
chick 50

The Chick-50 is the lowest priced 50 cc Japanese bike in the country (unless, of course, you want a pedal machine). It's just loaded with Fun—Fun—Fun! And you CAN afford it. What you may not realise is WHY you can. It takes years of motorcycle engineering to produce an economical bike like the Chick. From Yamaha's race-bred rotary valve engine to the famous Autolube system (with separate tanks for petrol and oil, gives great fuel economy—200 mpg—keeps the engine cool and clean, and is exclusive to Yahama), from safety to comfort, the Chick-50 gives a consistently better performance than any other 50 cc model. Check it with your local dealer to-day. And think about the special low insurance rates for Yahama owners only. The Yahama Chick Goes Cheap—the lowest priced 50 cc bike* in production.

Price £109.15.0.

the new

YAMAHA
chick 50

* When we say ' bike ' we naturally mean non-pedal assisted.

If you can't beat them

join them.

The only way to keep up with the Yamaha crowd is on a Yamaha. You see Yamahas everywhere — but not for long. Yamahas overtake, out-accelerate and out-corner anything. Yamaha riders spend less too — they can get up to 200 miles on a gallon. And if you don't see a girl friend on the pillion — she's got a Yamaha of her own (yes, Yamaha make a bike for girls too). So head for your local dealer and come away faster, on a Yamaha.

| YAMAHA 50 (YF · 1AK) | YAMAHA 50 (MF - 3D) |

Get places, fast, on a **YAMAHA**

Capri

Enjoy the clean luxury of a Capri. Zip through the traffic for fab trips to the country or beach.

Turn every weekend into a holiday !

Get the most out of life by getting your Capri Now.

Capri 50 c.c. — £132-0-0
Capri 100 c.c. — £155-0-0
Capri 150 c.c. — £175-0-0

BUZZ ALONG
on one of these fab
GARELLI
WASPS

It's just the job for nipping through the traffic — it's much faster than the bus and of course you don't have to queue — it'll take you from door to door in half a jiffy and costs less than ½d per mile to run. You'll be able to buy it out of the money you save on bus fares! Ideal for a quick run to the sea after work or for exploring at week-ends.

See it at your dealers now or get catalogue and confidential credit terms from the distributors.

61 gns

Agrati Sales (I.) Ltd.
21, MAIN ST., DONNYBROOK,
DUBLIN. 4.

The Garelli Concorde, price £97.00, fitted with legshields ensures easy clean travel at reasonably low cost (less than ¼ per mile) for those who can't be bothered wasting time in a bus or car snarled up in a traffic jam.

Motor Bike Adverts

All from New Spotlight

Top left: Yamaha Cork 1968

Top right: Yamaha Chick 1968

Middle left: Yamaha 50 1968

Middle right: Garelli Wasp 1967

Above: Capri 1971

Right: Garelli 1971

Good taste... Carrolls Number 1

LOW TO MIDDLE TAR As determined by Haskins Laboratories Europe Ltd.

GOVERNMENT WARNING: SMOKING CAN DAMAGE YOUR HEALTH

before you pay more than 4'1 for 20 cigarettes, make this test

Try Country Life. It's the obvious way to judge the quality that makes this cigarette the best value in smoking today

4'1 for twenty

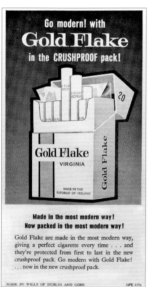

Go modern! with Gold Flake in the CRUSHPROOF pack!

Gold Flake VIRGINIA

MADE IN THE REPUBLIC OF IRELAND

Made in the most modern way! Now packed in the most modern way!

Gold Flake are made in the most modern way, giving a perfect cigarette every time . . . and they're protected from first to last in the new crushproof pack. Go modern with Gold Flake! . . . now in the new crushproof pack.

MADE BY WILLS OF DUBLIN AND CORK

Special friends. Special evening. What other cigarette could be so right?

John Player Special
The mild king size cigarette. 29p for 20.

move up to Kingsway

Kingsway king size filter

Move up to Kingsway, the cigarette that fits the mood of these exciting times so well. More length, more pleasure, more fine tobacco. At 4/6 for 20, Kingsway cost no more than plain ordinary-size cigarettes.

MADE IN IRELAND BY WILLS OF DUBLIN AND CORK

Adverts for Cigarettes

Top right: Country Life, Woman's Choice 1968

Bottom right: Kingsway, Woman's Way 1966

Bottom middle: John Player Special, Woman's Way 1972

Bottom left: Gold Flake, Model Housekeeping 1961

Top left: Carrolls Number 1, In Dublin 1979

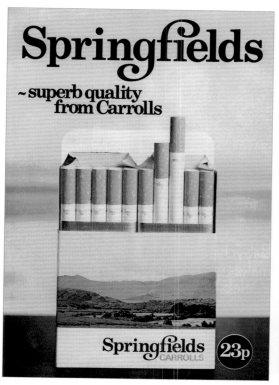

Adverts for Cigarettes

Top right: Albany, Woman's Choice 1971
Right: Springfields, Woman's Choice 1971
Bottom middle: Consulate, Woman's Way 1972
Bottom left: Escort, Woman's Way 1966
Top left: Springfields, Woman's Way 1971

Adverts for Harp Lager
Magill
Left: 1978
Below: 1979
Bottom right: 1977
Bottom left: 1983

The way to treat a lady

Strong, Cool Lancer Lager

Good beginning to a lively lovely evening.
Something special for someone special.
Definitely the way to treat a lady.
BREWED BY HARP

Adverts for Beer and Lager
Left: Lancer, Magill 1980
Bottom right: Satzenbrau Pils, Executive 1979
Bottom left: Smithwicks, Magill 1980

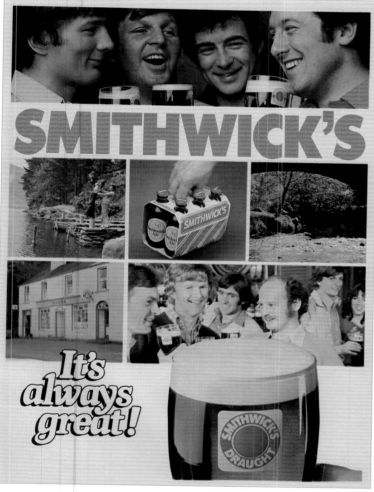

SMITHWICK'S

It's always great!

SMITHWICKS DRAUGHT

IF YOU'RE LOOKING FOR SOMETHING DIFFERENT

YOU'RE LOOKING AT IT

Satzenbrau
Pils
STRONG LAGER

SATZENBRAU
LAGER WITH A DIFFERENCE

How do they say vodka?

Photographed at the Richie Hendriks Gallery, Dublin.

Smirnoff!

In the east, a Smirnoff Screwdriver: Smirnoff with fresh orange juice. In New York, they prefer a Bloody Mary : Smirnoff with tomato juice. Sydney, Australia is the city for Smirnoff Gimlets, with a dash of bitters, lime juice and a big swoosh of soda. One thing is favourite with them all : Smirnoff, the vodka with the clean, exciting taste. Have an adventure to-night; try Smirnoff with something new.

clean round the world

Show your style

clearly

with your favourite tonic, or a dash of orange, red, lemon or lime.

Cork Dry Gin

The one and only.

Kiskadee
That's the way
the playground swings

Alfresco in August. Kebabs. And Kiskadee, the white rum to make a Caribbean of any beach. Cool it with Coke. Lace it with Lime. Tinge it with Tonic. And watch the sun go down through the ice at the bottom of your glass.

Adverts for Spirits

Top right: Smirnoff, Woman's Choice 1969
Bottom right: Kiskadee, Woman's Choice 1971
Above: Cork Dry Gin, Irish Business 1978

The Smirnoff advert was photographed at the Richie Hendrik's Gallery, 119 St Stephen's Green, Dublin 2.

Is This The Wine The Romans Banned?

'Tis said that Roman soldiers while guarding the banks of the Rhine were enticed away, never to return, by the golden wine of the Rhine Maidens, that one sip was enough to lure a man to their voluptuous embrace, and certain death. It's suggested that as a result, the Romans were forbidden to drink the delightful Liebfraumilch of the area and for years many thought the secret of the golden wine was lost forever. But it was kept and treasured, hidden in traditional stone crocks.

Today the soft, light refreshing wine is bottled in a replica of the stone crock of Roman times and can be enjoyed as an aperitif or with good food.

However should you be spending an evening on the banks of the Rhine…

Black Tower

LIEBFRAUMILCH QUALITATSWEIN
The wine of the Rhine Maidens

Adverts for Wine
Left: Black Tower, Magill 1978
Below: Blue Max, Executive 1979
Bottom left: Quinnsworth, Magill 1977

Your guided tour of the best wine producing countries …

…starts and ends at Quinnsworth

As it takes you to the best wine-producing districts, you'll see many quality names. Beaujolais Berard and a great range of Bordeaux wines from the famous House of Cruse. Rudolph Müller's Liebfraumilch and the Bishop of Riesling from the Rhine and Mosel valleys. In Italian wines, Bolla's Soave Classico and Ruffino's renowned Chianti. And that's not all. You'll see some superb sparkling wines, Dom Perignon champagne plus fine chateau wines like Chateau D'Issan. What does the tour cost? It depends, of course, on how many stops you make. But overall it comes at a bargain price because in most cases Quinnsworth import their wines directly. And to think it's a tour you can take any shopping day . . . .

Let's get it all together at

Quinnsworth

At Quinnsworth we stock the widest possible range of wines. And many are imported directly to give you the best value possible. All the wines illustrated are direct imports and therefore exceptional value.

Blue Max is a liebfraumilch new to Ireland. It is a really superb quality Rhine wine retailing at around £1.99, making it a very real alternative. **Blue Max** is here to stay. Ask for it today. Now you can buy a top quality liebfraumilch at a realistic price.

look out for **Blue Max**

Exclusive in Ireland to
Murphys Brewery Wines & Spirits Ltd.

Magill
January 1979

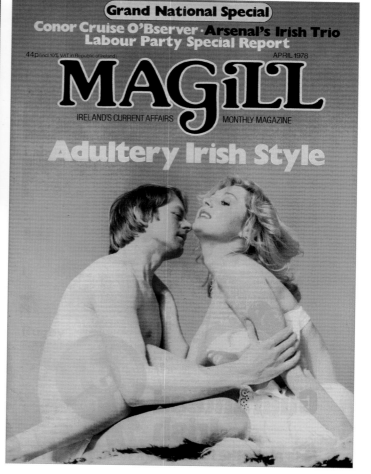

Magill

Top left: Nuclear 1978

Top right: The North 1978

Right: Adultery 1978

Bottom middle: Garda 1978

Bottom left: Gay Byrne 1979

A newsmagazine for women

Magill Publications Ltd. will publish a monthly newsmagazine for women from February 12 next. The editor will be Marian Finucane, who is currently presenter of the RTE Radio One programme, "Women Today".

Marian Finucane

Status will report on news events of interest to women, it will undertake investigations into issues related to women, it will include sections on health, consumer affairs, clothes, sport, finance, interior design, food and the arts.

Status will have a targeted circulation of 30,000 copies per issue, with a readership of 150,000 people.

Advertising manager for Status will be Pat Quinlan, who has been with Magill since last April.

Status, 14 Merrion Row, Dublin 2.
Telephone: 606055.

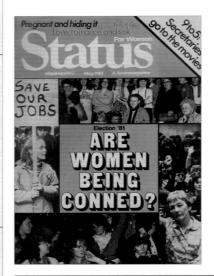

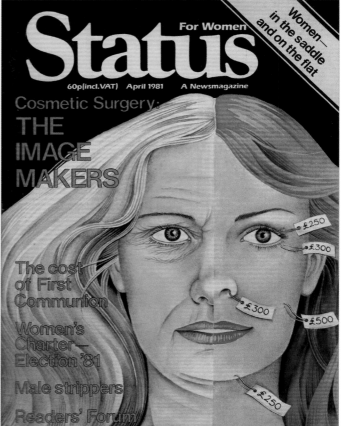

Status

All issues 1981

Top left: Notice for commencement of Status, Magill 1981. Marian Finucane was the original Status editor with Pat Brennan later taking over the role.

Status

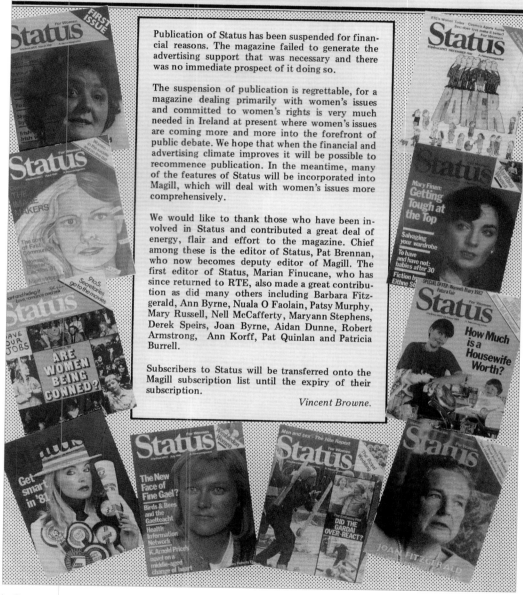

Publication of Status has been suspended for financial reasons. The magazine failed to generate the advertising support that was necessary and there was no immediate prospect of it doing so.

The suspension of publication is regrettable, for a magazine dealing primarily with women's issues and committed to women's rights is very much needed in Ireland at present where women's issues are coming more and more into the forefront of public debate. We hope that when the financial and advertising climate improves it will be possible to recommence publication. In the meantime, many of the features of Status will be incorporated into Magill, which will deal with women's issues more comprehensively.

We would like to thank those who have been involved in Status and contributed a great deal of energy, flair and effort to the magazine. Chief among these is the editor of Status, Pat Brennan, who now becomes deputy editor of Magill. The first editor of Status, Marian Finucane, who has since returned to RTE, also made a great contribution as did many others including Barbara Fitzgerald, Ann Byrne, Nuala O Faolain, Patsy Murphy, Mary Russell, Nell McCafferty, Maryann Stephens, Derek Speirs, Joan Byrne, Aidan Dunne, Robert Armstrong, Ann Korff, Pat Quinlan and Patricia Burrell.

Subscribers to Status will be transferred onto the Magill subscription list until the expiry of their subscription.

Vincent Browne.

Status

Notice of the closure of Status, Magill, January 1982

A BIT OF STICK NEVER DID ANYONE HARM, NOW DID IT?

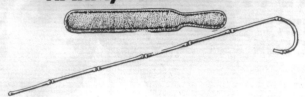

Have your prejudices been lashed lately?

Or your ideas knocked about? We think a newspaper should make people think. Upset people. Create controversy. Controversy? In The Irish Times? We like to feel we're the most controversial newspaper around. Because we try to show the world to the world as it is. And when that means shaking up people, or ideas, or prejudices, we do it with as much vigour as anybody.

But with more thought, more facts, more research, more depth.

Maybe we could shock you. Or make you disagree violently with us. Or make you glad we spoke out.

We'd like the chance.

Each weekday morning.

If you miss THE IRISH TIMES you miss part of the day

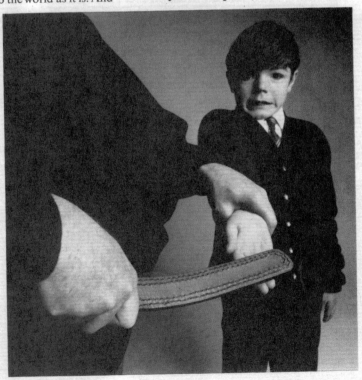

Irish Times Advert
Woman's Way 1971

MY LIFE WITH JACQUELINE KENNEDY

She worked with her during the White House years.
She knew her as a wife, mother and perfectionist.
She was at Jacqueline Kennedy's side on that fateful day in Dallas.
Now Mary Gallagher who was personal secretary to Jacqueline Kennedy has written an outspoken account on the devastating and wonderful events of these years.
The Sunday Independent will commence publication of this fascinating series next Sunday. Don't miss it.

Sunday Independent

Evening HERALD

Gay Byrne, Ireland's foremost television personality, has something controversial or witty to talk about every week in the Evening Herald. His sparkling column appears on Tuesdays.

Newspaper Adverts

Above: Evening Herald, Woman's Way 1969
Top left: Sunday Independent, Woman's Way 1970
Right: Sunday Tribune 1985

The Sunday Tribune is two years old today. Join the party with...

EAMON DUNPHY on Television and Soccer

DEIRDRE PURCELL Woman Journalist of the Year

DERMOT MORGAN on Low Life

EMILY O'REILLY on People

FINTAN O'TOOLE on Theatre

RUTH BUCHANAN on High Life

MICHAEL DWYER on Cinema

GRAEME COOK Property Editor

EUGENE McGEE on Gaelic Sports

DEIRDRE McQUILLAN on Fashion

WENDY SHEA O Brien Cartoonist

JOHN O'CALLAGHAN on Taxation

Ireland's Colourful Sunday

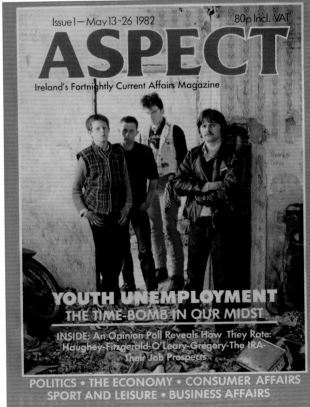

Various Magazine Covers

Top left: USI News 1989
Top right: Yes 1965
Middle right: Phoenix 1985
Above: Nusight 1969
Left: Aspect 1982

Various Magazine Covers

Above: Scene, illustrated by Jim Fitzpatrick 1968

Top left: Social & Personal 1994

Top right: d'Side 1995

Middle right: Big Issues 1994

Right: Bull Magazine, illustrated by O'Brien 1983

Adverts for Banks

Above: Bank of Ireland, Magill 1978

Top right: Hibernian Bank, Miss 1968

Top middle: Ulster Bank, Image 1984

Top left: Bank Giro, Woman's Choice 1969

Middle right: Bank of Ireland, Woman's Way 1974

Bottom right: AIB, New Spotlight 1972

Comics and Humour

Left: Gakbag 1984

Below: Dublin Opinion 1959

Bottom right: Yellow Press 1991

Bottom left: Fitz 1995

Gakbag was created and edited by award-winning Irish comedy writer and Drogheda United fan Arthur Mathews along with Mick Nugent. One of the strips, 'Jimmy's Boots', is featured in the sport chapter.

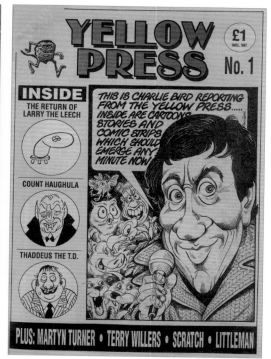

Too Late

Above: Too Late 4 1981
Left: Too Late 2 1980
Top left: Too Late 3 1980
Top right: Too Late 5 1981
Middle right: Too Late 1 1978

BRAND NEW RETRO

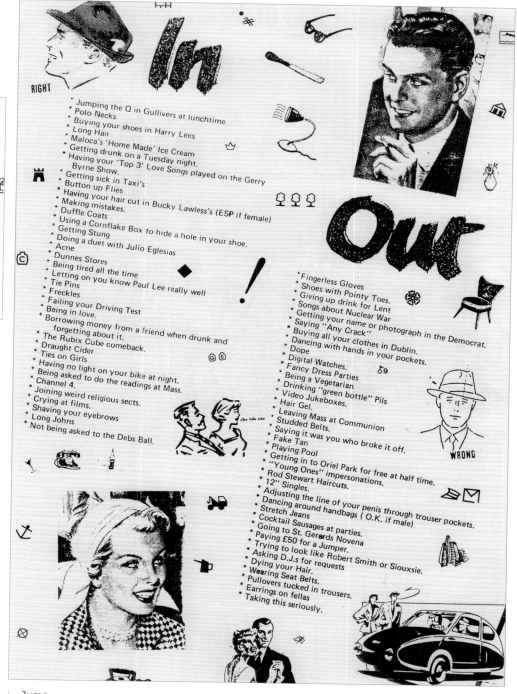

Jump

Issue 1 1984

Too Late (opposite page) was the first magazine I digitised for the blog. The choice was highly personal as I had co-produced the first issue with my brother, Eamonn, from our bedroom back in winter 1978. He went on to produce a further four issues with the help of a number of our friends. The first issue was heavily influenced by the punk fanzine culture of that time. The magazine later evolved into a humorous digest of the 'youth scene' in Dundalk during the period 1979 to 1982.

Jump was a single-issue sister magazine which continued the same theme but with slightly higher production values.

Food Adverts

Top right: Chef Sauce, Woman's Choice 1971

Above: Melville Milk, Model Housekeeping 1961

Left: Butterkrust Bread, Woman's Choice 1971

Top left: BIM Bord Iascaigh Mhara, Woman's Way 1967

Top middle: Green Isle, Women's Way 1969

Sausage Adverts

Above: Denny, Woman's Way 1967
Left: Clover, Woman's Choice 1968
Top left: Clover, Woman's Choice 1967

Adverts for Cheese
All from Woman's Way 1970

WEEK·END
completes that weekend feeling
with chocolates and candies in a smart new box.

A Mackintosh product · Made in Ireland.

Adverts for Treats and Soft Drinks

Left: Weekend, Woman's Choice 1968
Below: Tanora, Cork Holy Bough 1980
Bottom right: Miwadi, Woman's Way 1968
Bottom left: Batchelors Strawberries, Dublin Opinion 1959

In Enda Walsh's play Disco Pigs, Pig orders 'Two battur burgurs! Two sauce! Two chips! Two peas! Two Tanora!'

Things keep changing... but the good things stay the same. **Tanora** SPARKLING TANGERINE DRINK

"I ALWAYS *INSIST* ON B........S." **Batchelors**

"Because for flavour and quality Batchelors cannot be beaten. Just taste Batchelor's new season's Strawberries. You have? Then you know all about their specially wonderful flavour. No other Strawberries taste quite so delicious, quite so sun-ripe and juicy... right down to the last luscious mouthful."

SELECT IRISH **STRAWBERRIES**

Mi-Wadi makes Christmas The Real Thing

Mi-wadi ORANGE DRINK

33 50
60
45 50
60 STROBE

DIRECT DRIVE FULL AUTOMATIC
STERO TURNTABLE

ANTI SKATE

Music & Showbiz

'Alright the Scheme, it's your turn now' shouted Bono at the end of U2's soundcheck. We were a Dundalk group supporting U2 at Dublin's Dandelion Market and it wasn't often we were acknowledged by the main act, never mind allowed time for a soundcheck. It was September 1979, the gig was packed, brimming with energy, and U2 were about to release their first single.

A week later the Pope arrived. Ireland embraced the whole shebang and firmly pressed pause on the social and cultural change button.

MANUAL

12	30
10	25
7	17

SIZE

UP

DOWN

ARM
ELEVATION

START   STOP   REPEAT

Showband Snaps
New Spotlight 1966
Top: The Freshmen
Middle: The Plattermen
Bottom left: The Arrivals
Bottom right: The Drifters

THE MIGHTY AVONS

Showband Snaps

Left: The Mighty Avons
Bottom left: The Jim Farley Showband
Below: The Clubmen
Bottom right: The Royal Blues

All from the New Spotlight Annual 1967 which was published for Christmas 1966. Photographer with New Spotlight at that time was Roy Esmonde.

THE CLUBMEN

FARLEY SHOWBAND

THE ROYAL BLUES

Group Pin-Ups
New Spotlight

Left: Clouds 1969

Below: Candy 1970

Bottom left: Sands 1967

Bottom right: Granny's Intentions 1968

The pin-up page appeared either on the back or inner back cover of the weekly magazine.

New Spotlight pin-up: THE GENTRY

New Spotlight pin up: FIREHOUSE

Group Pin-Ups

New Spotlight

Top left: The Sahara 1970

Top right: The Creatures 1967

Above: Gentry 1970

Left: Firehouse 1970

New Spotlight Pin-up:
GREGORY OF THE CADETS

BRIAN COLL

Solo Pin-Ups

New Spotlight

Right: Brian Coll 1970

Above: Peter Adler 1966

Top left: Merv Allen 1971

Top right: Gregory (of the Cadets) 1970

Peter Adler, the guy with the shades, was the son of US musician Larry Adler and came to study in Trinity College. He was a member of Dublin beat group the Action in the mid sixties.

New
Spotlight
JOHN
McNALLY

Solo Pin-Ups
New Spotlight
Left: Butch Moore 1966
Above: Shay O'Hara 1968
Top right: Billy Brown 1968
Top middle: Johnny McEvoy 1968
Top left: John McNally 1968

● "Pussy's Parlour," described as a new excitingly different cabaret room, has opened at the Baggot Inn, Dublin. Star of the show is 'Mr. Pussy' himself/herself alias Alan Amsby who has arrived on the Dublin scene via London and Belfast.

Mr Pussy

Above: Alan Amsby, New Spotlight 1970

Left: With cartoonist Terry Willers and Mr Pussy's personal hairdresser, Showcase 1971

Top left: Mr Pussy, Showcase 1970

Top: Advert celebrating a one-year run at the Baggot Inn, Showcase 1971

Top right: Live, Showcase 1971

Mr Pussy (real name Alan Amsby) moved to Dublin from London, via Belfast, in 1969. A drag artist, he became a renowned figure in Irish cabaret. Donal Corvin said that 'if Danny La Rue is the sophisticated older woman, Pussy is the young mod girl giving everyone the come-on'.

Showbiz Snippets

Left: Ruth Buchanan, Scene 1968. Photo by Walter Pfeiffer

Below: Albert Reynolds at his Showboat cabaret club in Malahide, New Spotlight 1968

Middle right: Mark and Peter Keaveney, founders of Peter Mark hairdressers, Model Housekeeping 1965

Bottom right: Wedding of Bill and Hilary O'Herlihy, Woman's Way 1971

Bottom left: Milo O'Shea at Mosney with Danny Cummins and Joanne Walsh, Showcase 1968

Middle left: Adam Faith and John Bowman, RTE Guide 1962

Adam Faith chats with John Bowman, the compere of R.E.'s Come Dancing.

MARK and PETER KEAVENEY . . . . Not spoiled by success.

Danny Cummins, currently heading the Revue Company at Butlin's Holiday Camp, Mosney, Co. Meath, announced his engagement to Royalette, Joanne Walsh, Pimlico, Dublin. Milo O'Shea here congratulates the happy couple on a flying visit to the Camp.

Bill and Hilary O'Herlihy with Father Jerome O'Herlihy at the reception in Dublin's Shelbourne Hotel.

OUT NOW!

TERRIFIC
NEW
SINGLE FROM
KELLEY

M MOTHER'S LOV

c w I LOVE ONLY YOU on Target

DON'T TAKE ADVANTAGE OF ME

MURPHY and the SWALLOWS

Adverts & Promotional Shots

Top left: Advert for Kelley, New Spotlight 1970

Top right: Advert for Murphy and the Swallows, New Spotlight 1972

Above: Anne Byrne and the Pattern in Merrion Square, Dublin 2, Showcase 1970

Bottom right: Betty Anne and the Teenbeats, New Spotlight 1967

NATIONAL SONG CONTEST 1970

National Song Contest

New Spotlight 1970

Contestants for the 1970 National Song Contest outside RTE Studios in Donnybrook.
Dana, on the extreme right, would go on to win the Eurovision.

Heat

Left: Boy Scouts 1978
Below: Bob Geldof 1978
Top left: The Clash 1977
Middle left: The Hulk 1977
Bottom left: Radiators 1977

Heat, created by Jude Carr and Pete Price, began in 1977. It was fun, stylish, Irish - and streets ahead of all Irish and UK fanzines.

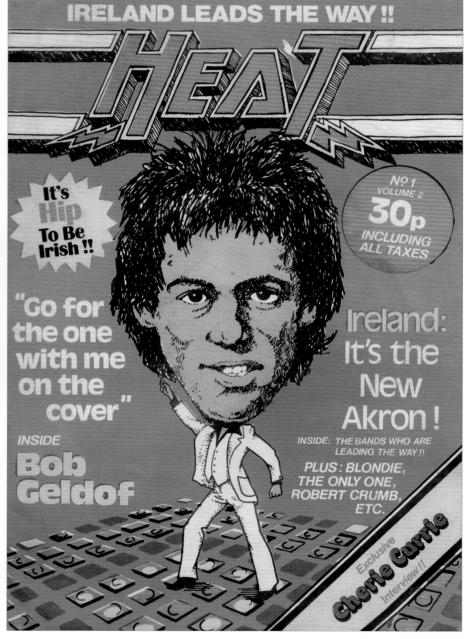

Fanzines

Above: Black & White 1979

Top left: Vox 1980

Top middle: Imprint 1980

Top right: Pop Tones circa 1982

Bottom right: Almost News 1985

It's interesting to see where those involved with fanzines ended up. Take the team from Almost News for example. Its editor Tony Clayton-Lea later joined the Irish Times. Shane Harrison joined the BBC while Kelly Fincham became a US college professor in journalism. Arthur Mathews did Toast of London, Father Ted, and loads more. Paul Eustace worked for iD and Dr Enda Murray is a filmmaker in Sydney.

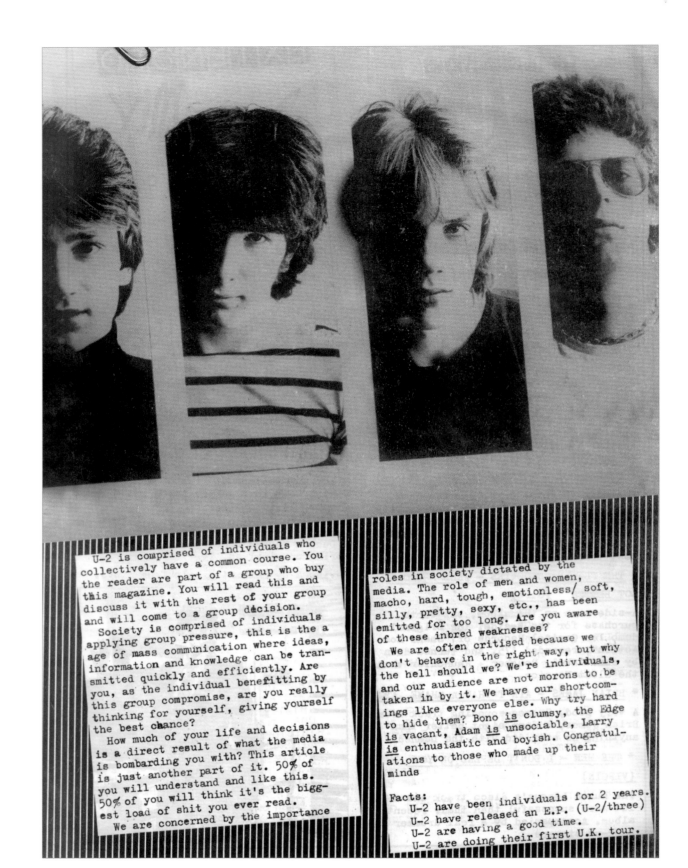

U-2 is comprised of individuals who collectively have a common course. You the reader are part of a group who buy this magazine. You will read this and discuss it with the rest of your group and will come to a group decision.

Society is comprised of individuals applying group pressure, this is the a age of mass communication where ideas, information and knowledge can be transmitted quickly and efficiently. Are you, as the individual benefitting by this group compromise, are you really thinking for yourself, giving yourself the best chance?

How much of your life and decisions is a direct result of what the media is bombarding you with? This article is just another part of it. 50% of you will understand and like this. 50% of you will think it's the biggest load of shit you ever read.

We are concerned by the importance

roles in society dictated by the media. The role of men and women, macho, hard, tough, emotionless/ soft, silly, pretty, sexy, etc., has been emitted for too long. Are you aware of these inbred weaknesses?

We are often critised because we don't behave in the right way, but why the hell should we? We're individuals, and our audience are not morons to be taken in by it. We have our shortcomings like everyone else. Why try hard to hide them? Bono is clumsy, the Edge is vacant, Adam is unsociable, Larry is enthusiastic and boyish. Congratulations to those who made up their minds

Facts:
U-2 have been individuals for 2 years.
U-2 have released an E.P. (U-2/three)
U-2 are having a good time.
U-2 are doing their first U.K. tour.

U2 by U2
Black & White fanzine 1979

Black and White fanzine emerged from the ashes of Heat fanzine. This issue came out in 1979, the year the Blades and U2 combined for a double-header weekly residency at the Baggot Inn. The U2 article was written by U2 themselves.

PAUL CLEARY

LARRY SCHREIBER

PAT LARKIN

THE BLADES: Perhaps the finest pop group Dublin has yet produced. Still raw slightly ragged as musicians, The Blades are developing at a rate of acceleration that far outstrips their local competition. And with several score songs that conduct the too-rare marriage of witty and perceptive lyrics with instantly memorable melodies, this Ringsend trio's preparations for an international breakout are nearing completion.

Already signed for Ireland to The Fledgling Guided Missiles label, The Blades have aroused much interest in London and Los Angeles, where their excellent four track demo has been well received, including two recording contracts and several publishing offers.

It is an auspicious start for so young a band (with barely seven months of gigging under their belts....) ; and The Blades have the talent and the drive to capitalize on it.

PAUL CLEARY: Prime mover of The Blades, Paul composes most of their songs, and possesses a manifestly sweet and expressive voice to sing'em with. 20 year-old Paul plays bass, and his favourite is blue.

PAT LARKIN: Already a legend in the Dublin Gas Works where he spends his week-days "drawing lines that represent pipes" onto blueprints, Pat is The Blades' ace stix'n'skins man. This 23 year-old Ringsender is also known for his cautious driving of the white Blades-mobile.

LARRY SCHREIBER: Known as the 'Lar' to the other two Blades, Larry is the group's guitarist. A reticent stage performer, Larry also sings backing vocals and is capable of writing fine pop songs when he can muster the self-confidence.

THE BLADES

The Blades
Black & White fanzine 1979

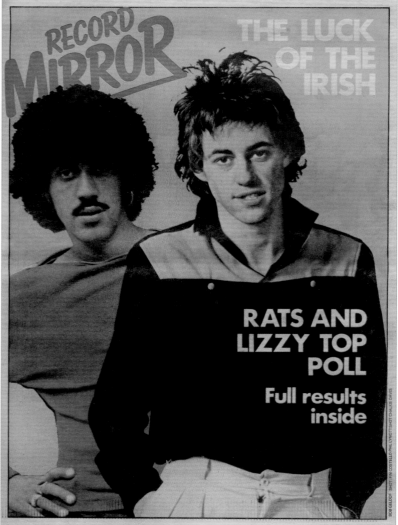

Phil Lynott Wedding
Record Mirror 1980
Top right: Phil Lynott, Caroline Crowther and
Lesley Crowther
Top middle: Phil Lynott and baby Sarah
Middle right: Brian Robertson and Bob Geldof
Above: Lemmy and Johnny Fingers
Top left: Mark Knopfler

Paula Yates wrote a weekly column for the Record
Mirror and in February 1980 she wrote about
her time at Phil Lynott and Caroline Crowther's
wedding. Caroline's father was comedian, actor
and game show host Leslie Crowther.

The Luck of the Irish
Record Mirror 1979

PLEASE LOOK AFTER THIS BAND

Twenty years ago, The Specials were the voice of a decaying Britain. But behind the hits lay a gang of damaged souls torn apart by their leader's unswerving political conviction. Alexis Petridis investigates. Meanwhile, on p.83, Lois Wilson looks at 2 Tone's other front-runners.

The Specials at Connolly Station
Mojo 2002

Mojo magazine ran a retrospective feature on the Specials in 2002. The photo was taken at Connolly Station, Dublin in November 1979. The two lads standing right behind Terry Hall are Odel Muckian and Shane Treacy from Dundalk.
Photo by Jill Furmanovsky

Depeche Mode in Dublin
NME 1983

Depeche Mode on the streets of Dublin before their gig at the SFX in September 1983. Andy Fletcher makes time for a pint.
| Photos by Adrian Booth.

Rod Stewart in Dublin
NME 1975

Rod Stewart was a tax exile in 1975, which meant he couldn't spend more than three months a year in England. To promote his new album Atlantic Crossing, the British media were invited to interview him in Dublin. He conducted the interviews in the Elizabeth Taylor suite at the Gresham Hotel along with then girlfriend Britt Ekland.
Photos by Joe Stevens.

Madness in Dublin

Melody Maker 1985

Photographed at Madigans pub, North Earl Street, Dublin 1, on Monday 28th October. It was a Bank Holiday and Marathon day in the city. Madness were playing that night at the nearby Saint Francis Xavier (SFX) hall, described in the article by Barry McIlheney as 'the city's premier venue for visiting pop stars'.

Photos by Paul Rider.

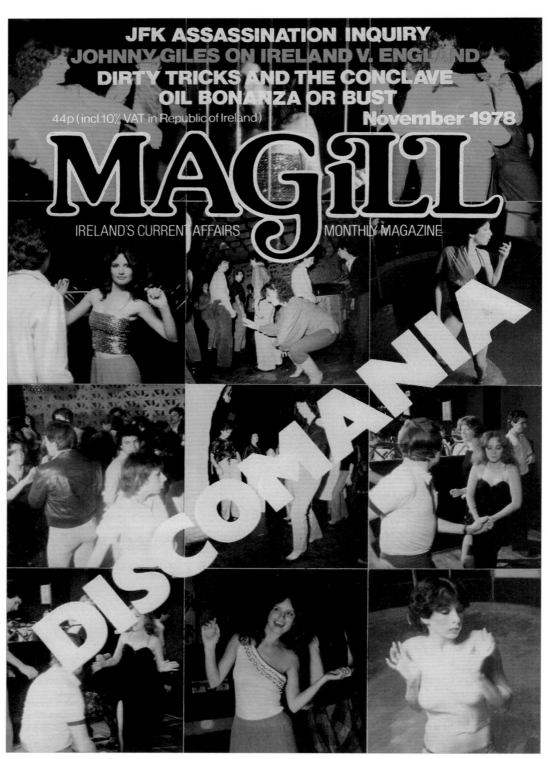

Discomania
Magill 1979
Photos by Tony O'Malley Studio

Dublin Nightclubs

Right: Membership card for Sloopys, 1971
Below: Sloopy's, Magill, 1979
Bottom left: Advert for Zhivago, Man Alive 1974
Bottom middle: Barbarellas, Magill, 1979
Bottom right: Advert for Club Cleo, Man Alive 1974
Magill photos by Tony O'Malley Studio.

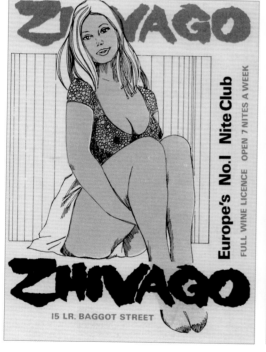

Revolution
NIGHT CLUB

Rutland Place

Top O'Connell St. opposite Gate Theatre.

Offers You

live entertainment from the world's top groups and D.J.'s. Atmosphere and lighting supreme. Full wine licence. Tudor-style restaurant where you may wine, dine and dance in intimate surroundings at reasonable prices.

BE SCENE AT

the newest-hottest spot in Cork

Swingers

NIGHT CLUB

Caroline St., Cork.

Now open Wed. thru Sun. from 10 p.m.

Gentle sensual swaying.
Live music from your favourite group.
Bittersweet glimpse of an old flame.
The sparkle of pre-dawn champagne.
Favourite foods taste better in the early a.m.
Chatting to celebrity disc-jockeys.
Hoping the night will never end.

The RIVERCLUB

It's a whole new scene

4 Batchelor's Walk · Dublin 1 · Phone 44746 42591 45732

Is your ballroom empty?
Let Star Trek help.

Star Trek has arrived ! The largest mobile discotheque in Europe. Star Trek will transform your Ballroom into a throbbing, exciting scene, with Go Go Girls, T.V. disc jockeys, a spectacular light show, and the latest pop records. Contact Star Trek, and let your Ballroom make money for you.

Star Trek

Monks Meadow, Portmarnock, Co Dublin. Tel 685 889

Nightclub Adverts

Above: The River Club, Bachelors Walk, Dublin 1, New Spotlight 1972
Left: Star Trek mobile disco, Showcase 1971
Top left: Revolution, Rutland Place, Dublin 1, Man Alive 1974
Top middle: Swingers night club, Caroline Street, Cork, Scene 1976

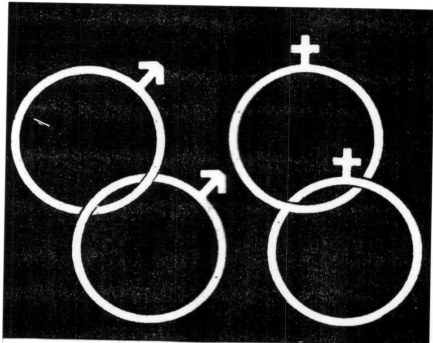

It would be impossible to say very much about **Flikkers** disco without making reference to the Hirschfeld Centre as a whole, for the disco is only one aspect of a most worthy, comprehensive and essential service for gay people.

Run by the National Gay Federation, the Centre provides for its members the support denied them by society. There are counselling facilities, the Tel-a-Friend service, a fine cinema/forum room and lounge space. The disco is on the 1st floor of this three-storey building. During the day it doubles as a restaurant so, by definition, it is functional rather than lavish. Taking into account the voluntary nature of the organisation and the financial burdens under which it operates, the facilities are remarkable and the relaxed atmosphere of people working together towards a common goal is immediately perceptible. What Flikkers lacks in lustre, it compensates for in its social function.

The ample dance floor, with modest lighting and surroundings, in no way detracts from the enjoyment of the participants, who on Saturday were mainly men. Thursday night is set aside for gay women. A splendid Bose sound system keeps you on your toes, disco and reggae being the main musical fare.

There is no alcohol on the premises (a fact which possibly contributes to the good vibe). At one end of the disco there is seating accommodation and a compact kitchenette. Here you can get delicious Bewley's tea or coffee, cakes, pies, curries, salads and soft drinks - all very reasonable. Flikkers gets an average attendance of 150 people a night, but they would hope for more when the projected decor and lighting improvements are completed.

The disco is confined to the Centre's members and their guests only and admission is £1.80 or £2.50 respectively. Members must be over 18. On Saturday, the age range seemed to be from 20 to 60 with more emphasis on the former. There is a special Youth counselling service for under 21s on a Sunday with a disco from 3 to 6.30 p.m.

According to the Federation's mag, In Touch, there are 'candlelit lunches at reasonable prices served to people of all persuasions' from 12.30 - 2 p.m. Times is hard, folks, the cause deserving; check it out.

Lynn Geldof

Gay Nightclubs

In Dublin 1980

Above: Review of Flikkers disco at the Hirschfeld Centre, Temple Bar, Dublin by Lynn Geldof

Right: Irish Gay Rights Movement, Phoenix Club advert

Top right: Flikkers Disco advert

Flikkers Disco

	Fri./Sat.	10.30 p.m. to 2 a.m.
buddys night	Sun.	9.30 p.m. to 1 a.m.
reduced rates	Wed.	10.00 p.m. to 1 a.m.

Flikkers Disco Hirschfeld Centre
10 Fownes St., Dublin 2. Tel. 710939
admission & membership reserved

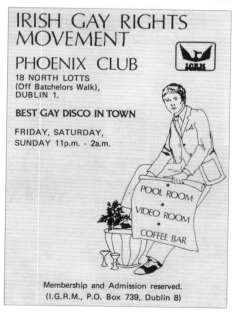

IRISH GAY RIGHTS MOVEMENT

PHOENIX CLUB

18 NORTH LOTTS
(Off Batchelors Walk),
DUBLIN 1.

BEST GAY DISCO IN TOWN

FRIDAY, SATURDAY,
SUNDAY 11p.m. - 2a.m.

POOL ROOM
VIDEO ROOM
COFFEE BAR

Membership and Admission reserved.
(I.G.R.M., P.O. Box 739, Dublin 8)

WEEKLY VOL. 2. NO. 4. WEEK ENDING JUNE 22. PRICE 1/2 (Incl. all taxes)

BIG BEAT COMPETITION:DUBLIN ENTERTAINMENT GUIDE:WORDS OF YOUNG GIRL

New Spotlight

1968

John Coughlan started Spotlight in Cork in 1963 as an 8 page foldover magazine printed on quality blotting paper. Issue 1 sold 2,000 copies and as readership grew the format changed to tabloid size and John launched Spotlight as a national pop monthly. Production moved to Dublin in late 1964 and 'New' was tagged on to the title. By 1966 New Spotlight had sales of 55,000 with 200,000 readers and in 1967 it went weekly.

Colourful and entertaining, New Spotlight set its own standards and provided a new and exciting platform for Irish entertainers. Of course it covered mainly Showband acts but it also featured articles from regular columnist Pat Egan, who championed new young Irish talent. Donal Corvin was there too and it is these articles, along with photos by Mark Nolan and Roy Esmonde and illustrations by Kevin O'Brien, that are fondly featured throughout the book and blog.

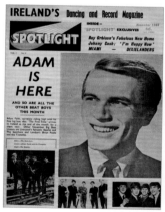

New Spotlight

Top left: Christmas 1970

Top right: Dickie Rock 1968

Bottom right: Dreams 1970

Bottom middle: Tina and Roly 1969

Bottom left: Spotlight 1963

National Showbiz Poll Results

This page: New Spotlight cover 1971

Opposite page: Poll results, New Spotlight 1971

FAV. IRISH MALE SINGER:
1, Joe Dolan; 2, Dickie Rock; 3, Big Tom; 4, Dermot Hegarty; 5, Gene Stewart.

FAV. IRISH GROUP:
1, Skid Row; 2, Taste; 3, Bye Laws; 4, Thin Lizzy; 5, Granny's Intentions.

FAV. IRISH RADIO D.J.:
1, Larry Gogan; 2, Terry Wogan; 3, Brendan Balfe; 4, Mike Murphy; 5, Gay Byrne.

FAV. IRISH GIRL SINGER:
1, Margo; 2, Dana; 3, Kelley; 4, Sandy Jones; 5, Clodagh Rogers.

FAV. FOLK GROUP OR SINGER:
1, Danny Doyle; 2, Dubliners; 3, Pattersons; 4, Johnny McEvoy; 5, Wolfe Tones.

FAV. IRISH CLUB D.J.:
I, Pat Egan; 2, Danny Hughes; 3, Larry Gogan.

FAV. IRISH C&W SINGER:
1, Big Tom; 2, Gene Stewart; 3, Brian Coll; 4, Dermot Henry; 5, D. Hegarty.

BEST YOUNG SHOWBAND HOPE FOR '71:
1, Arrows; 2, Freedom; 3, Virginians; 4, Gentry; 5, Hillbillies.

FAV. IRISH SHOWBAND OR GROUP MUSICIAN:
1, Billy Brown; 2, Rory Gallagher; 3, Clem Quinn.

FAV. WORLD MALE SINGER:
1, Elvis; 2, Tom Jones; 3, Cliff Richard; 4, Glen Campbell; 5, Englebert Humperdinck.

FAV. INTERNATIONAL C&W STAR:
1, Johnny Cash; 2, Slim Whitman; 3, Glen Campbell; 4, Hank Locklin; 5, Buck Owens.

FAV. INTERNATIONAL 'HEAVY' GROUP:
1, Led Zeppelin; 2, Deep Purple; 3, Blood Sweat & Tears; 4, Taste; 5, Jethro Tull.

FAV. WORLD GIRL SINGER:
1, Mary Hopkin; 2, Lulu; 3, Cilla Black; 4, Sandy Shaw; 5, Freda Payne.

FAV. INTERNATIONAL GROUP:
1, Tremeloes; 2, Christie; 3, Creedence Clearwater Revival; 4, Beatles; 5, Bee Gees.

BEST BRITISH DISC JOCKEY:
1, Jimmy Saville; 2, Tony Blackburn; 3, Terry Wogan; 4, Tony Prince; 5, Alan Freeman.

Joe Dolan in Israel
New Spotlight 1970

Joe Dolan wrote a personal account of his trip to Israel, where he and the Drifters played in front of a crowd of almost 100,000 people. 'Tel Aviv is a long way from Mullingar... I had no idea that my hits had created such an impression in Israel. Of course, "Make Me an Island" made No. 1 there. "Teresa" had also done very well. Though that surging crowd was frightening for a moment, it was really one of the big thrills of my life'.

JOE IN ISRAEL

New Spotlight EXCLUSIVE

Israel may be involved in what might be called a running war with several Arab countries, but Drifter JOE DOLAN found the capital, Tel Aviv, a place of sunshine and happiness when he went there to sing at a pop festival. In fact, he says, he had only one nervous moment in all the time he spent there. He tells about it in the article over-page which he wrote exclusively for us

A familiar face on the streets of Tel Aviv.

Joe escorts an Israeli woman soldier. Below : Shopping in the market place.

100,000 Israelis turned up to hear Ireland's top pop singer.

JOE DOLAN OFFERS

£500 REWARD

Dominick Street,
Mullingar,
County Westmeath.
6th June, 1968.

It has come to my notice that rumours are being widely circulated about me concerning imaginary happenings with which I am supposed to have been associated.

These rumours are false and malicious in every detail and are an obvious attempt to injure me in the public eye.

Through my solicitors, J. A. Shaw & Co., Mullingar, I have requested the local Superintendent of the Garda Siochana (who has assured me that he believes the rumours to be groundless) to endeavour to trace the source of these malicious and unfounded stories.

I now hereby offer a reward of FIVE HUNDRED POUNDS to any person obtaining true information to enable me to successfully prosecute some or even one of these malicious scandal mongers.

Signed ....

JOE DOLAN

Joe Dolan Reward
New Spotlight 1970

This half-page advert was placed in New Spotlight magazine in June 1968. Elsewhere in the same issue there was an article entitled 'Joe Hits Back at Rumour Mongers' stating that Joe is 'offering a £500 reward to get to the bottom of vicious rumours being circulated about him. Normally Joe is cool, calm and unruffled, but the totally unfounded stories that have gained currency about him have hurt and angered him'.

Advert for The Chessmen

New Spotlight 1968

'Bang Shang A-Lang' was a seven-inch single released by Dublin
group the Chessmen, who were managed for a time by Noel Pearson.

Terry Wogan Interview
New Spotlight 1970

'It's good to be home for a while. But I see that the showbands are as bad as ever'. Donal Corvin chats with Terry Wogan back home in Ireland on a break from his regular afternoon BBC radio show.

TERRY WOGAN, currently one of Ireland's most successful exports, leaned his elbow on O'Connell Bridge, gazed down the Liffey towards the sea and said: 'It's good to be home for a while. But I see that the showbands are as bad as ever.'

He was on holiday from the BBC and his daily two-hour record programme. And he was talking on what used to be one of his pet subjects; the sad quality of some of our showbands and the country and western music that he detests.

Terry doesn't set himself up as a judge when he's talking about music but he knows a bummer of a song when he hears it. He plays a few bummers on his show and is the first to admit it.

'I don't pick the records for the programmes,' he says. 'The producer looks after that. They wouldn't be my choice and they aren't the producer's personal choice either. We're both catering for an audience of housewives and we play what we think they want to hear. If I happen to like a record that I play, I endorse it. Otherwise I just announce it and say nothing about whether I like it or not.'

He would like to do a programme of the music he likes. But meanwhile he's quite happy doing what he is good at— a chatty sort of show. He has a television show in his sights too. And the chances are that he'll get it all right—doing a sort of Eamonn Andrews routine.

Eamonn Andrews, I thought . . . Eamonn, Dave Allen, Terry Wogan. Three Irishmen with the gift of the gab who have done very well in a country where Irishmen normally just dig the roads.

● Did Terry think that being Irish had been a help to him in England? . . . 'Oh, definitely,' he agreed quickly. 'Having an Irish accent has been a great advantage so far. It's a classless accent in England and because of that you can appeal to a wider variety of listeners.'

'But', he warned, 'there have been so many bomb scares in England and the CS gas affair in the House of Commons and raids on people found with arms— all of them connected with Irishmen. This could affect people in my position. While this sort of thing is happening— and associated with Irishmen— English listeners might resent having an Irish accent on their national radio station for two hours every afternoon.'

Terry has been living in England for almost a year. With his wife and two young Wogans, he lives in a house about twenty miles outside the smoke of London. He likes it there, enjoys his work and has a good social life.

● Most of his friends are disc jockeys who work along with him in the Beeb. But I gather that Jimmy 'What's the recipe today?' Young doesn't figure on his list.

Terry isn't one of your 'cabbage' DJ's who can waffle like mad into a mike but can't string two words together when you try to talk to them. He's well stocked up with the old grey matter, probably as a result of eating a lot of sardines when he was young. He is an intelligent bloke, a good conversationalist who really has got something to talk about.

Donall Corvin.

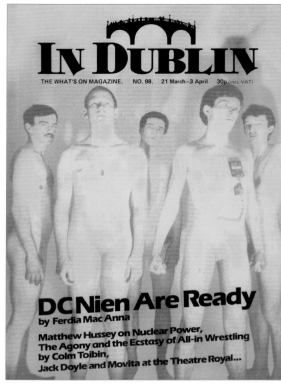

In Dublin

THE WHAT'S ON MAGAZINE.   NO. 98.   21 March–3 April   30p (incl. VAT)

DC Nien Are Ready
by Ferdia Mac Anna

**Matthew Hussey on Nuclear Power,
The Agony and the Ecstasy of All-in Wrestling
by Colm Toibin,
Jack Doyle and Movita at the Theatre Royal...**

35p (incl. VAT)   No.123   What's On 20 March–2 April

In Dublin

TOM WAITS, LOW-LIFER WITH CLASS
talks to John Little

WHAT'S ON 7–20 Feb   75p (incl 23½ VAT) No. 222

In Dublin

THE IRISH DISEASE:
BEGRUDGERY!
PLUS: ONLY FOOLS AND HORSES
- Coal Wars in the City by Padraig Yeates

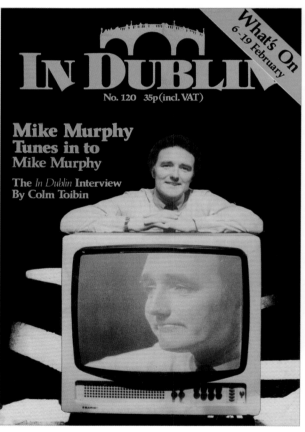

In Dublin

What's On 6–19 February

No. 120   35p (incl. VAT)

Mike Murphy
Tunes in to
Mike Murphy

The *In Dublin* Interview
By Colm Toibin

In Dublin

Vol 18 No 4 17 FEB–3 MAR '93

COMIC HEROES
KEVIN MCALEER
DENNIS LEARY
RAB C NESBITT

MUSIC
PADDY MOLONEY
CARTER USM
THE FRANK AND WALTERS

THE TRIALS OF
DERMOT MORGAN

In Dublin Covers

Top left: DC Nien 1980
Top right: Tom Waits 1981
Middle right: Begrudgery! 1985
Above: Dermot Morgan 1993
Left: Mike Murphy 1981

In Dublin began in April 1976 as a pocket-sized 'What's On' for the city. It later moved to standard A4 size. In 1986, its ten-year retrospective stated that 'it never set out to overthrow the face of journalism or even to make a fortune. You look back over ten years at a downright weird collection of articles, some radical, some grindingly conservative, some entertaining, some pompous as hell. Sometimes it seemed to matter, sometimes it seemed to wilfully ignore the serious stuff of the moment'.

DUBLINER Luke Kelly, known for his outspoken comments, takes the seat this week in an interview that takes you into the minds of the pop people who make the news . . . Pat Egan asks the Questions.

Q. How important is drinking to you?

A. It's a pleasure. Give me more and more and more. But I'm not so happy with the way they are changing all the auld pubs around, all this carpet and all these fancy seats. It's claustrophobia. My favourite pubs are McDaids in Grafton St., and Andy Cronin's, Kinnegad, and the Wren's Nest . . .

Q. Can you recall the happiest and most thrilling day of your life.

A. The day I made my first Holy Communion. Just think of the money I got, it was a great scene.

Q. Can you recall the most horrifying and ugliest day of your life?

A. The day I realised I was ugly and in no way attractive to women, and believe me, things have not improved since then. Seriously, it must have been the first time I saw films of Hiroshima. It was sickening how mankind could stoop so low. Those B Specials—they're horrifying too.

Q. Your views on the following people:
(1) Major Chichester Clarke, (2) Ian Paisley, (3) Bernadette Devlin, (4) The Pope.

A. Chichester Clark—He's non-existent and an accident. A very unimportant person.

Ian Paisley—Even a bigger accident. I have no time for the man at all.

Bernadette Devlin—I' dlike to marry her. She does all her talking in public and is probably a very quiet girl in private.

The Pope—He's a nice gentleman. I don't think he's as able to fulfil his role as well as Pope John was.

Q. Do you believe in love at first sight?

A. Love at first sight. No, but I believe in love for one night. Sure, I don't know what love is. I'm a married man, but I've no children. Nah! love is only for teenagers. I don't know anything about it.

Q. What does it take to make you happy.

A. I'm a very happy man at present. To sing well, a game of golf, a drink. I'll go on singing to my dying day. I more than likely will sing at my own wake. How about that.

Q. If not Luke Kelly, who would you like to have been.

A. Oh! Georgie Best. Look at the birds he has and all the ball's as well. Sure a footballer has a great life . . . Oh sure I had dreams about being a classical violinist or a great conductor.

The Dubliners and Tom Jones at the TV Club
New Spotlight 1967
Top: Luke Kelly, Tom Jones and Ciaran Bourke.
Centre: Jim Aiken, Tom Jones, Michael Hand and John Coughlan of New Spotlight with his wife Margaret.
Left: Michael Ryan (Evening Herald), Ronnie Drew, John Coughlan and Bill Troy, who was art director at New Spotlight at the time.

Music Adverts
Below: Big Tom, Christmas tour, New Spotlight 1968
Top right: Michael Landers, New Spotlight 1971
Bottom right: BP Fallon, Miss 1967
Bottom left: The Venturers, New Spotlight 1969

Best wishes for a Happy Christmas & New Year to our fans, friends and business associates from

BIG TOM AND THE MAINLINERS

Sun. Dec. 22nd TOOREEN	Fri. 27th NAVAN
Christmas Night MAPLE, ROCKCORRY	Sat. 28th DUNGANNON
St. Stephens Night PAVESI, DONEGAL	Sun. 29th KINGSCOURT

5-year-old sensation
Michael Landers
and his fantastic 9-piece band

THE YOUNGEST RECORDING ARTIST IN THE WORLD

great new release

'If I could be a sailor-man'

c/w 'MR. TAXMAN'

ON RUBY 131

Enquiries: Managers Note Phone 45284

THE PILLAR IS GONE—
BUT B. P. FALLON IS STILL WITH US

READ HIS COLUMN FOR POPSTERS
every week in
TOP TEN
PRICE 9d.

THE ONLY MAGAZINE WITH THE OFFICIAL IRISH TOP TEN

A great new release from the
VENTURES

'Where has all the love gone'

c/w 'Dear John'
ON RELEASE
in your record shops now

The Facts on

LARRY GOGAN

REAL NAME: Lorcan Gogan.
BIRTHDAY: 3rd May, 1892.
BIRTHPLACE: Rathgar, Dublin.
EDUCATED: St. Mary's College, Rathmines.
SISTERS: Maire and Eileen.
BROTHERS: Gerard, John, Tom, Bernard and Nia'l.
FORMER OCCUPATION: Actor.
HEIGHT: 5 ft. 10 ins.

HAIR: Brown.
EYES: Blueish Green.
AGE ENTERED SHOW BUSINESS: 14.
FIRST APPEARANCE: Gaiety Theatre in play "Life with Father."
FIRST RADIO BROADCAST: Playing part in a serial "District Nurse" 1961.
FIRST DEE JAY BROADCAST: "Morning Melody" 1961.

FIRST TV SHOW: "Shall We Dance" 1961.
HOBBIES: Records, Films.
FAV. FOOD: Steak and Chips and Ice Cream with cream.
FAV. DRINK: Lager.
FAV. DISC JOCKEYS: Alan Freeman, Dave Cash, Dave Symonds.
CAR: Fiat 124.
DISLIKES: Overbearing rude people.

LIKES: Relaxing over a few jars with friends, blondes.
FAV. SINGERS: Dusty Springfield, Tom Jones.
FAV. GROUPS: Bee Gees, Beatles, Blood Sweat and Tears.
FAV. ACTORS: Steve McQueen, Milo O'Shea.
FAV. TV PERSONALITY: Frank Hall.
AMBITION: To Keep it Swingin'.

The Facts on Larry Gogan

New Spotlight 1969

Larry's parents owned a newsagents in Fairview. I'm reliably told that, even before he entered showbiz, the local girls were always happy to run an errand to the shop for a chance of bumping into Larry.

RTE Guide

Top right: Bunny Carr 1976

Bottom right: Hal Roach 1962

Bottom middle: Forfeit 1962

Left: Aine O'Connor, Tom McGuirk 1975

Middle left: Hall's Pictorial Weekly 1976

Top left: Arthur Murphy 1975

Now almost 55 years old and still going strong each week, the first issue of the RTE Guide came out in December 1961.

RTE Guide

Top left: Barry Lang, Ruth Buchanan 1983
Top middle: Sheeba 1981
Top right: Gay Byrne 1984
Bottom right: Gerry Ryan 1988
Bottom left: Joe Lynch, Dermot Morgan, Twink, Ruth Buchanan 1983

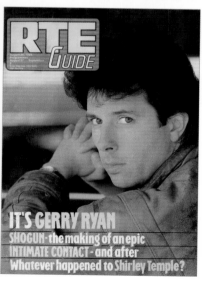

"It all started when I was still in school," said 19-year-old Dublin-born Philip Lynott, lead vocalist with that exciting new group, Orphanage.

"You know the sort of thing—a group of kids very impressed by the Beatles. We all bought guitars, formed a group called the Black Eagles, played anywhere we could, then split up and joined various groups. The only record I've made was with Skid Row—'New Places, Old Faces'." He laughed. "It only sold six hundred copies. Hope my next one does better."

I'd say it will. Though not long on the Irish beat scene, Orphanage are already very popular all round the country and have appeared on R.T.E.'s "Like Now" and U.T.V.'s "Zoom-In."

What of Philip? He's strong-minded, confident, outspoken, and says, "What do I like? Sexy females, especially strawberry blondes. Cars—I'd like to have one, just something that goes and is kinky; nice people, but above all, music. That's the ultimate for me—the big thing in my life and it comes before anything else. I spend hours playing and listening to music and writing songs, then I'm happy.

"I'll tell you what I dislike most of all too—those superior types who look down on any girl who hasn't got the same views. What right does anyone have to be so critical? We're all got our own lives to lead and different ideas on how to do this. The place money has in people's lives annoys me too. O.K., I know it's essential, but at the moment it's all-important to too many people. Another thing is social injustice. No. I'm not going to say anything about racial discrimination because people just say, 'Oh, another coloured fella with a chip on his shoulder. Take all the things Bob Dylan writes about though—housing problems, people starving and dying, wars. I sometimes get very frustrated because I feel so strongly about these things and can't do anything about them."

He glares. "I'd like to put all the oppressors into the oppressed position.

"Do you know what else I'd like to do? Adopt a kid. Now why can't single people do that? I'd like a kid and I'd be good to him and look after him and give him a good life—better than he'd have in an orphanage and no pun intended!' '

He grins. "I don't particularly want a wife, because I'm a bit of a flirt!"

Who are his favourite singers?

"I've lots of favourites in different styles. From Frank Sinatra to Frank Zappa of the Mother's Inventions and from Aretha Franklin to Rudy Valli to that great female Tiny Tim."

His favourite place is Dublin city, "dirty or not I love it." He likes anything from the hippy mode in clothes to the neat French look and has a current craze for spaghetti.

If he could change places with someone for two weeks it would be, "Eric Clapton of the Cream, I'd like to see what he thinks" and if he's one wish it would be that "every time I'd make a wish it'd come true."

An Afternoon with Rory Gallagher
New Spotlight 1971

Pictures of Rory Gallagher in an afternoon in Dublin
with New Spotlight journalist Donal Corvin. That's
Donal beside Rory in the top right picture. In his
article Donal writes, 'Gallagher is a genius. You know
it as you sit and watch him out of the corner of your
eye. You don't want to appear too obvious about it
all. But Gallagher has that aura, that magical ring of
confidence, that sets him out from ordinary mortals'.
The illustration of Rory and Taste is by Kevin O'Brien.

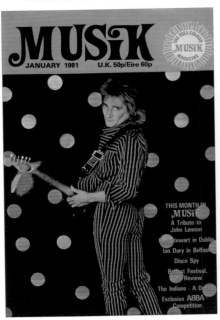

Showbiz Magazines

Above: Starlight 1978
Left: Showcase 1969
Bottom left: Musik 1981
Middle left: Scene 1976
Top left: Top Rank 1974

'Scene is like a magazine version of Melody Maker – it's terrific.' Marc Bolan's manager said that. Well, so says the Scene editorial in 1976. Pat Egan worked for Scene, as did Hot Press chief Niall Stokes and Dave Fanning. Scene had more of a 'rock' angle than the other Irish weekly from that time, Starlight.

Zig and Zag

Hot Press 1988

Featuring an interview by Graham Linehan with the aliens from Zog.

Sport

'And now… live in the studio, it's this week's number 1, it's the England World Cup Squad with Back Home'. I had no interest in Top of the Pops and ignored it until I was 10, when, for the first time, in May 1970, I switched it on just to see Peter Bonetti with the England World Cup squad perform their catchy Mexico 70 hit. As it was number 1, I had to sit through all the other acts before they came on. But, to my surprise, I enjoyed the show. After that, I tuned in every Thursday night at 7.30 and from then my obsession with football waned, giving way to the new god, pop music.

Did you know that Back Home was co-written by Derry man Phil Coulter and that his son Ryan played League of Ireland for Sligo Rovers?

BACK ROW (left to right): Joe Burke, Ashley Grimes, Niall Shelly, Mick Smyth, Noel Mitten, Padraic O'Connor.
FRONT ROW: Gerry Ryan, Eddie Byrne, Turlough O'Connor (captain), Pat Byrne, Fran O'Brien, Eamon Gregg, Tommy Kelly.

League of Ireland Champions
Shoot Magazine
Top: Bohemian FC 1975
Bottom: Shamrock Rovers FC 1985

Each summer Shoot magazine would do a feature on the current League
of Ireland champions with a colour team picture and some key club facts.

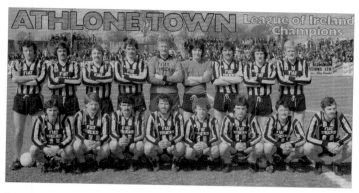

League of Ireland Champions
Shoot Magazine
Top: Athlone Town FC 1981
Above: Dundalk FC 1979
Left: Sligo Rovers FC 1977
Bottom: Limerick Utd FC with
comedian Karl Spain as mascot 1980

Jimmy's Boots by Arthur Mathews
Gakbag 1984

George Best

Left: George with his mother, New Spotlight 1970
Below: Focus On, Shoot 1970
Bottom left: Goal 1971
Bottom middle: Opening of Penneys, Dublin New Spotlight 1970
Bottom right: Sinead Cusack, New Spotlight 1971

FULL NAME: George Best
BIRTHPLACE: Belfast
BIRTHDATE: 22nd May, 1946
HEIGHT: 5 ft. 8½ in.
WEIGHT: 152 lb.
PREVIOUS CLUBS: None
CAR: 12-cylinder E-Type Jaguar
FAVOURITE PLAYER: The former Real Madrid star Alfredo Di Stefano
FAVOURITE OTHER TEAM: Spurs
MOST DIFFICULT OPPONENT: None
MOST MEMORABLE MATCH: Against Benfica in the Quarter Final of the 1965-66 European Cup. We won 5-1
BIGGEST THRILL: Every time I score
BIGGEST DISAPPOINTMENT: Not being able to play in World Cup Finals

BEST COUNTRY VISITED: U.S.A.
FAVOURITE FOOD: Chinese
MISCELLANEOUS LIKES: Reading, watching most sports, travelling
MISCELLANEOUS DISLIKES: Miserable people, delays at airports and railway stations
FAVOURITE T.V. SHOWS: Flip Wilson show, Marty Feldman show
FAVOURITE SINGERS: Tom Jones and Lulu
FAVOURITE ACTORS/ACTRESSES: Dustin Hoffman, Richard Harris, Steve McQueen, Rod Steiger, Catherine Ross and Julie Ege.

BEST FRIEND: My Bank Manager
BIGGEST INFLUENCE ON CAREER: Sir Matt Busby
BIGGEST DRAG IN SOCCER: Postponed games
INTERNATIONAL HONOURS: Apart from N. Ireland caps, none
PERSONAL AMBITION: To be happily married with kids
PROFESSIONAL AMBITION: To do well in the next World Cup
IF YOU WEREN'T A FOOTBALLER, WHAT DO YOU THINK YOU'D BE? I honestly don't know
WHAT PERSON IN THE WORLD WOULD YOU MOST LIKE TO MEET? Either Brigitte Bardot or Cassius Clay

Is GEORGE BEST too big for his golden boots?

To find out, just turn over

GOAL
THE WORLD'S GREATEST SOCCER WEEKLY

JANUARY 30, 1971
No. 130
1s 6d (7½p)

GOAL takes a cool look at Soccer's Mr. Controversy as he comes back to the game that can't do without him

GEORGIE IN DUBLIN NEXT WEEK

GEORGIE BEST, Belfast's glamorous football star, flies into Dublin next Tuesday to officially open a new Food Hall at Penney's in Henry Street. He'll be there at 3 p.m.

George's current girlfriend, blonde Swedish beauty Sive Hederby, arrived in England last weekend to spend a short holiday with the Belfast boy. She will very probably fly to Dublin with George in the chartered plane that is being laid on for his visit.

Best girl

This is beautiful Irish actress Sinéad Cusack, who stole the heart of super football star Georgie Best. She is working on a new British film 'Revenge' in which she co-stars with James Booth and Ray Barrett.

SO YOU WANT TO BE A GEORGIE BEST

Irish international
pro soccer player
EAMONN DUNPHY
tells it
like it really is

*Whither is fled the visionary gleam
Where is it now, the glory and the
dream?*

THE lines from Wordsworth are appropriate now, as the British football scene kicks off. The dreams and heartaches of last season are forgotten as we think of the triumphs that will be ours this year.

We are like men re-born. The smell of new mown grass, the warm sunshine as we train for fitness. And our thoughts of glory. Maybe they are the same dreams we had 10 years ago . . . and every year since.

You see, for every Georgie Best being raved about by the masses (not to mention the Dolly Birds), there are hundreds of common or garden footballers; players whose only female attention is the odd wink from a friendly barmaid!

But in every player's mind is the hope that this year he will catch the elusive star. Most would settle for promotion or a good run in the Cup.

These are the optimistic days. We are all giants—and the agony of an open goal missed last year is buried in the dreams of games to come.

To-day, I'm certainly bottom of the sun tan league. I've spent a couple of months in Dublin, but my team mates have the Continental look. Still, I have the memories of The Dubliners and Liam Clancy and

> Eamonn Dunphy is 23 and has been a professional soccer footballer for nine years. He went to Manchester United around the same time as George Best, still one of his best friends. To-day, Eamonn is one of the star's of Millwall, the London Second Division Club. He has 23 caps for Ireland. Here, in a special article for New Spotlight, he talks about life as a player and has a bit of advice for the many young men who think that all is glamorous on the football pitch.

Paddy Reilly and our songs of heroes and villains. I reckon I'm top of the culture league!

So you want to be a professional footballer? It's a tough life, and make no mistake about it. On a typical day, pre-season that is, we'd run seven miles in the morning and have a two-hour football session in the afternoon.

And while we're logging up the miles, our manager is clocking them up verbally. He tries to convince all players that this is "your year". He's already convinced the club directors of this . . . and we're only too willing to be.

For the benefit of the press, every manager in the land generally starts the new season with a quote like: "My boys are

very fit. We have worked hard and we learned a lot last year. Now we're poised for the promotion push and look to Europe at the end of it all."

I would love to see just one manager being honest and saying to newspapers something like this: "My players are a lazy bunch of chancers. We haven't done a stroke all year, and if you think for one minute that we're going to win anything this season, you must be daft."

Naturally, he'd lose his job . . . but he would certainly be welcome in my house!

Still, here are a few predictions for the coming football season.

★ George Best will become engaged to a Scandinavian blonde . . . and they will part after two weeks, remaining good friends.

★ "Hooligans" will continue to disrupt football occasionally. Perhaps if the game was a bit more exciting, they wouldn't have to wreck trains for their kicks.

★ Referees will remain the most hated men in football.

★ I fear that this will be the most vicious year yet on the playing park. Following Arsenal's much admired "aggression", watch out for cruder copies from other clubs.

★ Finally, my own club, Millwall, are a good bet for Division One next year . . . honestly.

Eamonn Dunphy

Above: New Spotlight 1971

Left: At Milltown with Shamrock Rovers, Magill 1977
Photo by Fergus Bourke

GOAL

THE WORLD'S GREATEST SOCCER WEEKLY

DECEMBER 12, 1970
No. 123

Why Arsenal are killing their ace scorers

JOHNNY GILES
Leeds and
Rep. of Ireland

Luton's Macdonald, the man they all want

ENGLAND
IN MALTA
—GO WITH
GOAL

SPECIAL SURVEY ON
GOVERNMENT
PERFORMANCE

MAGiLL

IRELAND'S CURRENT AFFAIRS MONTHLY MAGAZINE

JOHN GILES:
HALFWAY TO GREATNESS

THE TORIES AND NORTHERN IRELAND

"Every team needs supporters. That's why it's so important that we all support our own products in the shops. Because we're all part of the Irish team… and we can't afford to lose at home."

Guaranteed Irish

Let's make the future work for everyone.

Johnny Giles

Top Left: Goal 1970
Above: Magill cover 1979
Left: Guaranteed Irish advert, Magill 1978
Far Left: At Milltown, Magill 1977
Photo by Fergus Bourke

LIAM BRADY
Rep. of Ireland
and Arsenal

SHOOT!

Liam Brady

Above: Shoot 1979

Top right: PFA Player of the Year, Shoot 1979

Right: Focus On, Shoot 1984

Previous clubs: Arsenal, who signed me from school. And Juventus, who brought me to Italy for about £600,000 in 1980.

Nickname: "Chippy" died a natural death when I came out here. I haven't got one now.

Team you supported as a boy: None! A lot of sides impressed me, but I didn't follow any one in particular.

Football heroes of childhood: Again, a lot. But especially George Best, Bobby Charlton and Johnny Giles.

> **Most memorable match:** The 1979 F.A. Cup Final at Wembley, when we beat Manchester United 3-2. And the last match of my first year with Juventus, when we clinched the League title.

Biggest disappointment: Having to leave Juventus. Let's just say I felt very disenchanted.

Superstitions: None whatsoever.

International honours: I don't remember the exact number, but more than 40 caps for the Republic of Ireland.

Club honours: One F.A. Cup winners' medal and two

Favourite other sports person: I'd pick out Lester Piggott (below), Ian Botham and Jack Nicklaus because they're very much their own men. Their strong personalities sometimes get them into trouble, but they're the top experts in their fields.

runners'-up. A runners'-up medal in the European Cup-Winners' Cup. And two League titles with Juventus.

Favourite other sports: Well, I can play golf over here. But they've never heard of my other favourite, snooker.

Hobbies: Reading, mostly historical novels. And listening to practically any type of music.

Favourite actor or actress: Difficult, because we haven't been to the cinema for ages. Humphrey Bogart maybe,

because I'm beginning to prefer the old films to modern ones.

Favourite TV show: All the sports programmes, and we get a lot of sport on TV over here.

Favourite musician: Bob Dylan.

Biggest influence on career: I think we'd have to start with the coaches at St. Kevin's Boys Club in Dublin. Then, when I turned pro, Don Howe and Johnny Giles.

Favourite current players: Michel Platini, even though he took my place at Juventus. And I don't agree with people who say he didn't deserve his European Footballer of the Year award. Scoring 18 goals from midfield in Italy isn't easy! Then Zico, who hasn't hit top form with Udinese but is still top of the scoring charts. The other Brazilian, Socrates. And I wish I could see more of Maradona.

Ambitions for 1984: To get Sampdoria into Europe.

Long-term ambitions: To remain fit and healthy, to help the Republic of Ireland qualify for the World Cup Finals and to continue in football after I've retired. Until then, I wouldn't mind staying on in Italy.

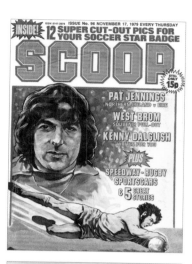

SUPER GOALIE

Britain's footballer of the year is an Irishman from Newry—Tottenham Hotspur goalkeeper — Pat Jennings. On May 3 he will accept his award in front of 700 footballing people at a special function. Pat, who is 27, joined Spurs from Watford in June '64 for the paltry sum of £25,000. Now his price on the transfer market would probably run to £300,000. Since joining Spurs he has made well over 300 league appearances, missing only three senior games in as many seasons. Rated one of the world's greatest 'keepers, Pat began his career with Newry town. He has represented Northern Ireland on 41 occasions. A keen Gaelic footballer earlier he played the code with Abbey C.B.S., Newry. During his term at White Hart Lane, Pat won an F.A. Cup, League Cup (twice) and U.E.F.A. cup winners' medal. Pat is married to former Hilton showband singer, Eleanor Toner, from near Newry. She too went to London to pursue a solo career and appeared at the London Palladium.

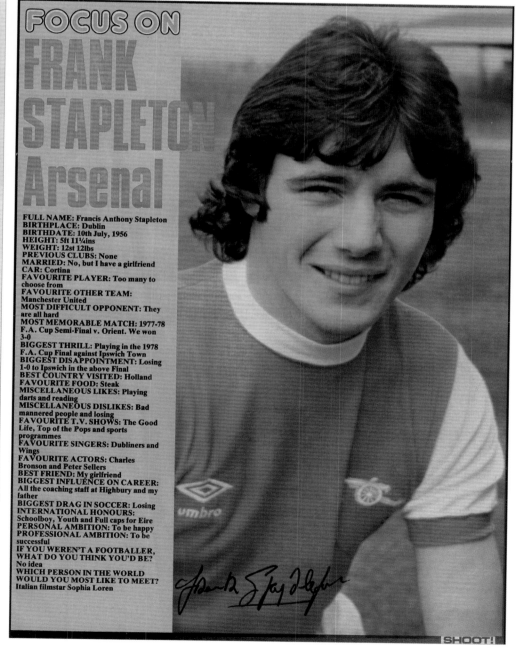

FOCUS ON FRANK STAPLETON Arsenal

FULL NAME: Francis Anthony Stapleton
BIRTHPLACE: Dublin
BIRTHDATE: 10th July, 1956
HEIGHT: 5ft 11¼ins
WEIGHT: 12st 12lbs
PREVIOUS CLUBS: None
MARRIED: No, but I have a girlfriend
CAR: Cortina
FAVOURITE PLAYER: Too many to choose from
FAVOURITE OTHER TEAM: Manchester United
MOST DIFFICULT OPPONENT: They are all hard
MOST MEMORABLE MATCH: 1977-78 F.A. Cup Semi-Final v. Orient. We won 3-0
BIGGEST THRILL: Playing in the 1978 F.A. Cup Final against Ipswich Town
BIGGEST DISAPPOINTMENT: Losing 1-0 to Ipswich in the above Final
BEST COUNTRY VISITED: Holland
FAVOURITE FOOD: Steak
MISCELLANEOUS LIKES: Playing darts and reading
MISCELLANEOUS DISLIKES: Bad mannered people and losing
FAVOURITE T.V. SHOWS: The Good Life, Top of the Pops and sports programmes
FAVOURITE SINGERS: Dubliners and Wings
FAVOURITE ACTORS: Charles Bronson and Peter Sellers
BEST FRIEND: My girlfriend
BIGGEST INFLUENCE ON CAREER: All the coaching staff at Highbury and my father
BIGGEST DRAG IN SOCCER: Losing
INTERNATIONAL HONOURS: Schoolboy, Youth and Full caps for Eire
PERSONAL AMBITION: To be happy
PROFESSIONAL AMBITION: To be successful
IF YOU WEREN'T A FOOTBALLER, WHAT DO YOU THINK YOU'D BE? No idea
WHICH PERSON IN THE WORLD WOULD YOU MOST LIKE TO MEET? Italian filmstar Sophia Loren

SHOOT!

Mick Martin

Left: With Kevin Keegan 1983

Below: With Gerry Daly outside Old Trafford 1973

Middle left: With Pat Crerand circa mid 1970s

All from Mick's international testimonial programme 1983.

Young hopefuls

Two young hopefuls, Gerry Daly and Mick Martin, arrived at Old Trafford from Bohemians.

Mick Martin

Above and right: Fashion shoot in Dalymount Park, New Spotlight 1970

Fullam's farewell

Soccer Snippets

Left: Johnny Fulham with Athlone FC at Milltown, Soccer Reporter 1981

Middle left: Richard Harris with Rodney Marsh and Dave Webb, Shoot 1972

Below: Don Givens, Shoot 1971

Bottom left: Martin O'Neill, Shoot 1971

Bottom middle: Steve Heighway advert, Shoot 1971

Bottom right: Blackthorn boot advert 1971

Bearded Richard Harris shows his footballing skill to Rodney Marsh (right) and Dave Webb at a screening of the soccer film "Bloomfield".

DON GIVENS Luton Town

SHOOT!

The Republic of Ireland's glory boys pictured before their shock 1-0 victory over England.
BACK ROW (left to right): Frank Stapleton, Mick McCarthy, Pat Bonner, Paul McGrath, John Aldridge, Tony Galvin.
FRONT ROW: Ronnie Whelan, Ray Houghton, Chris Hughton, Chris Morris, Kevin Moran.

Euro 88

Above: Ireland team, Shoot 1988

Top right: Evening Press Euro 88 Guide 1988

Top left: Shoot cover, 1988

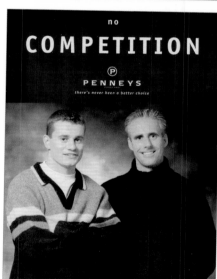

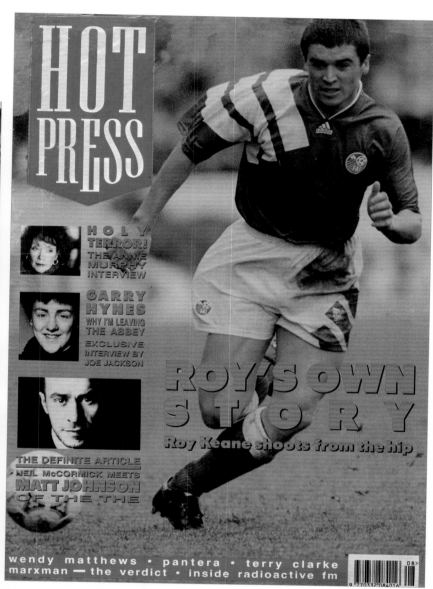

HOT PRESS

H O L Y TERROR! THE ANNE MURPHY INTERVIEW

GARRY HYNES WHY I'M LEAVING THE ABBEY EXCLUSIVE INTERVIEW BY JOE JACKSON

THE DEFINITE ARTICLE NEIL McCORMICK MEETS **MATT JOHNSON** OF THE THE

ROY'S OWN STORY

Roy Keane shoots from the hip

wendy matthews • pantera • terry clarke
marxman — the verdict • inside radioactive fm

THE '94 WORLD CUP KIT NOW AVAILABLE AT ALL LEADING SPORTS STORES

adidas

no
COMPETITION

Ⓟ PENNEYS
there's never been a better choice

[great *style* whatever the season]

Ⓟ PENNEYS

International Soccer Snippets
Above: Roy Keane, Hot Press 1993
Left & far left: Penneys advert,
match programme 1997
Top left: Adidas advert 1994

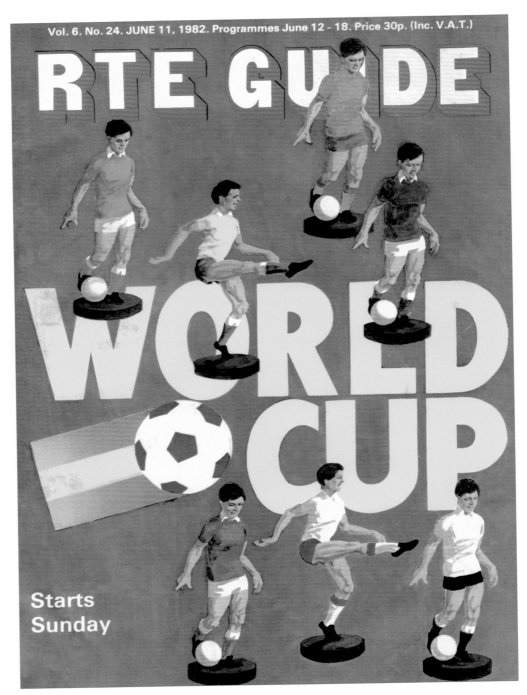

World Cup
RTE Guide 1982
Illustration by Alan Corsini

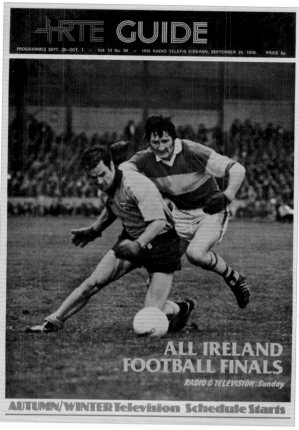

RTE Guides

Left: All Ireland Football Finals 1975
Bottom left: All Ireland Hurling Finals 1976
Below: All Ireland Football Finals 1976
Bottom right: Michael O'Hehir 1963

JIMMY BARRY MURPHY (Cork)

Full name: James Barry Murphy.
Address: Allolee, Laburnum Lawn, Cork.
Date of birth: August 22, 1954.
Weight: 12 st.
Height: 6' 0".
Club: St. Finbarr's.
Club colours: Royal blue.
Favourite position: Right corner forward.

Most difficult opponent: Brendan Colleran.
Most memorable game: 1973 All-Ireland Final versus Galway.
Biggest thrill: Scoring two goals in that final.
Hobbies: Greyhounds.
Favourite TV show: The Onedin Line.
Favourite actor: Charles Bronson.
Favourite type of music: All types of folk music.
Favourite holiday resort: Owenahincha, Co. Cork.
Who influenced you most: Br. Lambert of the Presentation Brothers.
Greatest ambition: To win the County Championship with my club.
Favourite referee: John Moloney.
Favourite grounds: Athletic Grounds in Cork, Croke Park and Thurles.
How often do you train: Four nights a week for big games.
Favourite other team: Kerry.
Favourite player: Sean O'Neill.
Person you admire most in Ireland: Bernadette Devlin.
Person you would most like to meet: Bobby Charlton.

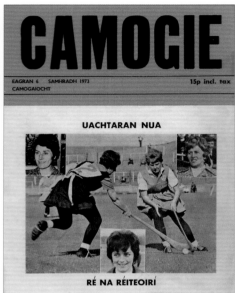

CAMOGIE

EAGRAN 6   SAMHRADH 1973
CAMOGAIOCHT   15p incl. tax

UACHTARAN NUA

RÉ NA RÉITEOIRÍ

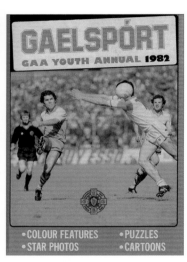

GAELSPÓRT
GAA YOUTH ANNUAL 1982

• COLOUR FEATURES   • PUZZLES
• STAR PHOTOS   • CARTOONS

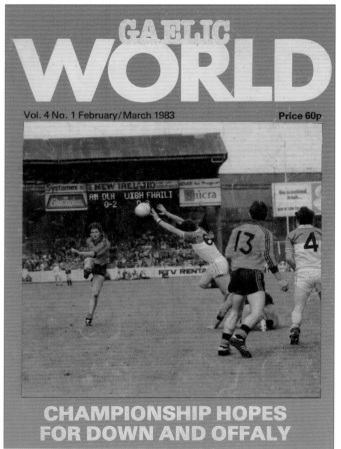

GAELIC WORLD

Vol. 4 No. 1 February/March 1983   Price 60p

CHAMPIONSHIP HOPES FOR DOWN AND OFFALY

GAA Publications
Above: Gaelspórt 1982
Left: Gaelic World 1983
Far left: Jimmy Barry Murphy, Boys Own 1973
Top middle: Camogie 1973

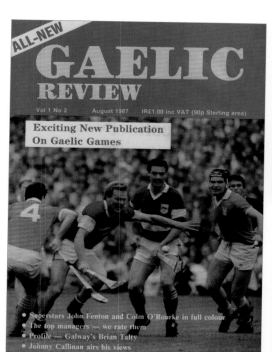

NOEL SKEHAN
(Kilkenny)

● JIMMY
DOYLE

● MARTIN
NEWELL

SPORTS STAR OF THE MONTH

Full name: Noel Skehan.
Address: 12 Woodlawn, Bennettsbridge, Co. Kilkenny.
Date of birth: December 6, 1944.
Weight: 11st. 7 lbs.
Height: 5'7½''.
Married: Yes.
Children: Two boys — Brian and Niall.
Club: Bennettsbridge.
Club colours: Green and gold.
Favourite position: Goalkeeper.
Most difficult opponent: Ray Cummins.
Most memorable game: 1972 All-Ireland Final.
Biggest thrill: Receiving the McCarthy Cup in 1972.
Greatest disappointment: 1973 All-Ireland Final.
Hobbies: Squash and badminton.
Favourite TV show: Late Late Show.
Favourite actor/actress: George Peppard, Liz Taylor.
Favourite type of music: Pop.
Favourite holiday resort: Salthill, Co. Galway.
Who influenced you most: My uncle — Dan Kennedy.
Greatest ambition: To win a National League medal.
Favourite referee: John Moloney.
Favourite grounds: Croke Park and Nowlan Park.
How often do you train: Three nights a week.
Favourite other team: Cork.
Favourite player: Pat Hartigan.
Person you admire most in Ireland: Garrett FitzGerald.
Person you would most like to meet: Ted Kennedy.

GAA Publications

Above: Gaelic Sport 1966
Top left: Gaelic Review 1987
Far right: Noel Skehan, Our Boys 1974

MICK O'CONNELL

QUESTIONNAIRE

Full name: Mick O'Connell.
Age: 36.
Height: 6' 0".
Weight: 13-4.
Schools: Valentia N.S. and Cahirciveen C.B.S.
Married: Yes.
No. of Children: One.
Occupation: Farmer, boatman.
Name of Club: Waterville.
Club Colours: Red.
Favourite position: Midfield.
Most memorable game: National League final v. Derry, 1961.
Biggest thrill: Putting a 70 yds. free over the bar in Killarney, 1963.
Greatest disappointment: 1959 All Ireland Final although on winning side — did not play well and was also injured.
Player you admire most: At present time, Seán O'Neill.
Play any other games: No.
Any hobbies: Hunting, fishing and gardening.
Any sporting ambition: Keep active as long as possible.
Favourite Sportswriter: None in particular.
Favourite Referee: None in particular.
Favourite T.V. Show: Harry Worth.
Favourite singer: I thought "Dana" quite good.
Person you like to meet most: Bobby Charlton.
Advice for beginners: Practise always and look at good adult players frequently.

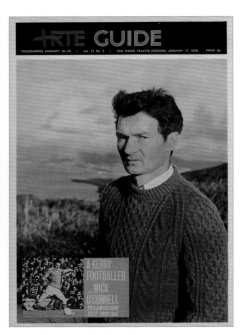

Mick O'Connell and Steve Staunton

Above: Mick O'Connell, Our Boys 1974

Top right: Mick O'Connell, RTE Guide 1975

Bottom right: Steve Staunton playing for the Clans, Dundalk v Kilkerley in Louth SFC semi final, The Argus 1986

Photo by Ken Finnegan

Hey Ref!
Gaelic Youth Annual 1982

Another Point !

A most important point, too! **Security !** Certain Insurance Policies give you this security, and the point about New Ireland Life and Endowment Policies is that they give you DOUBLE benefits in case of fatal accident—**without extra premium**—in addition to all the usual benefits. To be **doubly** assured of security, insure with

NEW IRELAND
ASSURANCE COMPANY, LTD.
Head Office—12 DAWSON STREET, DUBLIN.
M. W. O'Reilly, P.C., F.C.I.I., Managing Director.

GAA Adverts

Left: New Ireland, Croke Park match programme 1956
Below: Munster & Leinster Bank, Gaelic Sport magazine 1966
Middle upper: Asbestos, Gaelic Sport magazine 1966
Middle lower: Clerys, Croke Park match programme 1957
Bottom left: Club Lemon, Croke Park match programme 1956

TAKE ROOFING, FOR INSTANCE . . . .

ASBESTOS CEMENT products are incredibly versatile (some of its uses haven't been discovered yet!). Maybe you can think of a few. In the meantime we'll be glad to tell you how Architects, Builders, Farmers, Gardeners and householders all over the world are using modern ASBESTOS CEMENT products to advantage.

Asbestos

ASBESTOS CEMENT LIMITED
19 LOWER PEMBROKE STREET
DUBLIN 2.

Croke Park—G.A.A. Headquarters

Clerys

Ireland's Shopping G.H.Q.

Get all your Sports needs in this famous section of Clerys where, as elsewhere throughout the Store, prices are marked on the Small-Profit Policy.

Meet your friends in Clerys Restaurant. Two great floors, fully licensed. Popular 4-course Luncheons served 12.30 p.m. to 3.30 p.m. Tea 4 p.m. to 7 p.m. A la Carte 10 a.m. to 10 p.m.

Half-time......
Full-time......
Time You had a
CLUB ORANGE
OR
CLUB LEMON

On sale in all the best Bars and Clubs

Marketed only by
MINERAL WATERS DISTRIBUTORS LTD.
45 KILDARE STREET, DUBLIN

ONE WAY TO **SAVE**

Another good way to save is with the M. & L. Open that Savings Account now!

THE
MUNSTER & LEINSTER BANK
LIMITED
Branches throughout the country

THE GREATEST THING SINCE THE ASH!

camán wavin

Approx. 18 ounces. 32 inch.
Ideal for boys or girls 12 to 15.
Practically unbreakable!

Trade Enquiries:
Wavin Pipes Ltd.
Balbriggan Co. Dublin.

IN ANY EVENT
O'NEILLS ARE
ON A WINNER

**Supergear
for Superstars**

O'neills

GAA Adverts
Above: Wavin, Magill 1978
Middle right: O'Neills, Gaelic Youth Annual 1982
Right: Afton Cigarettes, Croke Park match programme 1956
Top: Afton Cigarettes, Croke Park match programme 1957

Ireland v Wales

Rugby international match programme 1958

IRISH
RUGBY FOOTBALL UNION

IRELAND v WALES

LANSDOWNE ROAD

Saturday, 15th March, 1958

OFFICIAL PROGRAMME
ONE SHILLING

Secretary

THE IRISH XV
(AS ORIGINALLY SELECTED)

J. G. M. W. MURPHY

J. G. M. W. MURPHY (*London Irish*). Born in Bangor, Co. Down, 20/8/26. 12 st. 8 lb., 6 ft. Educated at Methodist College, Belfast, and Dublin University. John Gervase Maurice Walker Murphy is a chaplain with the British Army. Stationed at Woolwich Garrison, London. Gerry was first capped for Ireland against the South Africans in 1952 and that Season he played against England, Scotland and Wales. While playing with Lurgan, he was capped again in 1954 against the New Zealanders. Has been playing great stuff this Season for London Irish and replaces Berkery, also of that Club, for his sixth cap to-day.

A. J. F. O'REILLY (*Old Belvedere*). Born Dublin, 7/5/36. 13 st. 12 lb., 6 ft. 2 in. Educated at Belvedere College, Dublin. Tony is an undergraduate at University College, Dublin, studying for the degree of B.C.L., and also a final year Solicitor's apprentice. Playing as wing three-quarter for Ireland this Season Tony has shown tremendous power and resourcefulness. Not content to await developments, he keenly watches for the smallest chance to turn any movement into all-out attack. His well placed twenty-five yard drop kicks, in the Scottish game, was further evidence of his all-round competence. He gains his sixteenth cap to-day.

A. J. F. O'REILLY

N. J. HENDERSON

N. J. HENDERSON (*North of Ireland F.C.*). Born in Drumahoe, Co. Derry, 10/8/28. 14 st., 5 ft. 11½ in. Educated at Foyle College and Queen's University, Belfast. Noel Joseph Henderson is a B.Sc., and a Sales Superintendent with a Petroleum Company in Belfast. To-day is Noel's thirty-fifth cap, passing Eugene Davy by one appearance. He now ranks third in the list of caps won, to George Stephenson and to his brother-in-law Jack Kyle. First capped against Scotland at Murrayfield in 1949, replacing T. J. Gavin, later that Season playing against Wales at Swansea in our Triple Crown decider. Captain of the Irish XV to-day.

D. HEWITT (*Queen's University, Belfast*). Born in Belfast, 9/9/39. 11 st. 6 lb., 5 ft. 9 in. Educated at Royal Belfast Academical Institution. David Hewitt is studying Law at Queen's. His first year in Senior Football and his fourth International cap for Ireland to-day. Earlier in the Season David played brilliant Rugby for the Combined Universities against the Rest of Ireland. He is capable of producing lightning thrusts and shows immense speed off the mark. His defence against Scotland was good. Now 19 years of age, David has a fine future in International Rugby.

[*Irish Times*

D. HEWITT

A. C. PEDLOW

A. C. PEDLOW (*C.I.Y.M.S.*). Born in Lurgan, County Armagh. 20/1/34. 14 st., 6 ft. Alexander Cecil Pedlow was educated at Campbell College, Belfast, and Queen's University. He is a Dentist in Belfast. Cecil is the heaviest of the three-quarters playing to-day. His two tries against Scotland a fortnight ago showed all the technique of wing three-quarter play. His use of weight, speed, good hands and most determined running made him easily the most outstanding player on the field against Scotland. Twentieth cap to-day, a remarkable tally for his 24 years of age.

R. H. WILLIAMS

W. R. EVANS

R. H. WILLIAMS (*Llanelly*). Second row. Age 27 years. 6 ft. 2 in., 15 st. 7 lb. Rhys Williams established himself as a great line-out forward, in the true Welsh tradition, while on Tour of South Africa in 1955. Captain of his Club this Season he led the "Sospans" when on Tour in Moscow last Summer. A great worker, Rhys directs the Welsh "slipping" strategy in the line-outs. First capped in 1954, to-day will be his seventeenth cap. Some two pounds heavier than Billy Mulcahy, his opposite number to-day.

W. R. EVANS (*Cardiff*). Second row. Age 24 years. 6 ft. 2 in., 16 st. Born in Porthcawl. Roddy Evans was educated at Cowbridge Grammar School, Cambridge University and is presently a Solicitor's Apprentice. First capped this Season against the Australians he was honoured last month by being selected for the Barbarians against the Tourists. An outstanding line-out forward, ranked with England's Marquis as the best playing to-day. Very mobile for his 16 st. Gains his fourth cap to-day.

J. FAULL (*Swansea*). Lock forward. Age 24 years. 6 ft., 15 st. A bustling, intelligent forward, John Faull played as a centre three-quarter while at school at Bronisgrove. He played centre for Swansea against the 1953 All Blacks. Deputy goal kicker to star full back Terry Davies. First capped last Season against Scotland and gained his second against Ireland. At lock he keeps Russell Robins out of this Welsh XV. The son of International Board member and former International referee, J. W. Faull. His sixth cap to-day.

R. C. C. THOMAS

H. J. MORGAN

R. C. C. THOMAS (*Swansea*). Blindside wing forward. Age 28 years. 6 ft. 1 in., 14 st. Educated at Blundells. Clem Thomas is a wholesale butcher. First capped against France in 1949 he gained a "Blue" at Cambridge that Season. Played only once for Wales last year, against England and has made a tremendous "come-back" this Season. Gains his "21st" cap to-day and hopes to celebrate his International "Coming of age" by leading Wales to victory. Switched from onside to blindside wing forward after Wallabies game. To-day's Welsh captain.

H. J. MORGAN (*Abertillery*). Openside wing forward. Age 21 years. 5 ft. 9 in., 13 st. 10 lb. As a newcomer to the International scene this Season Hayden Morgan in his debut against England at Twickenham had an outstanding game. This first cap confirmed his excellent showing in the Welsh Final Trial. Was not selected against Australia. Presently undergoing his National Service with a Parachute Regiment. Played on the winning Barbarians XV against the East Midlands in the Mobbs Memorial match at Northampton ten days ago. His third cap to-day.

J. FAULL

Ireland v England
Rugby international match programme 1977

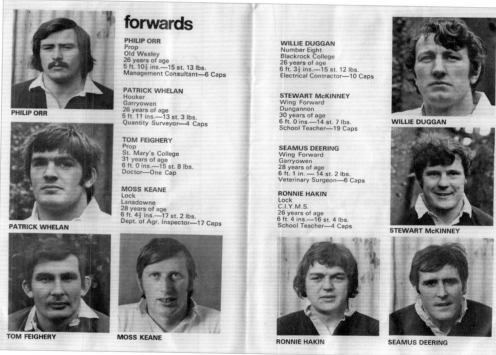

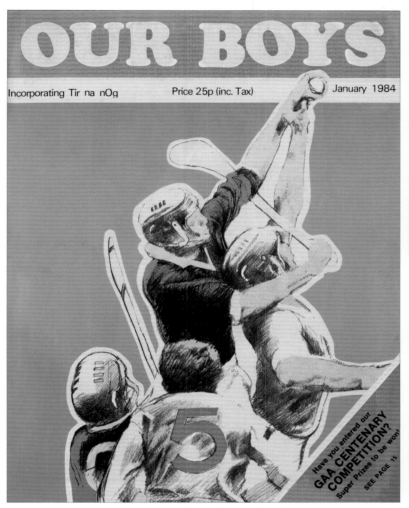

Our Boys

Left: 1964
Top left: 1984
Above: 1974
Top right: 1979

Our Boys was published by the Christian Brothers and the Educational Company of Ireland. It started in 1914 and continued through to the early 1990s. Aimed at young and teenage boys and based on its UK counterpart, Boy's Own, it had cartoons and stories covering adventure, sport, nature, science and more. Some of the content, such as the cartoon series Tír Na nÓg, was in Irish.

Focus on:
EAMONN COUGHLAN

Full name: Eamonn Coughlan
Birthplace: Dublin
Birthdate: 21-11-78
Height: 5'10½"
Weight: 140 lbs
Married: Yes
Car: Capri 3,000 GXL
Most difficult opponent: Steve Ovett/John Walker
Biggest thrill: Winning a silver medal in the 1978 European Championships
Biggest disappointment: Finishing 4th in Montreal Olympics.
Best country visited: U.S.A.
Favourite food and drink: T-Bone steak and Harp Lager
Miscellaneous likes: Relaxing at home not having to worry about training.
Miscellaneous Dislikes: Sitting around ariports waiting for delayed planes
Favourite TV shows: No particular TV show.
Favourite actor/actress: Cheryl Ladd
Favourite singers: Linda Ronstadt
Favourite venue: San Diego, California.
Favourite sports writer: none
Biggest influence on career: My wife Yvonne.
Personal ambition: To win an Olympic Gold medal
Professional ambition: To be as succesful in business as I am on the running track.
If you weren't a runner what do you think you'd be?: No idea
Which person in the world would you most like to meet?: Mohammed Ali

Athletics

Top left: Focus on Eamonn Coughlan, In Dublin 1978
Bottom left: Eamonn Coughlan and Mary Purcell, Man Alive 1975
Top right: The Irish Digest 1957
Above: Irish Runner 1988
Above right: Marathon 1983

The Irish Digest cover from 1957 shows Ronnie Delaney winning the 1500 metres at the Melbourne Olympics a year earlier.

The Focus On Eamonn Coghlan has his birthdate year wrong, it should be 1952. And that's my brother Eamonn on the left on the cover of Irish Runner.

IRELAND'S CHAMPION SWIMMER
Donnacha O'Dea (Columcille Club) who won nine gold medals and established
four records during the Irish National Swimming Championships held at
Mosney in 1964.

Other Sports

Right: Alex Higgins, RTE Guide 1984

Top left: Advert for Squash Ireland,
Man Alive 1974

Top right: Advert for Stillorgan Bowl,
Woman's Choice 1969

Above: Donnacha 'The Don' O'Dea at
Butlins 1964

Donnacha, who would later represent
Ireland at the 1968 Olympics, is now a
professional poker player.

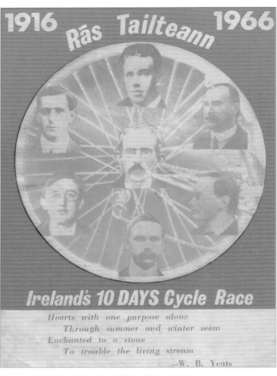

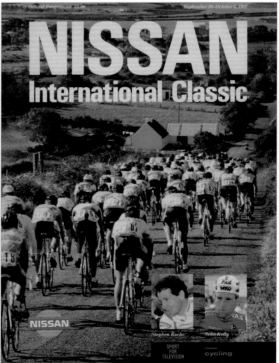

Cycling

Above: Advert for milk, RTE Guide 1982

Right: Nissan International programme 1987

Top right: Rás Tailteann progamme 1966

Top left: Advert for Dunlop, Rás Tailteann programme 1966

Big 8 wish Muhammed luck for his Dublin fight

MUHAMMAD ALI, now looking forward to a return fight with Joe Frazier for the heavyweight title he once held, is training for his bout with Al (Blue) Lewis in Dublin later this month . . . The former champion will come here with a good-luck wish from the manager and three of the stars of the Big 8 now playing in Las Vegas. Seen here with the fighter are (l. to r.) Tom Dunphy, manager T. J. Byrne, Brendan Bowyer and Paddy Cole.

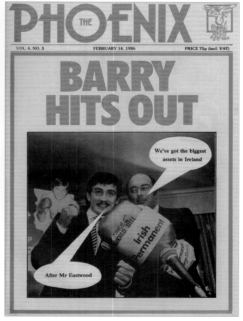

Boxing

Above: Barry McGuigan, The Belfast Review 1984
Photo by Bill Kirk
Top right: Muhammad Ali and the Big 8, New Spotlight 1972
Right: Barry McGuigan and Barney Eastwood, The Phoenix 1986

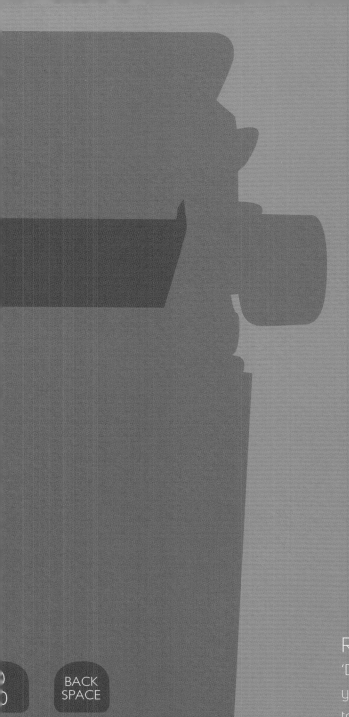

Readers' Lives

'Dear Brian, Thank you for your letter. Please find enclosed your record token for £1.50'. Like Morrissey, I too wrote letters to the NME. Unlike Morrissey, they did not publish any of mine. Nor did Melody Maker, who I strategically targeted in order to win an album token for 'letter of the week'. I did, eventually, get a letter published in Starlight in 1975, winning a record token.

I never wrote to Problem Pages. Little point, when I could see from the replies to others, that the advice to me would probably be to 'discuss with a priest' or send off for that special book from Easons.

Irish Spotlight

Top right: Irish 1964

Bottom right: Women 1965

Bottom left: Sport 1965

Top left: Pot 1969

Top centre: Gardaí 1969

Irish Spotlight, not to be confused with New Spotlight, was published monthly by the Irish Dominicans during the 1960s. Smaller than A4 size it covered a wide range of issues of the day. It was voted by Hibernia as 'Ireland's best religious magazine, being fresh interesting and attractively produced'.

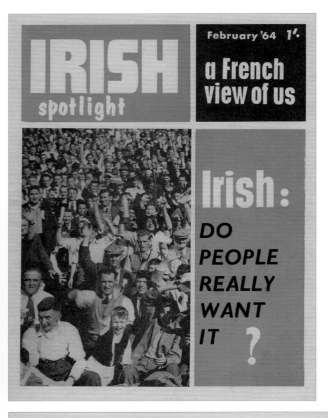

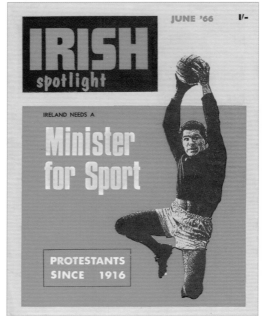

Sunday

APRIL 9, 1961 Vol. 5 No. 177 5d.

Review

31 Westmoreland St., Dublin, Phone 75871

A 22nd CHILD FOR JOHN JOE — AT 86

IRISHMAN ON BOARD BLAZING LINER

A Kilkenny widow last night sat waiting anxiously for news of her radio officer son, shipwrecked in a Persian Gulf liner disaster in which 49 are still missing.

During the day Mrs. G. McGrath, of 9 St. Francis terrace, Kilkenny, had received a terse telegram telling that her son Billy's ship, the cargo-liner Dara, was on fire. It had no news about the fate of the Kilkenny man.

Late last night, British and American freighters and warships combed the sea for the survivors. After a day of conflicting reports news came in of landing of survivors at various ports where hospital crews rushed to meet them.

But there was no specific news of the tall dark 21-years-old Irishman.

The disaster took place 300 miles from the port of Bahrein. The Dara apparently was in collision with a ship which dragged her anchor, according to the London spokesman of the controlling company.

She then put to sea because of rough weather intending to return later.

However, fire broke out while she was at sea in circumstances not yet clear.

Distress calls were sent out to say the liner was ablaze, and as flames swept the ship the passengers and crew—a total of 550—abandoned ship.

Unidentified

One person not yet identified died.

First ship on the scene was the 4,000-ton British ship, Empire Guillemot. She picked up close on 500 passengers and crew of the crippled Dara.

United States airforce and British Navy frigates are helping in the rescue operations.

In Kilkenny last night Mrs. McGrath said that her son had been at sea for about two years. Before the Dara he had been on the Southern Cross and visited home during the summer.

Billy McGrath was educated at the local C.B.S. and learned his radio-telegraphy at the Atlantic College, Dublin. His father was Garda Christopher McGrath. He is unmarried.

People in Kilkenny last night made several calls to the SUNDAY REVIEW anxiously seeking news of the safety of the "quiet and reserved" officer.

Picture by Jack MacManus

FULL STORY Page 3

John Joe at 86

The Sunday Review 1961

The Sunday Review was a weekly tabloid newspaper published in Dublin from 1957 to 1963. This cover story refers to John Joe of Sligo who, according to the paper, 'refused to accept the loneliness caused by the emigration of all his 11 children and the death of his wife.'

Become a
fashion shoe
model
for Tylers

£1,500
in prize money,
modelling courses,
modelling contracts
and wardrobes of
Tylers shoes to
be won in

TYLERS
MODEL GIRL COMPETITION
ENTER NOW!

Winners of the Tylers Model Girl Contest (l. to r.): Brigid
O'Sullivan, Sheelagh Moloney and Pauline Buckley from
Limerick.

FOOTING IT
TO STARDOM

THESE three pretty girls are good-looking all over,
but it is their feet that may make them famous,
for they are the winners in Tyler's National Model
Girl competition and contracts to model Tyler's shoes
are part of their prizes.

Denise Lavaud, Mairead Gallagher and Bernie Battles were chosen from competitors who had taken part in ten area heats at fashion shows throughout the country and Colonel H. W. H. Tyler, chairman of Tyler's, flew from England to present the prizes at the Model Girl ball in Dublin last month, Proceeds from the ball, by the way, were donated to the Irish Society for the Prevention of Cruelty to Children and all profits from the local fashion shows went to charity.

Each girl was presented with a cheque for £250, a wardrobe of Model Girl shoes and an Innoxa travel beauty case as well as her modelling contract.

Good luck to the future fashion - footers, Denise, Mairead and Bernie!

Julie Mahoney, Galway, Barbara Kidney, Dublin and Mairead Gallagher, Galway, winners of the Galway heat of Tylers' Miss Model Girl Contest.

IRELAND'S SUPER SOFT SUPER GIRL 1971

free competition

✳ **Bristow's** *star spray*
l♥vely hair contest

They're all after the big prize

✳ **FIRST PRIZE** **£100** CASH   ✳ **SECOND PRIZE** **£50** CASH   ✳ **THIRD PRIZE** **£25** CASH

plus a free week's holiday at Butlin's Holiday Camp, Mosney.

Miss Anne McDonagh 22 Bourke Ave., Lord Edward St., Limerick.

Mrs. Mary Egan 12 Shanard Road, Whitehall, Dublin 9.

Miss Margaret Hegarty 19 St. Anne's Road, Killarney.

Mrs. Lorraine O'Donnell Lissadell, Fermoy.

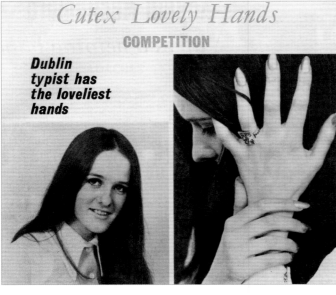

Cutex Lovely Hands

COMPETITION

Dublin typist has the loveliest hands

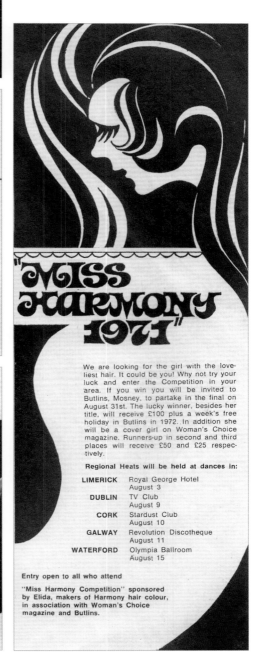

"MISS HARMONY 1971"

We are looking for the girl with the loveliest hair. It could be you! Why not try your luck and enter the Competition in your area. If you win you will be invited to Butlins, Mosney, to partake in the final on August 31st. The lucky winner, besides her title, will receive £100 plus a week's free holiday in Butlins in 1972. In addition she will be a cover girl on Woman's Choice magazine. Runners-up in second and third places will receive £50 and £25 respectively.

Regional Heats will be held at dances in:

LIMERICK	Royal George Hotel August 3
DUBLIN	TV Club August 9
CORK	Stardust Club August 10
GALWAY	Revolution Discotheque August 11
WATERFORD	Olympia Ballroom August 15

Entry open to all who attend

"Miss Harmony Competition" sponsored by Elida, makers of Harmony hair colour, in association with Woman's Choice magazine and Butlins.

Hair and Hands Competitions
Above: Lovely Hands winner, Woman's Way 1969
Far right: Miss Harmony advert, Woman's Way 1971
Top: Super Soft Super Girl with Mike Murphy, Woman's Choice 1971
Middle: Lovely Hair, Woman's Way 1966

TEEN QUEEN '68'

Beauty Competitions
Left: Teen Queen, New Spotlight 1968
Below: Terylene advert, Woman's Way 1967
Bottom left: Miss India Tea, New Spotlight 1967
Bottom right: Miss Dublin, New Spotlight 1969

A KISS of congratulations from deejay Larry Gogan for the 1968 Teen Queen, lovely Marina Perini of Dublin. She was chosen at "New Spotligh's Night Out" in the Television Club. And the prize in the contest organised by Vick International Limited (makers of Clearasil Medication and Soap) is a holiday for two to the value of £200 . . . a whole week in Paris in Spring.

Marina was chosen for her personality, charm and perfect complexion. A model, she was crowned as the first beauty queen of 1968. And a worthy queen, too.

Winner of second prize (£50 in cash) was another lively girl, this time from the South Rachel Williams from Cork.

Helen McMahon reigns 'Miss Ireland' in 'TERYLENE'

Helen McMahon picked 'Terylene' for her Bonnie Sue dress. Naturally. Because crease-free carefree 'Terylene' makes the most of dresses, the best of clothes. But then, it's the most internationally known name in womenswear today. Ask Helen McMahon. Or any other well-dressed girl.

ICI

'Terylene' and 'Terylene' are registered trademarks of Imperial Chemical Industries Limited, London.

Dublin Winner :
LINDA YOUNG

Derry/Donegal Winner :
MARIEAD McCOURT

Offaly Winner :
MARIE CRINNIGAN

'MISS INDIA TEA' HEAT WINNERS

Tim Hickey (Benjy) with Miss Dublin winners at TV Club.

beauties from the ballrooms

These pretty girls who went dancing in Cashel's Tippland ballroom won the first heat in the Miss Tipperary contest, winner of which goes forward to Ireland's first Beauty Congress which takes place next month in Belfast.

There she stands a chance of joining Ireland's international beauty team who will compete for the titles of Miss Europe (Morocco in May), Miss Universe (Miami Beach, Florida in July), Miss International (Tokyo in September) and Miss World (London in November).

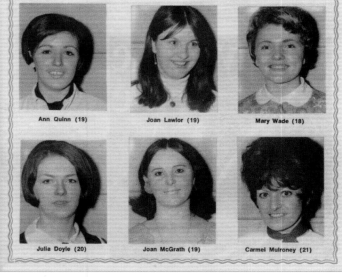

Ann Quinn (19)   Joan Lawlor (19)   Mary Wade (18)

Julia Doyle (20)   Joan McGrath (19)   Carmel Mulroney (21)

WINNERS AT BUTLINS

Recent winners of the weekly Miss Harmony and Miss Elegance competitions being held this summer in conjunction with Woman's Way in Butlin's Holiday Camp, Mosney, Co. Meath.

MISS HARMONY
Seventeen-year-old Brenda Guidon, 73 Blackditch Road, Ballyfermot, Dublin. Dark brown hair drawn back from the forehead and falling in ringlets.

MISS ELEGANCE
Mrs. Mary Coburn, 115 Ard Easmuinn, Dundalk whose black and silver Lurex coat is worn with a checked Lurex toning dress and teamed with black accessories. ●

Eight of the prettiest girls in Ireland in one picture! All of them will take part in a gala fashion show in the Gresham Hotel Dublin on Monday, November 28. They will be featured in a cabaret with top showband stars. In this photograph are Miss Ireland, Miss Mod, Miss Chelsea, Queen of Hearts, Girl of Future, Miss Victor and Miss Spotlight.

Beauty Competitions
Above: Various winners, New Spotlight 1967
Left: Winners at Butlins, Woman's Way 1968
Top: Beauties from the Ballrooms, Woman's Way 1969

A figure the girls will envy— a figure the boys will love!

A special delivery of continental health aids to a beautiful figure highlighted by an ideal bustline has now arrived in Ireland! Now you can control the size and shape of your bust safely, simply and without strenuous exercise. New beauty and confidence can be yours—you will be amazed and pleased with the quick results. A must for women of all ages, *The' MEDICIN' BUST MASSAGER for a beautiful bustline.* Price £5/5/0.

GET RID OF UGLY FAT BULGES !

Most girls are not too fat and slimming overall will not solve their problem but every woman needs to control certain parts where fat has developed. Now the continental MASVELT Massage apparatus will enable you to remove any excess from whatever part you require. Full details on request. 2 models available.

(1) Masvelt Double for faster results £5 15s. 6d. (2) Masvelt Single, £4 14s. 6d.

Post Coupon NOW

▬ ▬ ▬ ▬ ▬ ▬ ▬ ▬

FEMININE

Health & Beauty

Suppliers of specialist aids to Beauty and Body Culture,
8 Anglesea Buildings, Upr. George's St., Dun Laoghaire, Co. Dublin.
Phone 809571 (if engaged—801489, Ext. 1)

Please send me details of
Medicin' Bust ☐ Masvelt Massage ☐

NAME ....

ADDRESS ....

....SP26

Are you going to stay SKINNY for another unhappy summer?

Take SUPER WATE-ON

You can have an attractive figure that will put you right back where the fun is. You can put on pounds and inches of firm healthy flesh—by taking SUPER WATE-ON.

SUPER WATE-ON is a fruit flavoured concentration of weight-building calories, fortified with vitamins B1, B2, B12 and D2. It helps build up your whole body. You *look* better. You *feel* better. And the extra weight even gives you extra energy and go.

Get a beautiful figure, and come out of your shell. Start a course of SUPER WATE-ON today. Buy SUPER WATE-ON at your chemist. Recommended prices: Emulsion (strawberry flavour) or tablets (banana flavour), 26/- per large packet. Also regular WATE-ON, 22/- per packet.

GILLESPIE & CO. LTD., Dubber Rd., Finglas, Dublin 11

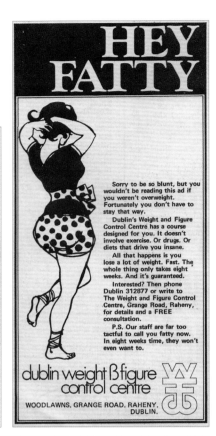

HEY FATTY

Sorry to be so blunt, but you wouldn't be reading this ad if you weren't overweight. Fortunately you don't have to stay that way.

Dublin's Weight and Figure Control Centre has a course designed for you. It doesn't involve exercise. Or drugs. Or diets that drive you insane.

All that happens is you lose a lot of weight. Fast. The whole thing only takes eight weeks. And it's guaranteed.

Interested? Then phone Dublin 312877 or write to The Weight and Figure Control Centre, Grange Road, Raheny, for details and a FREE consultation.

P.S. Our staff are far too tactful to call you fatty now. In eight weeks time, they won't even want to.

dublin weight ß figure control centre

WOODLAWNS, GRANGE ROAD, RAHENY, DUBLIN.

They'll never call you SKINNY again!

WATE-ON offers you a quick way to put on extra pounds and inches of firm, healthy flesh—safely.

WATE-ON provides nourishment, helps to improve appetite and increase vitality and contains Vitamins D, B_{12}, B_1 and B_6. You can give it to children over five with confidence.

Start taking a course of WATE-ON *now*-and you'll be fit and ready to enjoy those summer beaches and swimming pools. *Get WATE-ON from your chemist today.*

FOR MEN, WOMEN AND CHILDREN

WATE-ON

Emulsion or tablets - 21/6 per pack

TRADE ENQUIRIES · GILLESPIE & CO LTD DUBLIN 11

Weight & Figure Adverts

Above: Wate-On, Miss Magazine 1966
Top middle: Super Wate-On, New Spotlight 1967
Top right: Hey Fatty, Woman's Choice 1970
Left: Health & Beauty, Woman's Way 1968

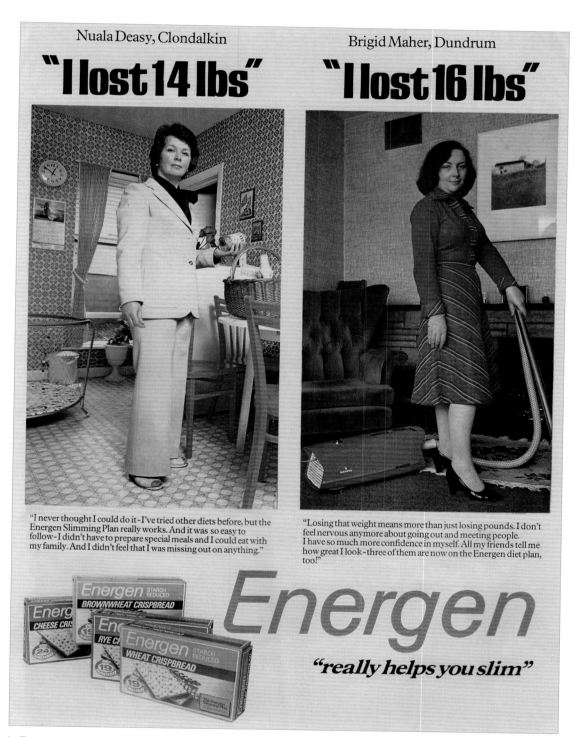

Nuala Deasy, Clondalkin

"I lost 14 lbs"

"I never thought I could do it – I've tried other diets before, but the Energen Slimming Plan really works. And it was so easy to follow – I didn't have to prepare special meals and I could eat with my family. And I didn't feel that I was missing out on anything."

Brigid Maher, Dundrum

"I lost 16 lbs"

"Losing that weight means more than just losing pounds. I don't feel nervous anymore about going out and meeting people. I have so much more confidence in myself. All my friends tell me how great I look – three of them are now on the Energen diet plan, too!"

Energen

"really helps you slim"

Energen Crispbread Advert
Woman's Way 1978

Club Milk, Club Golf,
Club Nutana, Club Orange.

where the action is

Advert for Club Milk
Woman's Way 1971

Rave Girls

All from New Spotlight 1970

From Pat Egan's 'Where it's at' column, the 'Irish Rave Girls' mini feature launched in 1970 with Pat and photographer Mark Nolan heading out on the town to shoot 'the best looking girls in town'. Almost all photos by Mark Nolan.

DOING HER OWN THING . . .

Pauline Carolan is a twenty-two-year-old young lady with a lot going for herself. Within the next few weeks she will open Encore Boutique in Dublin's plush Grafton Street. Encore, she tells me, is 'Antiques and Jewels.' 'We are going to sell exactly what the young people in Dublin are looking for. I hope also to have a post order dept. for country people who will be interested in the kind of clothes we will be selling.' Encore is at 87 Grafton Street (first floor). Even if you're not buying, Pauline invites you to look around. So all you swinging cats who feel Dublin has little to offer on the gear scene, get going. Pauline, who hopes to be a millionairess before she's forty has her finger in a number of pies. She also handles the catering for a number of Dublin clubs. So, as you can see, here is one young lady who knows Where It's At.

Rave Girl

This is beautiful Tina De Cora (real name Tina Doyle) from Inchicore in Dublin. A record spinner, she has appeared in Sloopys, Zhivago and the Star clubs in Dublin. She is hoping to be the Anne Nightingale of the Irish pop scene (Anne is the only girl disc jockey on Radio One).

Rave girl

Wow! that's what I said when I first saw this beautiful young lady Gay Flavin. Gay is nineteen and comes from Sandymount in Dublin. She's a model with the Impact agency and just loves her job. She likes horse riding and fencing, is currently dating a boy from Scotland and is very happy with life at the moment. Gay's favourite man is film star Robert Redford of Sundance Kid fame. She thinks he's the greatest.

Rave girl

Breda Joyce is one of those girls everybody likes. She's not telling her age but our guess is about 21. A model with the Ann Murray Agency, she's also a disc jockey. Likes tall slim men who don't talk too much but will listen. Her favourite: Robert Redford ('The Sundance Kid') . . . 'He's a real doll', she says. Breda likes fast cars, walks, good food and sincere people.

Rave girl

She's 19?year-old Carol Dickson—
a model with the Impact Agency in
Dublin. I found her picture in the
fashion file and just had to find out
all about her. When she's not
modelling, Carol likes to write
short stories or go off into the
open country on a hike. She's
hitched all over Europe. Folk music
is her special favourite and she digs
people like Bob Dylan and Simon
and Garfunkel. Men? 'I like big
strong fellows with a Steve
McQueen image', she said.

Rave girl

Nice to say welcome to a young
Irish girl living in London. Hi to
Marie Allen, born in New Ross,
Co. Wexford. She has been in
London for the last few years mak-
ing a name for herself as a model.
This lovely girl likes ice skating
and has a soft spot for Spotlight's
London columnist, Paschal Mooney.
Marie hopes to reach the top of
her profession and to travel the
world . . .

Rave Girl

This is beautiful Marguerite Shortt,
who's 19 and a student at Dublin's
College of Art. I caught her
dancing at the Star Club and,
boy, did she look freaky.
Marguerite digs boys with fuzzy
hair and dark skin, just loves
Indian music and could listen to
Ravi Shankar and Alla Racha all
night long. Her favourite group
are Blind Faith and she confesses
to never having heard a
showband. Hopes to be a
highly successful artist. She likes
to keep changing her men
around.

Rave Girl

Meet Mary Healy from Cork, who
works in the Sound of Music record
shop in Dublin. This beautiful
young lady loves life in the big
city. Mary—who's 19—was brought
to our notice by a number of customers at the Sound of Music. She
likes dancing, going to good films,
and dating nice boys (she has a
very steady boy at the moment).
Now and then she gets homesick
but thinks that when she marries
she will live in Dublin.

RAVE GIRL

Is nineteen-year-old Dee Healy, a
commercial artist from Dublin, who
is also one of the only female disc
jockys on the Irish club scene. She
raves over boys with long hair and
dark brown eyes, loves to go on
camping week-ends and will try
anything for a laugh (well, almost).
Tells us she is very lonely and can't
wait to meet Mr. Right. Her favourite star is Robert Wagner and
she just loves Stevie Ellis. Her
favourite long-haired man is Rory
Gallagher of Taste . . . That's Dee.

Wendy and Michelle

RAVE

Like Now dancers Wendy Hutchinson and Michelle are happy to be part of a dancing world. You can catch them on stage any night, boys. At Sloopy's, Countdown, or any of the 'in' clubs. Wendy is 16 years and digs Jetro Tull, Dionne Warwick and the Dreams. Michelle is 18 years, loves the Taste and Eric Clapton, and her fave Irish band is the Real McCoy.

RAVE GIRL

This week's rave lady is Pat Harrison, an 18-year-old beauty from Killiney, Co. Dublin. Someday she's hoping to meet a nice young man and settle down but at the moment she's much too busy making the scene to worry about love. Pat who does part time modeling and dancing works as a receptionist in a big city travel agent's. She digs American group Charigo and just loves Cilla Black Her favourite record of the moment is 'Friends' by Arrival. Her favourite Irish band is the Real McCoy and the man in her life is Steve McQueen. Watch for her dancing on the new all-girls show on RTE. She's a sight for sore eyes......

Rave Girl

Martine Kelly is a model with the Impact agency. She's eighteen years of age and wants to reach the top of her profession. When not on the fashion scene Martine likes to rave it up around the clubs. Likes tall slim men (very slim) with black hair. She has a favourite man but won't give his name. Loves Tom Jones, "he's the greatest singer there is" she says. Hopes to get married someday but not yet as she wants to see what's happening around the world.

RAVE GIRL

Our "Where It's At" rave girl this week is nineteen-year-old secretary, beautiful Anne Pentony. Anne, who's also a go-go dancer in her spare time is, we feel, one of the grooviest and most with-it dancing girls around. Ann, whose hobbies are swimming, dancing and horse-riding, has wide ambitions to travel the world. Her tastes in music are very with-it and she just loves the new Canned Heat record "Let's Work Together" . . . She won't talk about men but the guy who catches her will be the lucky one.

RAVE GIRL

Our lady of beauty and fashion this week is twenty-year-old Dubliner Irene Greeley—a model. You may recall she was on the cover of the controversial "This Week" magazine when they ran a feature on the pill. Oh boy! She did look well, and as you can see she always does. Irene, who's a big fan of both jazz and underground music, is looking forward to her holidays—three weeks in the Greek islands. She admits to having a man in her life "but then what girl hasn't" she says. Her hobbies are horse riding and dancing and just meeting people. Her ideal man? Paul Newman . . .

Sue won't be going to the dance tonight

Someone went through her flat with a fine-comb.
A new dress ruined. Handbag stolen.
Lots of other items missing.
Like most girls of her age, Sue Riley never thought
about insurance. Don't make the same mistake.
Call on Hibernian for peace of mind.

 **HIBERNIAN INSURANCE**

in association with Commercial Union Assurance Group, Hawkins House, Hawkins Street, Dublin 2. Tel. 772911. And thirty-three local offices throughout the country.

WILSON HARTNELL
WOMAN'S WAY, 22nd MAY, 1970

Advert for Hibernian Insurance
Woman's Way 1971

An Gael Óg

Top left: 1971
Top right: 1972
Middle left: 1972
Middle right: 1970
Bottom left: 1973
Bottom right: 1972

An Gael Óg was published by the Christian Brothers in Dublin. Illustrations for all the covers featured here were done by Sean O'Slatra (Slattery).

PLEASED TO MEET YOU

THIS week we publish more pictures of members of our Readers' Club who would like to make new friends through this column.

(1) Ann Gargan, Ballyburr, Cuffes Grange, Co. Kilkenny. Age 21. Hobbies: Dancing and sports.

(2) Carmel Owens, 59 Belgium Park, Monaghan. Age 18. Hobbies: Dancing, skating, indoor football, listening to the Freshmen and boys.

(3) Maureen McGlinchey, Doohan, Castlefin, Co. Donegal. Age 19. Hobbies: Dancing and listening to pop records.

(4) Noreen Mulvaney, 1A St. Marnocks Ave., Portmarnock, Co. Dublin. Age 17. Hobbies: Dancing, sailing, stamp collecting and swimming.

(7) Michael O'Connor, Agricultural College, Mount Bellew, Co. Galway. Age 19. Hobbies. Gaelic football, dancing, current affairs.

(8) Tom Dromoey, C/O St. Brendan's College, Killarney, Co Kerry. Age 17. Hobbies: Sport, pop music, listening to the Debonaires, food and meeting funny people.

Readers' Club

New Spotlight 1968

The Readers' Club feature began in January 1968 and ran intermittently for 2 years. A sort of Bebo/Facebook for the 1960s.

PLEASED TO MEET YOU

(1) Raymond Walsh, Graffogue, Scramogue, Co. Roscommon. Age 18 years. Hobbies: GAA, bowling, international Rugby, watching TV, pictures and pop music.

(2) Brendan Healy, Windsor, Victoria Road, Cork. Age 18 years. Hobbies: Films, reading, boating, watching TV.

(5) Christine Hennessy, Clonbrien, Athlacca, Kilmallock, Co. Limerick. Age 15 years. Hobbies: Reading, painting, embroidery.

(6) Theresa Gill, 56 Upper Mount Pleasant Ave., Rathmines, Dublin 6. Age 17 years. Hobbies: Dancing, tennis, films.

(3). Anne Maria Byrne, 12 Merton Park, S.C.Rd., Dublin 8. Age 18. Hobbies: Dancing, films, radio.

(4). Miss P. O'Sullivan, Ballinacara, Ballindangan, Mitchelstown, Co. Cork. Age 16. Hobbies: Dancing, reading, collecting showband pics, listening to pop records.

Readers' Club

1. Kathleen Ahern (19), "Coola-
leen," Broadford, Co. Limerick—
Hobbies: Reading, dancing, films,
music.

5. Stephanie O'Mahony (19), 138
Farranferris Ave., Farranree, Cork.
Dancing, films. Fav. singer: Dickie
Rock.

2. Ann Cronin (17), Milleens,
Coolea, Ballyvourney, Co. Cork.
Dancing, reading, music, camogie.

6. Ethel Scott (25), 8 St. Patrick's
Tce., Mostrim, Co. Longford. Collecting records, dancing.

3. Edward O'Reilly (21), 13
Keeper Rd., Crumlin, Dublin 12.
Dancing, pop music, T.V., and all
sports.

7. Christy Cox (22), 26 Pearse
Sq., Dublin 2. Football, walking,
films, records.

Eamon Kirby (15½), 29 St. Brendan's
St., St. Mary's Park, Limerick.
Hobbies: Pop music, stamp collect-
ing, dancing.

Marion Carolan (14½), 10 Linenhall
Prde., off North King St., Dublin 7:
Dancing, swimming, films, table
tennis.

Seamus Henchy (15), The Square,
Ennistymon, Co. Clare: Football,
music, films.

Eddie Long (20), Carrigcloney,
Glenmore, Co. Kilkenny: Dancing,
reading, playing guitar.

READERS' CLUB

Rebecca Boyle, 3 Chelmsford Road,
Road, Ranelagh, Dublin 6: Swimming, reading, dancing, films,
records.

Thomas McNulty (18), Killenarden,
Tallaght, Co. Dublin: Singing, television.

Noel Dobbyn (17), Granagh, Carri-
geen, Waterford: Dancing, reading,
listening to radio.

Breda Roche (16), 101 Rockenham,
Ferrybank, Waterford: Dancing, pop
music, tennis.

RELIGION

How relevant is it to young people in Ireland today?
PAT EGAN has been asking this very pertinent question.

CATHERINE SMITH (age 21), Drogheda.
Religion is not really important to me anymore. I go to Mass most Sundays but I don't have a lot of interest in what's going on. Some of the idea the Church put over are very old fashioned . . .

BREDA FENNELL (Age 21) Dungarvan.
I go to Mass, but not all the time. I am not that religious but I think it's important to have something to hang onto. I pray when I want to give thanks for things or anything at all really.

EILEEN O'CONNOR (Age 20), Omagh.
Yes, I think it's very important to be religious. I never miss Mass. I pray all the time for everything. I would bring my children up as I have been brought up. I see nothing wrong with the way I have turned out.

NUALA McGURN (Age 18), Omagh.
I am not really very interested in religion and I would marry for love and not bring religion into it. Yes I pray. Everyone does. I don't think the church is right to tell people how to kiss and how not to kiss. Everyone has his own mind.

PHILOMENA McCONVILLE (Age 20), N. Ireland.
I grew up in a Catholic family so that's mainly the reason I go to church. I have no set ideas on what's right or wrong. I pray in time of need. It's nice to have someone to turn to who seems to understand all our problems.

NORA COYLE (Age 21) Donegal
I don't pray very much any more so I really don't care too much about religion. I feel by doing good I am leading a proper life and to me thats what's most important.

DANNY MURRAY (Age 25), Mullingar.
Religion is not important anymore. Let young people live as they want to live. I go to Mass because it's nice to give up me for someone else.

KATHLEEN McGUINN (Age 19), Omagh.
Some of the things the Church teaches are old hat but that's no reason to knock my religion. Yes I go to Mass and I pray. Now and then I might get browned off with the whole thing but everyone comes back to God.

HUGH FITZSIMONS (Age 20), Dublin.
Yes I have an interest in religion, mainly because I was brought up that way. Life means a lot to me and I would like to know some of the answers. I don't know about life after death. There is something there but it's anyone's guess.

CHRISTY WALSH (Age 22), Dublin.
I believe in God because I am afraid of his power but I am not interested in religion. I know there is something behind my being. My children could lead their own lives and discover life and God for themselves.

BREDA FOLEY (Age 22), Waterford.
Oh yes I go to Mass and I believe in God and his goodness. When I have children I will see that they are brought up as good Catholics . . .

THOMAS BENT (Age 20), Wexford.
Yes I think religion is important to the young because they need something to believe in. I go to church because this is the way I was brought up. God is real . . .

MARIE O'CONNOR (Age 18), Omagh.
I would not marry a boy if he was not a Catholic. The church is not strict and every young person should go to Mass. But every man is his own worry and will have to answer to God one day.

CHRIS GRANT (Age 20), Newry.
I am a Catholic, but I would marry for love. I pray because it gives me comfort and shows I believe in something other than myself. Everyone should have some kind of religion.

SEAN KINSELLA (Age 21), Dublin.
I don't believe in God, not in the image I was told about at school. Religion means nothing and I will never be interested in what the Pope and Church have to say . . .

Vox Pop Religion

New Spotlight 1970

In 1970, Pat Egan took to the streets with photographer
Mark Nolan to run a series of Vox Pop interviews.

VOTES AT 18?

Do young people want votes earlier?
Pat Egan has been out asking them

Pics/Mark Nolan

IMELDA CUMMINS (age 20), shorthand typist.
Yes, the idea is quite right. It gives the young a sense of responsibility. After all, you know as much at eighteen as you do at twenty-one. I know who the Prime Minister is but I don't really care about who's in power once nothing happens to the country.

T. CONNORS (age 21).
Yes, of course there should be votes at eighteen. You're old enought to understand anything at that age. I don't have any real interest in politics, but votes at eighteen are a must.

IRIS JACKSON (23), secretary.
If young people want to vote at eighteen let them. Most of them are old enough. No, I have no interest in politics. I have never used my vote yet, it's too much trouble.

ISABEL COX (age 14), student.
I would like to vote at eighteen. Even now I have a fair interest in politics and after all it's the young people who matter. I think I would vote Labour.

JOYCE McCARTHY (age 18), office worker.
Oh yes, it must come soon. After all, if you're old enough to marry at eighteen surely you should have a vote. I don't really know much about politics but I have a passing interest.

WILLIAM GRAHAM (age 18), sheet metal worker.
Yes, eighteen is the right age for voting. After all if the government take your money in taxes when you're only earning seven or eight quid you should have some say in who's running the country.

MICHELLE MARCELLIN (age 20), student.
Yes, there should be votes at 18, it's only right after all if you do anything wrong at eighteen or any other age they don't let you off because you don't have a vote. Yes, I am interested in what's happening in Ireland.

MONICA PRIZEMAN (age 16), worker with cosmetic company.
Yes, there should be votes at eighteen. After all it's in across the water now and if the English teenagers are good enough to vote then so are the Irish. I'm all for it, we should have a Bernie Devlin down here in Dublin.

JIMMY O'NEILL (22), house painter.
If you're old enough to join the army and get yourself killed fighting, well it's only right you should have a vote. It's about time the young people had their say. No, I have no real interest in politics.

ANN KAVANAGH (age 17), student.
Most young people know what's happening in their own country by the time they are eighteen and they should have a vote. I am interested in what way the country is run, after all I have to live in it . . .

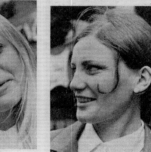

ANN FAGAN (age 21), shorthand typist.
No, I don't think so. After all, what do young people of eighteen know about the running of the country. I don't have any interest in governments or politics.

PATRICIA ADAMS (age 14), student.
Of course young people should be able to vote at eighteen. It's only fair if you're working that you should have a vote. I don't have any real interest in politics but I still think young people should have a vote.

Vox Pop Votes at 18?
New Spotlight 1970

MEDICAL EXPERTS DIFFER ON THE EFFECTS OF MARIJUANA. SOME SAY IT CAN LEAD TO DEPENDENCE AND A MOVE ON TO HARDER DRUGS, ESPECIALLY FOR YOUNG PEOPLE WITH MENTAL PROBLEMS. OTHERS SAY IT IS FAR LESS HARMFUL THAN NICOTINE OR ALCOHOL AND THAT IT SHOULD BE LEGALISED. PAT EGAN HAS BEEN ASKING YOUNG PEOPLE IF THE DRUG, COMMONLY KNOWN AS 'POT', SHOULD BE MADE LEGAL.

pot

SHOULD IT BE LEGALISED?

Pat Egan has been asking young people this very controversial question

Breda O'Brien (23), sales assistant, Kilkenny:

It should not be made legal. I would not smoke pot nor take any kind of drugs. There is no need at all for people to do so . . . Life is fine without them.

Justin MacInnes (19), office manager, Dublin:

Yes. It could be sold in chemists' shops to people over 18.

Mary McGuinness (24), typist, Edgeworthstown:

Under no circumstances should drugs be approved — not even soft drugs like hash. They are so much worse than drink because it's so easy to get hooked.

Mick Carwood (21), musician with Others:

It should not be legalised. I feel sorry for people who get hooked. Anyone who knows a friend who is hooked, or even smoking, should do everything possible to get them straight.

Kay Hughes (20), shorthand typist, Longford:

It's up to each individual whether they should smoke or not. It's a matter of conscience. I don't think it's right to jail people on drugs.

Renee Gaffney (21), Mullingar:

If people want to smoke pot it's their own business. Personally I wouldn't, but it would make little difference to me if a boy I was dating was smoking pot. If it was harming him I would try to get him off it.

Brian O'Connell (21), Clerk, Cabra West: Why spend 10/- on a single when you can get an album for 13/-? Singles are on the way out. It's months since I bought one and 7/- is as much as I would pay for a single.

Marion Kenny (17), Ballyfermot, Dublin: Records are too dear. I just don't have the money. I like Dean Martin but I haven't any real interest in the top ten. At 10/- singles are very expensive.

Kay Reddy (22), insurance clerk, Templeogue: My record player is not working so I haven't bought any records lately. 10/- is just crazy for a single. I like anything on Tamla Motown but I would have to like it an awful lot to pay ten shillings for it.

Jacqueline Lee (18), Dun Laoghaire: It's far too much for just one record. You don't get value for your money. If I really liked a record I would pay it but it's highway robbery. The last record I bought was Melanie's Ruby Tuesday. That was worth 10/-.

Bernadette Summer (16), student, Dublin: No, no, no. I would never pay 10/- for a record. I hardly get that much pocket money a week. The last record I bought was an album by Led Zeppelin but I will never buy singles at 10/-.

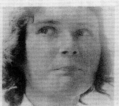

the price of pop

IS 10/- TOO MUCH TO PAY FOR A SINGLE?

Pat Egan has been asking the question.
Mark Nolan took the pictures.

Martin Malone (21), Garage assistant, Dublin: It's a long time since I bought a record. Anyone who pays 10/- for one is crazy. If everybody left them in the shops the price would soon drop back to about 6/- which would be still too much. I wouldn't mind if the singer and songwriter were getting the money but the Government and record shops get the best deal.

Susan Gordon (16), student, Whitehall, Dublin: Ten shillings for a record? Never! I just don't have that kind of money. It's madness to expect teenagers to pay something they just don't have. There was a time I used to buy records every few weeks, but not any more.

Tina Condell (18), drapery assistant, Dun Laoghaire: People can't afford to pay these prices for records. Everything has gone sky high. If I really like a song I may think about buying it but the price nearly always puts me off. I bought 'Which Way You Goin' Billy' but that was a great one.

Helen Quinn (20), Wages clerk, Dublin: I think 5/- or even 6/- would be plenty for a single. After all, the companies would sell more records if they were cheaper. I paid 10/- for Don Fardon's record only last week.

Mary Nolan (18), factory worker, Dublin: Where would I get 10/- for a record. The last time I bought one they were 7/6, which nearly broke me. Anyway, I can hear them on the radio just as often as I would have time to play them.

Diana Bowes (18), Dublin: If there was a refund on old records it might reduce costs. Most of the pop stars want records to be sold more cheaply so why don't they refuse to record songs until the companies bring down the prices.

Mike Finnegan (18), Motor mechanic, Dublin: I don't buy records but if they cost so much I am glad I don't. You don't get value for your money. I can see the sales of discs falling very low if they go past 10/-.

Vox Pop The Price of Pop
New Spotlight 1970

Social know-how

Jean Begley's advice column to guide you smoothly through the modern scene.

Is it acceptable to talk and make jokes about sex in mixed company?

ATTITUDES are very relaxed today, but in mixed company it is wise to remember there may be sensitive people who would be offended by crude conversation.

My daughter is getting married soon. Who should be at the hotel to receive the guests after the church ceremony?

THE bride's parents must arrive first at the hotel where the reception is to be held and as host and hostess they greet the guests as they arrive.

I usually accompany my wife and children to Mass on Sundays. Should I walk down the aisle first and enter the pew, followed by my wife and children?

YOU should walk in front of your family going down the aisle of the church. When you reach a suitable pew you stand aside, allowing your wife and children to enter first and then you take your place on the outside of the pew next the aisle.

My daughter has just got engaged to be married and we have not yet met her fiancé's parents. My husband and I wonder if we should invite them to visit us first, or if it is up to them to ask us so that we can all get acquainted.

WHEN the engagement is announced and the families do not know each other, it is for the mother of the prospective bridegroom to invite the girl's family to visit her, but this rule is not strictly adhered to these days.

I am a very bad correspondent and when I sit down to write a letter I never know what to say, therefore my letters are always very short and dull.

LETTER-WRITING is merely an expression of thoughts on paper, so when you write a letter, try to picture the person to whom you are sending it and express your thoughts on paper as if you were talking to that person.

How does one eat lobster?

USE a fish knife or special lobster fork. Hold the claw with your fingers and use the fork to get the flesh out.

Bad Habit

Q *Please could you tell me if masturbation would ever stop me from from becoming a father? Is it harmful? I am a boy of 15, and very worried about this.*

A Masturbatiin is one more of those bad habits of adolescence which creates so much unhappiness and guilt in the minds of young people. To answer your question bluntly, no, it will not prevent you from becoming a father, and no, it is not harmful.

But like any bad habit, it is an abuse of a good quality —in this case man's ability to procreate: If you abuse this ability, you lose respect for it gradually, and forget its real purpose.

Continued indulgence in this now could lead to a situation in which you would have no interest in legitimate sexual relations, with the result that your inclination to fatherhood would be affected. Similarly, when I say that masturbation is not harmful, I have also to point out that this is in the strict physical sense. Emotionally, if you came to depend on it as a release of tension and frustration, it could mean that you would not need the affection and love of a woman; psychologically, it could mean that your mental attitude to sex might be affected by some hangover sense of guilt later on in life.

Like all bad habits, it would be best if you could stop practising it. Best for yourself.

Are bikinis immodest?

I MAY as well say that most of the bikini-clad girls I saw on Irish beaches must never have looked at themselves in a mirror, from the point of view of beauty or modesty.

Their pasty, flabby midriffs, bony ribs, or spare tyres looked revolting.

I also saw couples openly courting on beaches. Was it a coincidence that most of the girls so involved were bikini-clad?

Problem Pages

Various magazines from 1967-1972

'What is French kissing and if you do it, can you get pregnant?' This was the most popular question asked by teenagers in the late 1960s. You'll find the answer here in our selection of letters to agony aunts from 1966 to 1972 taken from New Spotlight, Woman's Way, Miss and Woman's Choice. The Social know-how section was a weekly feature in Woman's Way.

My husband is good to me and the family, but I resent the fact that he is a mouse. I have to take the initiative in everything. He is unambitious and never gets anything finished. There has been a half-made cupboard in the kitchen for four years! He is untidy and forgetful and is getting worse as he approaches middle-age. I get so tired always having to take responsibility in the training of the children and all plans and arrangements of the household. I have to see that bills are paid and so on. Women in Ireland have it very tough. What can you say to help me to accept this situation?

GRIN and bear it—with particular emphasis on the grin bit! You won't change him now. If he were the organising type you might have quite a few clashes, because you seem to be quite an organiser yourself. It's getting you down because you feel that you have an over-dose of responsibility, but now and again, when things are getting a bit much, announce that you feel over-tired and are taking a morning in bed.

As you have no babies, you should leave it to your husband and children to get themselves out to work and school occasionally. Do remember to delegate authority. Each of the children should be able to undertake household tasks and you could ask your husband if he would encourage them in this. Ask him to show the lads how to clean shoes and carry in coal, cut grass and do carpentry—such as finishing the kitchen cupboard! Tact and that grin do more than nagging.

Where can I meet a beautiful girl?

Please tell me the right place to meet a beautiful girl. Outsiders find this town very clannish.
I did see one at a dance. I didn't ask her for a dance at first and later I approached her, but she turned away. I am almost twenty-two.

DON'T aim at getting a "beautiful" girl, just be friendly with any girl. They won't all turn away. Very often those who are more homely-looking are the nicest, so don't be choosy. You have written about this before, so I'm beginning to feel that perhaps you are too ambitious to win a glamour girl.

Q **I am 16 years of age and I work as a shop assistant in Dublin. I am very worried about something, and wonder if you can help me. I have a forewoman and at first I thought she was being friendly with me. But last week she kissed me, and yesterday she asked me would I go home to the flat and sleep with her. What should I do?**

A Well, I think the first thing you must do is absolutely refuse to go **anywhere** with her. This is not normal behaviour (I'm sure you know that), but when you are a little older you'll realise there are a lot of women in the world like her. They are unfortunate mis-fits, trying to squeeze out some kind of happiness for themselves. For your own sake, I must tell you that women of this kind rarely take a hint; you will probably have to show her very definitely that you are just not interested—at all—before she will let you alone, and even then you will have to be careful, and try never to be alone with her. I don't suppose you are the only girl in the shop she has been interested in, and maybe when you make a good friend there you can confide in her. At the moment it might be dangerous to tell the other assistants about this woman's overtures to you. Don't forget your suspicions, but you must be sensible about them, and realise that you have to work under this woman. Your rejection of her may make her angry, or upset, (it could even be that she doesn't know how much she is disturbing you) and you will have to risk her showing her displeasure in various ways. You will have to be very grown-up about, it quiet and practical, but if you find that her attentions continue to the point of really upsetting you, you will have to tell somebody who can help you by warning her off. Try to be careful who you tell. It will have to be someone who will take you seriously, and who will not talk to anyone else about it. But I feel it will not come to this; once you let this woman see, quite definitely, that you do not share her tendencies, I expect you will be left alone.

I am eighteen and don't know much about the facts of life. I met a very nice fellow at a dance last Sunday and he has dated me again. It's time I learned a bit.
Now I hear the girls where I work talking about "French kissing" and "French letters". I don't know what they mean and I wouldn't like to ask them because the girls would just laugh. Could you please tell me and give me the name of a book I could read? My mother is dead and I have nobody to turn to. In the office here all the others seem to have all the answers.

YOU are not the only one asking these questions. "French kissing" is prolonged kissing which arouses passion and it is wrong for unmarried people. "French letters" are artificial contraceptives—also forbidden by the Catholic Church. I do not know why the French are linked with these two abuses!

To sum up, I quote from Lynn Alexander's book, "About Dating" (Franciscan Publishers, Wisconsin, U.S.A.): "Necking is indulging in prolonged and passionate kissing. Petting, to put it bluntly, is allowing a boy to place his hands on the intimate parts of the body. Both, I am sure you know, are sinful. They are sins against chastity. They are the deliberate assumption of privileges and rights which have no place outside of marriage."

The C.T.S., 7 & 8 Lower Abbey Street, Dublin 1, have published a sixpenny booklet by Dr. Thomas Finnegan, entitled, "The Girl's Own" (Questions Young Women Ask). The author deals well with many of the problems of young girls and also suggests some helpful books. Send 6d., plus 4d. postage, to the C.T.S. for a copy of this booklet.

Right Thing

Q: *I am 17, and was going with a man of about 26 for two months. I loved him very much and he had great respect for me and he was very good to me. One day, I met his brother by accident, and I got an awful shock when he told me that his brother (my boyfriend) was married. I just couldn't believe it as he had been so nice to me and never kept me out late and you would think that a man like that would want something more than just a kiss—and sometimes we didn't even kiss, just talked. I told him that I never wanted to see him again, and that he was doing a terrible thing to his wife. Then he explained everything to me, and apologised for what he had done. He has written to me and asked me to go out with him again, but I have refused. I see him nearly every week, and he keeps asking me out, and I still refuse him. What can I do about him? I still love him, and hate to refuse him, but I don't think this is a bit fair to his wife, as it is with her he should be, and not with me. (Heart Broken)*

A: You've done the right thing, and now you must stick to it. No decision, once taken, is ever just finished with painlessly; unfortunately, there's always a period of distress and unpleasantness for a while afterwards, but you should find courage in the knowledge that you *have* behaved properly, and have nothing to reproach yourself with. You won't be able to forget about this man just like that. But you can learn from the experience, and gradually the strength of character that helped you make the break will also help you understand the situation and come to terms with it.

Go-Go Girl

I AM WRITING to know can you get me a job as a go-go girl or a singer in a showband. I do not know where to write for the names of band managers. That is the only dream I want to come true

Each week "New Spotlight" is full of the names and addresses of Showbands and their Managers. You could write to several of them asking for information on the possibility of getting a job like this, and their replies will indicate whether or not you have any hope of realising your dream.

What a Question !

Q: *Last week, my boyfriend asked me was I sexy". I did not tell him, as I don't know what this means. Please tell me what it means, and if you are "sexy" what do you feel? (Puzzled)*

A: I think that what that boyfriend probably meant was whether or not you would allow *him* to feel "sexy" about you. That means that he would behave to you almost as though you were married, but with one very important difference. A husband and wife love one another—that's why they got married. A boyfriend who wants the same physical intimacy with his girl without bothering about marriage is showing neither love nor friendliness.

But he is showing strong symptoms of selfishness, and also of a strange, callous lack of appreciation of you, as a person. The question was insulting. A boy worth calling a boyfriend would know, through his affection for you and knowledge of you, what you were really like.

He would not be interested in applying to you a term which is usually used to describe people of rather poor moral standards or careless personal behaviour. For "sexy" means interested in sex, or physical intimacy for its own sake, and with all comers.

Is it only virgins who can wear white when getting married ? If so, is it a sin for others to do so ?

WHAT you wear getting married is a matter of taste and has nothing whatsoever to do with the kind of life you have been leading. A girl is hardly going to announce her private weaknesses by the clothes she wears at her wedding !

Traditionally, white is a symbol of purity, but the important thing for a bride is her intention to be faithful to her marriage vows.

•   •   •

DESPERATE PROBLEM

I have a desperate problem. I met a boy at the weekend and I found him very generous and thoughtful. He took me home around 11 and I just thanked him for the evening. At about 2 o'clock there was a knock on the door. When my flatmate answered it she found this fellow outside, saying that he had to speak to me urgently. She left him in and he came over and sat on my bed and took his shoes off and made himself comfortable. I told him to get out but he would not. He got into bed beside me. I don't think he did anything to me but I am not sure and now I am afraid that I might be pregnant. What is the quickest possible way for me to find out whether I am or not ?

All you have to do is wait. If you miss a period it will be certain enough for you to go to a doctor, and then the usual test will be carried out and you will be told whether or not you are pregnant. What I can't understand is why you allowed this boy not only to walk into your flat but to get into your bed—could you not have got out of it? If the boy had refused to leave the flat you could have rung for the gardai—they do help you know. Don't try to pretend that this was all the boy's fault—you certainly seem to have allowed him to do as he liked.

Q I have a very short but serious problem. I do not know what a "French Letter" is.—(Sligo.)

A It's a contraceptive.

Long line trouble

DOING A LINE with a fellow for six years we got engaged last year, but since then he has lost all control of his emotions. This has also happened to me and on one occasion he asked me to sleep with him. I refused but he still insists. I love him very much, so please tell me what to do because we have no plans about marriage.

● Make them, because it's a bit much to ask this man to remain celibate indefinitely, and it's going to be rough on you too. A man and a woman who are in love usually want to be intimate, and to have children, and marriage offers the opportunity for this kind of fulfilment. Six years may not mean much, if you began doing a line at 14 or so. But if you did start going together so young the time has now come for the relationship either to enter the next logical phase—marriage—or to peter bitterly out.

Love, in your circumstances, becomes a kind of shamefaced excuse for sex. It's wrong to allow things to develop like that. Such development, which leads in the end to wickedness for its own sake, can only do you both serious damage. Your fiance's loss of control (as you put it) is an indication of the need for a change. Discuss it, talk marriage, and start planning.

Madly

Q I am madly in love with a certain boy who is, I think, chasing me. His friend tells me he is chasing me, but anytime I go near him or say anything to him he tells me to get lost. What should I do? (M.C.)

A Take his advice, and ignore his friend.

Q. I have been going with a very nice boy for six months and I like him very much. I am eighteen and he is twenty. I go to Confession and Holy Communion once a week but last Sunday our Parish Priest gave a sermon and said he did not think it necessary to go to confession every week. What worries me is that when I go out with my boyfriend he usually kisses me a few times and then I think I must go to confession before I go to Holy Communion. Is it necessary for me to go to Confession after every date before going to Communion? (Hopeful, Carrick-on-Suir).

A. I would like to think you could ask the P.P. who gave this sermon to advise you on this problem. My opinion is a very personal one, and it depends on what you think is a sin. You must not receive Communion if you believe you have a sin on your soul. "A few kisses" couldn't amount to sinning, unless you believe you were doing wrong. You know that you don't commit a sin without knowing it—the knowledge is what makes it sinful. If you feel guilty about your behaviour on a date, go to Confession, and then discuss your conversation with the priest with your boy friend. Be sure to let him in on your worries. But I don't think you need worry too much.

Q I am a girl and I am nearly fourteen. I had french kissing with another girl just for fun. Could this lead to pregnancy? (no name supplied).

A Straight answer to crooked question: No. Now the pair of you would want to get wise to yourselves. If you're prepared to experiment, "for fun," with something you obviously don't underestand at all, you're not just a pair of stupid babies, but two ignorant little girls who know well that something is wrong and are still prepared to try to find out what it feels like. Forget tbout this stupid fun of yours, and the next time you want to know something, ask someone older, and wiser than yourselves. It's time you started asking!

Grooming problem

PLEASE TELL ME where I could get a lady's razor and blades, and how much they cost. How often do you think one should shave under-arm hair?

● You'll get a lady's razor and blades at any chemist's or even at a general store. They can cost anything from cheap ranges for 10/- or so to much more expensive ones. Under-arm grooming is a matter of preference, but if you do it at all you may as well do it properly. That means you shave each time the new growth becomes obvious.

COLETTE has quite a different problem. "I am friends with a nice girl, but the other day she told me her Dad was a bin-man. My mother believes her, but I do not, and now Mom has told me to drop her as she is not my class. Can you advise me what to do?

ME: Colette, I don't think the problem is yours, but your Mom's. The thing that matters where friends are concerned is kindness and loyalty, not what their Dad does for a living.

I've known the greatest bounders of all time who came from the top drawer and whom I wouldn't bother to invite to my home. This kind of snobbery is regrettable and I trust you won't develop it within yourself. Wise up your Mom to the facts.

ASK RUTH

Q My parents don't like my boyfriend. They're always going on about his long hair and his mod clothes. And they won't let him come near the house. They told me not to go out with him . . . they said I was too good for him. But I really do love him . . . he's awful generous and great fun to be with and we never do anything wrong. How can I get my parents to like him?—**Marion, Rathmines.**

A Funny how much more class-conscious parents are. You may not be able to get your parents to like your boyfriend . . . even if he cut off all his hair and wore suits and carried an umbrella. But you could get them to tolerate him. With a little assistance from himself, of course. Get him to offer to mow the lawn. Or clean the windows for your mother. Or wash your father's car. Anything that will show he's not a lazy good-for-nothing . . . parents always think that anything in mod clothes and long hair is a lazy good-for-nothing. They'll be grateful for his help and they'll be obliged to invite him in for of tea afterwards. The rest is up to him. If he's really generous and good fun, they'll soon see it. And they'll probably invite him again. If only to mend a pane of glass or something! Remember one thing though! Parents, especially fathers, never really like their daughters' boyfriends. They never think they're good enough. From your letter, I gather that you're quite young still. So be patient with your parents . . . they're going through a difficult stage.

I'm sick of mini skirts...

I'm a young man of twenty and sick of girls throwing themselves at me and seducing men by wearing ghastly mini-mini-skirts. I've never seen so many fat legs, but they are still cheaply seductive. Girls will have to answer for a great deal. Why have they no self-respect?

THAT letter speaks for itself, doesn't it? It says two things, first that men want to meet girls who have self-respect. Second that there certainly are good men left, but that they depend on the help they get from the girls to keep them on the right road. It's even better to have this said by a twenty-year-old man than by me!

Worry Word

Q *I am 19 and I would like to know what is the meaning of the word virgin? (Worried)*

A A virgin is a young person, who has not experienced sexual intercourse. It is usually applied to unmarried girls.

Q. We are two very mixed up girls. We are very much in love with a showband singer but it is just getting us nowhere. Every time we see him on television, or in a magazine, we just go off our heads. We were at a dance the other night and he winked at us. We were not able to dance for the rest of the night—we just sat with our mouths open looking at him, in the next world you might say. Don't mind my writing as I am looking at a photo of him and writing at the same time. (Trim).

A. Where do you expect your love for this showband singer to get you? One wink doesn't mean he's really noticed you, although I'm sure the sight of two young girls sitting with their mouths open in a dance hall must be pretty noticeable! And *think* of all the nice lads you might have danced with, but couldn't just because another man had (ugh!) *winked* at you . . . At you both, which makes it worse. You must be great pals to be so ready to share with one another this great passion. Poor "Trim", you've just got to work this out of your system. For a start, close your mouth, and turn that photograph to the wall. . . .

STRANGE ROMANCE

Q *I am a girl of 17 and I have been going out steadily with a man of 29 for six months. Lately he has been talking about the couple next door, who have been married seven years and have no children and asked me if I would have a baby for him. I really love him. I would marry him in the morning but my parents don't know about our affair. What shall I do? (G.T.)*

A Why don't your parents know? Let them know, for a start, by bringing this man home. If he doesn't want to meet them it indicates he isn't really taking his relationship with you very seriously. "The couple next door" have their own sad problem. I don't understand why your boyfriend should be suddenly taking such a great interest in their childlessness. I assume when he asked you if you would have a baby for him he meant when you were married? It all sounds a little bit odd and suspicious. I'd say you're much too young to have anything to do with this man—least of all marrying him "in the morning", especially as you don't say anything about his having asked you to.

Post and Paper Adverts

Above: Belvedere Bond, Woman's Way 1970

Right: Odlum's, Irish Spotlight 1964

letters

Write to:
New Spotlight,
Botanic Road,
Glasnevin, Dublin 9

LET THEM DRINK, BUT CHARGE THEM MORE

ON BEHALF OF a group of girls who go dancing both during the week and at week-ends, I want to draw attention to what is quite a problem. It's this: Large numbers of young men do not go to the dance halls until the publichouses have closed. Our suggestion is that promoters and hall owners fix different admission prices, making it a bit higher after 10.30. This might induce the fellows to come in early and dance. Then we might not have so many girls just sitting around and waiting.—Miss R.M., Brookwood Crescent, Artane, Dublin.

WAKE UP!

DEAR Editor.—Upon read-in former issues of pop magazines and list ening to Irish pop programmes, I see that RTE haven't banned the Beatles latest L.P.

Know why? I'll tell you. Because in Ireland they are just beginning to understand sex in songs.

Because they don't know a thing—not one thing—about drugs and don't therefore, know when a song is "druggy".

They should have banned that L.P. and not the Dubliners' single! — "Wakey, Wakey." Carlow.

Dear Editor:

I believe you want something fresh for your magazine, well what could be fresher than " The Beatles in Dublin"? After all they got so much notice by the papers its just not "fair" that you should bypass them.

Let us just see what happened. Four young men came over from England. They intended giving a show in Dublin and by doing this to collect some money for themselves, which was perfectly all right. But what happened? Our Catholic, Irish Teenagers just went crazy. For what, I cannot understand.

Up to now Ireland has been looked on as one of the best if not the best country for bringing up young people, and now are we going to stand by, and let it down by a few hundred screaming teenagers? I am a teenager myself and I say "no"!

I have seen the "Beatles" on T.V. myself and what do I think of them? Well I think a child of five would have more sense.

As we now see, it's up to the few sensible teenagers that are left to make sure this doesn't happen again.

—Madeline Dolan (Roscommon)

Consolation letter

I WANT TO ENCOURAGE the girl who wrote to say that her friends jeered her about her Garda boyfriend who was 10 years older than her, and losing his hair from wearing his cap. I hope to get married next year to a Garda who is ten years older than me, and who is also losing his hair. But I don't mind about those things, because I love him very much. Before I met him I could not get a decent boyfriend—only those long-haired fellows who wanted nothing but sex. I like my boyfriend for what he is—hair has nothing to do with it. The girls at work always pass remarks about him, but I ignore their talk. He is so nice to me, and so good, that I don't care what they say. I just listen and don't say a word, so if you could print some of this letter it might help that other girl not to pay any heed either.

Dear Editor :

Why don't you send a copy of the January Spotlight to President Kennedy's widow? I really think she would be interested. That really superb sermon by Fr. G. Bowe, O.P. might console her, as it consoled me. It is one of the finest tributes to the late President which I have read.

—Miriam O'Brien (Dublin)

CATCHER IN THE RYE

Dear Editor :

I'm reading the Catcher in the Rye at the moment, just because I found an article about Salinger in IRISH SPOTLIGHT. Until then I thought it was a nasty book, and I stopped my daughter reading it.

It's not nasty, it is very pathetic especially if it's a picture of an average American youth. The descriptions are extraordinary lifelike and very biting. It's quite a book! I'll tell my daughter she can read it.

—Mrs. J. Keraudren

DEAR EDITOR — Would it be too much to ask the showbands to avoid playing "Merry Ploughboy." "Muirsheen Durkin," etc., at a dance when the floor is OVERCROWDED. I enjoy dancing to these records very much as the beat is terrific, but it is impossible to dance to them when the floor is full without the fear of a stiletto heel piercing your foot, or without being pushed and shoved.— Badly Bruised. Co. Monaghan.

THIS WEEK'S PRIZE BOND LETTER

Women, no matter how valuable or efficient they may be in Civil Service or local government posts, must resign on marriage. While I agree that a woman's first duty is to her family, I think that she should be allowed to go on working if she wants to. It would be a boon to most women to have a job for the first few months of marriage for it is very difficult for a young couple to get on their feet in these days of high prices.

If a family falls upon hard times (if, for example, the husband falls ill), the wife's earnings would be a great asset. I hope that the Commission on the Status of Women will do something to improve this deplorable state of affairs.

(Miss) K.H., Roscommon.

DEAR EDITOR,—The Dubliners are really great. But why do they have to dress so horribly? Come on Ronnie, Luke and the rest of you and let's have a bit of style. You might then win even more admirers.—Mary Greer, Ballydarragh, Cranford, Gorey, Co. Wexford.

Letters

Various magazines from 1964 to 1972

A selection of letters and hints taken from New Spotlight, Woman's Way, Irish Spotlight and Woman's Choice.

HOW DARE YOU KENNY !

Congratulations to Joe Dolan and his great new hit record 'It Makes No Difference'. Joe should be very grateful to Radio Luxembourg for giving it a Power Play. So far 'Make Me an Island', 'Teresa' and 'Good Looking Woman' were all Power Plays and great hits because of it. But how dare Kenny Everett slam his new disc. It was about time he was taken off the BBC anyway!
—James McNichalas, Rinmore, Cloghans, Ballina, Co. Mayo.

COWBOYS GO HOME

DEAR Editor, — Showband originality strikes again! Just when I thought the scene was starting to progress some fool comes up with the most ridiculous idea—dressing six or seven grown men up in cowboy suits and calling them the you-know-whats. I have nothing against a band playing country and western because this type of music is popular in country venues, but these hideous uniforms and that name—Ugh! I did not think that in this age of progression anybody (even on the showband scene) could have such a lack of foresight and originality. For pity's sake keep the cowboys away from the British pop press or Ireland will be the laughing stock of the pop scene and we are bad enough as it is.—Noel Casey, Dublin 7.

Give your hands a beauty treatment before doing the chores. Put a few drops of olive oil into each finger of your rubber gloves and your hands, nails and gloves will be preserved.

(Mrs.) Mary Higgins, Dublin

HINTS THAT HELP

To prevent sausages from burning, dip them in boiling water before frying or grilling.

To avoid berets shrinking after having been washed, stretch them over plates to dry.

Mrs. M. Lalor, Portlaoise

I would certainly agree that every girl should know exactly what her fiance is earning before they marry. Knowing where they stand financially is essential to the plans of any young couple and most pre-marriage courses strongly advise frankness and money matters.

I do feel, however, that as the years pass, wives should be content to know only approximately how much their husbands earn. No man should be asked to account for every shilling in his pay packet. Being master of his own money keeps him from feeling downtrodden.

This harmless secrecy about the odd pound or two enables a husband to produce an unexpected gift or arrange an extra-special outing for his family. Some men are forced to deceive over-extravagant wives about their salaries in order to pay the monthly bills; some are over-anxious about the future and like to save quietly for a rainy day.

There are many justifiable reasons why the wife should not know the exact figure on her husband's pay cheque.

(Mrs.) M. T., Dublin 9

Her Pet Hates

My five pet hates are: tea-leaves in the sink, cooked potato jackets on the dinner table, unwanted milk bottles on the doorstep, a hearth covered with ashes and cinders when the fire has gone out and trying to dry dishes with a wet tea cloth.

(MRS.) J.L., Portlaoise

HINTS THAT HELP

If you have a tendency to leave your gardening tools lying outside when you've finished using them in the evenings, it's a good idea to paint the handles with luminous paint.

A garden rake, for example, can be a dangerous thing to stand on in the dark, but there's less risk of doing this if it is painted.

Don't paint the whole handle, of course. A couple of strips are sufficient.

(Mrs.) Sean Little, Enfield, Co. Meath.

HELPFUL HUSBAND

Dear Editor,

How often do we hear complaints from Irish women that their husbands are inconsiderate and unwilling to help in the home. I would like to suggest that the womenfolk themselves are largely responsible for this state of affairs. As a young married woman with two babies and a wonderful husband, I would like to share our experience of the past week with other readers.

On two occasions, being unable to go into town, two miles away, my husband kindly offered (a) to take my coat to the cleaners, and (b) to collect some baby food from the chemist. Imagine his intense embarrassment when the female assistants in both places regarded his requests with obvious surprise and amusement, then proceeded to titter among themselves while serving him. What a disgusting yet typical attitude. Is it any wonder then, that men, when faced with this female reaction, do come to the conclusion that any help within the home is beneath their dignity. Wake up, girls and give the men a chance. A little encouragement and appreciation will get you a long way.

"Satisfied," Kerry.

HINTS THAT HELP

Put old scraps of leftover toilet soap in a jam jar half-filled with water. After some weeks you will find that you have a lovely scented liquid shampoo, which is also ideal for blankets and woollens.

(Mrs) K. R., Carnew, Co. Wicklow.

Butlin's Family Photo
1964

Butlin's Holiday Camp opened in Mosney, Co Meath in 1948.
We stayed there a number of times in the 1960s and had a
fantastic time. This picture, taken in June 1964, shows my
mother, Patricia, and my father, Pat, along with my sister Sinead
at the breakfast table. I can smell the eggs frying in the kitchen
and I can hear the outdoor swimming pool fountains hissing
away in the background. This was the first photo to appear on
Brandnewretro.ie back in April 2011. It is also my favourite.

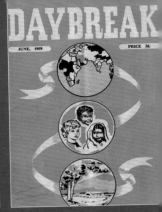